The Lenovo Affair

The Growth of China's Computer Giant and Its Takeover of IBM-PC

The Lenovo Affair

The Growth of China's Computer Giant and Its Takeover of IBM-PC

Ling Zhijun

Translated by Martha Avery

John Wiley & Sons (Asia) Pte Ltd

This publication is designed to provide accurate and authoritative information with
regard to the subject matter covered. It is sold with the understanding that the
Publisher is not engaged in rendering professional services. If professional advice or
other expert assistance is required, the services of a competent professional person
should be sought.

Other Wiley Editorial Offices

John Wiley & Sons, Inc., 111 River Street, Hoboken, NJ 07030, USA
John Wiley & Sons Ltd., The Atrium, Southern Gate, Chichester PO19 BSQ, England
John Wiley & Sons (Canada) Ltd., 5353 Dundas Street West, Suite 400, Toronto,
Ontario M9B 6H8, Canada
John Wiley & Sons Australia Ltd., 42 McDougall Street, Milton, Queensland 4064,
Australia
Wiley-VCH, Boschstrasse 12, D-69469 Weinheim Germany

Library of Congress Cataloging-in-Publication Data:

ISBN - 13 978-0-470-82193-0
ISBN - 10 0-470-82193-0

Typeset in 11-13 point, Goudy by Superskill
Printed in Singapore by Saik Wah Press Pte Ltd
10 9 8 7 6 5 4 3 2 1

CONTENTS

Introduction

Everyone is sleeping, the air is thin and it's hard to breathe. You wake up first, suffocating, feeling as though you're about to die. You find that the surrounding walls are made of steel: no way to pry them open.

Liu Chuanzhi quoting Lu Xun

The morning of June 22, 2004 witnessed an ambitious play by the computer company known in China as *Lianxiang* and in the West as Lenovo. In a courtyard at the foot of the Fragrant Hills outside Beijing, the Chairman's chat with a friend was interrupted by phone calls: five kilometers away a negotiation had entered final stages. The Lianxiang Group was trying to bring IBM's global personal computer business into its fold. The company's Executive Vice President, Ma Xuezheng, kept calling in to report developments. Negotiations were going back and forth between US$1.1 and US$1.5 billion. "Apologies for the interruptions," Liu Chuanzhi said to his friend. The intensity of his eyes betrayed the fact that this was less an apology than a moment of high drama.

The purchase, unique in Chinese commercial history, was more significant than the dollar value being discussed. The "plot by global western enterprises to gulp up a large share of the Chinese market" was, in the eyes of some people, being dealt a powerful blow. This broadly perceived "plot", whether true or a fabrication, had in the past twenty years become the foundation of nationalist sentiment in China. An underlying anxiety had increased the West's distrust of China which in turn fed Chinese antagonism toward foreign politicians. *Zhongnanhai*, the governing seat of China, had set the national direction and pace of China's foreign policy; it had been successful in leading China into the World Trade Organization (WTO). The name *Zhongnanhai* means "south-central lake" and describes an area west of the Forbidden City in the middle of Beijing, bordered by a string of small lakes. This is where China's senior power resides. To Chinese, the name is shorthand for "Central." The decision to enter WTO did not ease the conflicts. On the contrary, Chinese opposition to what was seen as Western multinationals' large-scale entry into China intensified.

This battle between China and the West to occupy commercial territory opened a pathway for one of China's outstanding business leaders, Liu Chuanzhi. He was able to align the mood of China with support from the government for his own company's long-term strategic goals. In the process, he facilitated the rise of Lianxiang as a major global corporation.

Liu Chuanzhi is generally recognized as being one of China's most creative and decisive business leaders. He is refered to as the "godfather of China's information industries." The American magazine *Business Week* has described him as a "World Business Leader", and ranked him among the twenty-four most famous global businessmen.

Liu Chuanzhi started in business in his forties. When he founded the company in 1984, he was an engineer, just one of 1,500 employees of the Computer Sciences Institute of the Chinese Academy of Sciences. When China first started setting up its computer industry in 1956, he was in his first year of middle school. His family had instilled in him a Chinese way of thinking and a traditional code of conduct. The events that were to occur in China contributed not only to his personal development, but also led to the formation of Lianxiang.

Liu Chuanzhi was born in 1944 in Shanghai. His grandfather had worked in a traditional Chinese bank in a place called Zhenjiang in Jiangsu province. Cautious and conscientious, his grandfather became Head of the bank and, with his savings, sent his son to Shanghai to get an education. Liu Gushu, Liu Chuanzhi's father, was an ardent student. When he passed an exam to be admitted into the Shanghai branch of the Bank of China, however, he took his father's advice, gave up scholarship, and joined the ranks of commerce. In the 1930s, the prosperity of Shanghai was world-renowned. More than two hundred banks were situated along the Whampoa River: Shanghai was known as "the finance center of the Orient." Liu Chuanzhi's father eventually became Chairman of the Board of the China Patent Agency Company, an entity formed under the banner of the Chinese Communist Party. Liu Chuanzhi's mother was born into a wealthy family in Zhenjiang and her father became Finance Minister under the regional warlord Sun Chuanfang. She was raised as a traditional Chinese woman, with a character that was both gentle and determined: she resolutely accompanied Liu's father through what were to be tumultuous changes in life.

This was a family with principles. Liu's father believed that the quality of a man was of primary importance—being honest and "upright" was far more important than being wealthy and famous.

The year after Liu Chuanzhi was born was notable not only in China but around the world. Roosevelt, Stalin, and Churchill signed the Potsdam Agreement and the Second World War came to an end. In Asia, the Japanese surrendered and both Communist and Kuomintang branches of the army in China began to move into Chinese cities. In America, at the University of Pennsylvania, with the support of the War Planning Office and US$400,000, a group of young electrical engineers developed the first digital computing machine in the world. This was the ENIAC, the "Electronic Numerical Integrator and Computer." ENIAC weighed thirty tons. It covered 1,800 square feet of space and used 19,000 electrical cables. Requiring a massive voltage of 175,000 watts, it was capable of computing 5,000 times per second. This is around one-ten-thousandth the computing power of a modern-day laptop computer. Initial development of the ENIAC was done in the interests of winning the war: it was meant to raise the accuracy rate of hitting a target. Now the war was over and the machine had no apparent military use, but the thinking that it encompassed—a "memory program" and "binary mathematics'—successfully brought the world into the age of electronic computers.

China had to wait many years for the dawn of the new computer era to reach its shores. In the mid-1940s, civil war was raging, while Americans were already shifting computer usage from military to commercial applications. Old conflicts had not disappeared between the political forces led by Mao Zedong and Chiang Kaishek. New conflicts were added to the old. Although Liu Gushu was employed by a Kuomintang bank, his inclinations were towards the Communist Party. Those inclinations led to secret communications with underground Party members.

In the fall of 1949, the Chinese civil war ended with the victory of the Communist Party. Liu Chuanzhi was five years old at the time. His family moved to Beijing where they lived in a *hutong* or lane, near Wangfujing, one of the most desirable districts in the city center. They had lost their wealth but were still a well-off family. Liu's father continued to work in the Bank of China and became an official member of the Communist Party. He maintained an approach of personal integrity. He believed that one should not be opportunistic or crafty, that one should work responsibly and be able to endure hard work as well as criticism, that one should have smooth, cordial relations with one's colleagues. Liu's father gradually built up his reputation in the field of banking. His integrity, sound reputation and stable relationships were attributes that were to serve his son well in the future.

The early 1950s was a glorious period for many Chinese—the country was being transformed and, though all were poor, all worked together to facilitate change. Years later, once Liu Chuanzhi was famous and successful, he thought back to the themes of those times—socialist transformation, opposing America and helping Korea, replacing the old currency with the People's Currency, the Renminbi (RMB), the "Three-Anti Five-Anti movement," the death of Stalin etc. Although he was only a grade-school student, these things made a strong impression on him. He did not realize that during this period rapid advances in mainframe computers were occurring in the West.

Just as the Second World War spurred tremendous investment in technical fields, the Cold War and the Arms Race became the impetus for scientific advancement. International Business Machines (IBM), began experimenting with silicon quartz conductors as a substitute for the vacuum tubes in its mainframe computers. Because of this, it became the earliest and the largest customer of Texas Instruments. The age of silicon conductors had arrived, but ended almost as soon as it began. In 1959, Robert Noyce, son of a minister in the state of Iowa, etched the various components of electronic circuits on a small silicon chip. Resistance, electrical capacity, diodes and triodes, all could now be arrayed on a very small space and connected under a protective layer of oxidized silicon. Noyce called the result an "integrated electric circuit." Together with two colleagues, he founded the company Intel in 1968. Three years earlier, a man named Gordon E. Moore had formulated the concept known as Moore's Law, that stated that the number of transistors the industry would be able to place on a computer chip would double every few years. In 1995, he updated his prediction to once every two years. Intended as just a rule of thumb in 1965, this Law has become a guiding principle for the industry— to deliver ever more powerful semiconductor chips at proportionate decreases in cost.

Liu Chuanzhi never met Robert Noyce or Gordon Moore. Only years later did he meet Andrew Grove, currently Chairman of the Board of

Intel. He was still a student in middle school when these men were opening the door to the digital age. The computer industry in China began in 1956. Zhou Enlai, Premier of China's State Council, led several hundred officials and scientists through the process of formulating a "Science and Technology Development Plan." Zhou Enlai intended to incorporate all sciences within this plan in a timeframe of twelve years. Among the items, Number 41 was the task of setting up "computing technology," and this was singled out as "urgent." Several computer experts from the Soviet Union became advisors for this Chinese effort. The urgency felt by the Soviets was impressed upon Chinese plans to the extent that China established four research institutes simultaneously—a Computer Technology Institute, a Semiconductor Institute, an Automatic Control Institute, and an Electronics Institute. The Computer Technology Institute was formally established on August 25, 1956. A former revolutionary with the requisite qualifications became its first Director. His name was Yan Peilin. Yan knew nothing about computers, but he was powerful, made things happen, and he was impartial and incorruptible. His administrative rank was Grade Nine—equivalent to being a provincial Party Secretary in the ranking of officials today.

China used military methods of "strategic deployment" to establish its computer industry. The Number One Command Post of this war was Building Number 3 in a set of buildings in western Beijing. Virtually nobody in China knew what computer technology was at the time. They didn't know about silicon memory devices, integrated circuits, ENIAC or IBM. Virtually nobody had ever seen a real "digital computing machine." The people who helped start the computer age in China had no contact with computers at all at the time and these people were the founding members of what was to become Lianxiang. Zeng Maochao was a third-year student at Shanghai's Jiaotong University. Ni Guangnan and Li Qin had just entered university. Liu Chuanzhu was in middle school. Yang Yuanqing and Guo Wei had not yet been born.

The first batch of forty-five Chinese "computer scientists" was assembled in the way an army allocates military personnel. In fact, these scientists were just students selected from three universities—Qinghua University, Shanghai Jiaotong University and Peking University. Since there was no such discipline as "Computing," all of them came from the "Automatic Control Department" of their universities. During a short training period, they learned what a computer was, then were sent one by one to the Soviet Union to see what computers looked like. Back in Beijing, they were placed in the new Computer Institute and, with the aid of Soviet diagrams, began to formulate China's very first computer. This first machine was called the "103." It was a small machine that did thirty calculations per second.

Zeng Maochao entered the Computer Institute in the fall of 1957 with a college degree. He later became the Head of the Institute and a key person in the founding of Lianxiang. By chance, the timing of his graduation saved him from being declared a "Rightist," a serious political liability.

Liu Chuanzhi's experience of Chinese political events in the late 1950s was less direct, although he too felt pressure from changes in his own home. His father, who persisted in expressing contrary opinions to the Leaders, had been given a "Warning." This Warning was a great reproach to his attitude of being straightforward, loyal and honest. The unfavorable atmosphere affected his son. Liu Chuanzhi's classmates began to pay attention to the position of their classmates' fathers: they became attuned to whether a classmate was from a capitalist family, or landlord, or professional, or worker, or cadre. Violent arguments erupted from time to time, but mostly students began to distance themselves from one another, and become silent.

Liu was not a child that liked silence. He had a great interest in national affairs. He particularly liked war novels. *Red Flag Waving* has dozens of volumes, detailing the exploits of army people of the Communist Party: Liu read these in detail. Then there were works of world-famous authors, there were the unofficial histories, there was the *Romance of the Three Kingdoms*, and *Water Margin*, also the *Collected Works of Mao Zedong*. Later he was to use primarily military analogies in discussing corporate strategy. Younger employees found this amusing—they did not understand the context in which Chinese of Liu's generation had lived.

The great movement to smelt iron and steel was a notable episode of that period that aroused people's passion. It remains a scar on the course of China's economic development, but one that has a certain ugly beauty. The good news about the country's "construction" was sent daily to *Zhongnanhai*, as well as advertised in newspapers. Within a few weeks, China had many millions of steel-smelting furnaces burning away to contribute to the Cause. Thick smoke billowed everywhere. Furnaces were built in Liu Chuanzhi's school and in the Bank of China where his mother worked. Everyone went home to search for metal that they could melt down—objects would then be smashed to pieces and the pieces stuffed into the furnaces. There was no central heating in Beijing at the time, nor any gas heating. All families relied on charcoal-briquet stoves to cook food and provide heat. A tubular metal ring was set over the fire on which one placed the family cooking pot. Lui and his mother smashed the vital household stove ring. They divided it into two parts and heroically marched out to deliver it to their respective furnaces.

It was a time of dreams and high emotions. After the steel-smelting came the "Rid the Four Harmfuls" which meant ants, mosquitoes, rats, and sparrows. Mao Zedong had said that sparrows ate grain and therefore were one of the "four bads." The central government decided that everyone in the country was to be given three days of vacation during which they were go outdoors and do nothing but kill sparrows. Liu Chuanzhi, with his teacher and fellow students, climbed onto the roof of the school. With a washbasin in one hand and a stick in the other, they beat the washbasins steadily day and night. The ringing of other washbasins resounded throughout the city, sparrows rose from their resting places in alarm. With no place to land, they exhausted themselves in the air and finally fell to earth, dead. People picked the spoils of victory off the ground and took them away to report the trophies.

The "fiery Red" years were passed in this manner. Soon afterwards, due to economic disruption, the entire country began to feel the pangs of hunger. Mao Zedong's method of dealing with this was to say, "Eat dry when you are busy, wet when you are resting. When you are neither working nor resting, eat half and half." Dry food meant more concentrated protein—watery soup had fewer calories. This did not work for the simple reason that many people had neither dry nor wet. They began to eat the leaves of trees and the roots of grasses. Soon these too were gone. In the three ensuing years, of the thirty million people who died of hunger or of disease caused by famine, most were in the countryside. People in the cities were better off, but available food was rationed. Officials were no exception. Department Heads were allowed a small amount of meat; Bureau Heads were allowed a ration of soybeans, and so they were called "Fish and Meat Cadres" and "Bean Cadres." Liu Chuanzhi's father was a Section Head, so he was a Bean Cadre. He was allowed beans to keep his family alive.

The Computer Institute did not set up a furnace in its courtyard, but dreams and high emotions were burning there as well. Young scientists drafted their own Great Leap Target Quotas. They decided to research and develop the very first Chinese mainframe computer that could calculate at a rate of 10,000 computations per second, and they named this goal the Number 104. They decided to have it ready by October 1, 1959. Zeng Maochao would always shake his head when relating this story in later years. "Setting target quotas on scientific research—I find it strange.

Factory workers can produce a certain number of manufactured items, but what kind of quota can you set on scientific research?"

Nobody said this at the time. Researchers in the Computer Institute, hungry as they were, worked long hours to bring Number 104 into existence. They wanted it to be their contribution to the Great Leap Forward of China and to have this recognized during the annual parade in Tiananmen on National Day. October 1, 1959 was the tenth anniversary of the founding of the People's Republic of China. The machine was paraded around the Square to tremendous cheers, but it had not been finished and was in fact completely useless. After the ceremony to "contribute the contributions," Zeng Maochao and his colleagues went back to the Institute and continued work. Nobody had any clear idea of how to make the Number 104 actually function, so they invited Soviet specialists to give advice. It was at this point that relations between the two countries evolved from friendship to outright enmity.

With no Soviet specialists to help, twenty-five-year-old Zeng was made Chief of the team developing the Number 104. As he was later to say, "When there is no tiger in the mountains, the monkeys call themselves kings." Under Zeng, its magnetic silicon memory system was improved, and its computing speed increased one hundred times.

The Number 104 was China's first mainframe computer. The central processor used 8,000 vacuum electron tubes. Vacuum electron tubes are almost non-existent now, but before the age of transistors they were the most important components of all electronic equipment. During the years that Zeng Maochao was using several thousand vacuum tubes packed inside the Number 104, transistors had already begun to be substituted for tubes. Annual sales of transistors in the American market doubled in one year to more than $400 million. Transistor mainframe computers became the darling of industry and commerce, and transistor radios soon became a consumer item in ordinary households.

China was in the process of trying to "catch up with and overtake the rest of the world" and the Number 104 became one of its "secret weapons." The machine accomplished all kinds of complicated calculations, including weather forecasting, dam engineering, and the arc of the roofline of the Great Hall of the People. It also did many things to do with atom and hydrogen bombs. But its operation was energy-intensive—the 8,000 vacuum tubes put out a tremendous amount of heat. In summer, researchers had to bring in quantities of ice cubes and keep fans blowing. If all the fans were blowing at once, they could keep the mainframe cool enough—the computer operated in this fashion for around twenty years.

On the other side of the Pacific Ocean, technology was moving forward at breakneck speed in the 1960s. A generation of people born in the West after the Second World War was coming of age and they had an insatiable appetite for electronic goods. Electrical engineering became a fashionable occupation. Two magazines, *Popular Electronics* and *Wireless Electronic Technology* began to influence people's views of the world. Farmers' children, who in the past had studied how to repair tractors, now migrated to cities and began to study anything to do with the commercial potential of small-scale electronic appliances. Screens, memory chips (RAM), Read-Only Memory (ROM), desk-top computers, all made their appearance in these years. Gordon Moore came out with Moore's Law; IBM held eighty percent of the computer market and set the standards; integrated circuits became the hot new thing for the global electronics industry and rapidly invaded the territory of transistors. The market was phenomenal: in 1966, the price for a package of 200 transistors was US$150. Five years later it had dropped to US$44. Integrated circuits were even better—in the same period, the price for an integrated circuit containing 200 transistors dropped from US$15 to US$2. By the early 1970s, the market for integrated circuits had reached US$1 billion, surpassing that of transistors.

These years were important for the Chinese people, but "important" at the time related exclusively to political events. They had been through the Anti-Rightist Movement, the Four Eradicates Movement, and the Great Cultural Revolution. All were intoxicated by the emotional fervor of politics. Liu Chuanzhi graduated from high school in the summer of 1962. His dream was to become a pilot in the air force. At that time, people in the military were near-sacred beings—all young people, boys or girls, wanted to become soldiers, but particularly to become pilots.

Liu Chuanzhi passed all his exams and became the only candidate from his school to be considered for a future as a pilot. Because a relative had been denounced as a "Rightist," however, he was declared unfit. Lui was devastated. His father consoled him, "No matter what you do in the future, whether it's great or just something ordinary, so long as you are an upright human being you will be my good son." The term "upright human being" comes from Chinese classical philosophy and the statement was, as Liu says, "carved into my bones." Liu Chuanzhi had always worshipped his father and now he understood why. It was not because of his father's position, or assets, or even the blood relationship between them. It was because of his father's character.

When fall began that year, Liu entered the Xi'an Military Electronic Engineering Institute as a first-year student. This school specialized in atom bombs and guided missiles. Though they admitted him as a student, the school believed that his political views were insufficiently "clean" to deal with these subjects, so he was assigned to study radar. This gave Liu Chuanzhi an introduction to the general field of computers, the business by which he would rock China in years to come.

Liu Chuanzhi wanted to enter the Communist Party but this met with resistance: his classmates from rural towns said he lacked the requisite "feeling for workers and peasants." The China of those days and of today is very different, but the gap between urban and rural people hasn't changed. The same conflicts exist. Liu Chuanzhi had trouble defining what this "feeling for the workers and peasants" was supposed to be, but he discovered that his rural classmates gained the trust of Party organizations more quickly than he could. They were dependable, they could take hard work and endure criticism, they had no great philosophy, they were loyal and dedicated. Their "mouths were slow and their hands were fast." These attributes were just what the Party needed.

Eighteen-year-old Liu Chuanzhi began to learn the art of compromise. He learned to listen with full attention to what other people were saying, how to control his own desires, how to hide his own emotions. He learned the art of what in Chinese is called "hiding a needle inside the cotton." He learned how to get along with people he did not like. He learned to do things with enthusiasm that in fact he detested.

In June of 1966, the waves of the Great Cultural Revolution crashed on into the school. Twenty-two-year-old Liu Chuanzhi was putting the finishing touches on his dissertation about his own work in radar studies and was about to graduate. Instead, incited by Mao Zedong's call to action, he became a member of the first group of what were called the "revolutionary faction." He could give speeches that were eloquent, emotional, and inflammatory. He was also adept at identifying his opponents' weak points and honing in on one such point while ignoring the rest. He seemed to possess all qualities necessary for a model political leader. His rebel faction did not have any specific responsibilities, but for a certain period he was their guiding spirit. This could be attributed to his debating ability, but also to his organizational talents. Like allocating soldiers in a battle, he had the ability to allocate resources in a political movement.

Liu Chuanzhi began to have doubts about all that was happening. He began to understand one important thing: the world around him had two kinds of people. One kind saw things clearly: they could get to the heart of the matter and find some opportunity and some personal benefit from it. The other kind were confused. They simply threw themselves into affairs in a great confused muddle. He did not want to be a muddle-headed person; he also did not want to be an opportunist. He felt that the opportunist route was not only improper—it was extremely dangerous. From being a die-hard member of the revolutionary faction, therefore, he became a member of the "unaffiliated" faction. A Red Guard commander soon denounced him as being a "retreatist from revolutionary consciousness." The commander was a passionate man who enjoyed being a political operator and he may have felt it a shame to lose such a capable supporter.

Liu Chuanzhi graduated in 1968 and was sent to Chengdu to do research in a Research Institute. In the late 1960s, there was talk about the possibility of a World War III. The United States had doubled its involvement in the Vietnam War, sending in large numbers of soldiers and equipment. The Soviet Union and China were involved as well, which increased everyone's anxiety about global war. Mao Zedong did not miss the opportunity to use war fears as a way to incite the power of the masses. Liu's first assignment was to bring in captured American radar systems, disassemble them and use the knowledge to devise ways to improve China's military radar systems. Several months later, however, *Zhongnanhai* sent down an order: all intellectuals were to go down to farming villages to do manual labor. Liu left radar and went to a commune near Macao in Guangdong province where his job was to plant rice seedlings. From there he was moved to a farm in Hunan Province, where political criminals and people to be reformed through hard labor were sent. In April of 1970, he was assigned to work in Beijing in the Computer Institute of the Chinese Academy of Sciences. Over a period of two years he traveled from Xi'an in China's northwest, to Guangdong in the southeast, to Hunan in the south and eventually back to Beijing.

On the morning that he returned to Beijing he walked out of the train station and saw that everything looked different. The square in front of the Beijing Railroad Station was no longer festooned with slogans or flags. He saw no Red Guards wearing red armbands and old military uniforms. The Big-Character-Posters on the walls had been replaced by warnings from the Public Security Bureau. The warnings announced that so and so was "now a counter-revolutionary," or had already been "summarily executed." There were many such notices at the time—every few days a new set of them would be put out, black characters on white paper and, in blood red, a big X over the offender's name. This signified that the person had already been shot. If the purpose of putting up such posters was to shock, it was successful. Liu Chuanzhi discovered that one of the red X's covered the names of Wang Shouliang and his wife. This man had been one of his language professors in middle school, a teacher who was particularly fond of Liu and would often praise his essays. The announcement stated that the crime of both husband and wife had been to communicate with the outside world, the evidence for this being that the professor's wife had previously worked in the Soviet Embassy in China.

The key qualities of the man who was to become the Computer King of China were now in place, forged during eight years of turmoil and destitution. Liu now excelled in dealing with complex human relations. At critical times, he knew how to get help from people in power. He had developed a kind of unbreakable spirit. He had honed his competitive instincts. Perhaps most importantly, he had become a believer in the ability to forge a new reality.

The 1970s began in an atmosphere of both hyper-stimulation and depression. More than ten million intellectuals had lost their pride and their will was broken. Many now carefully kept their minds empty other than to write self-criticisms and statements swearing loyalty to Party leaders. The winds of war seemed to be gathering. The country's most important tasks seemed to be to rouse the fighting will of the masses and to produce nuclear weapons. China's first atom bomb was produced in 1964 and its first satellite in 1970—these accomplishments gave hundreds of millions of Chinese a feeling of security, isolated as they were by the West. *Zhongnanhai* continued the programs with determination and secretly formulated a plan to research guided missiles and to send up satellites. Without doubt, this touched the most sensitive nerve of Western countries. The West was incapable of obstructing the determination of the Chinese people, but it could block the export of advanced technology to China. This situation led to China's once again fostering and protecting Chinese intellectuals. The Computer Institute of the Chinese Academy of Sciences was among the privileged.

When Liu Chuanzhi entered the Computer Institute, it already occupied a large area one kilometer to the north of Zhongguanccun. The Institute already employed several hundred people. The Number 104 had played a considerable role in the process of researching atom bombs and this gave Chinese the confidence to make even bigger computers. *Zhongnanhai* extricated the Computer Institute from the organizational structure of the Chinese Academy of Sciences and placed it under the Scientific Industries Commission of the Ministry of Defense. It was given a military designation:

"Jing Troop #116." The Jing stood for Beijing, which means northern Capital. Scientific personnel became plain-clothed army personnel. Rank-and-file soldiers with loaded rifles stood at the guard posts. Zhongguancun, the place that was to become famous as China's high-tech zone, was still empty land, but the Computer Institute was already becoming China's "Palace" of computer science.

The years that followed were turbulent. The "Workers' Class," generally known as the "proletariat" to Westerners, took power and occupied the highest levels of government. Deng Xiaoping returned to power, then was "rectified and reorganized," Hu Yaobang came to the Academy of Sciences to promise that he would oppose the move to overturn cases against "right deviationists", Deng Xiaoping again fell from power, Zhou Enlai died, the Tiananmen Incident occurred in 1976. All these events created uncertainty in the Computer Institute, as they did in China overall. In terms of scientific accomplishments, research never stopped, but researchers never even considered the commercial applications of their work.

Large sums were invested in the Institute for military purposes and the research now focussed on the development of transistor computers. The Number 109 machine was created in 1964. It could perform 60,000 calculations every second, five times the speed of the Number 104, but it still used electron tubes. One year later, the Number 109-B machine was created, the first mainframe transistor digital computer developed by Chinese themselves. After another two years, the Number 109-C was created, which could do 110,000 computations per second and which appeared to be quite advanced. By 1971, Number 111 was born, China's first integrated circuit computer, albeit still relatively small. China went through the "electron tube period" and the "transistor period" in the 1950s and 1960s. By the time Liu Chuanzhi left the Labor Reform farm in Hunan and joined the Computer Institute, China's computer technology was entering its own Third Generation.

In developed countries, computers were employed in commercial uses from the 1970s. Japan, despite going through extremely hard times after being defeated in the War, began quietly to rebuild her economy. While Chinese were on the lookout for class enemies, the Japanese were building computers that far surpassed those of China. Hitachi and Fujitsu were already a certain size and their production lines were already using mainframe computers from IBM.

Americans, meanwhile, had computers that did one million computations a second. The most historically significant thing to happen next was the creation of personal computers and, in addition, the tremendous move into software development. In the winter of 1974, the personal computer established by the Edward Roberts group—the Altair 8800—was the start of a new epoch in computer history. It ignited the computer assembly business. In the spring of the following year, Bill Gates and Paul Allen wrote the first-generation applied-editing language tool. At the same time they set up the company called Microsoft in English, directly translated into the name *Weiroan* in Chinese. Immediately behind them came a group of young people who were destined to make history. Andy Grove, who prevented Intel from taking a mistaken path of memory chips, began the course of monopolizing microprocessors. Steve Jobs, not yet graduated from college, founded the Apple Computer Company in a small broken-down garage and in the following ten years created a computer that sold faster than any other in American computer history.

Liu Chuanzhi was 32 years old in 1976. In his first few years at the Computer Institute, he felt stifled. The days were hard to endure. "All day long you had to be totally quiet. It was intolerable. If you were to mention what was going on inside yourself, how you felt about things, someone might report you. If anything got out, you would not just be in trouble but in danger. After a while I found two or three very good friends. We would lock ourselves inside a room and talk about national affairs and make ourselves feel better." He and his friends discussed issues such as the Lin Biao Incident, the Gang of Four, Mao Zedong's wife, Jiang Qing, the mistreatment of Zhou Enlai.

Zhou Enlai died on January 8, 1976. The death traumatized Liu Chuanzhi; "The Premier had a cruel fate," he told a friend. "I think I know this country pretty well." To epitomize that fate, he recited a sentence from one of Lu Xun's stories, about a person living inside an iron-walled room: "Everyone is sleeping, the air is thin and it's hard to breathe. You wake up first, suffocating, feeling as though you're about to die. You find that the surrounding walls are made of steel: no way to pry them open."

By the spring of 1976, China had reached the point at which steel walls no longer could contain people's emotions. In the week before the holiday known as *Qingming* in China, Tiananmen surged with crowds of people. This was the first time the Communist Party faced a popular revolt since it had taken power. It led to Mao Zedong's doubting Deng Xiaoping. Deng was repeatedly denounced, but he kept winning the people's support. At the time, this incident was called the "Tiananmen Counter-revolutionary Incident." After eight months, it received formal exoneration and the name was changed to "the Tiananmen Revolutionary

Incident." Liu Chuanzhi experienced this process of going from "Counter-revolutionary" to "Revolutionary." In April, 1976, during the Great Agitation, he wrote a poem mourning Zhou Enlai and went to Tiananmen to recite it. This was a clear challenge to Jiang Qing, wife of Mao Zedong. One day later, the masses in the Square were suppressed by police and many were arrested and jailed. Liu Chuanzhi's name was also on the blacklist, but fortunately he had gone to Tiananmen when it was dark and returned before dawn. He went alone. The photo of Zhou Enlai and his poem were safely inserted in an oilcloth package and hidden under the eaves.

At the beginning of 1978, Mao Zedong had been dead for over one year. After going through an initial period of grief, new hope emerged in China. On March 18, 1978, a national science conference was held at the Great Hall of the People. A total of 5,585 delegates came from all over the country, teachers, doctors, writers and scientists, and also 117 commissioners from Institutes. For many years all of these people had been considered "left over from the Old Society" or they were known as "those who had not been properly reformed." Mao Zedong called them "hairs" on a blanket. Many people referred to them as the "Stinking Old Nine." They had endured unremitting criticism, hardship, humiliation, and many had died. They now heard Deng Xiaoping say, "Intellectuals are a part of the working class." He said, "Those who work with their brains are a component of those who work."

China's "springtime for the sciences" marked a new period of history. China's Academy of Sciences already had one hundred and twenty-three Research Institutes. The Computer Institute had 1,500 people and other cities were setting up their own computer teams throughout the country, in Shanghai, Xi'an, Wuhan, Chengdu and in Shenyang. For twelve years universities had not taken in any students or graduated any students. The computer scientists educated in the 1950s were now all over forty years old. Zeng Maochao had taken over from Yan Peilin and become the second Head of the Institute.

The Altair 8800 had not attracted Chinese attention; instead everyone was fixated on mainframes, feeling that this set the standard and was the pride of Chinese computer science. Computer science research was still considered a "National Responsibility," yet the mainframe under development was to be the last one that the Institute developed. It had a mighty name: "Project 757." It possessed a mighty volume—more than 1,300 components, more than 20,000 logic components. It was distributed over two floors of a building with the central processor in fifteen cases in one room and subsidiary elements including magnetic disk, laser disk, input output, printer, etc., occupying some 800 square meters in other rooms. Zeng Maochao called the long process of developing this machine the "Eight-year War of Resistance," a reference to the War of Resistance against Japan. The 1,000 people who worked on it in the Institute began in 1976 and finished only in 1983. Testing and adjustments went on for another year. Project 757 had a computing speed of ten million calculations per second and it won the Important Science and Technology Achievements' First-class Award. Yet, Zhou Guangzho, Deputy Head of the Institute and later to be Head of the Chinese Academy of Sciences, admitted quite candidly, "This 757 was extremely hard to use."

Not only were mainframe computers hard to use, this line of scientific research appeared to be over. China's Academy of Sciences had around 90,000 scientists. Every year, it spent approximately RMB 300 million of the national budget, but rarely could any of its scientific accomplishments be turned into anything useful. By the mid-1980s, China was clearly changing. The fear of war was receding and production lines for military industries were being converted to general consumption. The "757" became the final song in the history of computer development in the interests of the military in China.

In 1984, while the country at large was bubbling with excitement, the atmosphere at the Computer Institute was decidedly cool. Liu Chuanzhi's mood was particularly bad. For years, thousands of people had poured their intelligence and passion into developing this mainframe computer. To have done it and then simply to put it aside and wait to develop the next was unacceptable. The Institute had developed over twenty of these computers but was not permitted to sell a single one. Liu Chuanzhi thought that was wrong. He felt that computer technology should be able to do more than collect a pile of medals and awards. He decided that this was not the life he wanted. He had followed the path of science for over ten years and had nothing to show for it. Liu had always been surrounded by people who followed him and he knew that he had the ability to lead. He wanted an opportunity to use this talent. He therefore left the Computer Institute to become a cadre in the Personnel Department of the Chinese Academy of Sciences. After several months he discovered that he had no passion at all for being an official. All had to be done according to Department directives, and the work was trivial. Anybody could do it. This was not going to prove his value.

The Institute in 1984 was nearly dormant. The Number 109-C was retired from service. For the past eighteen years it had been used exclusively for research on atom bombs, hydrogen bombs, guided missiles and satellites, and it had served well. Before being dismantled, the Science Commission of the Defense Ministry awarded it honors as though the Commission were decorating a loyal old soldier. The machine was given an honorary title for Meritorious Service, yet not a single scientist in the Institute received any kind of award. Over 1,000 people and dozens of organizations had contributed their efforts to the project—it would have been impossible to know who would be most deserving. To scientists in the Institute, this was unimportant anyway, for matters of graver concern were imminent. Now that their "meritorious old minister" had been sent to pasture, what exactly were they supposed to do?

The Head of the Institute, Zeng Maochao, felt a great burden in this regard. The finances of the Institute were precarious. There was no research plan from the Defense Ministry at all, and consequently no allocation of funding. More than 1,000 scientists and technicians and more than 500 workers had nothing to do. In 1985, funding for applied sciences was to be cut by 20%; within five years, funding was to be discontinued altogether. If this were true, it meant that 1,500 employees under Zeng's responsibility could no longer carry on scientific research and that even their food and housing would be in doubt.

Liu Chuanzhi believed that the old system was insupportable. He wanted to do something by which he could feel some hope for the future.

By now it was late fall, 1984. It was the end of a glorious and also tragic era. People were anxiously anticipating the next chapter, though nobody knew how and where it would begin.

Part One

(1984-1989): The Rebels

ONE FOOT EACH ON TWO DIFFERENT BOATS

History is a book that is bound together one page at a time.

Liu Chuanzhi

The Lianxiang Group began to think of itself as having a history only after becoming a large company. In the early 1990s, people began to collect documents and organize files and it was only then that they discovered that there was no record of the company's founding. There had been no documents, no media coverage, no ceremonial ribbon-cutting that could define the Start. Years after the fact, some Founders vaguely remembered that the beginning was in the month of October 1984. Others thought, however, that it might have been November.

As time passed and company resources and fame grew, the legend of Lianxiang grew as well. The company came to be regarded as a model of China's development, it became the ideal "China Story". The pioneers of the company came to be regarded as pioneers for China, rebels who opened up the path of reform for others to follow. These pioneers were now championed as being able to break through all obstacles with a toughness and stamina that allowed them to succeed. They also had a streak of idealism and, it was admitted, a large measure of good luck. As the legend went on, these qualities allowed them to forge the entire computer industry in China, not just create China's largest computer company. The tough qualities also gave the pioneers the means to escape from poverty and make themselves wealthy.

The Founders were described as heroes. They were perceived to be a group of intellectuals who pressed forward with a mission despite the lack of resources. These intellectuals somehow obtained RMB 200,000 and were thereby able to turn the first page of this legendary story. In fact, in the beginning, nobody had any idea of where the company was going or what it might become.

To give one example: in the fall of 1984, Liu Chuanzhi made a solemn vow to Zhou Guangzho, the Deputy Director of the Chinese Academy of Sciences from whom he had received permission to found the company. He stated, "I promise we will create a company that has annual revenues of two million yuan." What was then an astronomical sum, around US$250,000 at today's rate of exchange, should be seen in context: after the acquisition of IBM-PC Lianxiang has an annual turnover exceeding US$13 billion.

October 17, 2004

The company started out in a small building of twenty square meters that had two rooms, front and back. It stood in front of the Computer Institute Compound at Number 2 Academy of Sciences South Road. In China, such small one-storey buildings in front of a compound served as guard posts. This founding site has now been recorded in the archives of the company and it echoes the famous sites of Communist Party history— Nanhu, Jinggangshan, Zunyi, Yan'an, Tiananmen. By the winter of 2002, the Founders of the company were white-haired and the building itself was dilapidated. It was not in keeping with the skyscrapers that began to surround it. The new guard at the company wanted to demolish it; the old guard wanted to keep it as historical evidence. After tremendous debate about preserving Tradition as opposed to getting on with Development, everyone agreed that Tradition should submit to the needs of Construction, that is to say, building up China. All agreed to move the building to a new spot and put it in a handsome grassy space where it would be an eternal monument.

After much discussion, Lianxiang's current management set the official date of the founding of Lianxiang in this building as November 1, 1984. There is some evidence to support this. Papers requesting the establishment of the company were sent up to the authorities on November 1, and the documents were sent back with a stamp of approval on the same day. Jia Xufu, one of the Founders, states with a certain conviction, however, that the "meeting to set up the company" was on October 17, 1984. This was then known as "the first Conference in the Guard Post."

Eleven people attended. This was a company-wide meeting and so eleven represented the full staff. All were members of the Computing and Technology Research Institute, and all were "middle-aged." At forty, Liu Chuanzhi was the youngest among them. Wang Shuhe was the oldest, at forty-five. Wang was at the time Head of the Science and Technology Department—he was superior to Liu Chuanzhi in both position and qualifications. He had an acute intelligence and spoke with vigor and passion. He always wanted to do things differently from others. All of these qualities were similar to Liu Chuanzhi, and yet Wang Shuhe was to leave the company within one year and eight months. Wang was a man who "turned his head around to look backwards three times for every one step he took forward." Nowadays it is difficult to comprehend the psychology of people at the time. As older people in China know well, the effect of one's experiences and "background," or prior family social status, left indelible traces on a person's character. Wang's family had been wealthy in the 1940s and this became a crime in New China when the Communist Party took power in 1949. A nationwide judgment of "class standing" occurred in the 1950s and Wang's father was judged to be a Small Landlord. Because of this, Wang himself was persecuted during every political movement that followed. The first half of his life was spent in a state of terror and depression. By the 1980s, this had all become something in the past, yet he could not allow himself to feel free. When he left the company, he told friends that he felt like a coward. Young people today cannot hear the anguish in this statement—those who lived through those times know the sentiment well. The mere social position of one's parents was cause for either swaggering about or cowering in abject fear. As a result, Wang was one of those who always vacillated before taking action. Liu Chuanzhi's approach was different: he ensured that defenses were prepared in every conceivable direction and then he plunged ahead. He and others in the company at the time understood that there was no turning back. Wang, in contrast, was unwilling to become a rebel who could not be assured of the precise future in advance. Wang was enthusiastic about establishing the company; his departure less than two years later was a result of personal necessity.

Preparations for starting the company were simple. There was no business plan. Liu Chuanzhi and Wang Shuhe agreed that the first task was to find like-minded people among their most trusted colleagues.

The first person they wanted to gather into their fold was Zhang Zuxiang. Zhang was Deputy Director of the Institute's Number Eight Research Lab and was famous in his own right. This could be attributed to his efforts in broadening general knowledge about computer sciences: he frequently gave lectures to thousands of people. One of Zhang's fortunate traits was that he made the right decisions at his various turning points in life. In 1958, when he entered the Shenyang Machine Electronics Institute, the government was just setting up computer-science departments in universities. Zhang asked to go to the China Science & Technology University to study computers, which was a wise decision. After graduating, he was appointed to a research institute in Dalian, where he was to study machine-tool fabrication. He asked to be transferred to the Computer Lab, however—a second wise decision. By 1984, people both inside and outside the government had been trying to entice him to help set up factories and run them. The Head of the Computer Institute, Zeng Maochao, had also wanted him to become General Manager of a Scientific Instruments Factory under the Institute, but Zhang tactfully turned him down. When an employee of the factory named Jin Yanjing left to form his own company, called *Xintong*, he too asked Zhang to come with him. "What I do is technology," he responded. "I can't manage a company."

Several weeks later, Liu Chuanzhi visited Zhang's home, a room in the collective dormitory at the Chinese Academy of Sciences. This building was known as a "tube building" at the time. It dated from the early 1980s and had corridors lined with rooms in which several dozen families lived. Liu Chuanzhi had brought along his plan. He admitted that he didn't have much money, only the RMB 200,000 promised by Zeng Maochao to start the enterprise, and the use of the Guard Post as an office. He said that no matter how large the company became in the future, it would still belong to the country, not to them, but to Liu's way of thinking this was not a problem. He was full of passion and excitement as he asked Zhang to join the enterprise.

Zhang was familiar with Liu Chuanzhi as a person. Although Liu was much younger, "his personal magnetism, his abilities, his honesty and the ease of talking to him had long since attracted me," as he was later to say. These convictions led him to accept Liu's invitation. Many years later, Zhang was still highly moved as he remembered that moment. "I am not a man of great abilities and I often make mistakes in judgment, but on that day, I made the most intelligent decision of my life."

There were now three of them. Wang, Liu, and Zhang came together in Zhang's tiny home to discuss the future of the company. The consensus was that the most urgent task was "to call together soldiers and buy horses." They wanted their troops to have certain potential capabilities: to understand their duties and yet be proactive, to have accomplished things already and yet be unsatisfied, to be loyal and open minded yet have the spirit of rebels. These three men had been working in the Computer Institute for years; the people they were looking for would come from the circle immediately around them. They drew up a list of names right there and then.

In those days, anyone involved in "business" had a bad reputation. Any cultivated, talented person was presumed to be a scientist. The first scholars who took the plunge into business were forced to do it in desperation. It was not easy to draw up a list of names, and it was even harder to persuade the candidates on the list to join them. The three men divided the responsibility and agreed that within three weeks they should have assembled their initial group. In the history of *Lianxiang*, these people are pioneers but in the Institute's large compound they were not so special. They were merely individuals dissatisfied with their current reality. They were willing to raise the standard of revolt on their own and they felt it would be that much better to do it as a group. In addition to the three already mentioned, there were Jia Xifu, Zhou Xiaolan, Jia Wanzhen, Ma Wenbao, Li Tianfu, Xie Songlin, Wang Shiying, and Pang Dawei.

In the years to come these men would be called "Founders." They were to become highly respected and admired by others. The first plenary session was held in the Guard Post. The room was bare, except for the dust. The first decision of the meeting, therefore, was to sweep the floor. It was then decided to move in some chairs and tables and, after this was done, everyone sat down. Nobody had a specific position or duty, there was no General Manager or Deputy General Manager. The entire staff could be seated on three benches. There was no ceremony associated with this meeting; there wasn't anyone announcing that this was the start of the company. "And yet," Zhang Zuxiang was to say, "I figure that that was the moment."

The company did not yet have a name. Everyone therefore began to think of names. They argued for a long time but couldn't agree. Their lives had been exclusively concerned with scholarship and with technology up to now—they had no concept of what a "company" really was. They were oblivious to the fact that the crux of a good name was its brevity, the ease with which it rolled off the tongue, the way it promoted a sense of cohesion and identity among a company's members, and the way it influenced a broader public. They could not, as in the West, use their own initials. Everyone felt that the name had to contain the words Chinese Academy of Sciences—this "brand" was to them both stirring and practical. The name could also not be without "Computer Technology Research

Institute," since this was the sacred home of computer science in China. And it could not be without the implied meaning of the words "Strong Development" since that was the dream of everyone involved. By the time the meeting had adjourned, therefore, all had agreed to name the company the Chinese Academy of Sciences Computer Technology Research Institute New Technology Development Company.

These men then moved from the familiar old establishment of the Institute into the Guard Post. If they had not taken this one step they never would have gone through so many trials and tribulations, ridicule, pressure, and dangers, but they also would not have enjoyed so much success. Today the company has over 17,000 employees, prior to the IBM acquisition, and an additional 9,600 after the acquisition. Their average age is twenty-eight. The name has been changed to Lianxiang in Chinese and Lenovo in English. Lianxiang has become the most famous brand in China and Lianxiang computers have become the symbol of the Chinese computer industry to the Chinese people.

At the time, none of these Founders could have imagined this future. They were not pioneers in technology, nor did they have any money to invest. They had plowed the fields of computer science for years, but had no idea what a personal computer was. As they put one foot out for that first step they had no idea in which direction the step should go. At that point, they could not conceive of the company's future path. The story about a meeting in a Guard Post at #2 Academy of Sciences South Road is, in fact, largely the story of what took place in China over the past twenty years.

A Nation of material shortage
On October 20, 1984, *Zhongnanhai*, the governing seat of power in China, passed a decree entitled "Decisions Regarding Reform of the Economic System." Much of what was written in this document is self-evident today. At the time, it released energies that had been held back for years. The document stated, for example, that "Rampant egalitarianism is destroying the productive capacity of society." And it said, "[We] permit and encourage certain regions, certain industries and certain people to depend on their hard work and energy to enrich themselves." It also said, "[We want to] encourage more and more people, wave by wave, to move towards wealth."

The Party Leaders described "reform" as something that was now "urgently needed." This too was unprecedented. In the fall of 1984, the tenor of a new era began to seep into every corner of China, including the Chinese Academy of Sciences. The Physics Research Institute placed the cornerstone for a new experimental laboratory, and Deng Xiaoping and his colleagues from *Zhongnanhai* came to extend congratulations and to help in piling up the earth around the foundation. To Liu Chuanzhi, this event held great symbolic meaning. A new life was close at hand, literally as well as figuratively, for the foundation was only one wall away from his home.

The new building was east of the Computer Institute, outside the wall that surrounded its compound. On the inside of the wall was a structure that was two meters high and three meters wide. This had once been a bicycle shed. At a certain point in China's history it became "home" for a group of scientists. The progression from parking shed for bikes to a home for people characterizes how Chinese lived in those days. China was already a bicycle paradise by the late-1960s: as soon as people accumulated a little cash, the first thing they bought was a bike. The Computer Institute therefore carved out a patch of ground for people to park these bikes on one side of its compound. It put up some shingles for a make-shift cover and provided employees with free parking space. This was happening all over China—it was standard practice for every unit in every city. Later, when the Cultural Revolution began to wind down, all things previously neglected were to have their turn. Everyone had been waiting years for a peaceful place to live and a stable job. Organizations began to expand as a generation of baby-boomers grew up. Young people began to marry, middle-aged people began to move back to their registered places of residence. Military personnel guarding compounds moved their families into cities. The shortage of housing soon became a tremendous social problem. In the Computer Institute, a group of covetous people, jealous of others' housing, moved themselves into the space of the bicycle parking lot. They divided the shed up into room after room of small squares and made living quarters by constructing walls of packed mud and cement. On their eastern walls they broke out square holes to serve as windows. On other walls they broke out doors and set doorjambs in them. In the 1970s and early 1980s, more than forty families lived in this bicycle-shed space. They included workers, policemen, and also scientific personnel like Liu Chuanzhi.

By the late 1970s, the small living area at the base of the Computer Institute's eastern wall was quite organized. A narrow lane traversed it from head to foot, so the district was called the Eastern-suburb People's Lane. This name originally belonged to a quiet district in the center of eastern Beijing: forty years earlier foreigners had lived there; thirty years earlier it became the seat of the Beijing Municipal government, so people thought of it as a synonym for a wealthy area. There was a certain irony to the fact that a group of scientists had appropriated the name for their living quarters. People who lived through that period in China know all that it implied.

Liu Chuanzhi moved into the Eastern-suburb People's Lane in 1971. He and his wife pasted newspapers on the four walls. They added a layer of bamboo mats to the roof, and then they moved the family in. That was a happy day, for they had been living in separate dormitories. Though the new home had a low ceiling, was cramped and dilapidated, it was paradise to them.

The Tangshan earthquake occurred in the summer of 1976. Approximately 240,000 people were killed in this event and the city of Tangshan was levelled to flat land. All of northeastern China was terrified that it might happen again. Many in Beijing refused to go indoors at night—they slept and basically lived outdoors. In the several weeks following the earthquake, temporary earthquake-proof huts sprang up around the city like mushrooms after a rain. The danger of another earthquake soon receded, but the simple huts had tapped a deep well of instinctive creativity. People soon expanded the huts and made them stronger, till they became something approaching permanently livable architecture. The Chinese language did not yet contain the phrase "illegal building." The government realized that it had no ability to make homes for everyone, so it simply allowed the self-determination to continue. This situation further inspired those who lived in the Eastern-suburb People's Lane. Everyone now competed to enlarge his own little space. Researchers who normally worked in the realm of Computer Sciences now became enthusiastic bricklayers.

Liu Chuanzhi and his wife were still living in the Eastern-suburb People's Lane when Lianxiang was established in 1984. Their child was born here and they took in a niece named Fang Fang; Liu Chuanzhi's wife's parents moved up from Hunan to live with them. The small place became crowded, the one bed was turned into upper and lower berths and they added a folding bed that would be spread out at night and taken up during the day. Washing would be hung out over the stove: the way the sheets fell into the soup once has become part of family lore.

In the fall of 1984, Liu Chuanzhi's monthly salary was RMB 105. Researchers with longer tenure received RMB 115, younger engineers received RMB 97. Salaries of urban dwellers in China had not changed throughout the 1950s and 1960s—only in the late 1970s was there a one-time nationally synchronized action to raise wages by 10%. Gradually more and more items were available in stores, and they were cheap, but one still had to plan a few months in advance to save enough to buy a pair of cotton trousers.

By the mid-1980s, the pace of change was picking up. The government dissolved 52,789 Peoples' Communes in the countryside, and now allowed farmers to grow products for themselves. Agricultural production increased by 20% and it was suddenly hard in this impoverished country to sell grain. It was a stirring time: in 1984 China competed in the Olympics for the first time since 1949 and won 15 gold medals; China's first Antarctic research team headed for the South Pole; fourteen cities along the eastern coast of China were declared to be "open to the Outside;" two radical reformers from the cities became popular heroes; two courageous novels describing "reformers" became best sellers in the bookstores—*Heavy Wings* and *Elegy for Yan Zhao*. On October 1, 1984, at the ceremony for the thirty-fifth anniversary of the founding of the Peoples' Republic of China, 500,000 people sang and danced while Peking University students managed to work a sheet with "Hello Xiaoping!" written on it into their parade formation. The media leveraged this event and gave hundreds of millions of Chinese an unprecedented sense of relaxation and freedom.

Seeking a new life is ok

In an amazingly short time, China went from being a land of rippling wheat and fertile rice fields to being a land covered with factories and shops. The years of "Reform" became one of the most momentous periods of change in Chinese history. Under the impetus of consumer demand and commercial supply, a tremendous economic system welled up in the country. Buying and selling goods was now seen as the road to success for individuals, enterprises, and the entire nation. Advertisements that had disappeared for thirty years returned. Newspapers began to print stories about profits, capital, bonuses, things that had belonged strictly to the belief system of "capitalists." Superhighways began to stretch across the land: this great invention that had brought such wealth to Western countries now brought fundamental change to the Chinese transport system. The wave of change rolled outward from cities into every corner of China.

When future historians look back on the course of China's reform, the mid-1980s may be seen as a time when a first generation of entrepreneurs began to open up virgin territory. The names of eight or nine out of every ten of the wealthiest people in China today can be found in the record of those early days. They include, for example, Zong Qinghou who, together with two retired teachers started selling popsicles on the street at four cents a stick, and two years later founded the Wahaha Children's Nutrition Company, one of the biggest companies in China.

The media in China does not generally like to use the term "rebels" to describe these courageous and also sometimes reckless people. It prefers to use "reformers", or "pioneers", or "business founders", or "heroes". Journalists began to research the origins of these people. They discovered three incubating locations that were particularly well-suited to the development of the entrepreneurial spirit. These were the delta region of the Pearl River near Guangzhou in Guangdong province, the Golden Triangle in the southern part of Fujian province, and the Wenzhou region in southern Zhejiang province. One observer named Qin Shuo did not agree—in a book called *Bureau of Great Changes*, he put Zhongguancun into the list. He noted that it was unlike the others in one key respect: the three areas noted by others were fertile ground for traders, whereas Zhongguancun was the cradle of "intellectual heroes." Liu Chuanzhi and his colleagues happened to be living in the middle of this intellectual cradle.

The geographic position of Zhongguancun is advantageous. It is in the northwest corner of Beijing along a corridor that has been a route for military expeditions and campaigns from ancient times. The invasion route was used by northern nomadic tribes and later peasant leaders as they entered Beijing. In 1949, the army of the Communist Party used this route when they entered the city and then moved southward into the central plains. For the next thirty years, many adverse policies were imposed on the city: tearing down the old walls, dismembering the old city, inserting skyscrapers in old neighborhoods of courtyard houses, expanding the city outwards ring road by ring road. However, one positive policy undertaken by the government was to concentrate universities and institutions of scientific research in an area of roughly one hundred square kilometers around Zhongguancun. The name means "village by the central pass". For the rest of this book it will be abbreviated as ZGC. By the mid-1980s, this region already contained seventy universities and at least two hundred science and technology organizations, concentrating a population of 300,000 university students and 100,000 science and technology personnel. Nationwide, thirty-six out of every one hundred scholars lives in this area. In the words of Qin Shuo, "this may be the highest density of scientific intelligence in the world."

Lianxiang was established during this extraordinary period of impetuous change—this period of casting off the existing system and searching for the future. The early Lianxiang entrepreneurs used "technology-development" to differentiate themselves from mere traders. They relied on chaotic disorder in the system, and the inability of the government to set restrictive policies, to make a profit. They survived considerable hardship at the beginning but their computers eventually became a necessary part of peoples' lives. The "Lianxiang Spirit" came to be called the "China Spirit." The company represented a microcosm of China and Chinese culture. In the past twenty years, Lianxiang has accompanied China as it grew up. It has put its imprint on China and, one could say, it has put the national imprint on itself.

Lianxiang and Liu Chuanzhi were not the first of their kind, however. The first ones came some four years earlier. The youngest researcher in the Physics Institute of the Academy of Sciences was Chen Chunxian: he left for Silicon Valley in America for an experience that changed his life. He noted that American scientists and engineers always wanted to realize their inventions in patented technology and to put the results of their knowledge into products. As a result, they sometimes succeeded in creating new industries worth billions of dollars. He also noted that, relatively speaking, the density of human talent in ZGC was no lower than that in the San Francisco or the Boston area. When people living in darkness for a long time are exposed to a ray of light, nothing can stop them from finding ways to get more of it. Chen's company was founded on October 23, 1980. It was called the Advanced Development Technical Service Department of the Beijing Ion Association. He appears to be the first researcher to resign his post at the Chinese Academy of Sciences, according to Academy records. His company was the first *min-ying* or "people-administered" scientific enterprise in ZGC. Enterprises in China are referred to either as "people-administered" or "state-administered," depending on whether or not they are owned by the state. People-administered enterprises are not called private companies. Chen's company was the Chinese version of a story from Silicon Valley: seven young people, a debt of RMB 500, and an old garage.

Chen and his colleagues scraped together a meager investment and then distributed RMB 15 each as bonuses to top executives. At the time, this was criticized as highly improper behavior. It was seen as engaging in speculation and profiteering. Many were envious, however, and resigning from one's secure government-funded post became a trend. "Plunging into the ocean" became a common phrase. Companies began to spring up on the streets of ZGC. Four among them became the most famous in China: Xintong, Sitong, Jinghai, and Kehai, later also known as the Two Tong's and the Two Hai's. All four were started by people from the Chinese

Academy of Sciences: Wan Runnan, Jin Yanjing, Chen Qingzhen, and Wang Hongde. Wang Hongde, Founder of Jinghai Company, was an engineer at the Computer Institute. His departure preceded that of Liu Chuanzhi by twelve months and he was even less able than Liu to go back. His days at the Institute could be described, he said, by the phrase "you're not allowed to do anything but you're not allowed to leave." When he resigned his post, he made a statement about the four ways of leaving: being transferred to a different post, being invited to a different post, retiring, and being fired. His conclusion was that "It doesn't matter what form it takes, just so long as you get Out!" At the time, this was the unmistakable "Declaration of a Rebel."

By the time Lianxiang was established in October of 1984, there were already forty scientific enterprises in ZGC. Most of these were clustered around White-Stone Bridge, or *Baishiqiao*, along a narrow ribbon stretching from Haidian Street to ZGC Street. There was also already an Electronics Street to sell their products. In the reforms of the mid-1980s, many risk-taking former scholars were turning to commerce, tempting and also tricking customers to the extent that all of China ridiculed ZGC's Electronics Street as being a place you go to get cheated. The newly named China Academy of Sciences Computer Technology Research Institute New Technology Development Company seemed just a drop of water in the general sea of commerce.

Liu Chuanzhi's mind was set when he left his old job and from all appearances he was a rebel, but at the same time he had no intention of parting ways with the traditional system. The reason Liu Chuanzhi was able to gather together such a group in such a short time was his knack for leaving room to maneuver, preserving space to operate within the infrastructure of the old system.

After *Zhongnanhai* promulgated the "Decision Regarding Reform of the Economic System," an early wave of risk-takers resigned from their old jobs and, relying on their own funding, started businesses. The great majority, however, stayed in the traditional system. They wanted more, yet were anxious not to lose what they had. They complained about abuses and corruption while, in many cases, continuing to enjoy what it brought to them personally.

Liu Chuanzhi was not like Wang Hongde. He did not have that kind of desperate willingness to take risks and completely abandon his base. He did not write a declaration of independence. He also was not like Wan Runnan, the Founder of Sitong, who declared to all who would listen that his was a company administered by private people, an organization without anyone above it, no supervisory authority. At the same time, Liu was not a person who abided by all the rules. He remained a rebel, albeit one embedded in the old system. He knew that he had to find policies that would allow him to hold the commanding ground under any circumstances and, to him, that meant not severing ties with authority. He never forgot his guiding principle: "Do something, but at the same time don't become a sacrificial victim to Reform."

The Head of the Institute, Zeng Maochao, knew that now was the time for significant action. He could not undertake radical changes in the Institute itself but he also could not see how it would support itself. He knew he should not hold back the creativity of his staff; at the same time, he did not want to force them into taking too big a risk. He decided to have the Institute become the "boss" of the new company in terms of being its administrative supervisor. He gave the company three key rights: the right to control its own finances, the right to hire and fire people, and the right to make policy decisions about operations. These three rights enabled the company to be an organization "without a supervisory body exercising control over it."

How was this new company to be funded? Money allocated by the government for scientific research was earmarked for specific purposes: allocating it for other uses was not permitted. Banks too would not loan money to the company. Fortunately, Zeng Maochao had, for the past several years, been leasing out the use of the Institute's mainframe computer. He charged one RMB per hour, and this had allowed him to save up a small sum of money. Most organizations operated in the same manner. They would make a little money in one way or another but they generally used the funds as bonuses for employees, or to buy extra food for them at the end of the year. Zeng Maochao planned ahead. He intended to use his funds for longer-term purposes. He had RMB 200,000 saved up and he now gave this to the new company. Later, as Lianxiang grew, it returned millions to the Institute, proving that Zeng was a man of considerable foresight. Zeng's investment that year was clear evidence that the company's assets belonged to the State. By financial rules of the Institute at that time, however, it was unclear whether or not this saved-up money should have been handed over to the State. This was to remain a contentious issue.

Nonetheless, the company had received a Guard Post, three specific rights, and RMB 200,000. After Lianxiang's success, not before, this was all recorded in company records as the Starting Point and was broadly touted by Chinese media. So far as Liu Chuanzhi and his colleagues were concerned, though, other received benefits were more important. The beauty of the system instituted by Zeng Maochao lay in non-publicized matters. The company could call on the services of Institute personnel without restrictions, for example. It could send any person who was not effective back to the Institute, where he would continue to enjoy his salary. In fact, all people working for the company remained on the employee rolls of the Computer Institute, and continued to receive salaries allocated by the Ministry of Finance. Employees of the company also continued to enjoy various rights granted to professional personnel regarding compensation of other kinds. Research personnel could take the results of their government-funded research with them and allow the company to use those results. In addition to the Guard Post, the company was allowed to use all material resources of the Institute including offices, telephone, fax, and so on.

None of these details was written into the company bylaws. Instead, they lay in the cracks between old and new systems. They were profoundly significant. Because of them, the company was able to use the benefits of both systems—the stability of the old and the opportunities of the new, and to avoid the shortcomings of both—the rigidities of the old and the risks of the new. The resources of the traditional system were used to subsidize exploration along an entirely new path. This was a tremendous comfort to people who still harbored misgivings.

Where to look for that "first pot of gold"
The first employee roster was established on December 4, 1984. It delineated people's titles and responsibilities. Wang Shuhe became the company's General Manager; Liu Chuanzhi and Zhang Zuxiang shared the Deputy General Manager position. The "three-man core" then prepared to expand their troops. The talent that they were able to assemble in the early days came from the strength of personal relationships within the Computer Institute; it did not derive from any promises or accomplishments of the company. Before the first official recruitment of college graduates in the summer of 1988, almost all employees of Lianxiang came from the Institute. The process of recruiting in the early days was simple: there was no written exam, and no interview. Everyone had lived and worked in the same compound for years—if you wanted to avoid someone you put your head down, if you wanted to acknowledge them you put your head up. There was no formal procedure for hiring. If you ran into someone you wanted, you said, "Hey, come on over to our company!" Or you might say, "Hey, you can still be an Institute person, just come on over and help the

company awhile." Recruitment notices were sometimes put up on bulletin boards but their real purpose was to let people know that the company existed and was making progress.

The organizational structure of the company was decided after Chinese New Year, 1985. It included four departments: the Technology Development Department, the Engineering Department, the Administrative Department, and the Office. Wang Shuhe issued a public announcement to the effect that seven people had been appointed Managers and Directors. On February 16, 1985, for the first time the company let the outside world know of its existence. It put up a notice at the ZGC intersection, on the wall facing the sun, which was the company's first reliably documentable ad.

All of Lianxiang's early personnel were emerging from years of hardship. They knew how to economize, and in starting up the company, as they say in Chinese, they "cut every cent in two and spent the two separately." Since they agreed to postpone getting a dedicated phone line, the most important duty of the Manager of the Operations Department, Liu Chifeng, was to guard the old phone, hoping to gain some business. A few people came to the door looking for the address on the ad, but they discovered that the company was a room not much bigger than the ad itself, without so much as a sign outside the door.

In spring, everyone agreed that it was time to hang out a signboard. They found a graphic designer and a good piece of wood. By the last week of March, the "China Academy of Sciences Computer Technology Research Institute New Technology Development Company" sign was ready: letters in gold paint on a black background. This was hung to face the Academy of Sciences South Road, on the same level as the sign for the China Academy of Sciences Computer Technology Research Institute. In his capacity as General Manager, Wang Shuhe delivered a report to Zeng Maochao guaranteeing that this sign "would not fade or deteriorate with the scouring of the wind and scorching of the sun."

On April 2, the appointments of Wang Shuhe, Liu Chuanzhi and Zhang Zuxiang received formal approval from the Chinese Academy of Sciences. Zeng Maochao honored his promise and put a bracket after the name of each, indicating their administrative rank. Wang Shuhe was "First Chu," Liu Chuanzhi and Zhang Zuxiang were "Deputy Chu." In the old days this would have been the lowest level of what was called a Seven-Ranked Official; in Communist Party ranking it also would have belonged to lower middle. To the three men on that day, the ranks had no real value but they were highly significant to employees of the company. Not only had the Party organization not regarded these men as traitors, it had incorporated them into the ranks of revolutionary troops. It had confirmed this with a seal of approval in the form of an organizational role.

The new Heads of the company therefore had "one foot each on two different boats". They now could avoid the problems of the old system, and they planned to relax controls even more. Their plan was excellent but one key issue remained: nobody really knew what this company ought to do. Even the Core Team of three could not say for sure. Should they try reselling things for a profit? Exercise suits perhaps, or electric refrigerators? These things were considered, but eventually the company decided to resell color TVs instead. Color TVs were an extremely hot item at the time—everyone had to have one. The government determined the price at which they left the factory and by the time they reached the market, the price could be RMB 1,000 higher. Everyone believed that the opportunity to make some money had arrived. Quality control and commercial integrity were already proving to be problematic in the mid-1980s and a popular saying went, "there's more tricksters than there are color TVs." Liu Chuanzhi knew it did not hurt to be careful: he ordered his staff to make sure that they saw the television sets with their own eyes before they paid for them. One of his staff announced that he had personally seen the TV sets and they were legitimate, but unfortunately he was duped: there had indeed been TV sets but they disappeared as soon as the money left company hands. Of the original RMB 200,000 received from Zeng Maochao, 140,000 was gone.

The first question facing the company was one that every enterprise contends with: Where is your first pot of gold going to come from? In Western countries, this is known as "the capitalist accumulation of initial capital." In China it is known as "the socialist accumulation of initial capital." The words are slightly different but the effect is exactly the same. Just as an airplane needs a runway in order to fly, a steamship needs a wharf from which to set forth, no matter which country, which region, or which company, if you want to take off, the first thing you must do is gather capital. You can borrow from the bank, you can raise money from society, or you can get support from a venture capitalist. In China, however, these were things that came only in the 1990s. They did not exist when Lianxiang was founded. In the 1980s, in China, a small or medium-sized enterprise could not borrow from a bank and people had no concept of venture capital. Both ethical and even legal issues therefore lurked behind the initial investment in any new enterprise. One could set up a sweatshop and rely on cutting the wages of workers to earn money. One could raise the hours and the amount that laborers had to work. One could evade taxes. Or one could pursue "self-interest," i.e., become corrupt. One could also rely on certain unique features of the governmental administrative system, such as the "permission system" or the "licensing system." One could take advantage of critical needs in certain commodities and the two-track system of pricing at the time—the official price and the market price, which enjoyed a hefty margin between them. All of these, in terms of academic parlance, belonged to "crimes of privately administered enterprises in China." As the Chairman of the Board of Wantong Company, Feng Lun, once said, "This so-called original sin simply meant the problem of not having any legal recourse to investment capital."

Liu did not dare break the law, and he also did not want to do anything unethical. If there had been an opportunity, he might have tried to enter the grey area between legal and illegal, but at the time even this opportunity was not available.

Liu placed his hopes on the Computer Institute. After all, he had lived under a traditional system for two dozen years, and he lacked the bravado to "walk straight-backed into danger." He had not built up any personal reputation in banking circles. Although a main tenet of the company was to disassociate itself from the Institute, everyone knew that the most important resources for the company lay within the traditional system. The Academy of Sciences was sacred in the eyes of most people. The Computer Institute was the cradle of the computer industry in China. All of the most notable people in the field had emerged from this Institute.

The Institute's reputation contributed greatly to the company. In the early period the Institute also brought the company priceless research results: the connection essentially enabled Lianxiang to leave its competitors behind in the dust. Although this was early days, when Zeng Maochao called the Institute a "Golden Signboard" for the company this was no exaggeration. When the company eventually did borrow money from a bank, it was able to use the name of the Institute: the company was the Institute's contracted party in applying for the loan. The guarantor of the loan was the Development Bureau of the Chinese Academy of Sciences. As a further example of the usefulness of the Institute to the Company: on January 21, 1985, the Deputy Director of the Chinese Academy of Sciences, Zhou Guangzho, allocated US$200,000 dollars from its foreign exchange quota to the company. The foreign exchange quota was an economic phenomenon unique to the 1980s in China. One could not spend it recklessly, and if one did, the consequences could be severe. In the document written by Zhou that allowed for allocating this sum to the company, he noted, "This is a kind of special favor."

By December of 1985, just one year after the establishment of the company, many hoped that it could move towards becoming more independent. Some hoped it could have its own Board of Directors in order to get out from under the control of the Institute. Liu Chuanzhi refused. Two general approaches characterized relations between staff and the Institute at the time: pledging loyalty or declaring rebellion. The more Liu Chuanzhi believed that he was on a path of no return, the more he also felt he was becoming a "loyal official" and not a rebel. He announced in the Annual Meeting, "the company will not set up an independent Board of Directors. Working directly under the concern and supervision of the Leaders guarantees that all the actions of the company will be following a unified path of development." In the twenty years that were to follow, many people recalled this statement. Many had come to believe that the Company took unfair advantage: it received RMB 200,000 from the Institute and in return garnered tens of millions. This was seen as profiting by unfair means. Others, on the contrary, raised doubts about the way the resources of the company still appeared to belong to the State. Only Liu Chuanzhi argued on behalf of strong ties to the Institute.

In his address at the 1985 Annual Meeting, Liu enumerated the company's accomplishments over the past year. He described the business items that had brought the company profit, such as the management engineering software from Tianjin, the management engineering software of the State Planning Commission, the automatic management system of the Mudanjiang Iron & Steel Factory, and others. The four most profitable items were a direct result of affiliation with the Computer Institute. They brought the company RMB 3.5 million in revenue and RMB 2.5 million on profit. They were:

1. The KT8920 mainframe computer. This had been developed solely by the Computer Institute, which then transferred certain useful parts to the company. The company, in its own name, sold the research results to outside entities in twenty-five separate contracts, making RMB 600,000 in profit.
2. The Chinese Academy of Sciences bought 500 IBM computers and transferred the contract for repair and training to the company, so that the company earned RMB 700,000 in service fees.
3. The company earned US$70,000 in gross profit for various things done on behalf of the Beijing Central Agency of IBM.

4. The final item was the most important. The Researcher Ni Guangnan, Chief Engineer of the company, had brought his Chinese-character system into the company. Although a result of his own research, this system had been funded and developed by the Computer Institute over the course of ten years. Ni Guangnan and his Chinese-character system will be addressed in detail later, but one thing should be mentioned here. Within six months of being brought into the company, that system sold more than 100 sets and brought the company RMB 400,000 in gross profit. More than that, it allowed Liu Chuanzhi to see down the path to the company's future.

2

SOME PEOPLE STRING THE PEARLS

If the overall situation cannot be changed, work to change the immediate circumstances. If these too cannot be changed, adapt yourself to the way things are and wait for your chance.

Liu Chuanzhi

"Some people are like pearls," Liu Chuanzhi once said to a friend. "And some are not—they can't glow with their own beauty. On the other hand, some of these other people know how to string pearls together, to make a fabulous necklace." He was already forty years old and he was not going to be able to change himself, but he knew his strengths: "I think that I am a string that aligns the right pearls." Liu Chuanzhi also knew his shortcomings: in the realm of science, he was much less talented than people like Ni Guangnan and Chen Dayou. Yet through stringing pearls he had a qualification that others lacked; through it, he wanted to find a way to sell the inventions of the Institute and turn technology into profit.

The common dream of Liu Chuanzhi and Ni Guangnan
In early 1985, one of the pearls in Liu Chuanzhi's mind was Ni Guangnan. Ni was Deputy Researcher in the Number 6 Research Laboratory, and he was acknowledged to be an outstanding scientist in the Institute. The media later described the circumstances of his joining the company. The *S&T News* said he was "a Scientist with the thinking of a Reformer: he's willing to use the market to judge the success or failure of accomplishments". Another paper said he was a "pathfinder in the field of Chinese-character

information systems". One author, Liu Shaotang, said Ni's nature was like chrysanthemums, that "would rather grow old in solitude on a branch than accompany yellow leaves dancing in the Western wind." This last was a reference to the way Ni had refused an invitation to stay in Canada, and a high salary. Instead he took a flight back to China and as he came off the airplane at the Beijing Capital Airport he shouted out, "Motherland, I have returned."

Liu Chuanzhi and Ni Guangnan had known each other for ten years. The family circumstances of the two were radically different. Liu's father was a loyal Party member, which gave the family a sense of superiority, while Ni's father had belonged to the Kuomintang before the 1940s. A "KMT background" brought extreme pressure to bear on families. Ni Guangnan found it hard to escape from this unfortunate legacy and this was apparent in his personal characteristics of modesty, self-restraint, inflexibility, and self-doubt. On the other hand, Liu Chuanzhi was self-confident and open. For many years the two had a certain respect for and understanding of each other. When both were sent to the Xiaozhan commune on the outskirts of Tianjin to do labor, they created a certain bond. Though the two men have since parted ways, Liu Chuanzhi retains high regard for Ni Guangnan's scholarship and acute memory for details. Liu was in his element when talking to people, whereas Ni's manner of conversing with people was to grill them about tough technical problems.

Ni Guangnan was representative of people from a particular era in the development of China's computer industry. Five years older, he had just graduated from the Nanjing Engineering Academy and entered the Computer Institute when Liu Chuanzhi was entering university in 1961. The height of his personal career came in 1985 after he entered the company. Before that, he was quiet: the early period of the company sparked the radiance of Ni Guangnan. Because of this, some people felt that there would have been no Lianxiang without Ni Guangnan. Others held exactly the opposite point of view. Was Ni the achievement of the company or vice versa? The same could be asked about Liu Chuanzhi. All of these questions came as a result of that famous invention: the LX-80 Lianxiang-type Chinese character system.

In early 1985, Liu Chuanzhi had a premonition that this LX-80 presented an opportunity that would change China. Personal computers had been around for ten years. In America, the development of the Altair 8800 had provided a chance to make history: dreams were turned into reality by the efforts of a few notable people. Bill Gates said, "Let every desk, every home have a computer." The first "screwdriver" company in the world was invented, putting silicon chips and a pile of components into a box and starting the computer assembly industry. A series of successful chain stores called Computerland began: these and other developments in the West jumpstarted the modern method of selling computer systems. China had approximately 110,000 personal computers in 1984, almost all of which came from IBM. Computers were entering the lives of Chinese people, but unfortunately all of them operated in an English operating environment. Chinese were using machines that could not recognize Chinese. Language became a natural barrier. Enabling a computer to recognize Chinese characters became the goal of many Chinese scientists: this was, without doubt, the bridge that would allow 1.3 billion Chinese to enter the computer age.

Ni Guangnan's "Chinese-character system" was soon appropriately called a "Han-card". Han is another word for Chinese, while Han-zi is the term for Chinese characters. This card incorporated three circuit boards made up of electronic circuit silicon chips and an operating system and connected by cable. All of the standard Chinese characters were permanently stored inside the memory. When a Chinese character was entered into the keyboard, the operating system translated the character into a digital form that the computer could accept, then sent the digital message to the memory and the appropriate address, read it into the operating system, entered it in memory storage, and sent it to the display monitor or to the printer as a composed Chinese character.

Over ten Chinese-character systems already existed in China, with principles and operating methods that were basically the same. Ni Guangnan's Han-card was just one of many, but his had a "linked-thought" functionality. It capitalized on a special characteristic of Chinese characters. Generally a Chinese word is composed of a double-word compound. Each first-word of the compound has several second-word possibilities that form different meanings as a two-word unit. By inputting the first word in Ni's system, one had access to a list of possible compounds, arranged in order of frequency of use.

Twenty years ago this was quite an accomplishment. None of the available systems had come across the concept of word groups or compounds. They forced the user to input one character at a time. As a huge list of same-sound characters came up on the screen, one would have to scroll through them tediously to find the right one then go through the same process with the next. One aspect of all human languages is that one sound has many possible meanings and this is particularly true of Chinese. The sound "yi" has over 137 different characters, for example, each with a different meaning. Sound-redundancy becomes an impediment to efficiency and speed of operating. With the Lianxiang function, by selecting a two-character compound the work load was automatically decreased by 50%. If three characters, the number of possible word groups was lowered by 98%, and if four characters, then there was basically no duplication. The speed of entering Chinese characters was thereby doubled at the very least. Obviously, the "lian-xiang," or linked-thinking concept led to a tremendous advance in Chinese computer usage.

In early 1985, when Liu Chuanzhi heard this news and went looking for Ni Guangnan, this technology was already fairly mature and already named the "LX-80 Lianxiang-type Chinese character system." Transporting it to personal computers was the next step. This was a clear signal: the door to the huge market for personal computers for 1.3 billion Chinese was about to open, and Liu and Ni were standing shoulder to shoulder at the entryway.

Liu Chuanzhi knew that Ni Guangnan had prepared everything for the grand entry but lacked one final link—an organization that could use his sample as a prototype and move into mass production and sales. Liu gathered critical information from his colleagues at the Computer Institute. They confirmed that Ni Guangnan had already given his LX-80 to the Xingong Company in Beijing and the Zhong-han-ji company in Shenzhen and perhaps two or three more. Nobody had any idea of exclusive patents at the time and Ni Guangnan also cared nothing about money. His desire was to have the LX-80 sold to people—whoever sold it was fine with him. If they would sell it, he would form an alliance with them. Liu approached Ni Guangnan and solemnly vowed, "I guarantee that I will turn all of your research results into products."

Liu's words gave Ni Guangnan a tremendous boost. Several years later he wrote a book, *The Path of a Scientist*, and in one essay described his feelings at the time, "I had received medals and awards for my scientific research. I had labored over mainframe computer development and had received top-level results. I had been given the most important honors of the Chinese Academy of Sciences. Yet, regrettably, all of these accomplishments simply lay there in the form of awards. None had been made into actual products."

Liu and Ni were to have differences of opinion in the future. Back then, however, they shared the same dreams, the same frustrations. They had a tacit agreement that allowed their work to be complementary: neither trespassed on the rights of the other. Liu prepared in advance to meet any demands that Ni might raise when he asked Ni to join the company. Ni put forth three conditions. First, he would not be an official. Second, he would not attend meetings. Third, he would not allow interviews from journalists. Liu Chuanzhi told him that these conditions would not be a problem, and that Ni could do what he liked.

Dramatic changes followed. Bringing his LX-80 with him, Ni Guangnan participated enthusiastically in Liu Chuanzhi's company. He later was to say that in order to become the Chief Engineer of the company, "I resolutely put down the iron rice bowl." This "iron rice bowl" was a euphemism for being fed from State funds, as a State employee with total security. Ni's statement was an exaggeration for, as noted above, employees who joined the company did not in fact give up their iron rice bowls. The "Chief Engineer" title on the books had brackets around it, indicating that Ni's duties were concurrent with his old job. In terms of the organization chart he still belonged to the Institute as a Deputy Researcher and he still received a salary from the Computer Institute. Nevertheless, he also joined the market economy.

Li Qin appears on the scene

The company emerged from uncertainty in the summer of 1985. Ni Guangnan's entry into the group and the LX-80 that he brought with him were tremendously stimulating to all. Though most could not comprehend how marvellous the technology was, everyone felt that this was a good omen for the company.

New recruits could no longer be squeezed into the Guard Post, so Zeng Maochao allowed the company to start using what was called the Number 1025 Building. The Number 1025 was a mainframe computer developed in the early 1980s. Back then, the first step in making a new computer was to build a large building for it. The Number 1025 was a two-story building, each floor had at least 200 square meters of open space and several smaller rooms. The company took over one corner of the second floor and now, for the first time, provided a room for the General Manager. This was given to the triumvirate of Wang Shuhe, Liu Chuanzhi and Zhang Zuxiang.

Liu Chuanzhi could see that neither Wang Shuhe or Zhang Zuxiang was an ideal manager. Zhang was not adept at political maneuvering, he had been employed by the Institute for half his life and was not up to the job of developing relationships on the Outside. Wang Shuhe's character was indecisive. He was not the kind of man who could lead a company through danger and hardship.

Liu Chuanzhi was an implementer of strategy who had foresight and organizational capability; he was not a great engineer. He had persuasive powers and magnetism, but he lacked technical skills. He needed an engineer with superior technological skills and he needed a manager who could execute decisions. Ni Guangnan's entry into the fold satisfied one condition, but where was the best manager to be found?

Liu Chuanzhi then met Li Qin. Li was sharp, straightforward, and dared to get things done, that is, was willing to bear risks for others. Although he was said to be a technical person it was clear that he had a talent for management. He grew up in the southern outskirts of Beijing in a place called Mentougou and had the ability to relate to all kinds of people. His performance at the Computer Institute was so outstanding that he enjoyed the high regard of Zeng Maochao, who, at one point, wanted to appoint him as Director in the Sixth lab. Like Liu Chuanzhi, Li Qin was disappointed by the Institute's work, however, and applied for permission to leave. "It takes eight years to make a computer," he said, "That's a waste of time." He had also decided he was not cut out to be an official, "I like plain talk. If you are an official you can't say what you mean." Despite all this, Zeng Maochao saw that this man had the potential to be a leader and he refused to let him resign. Without permission from the Head of the Institute, Li Qin could go nowhere. At the time, lower-level employees could oppose their superiors, they could mitigate control by their superiors through negativism and a go-slow attitude, but they were not able to choose their own work. Senior management had no power to retire or fire people, but they had plenty of power to prevent anyone from leaving.

Liu Chuanzhi and Zhang Zuxiang got to work on the project. They first persuaded Li Qin to come into the company, then devised ways to persuade Zeng Maochao to let him go. Zeng finally agreed.

The road to personal computers

Li Qin's entry into the company brought a fierce "wind" into what had been a fairly gentle and cultivated group. It increased the company's attack capabilities. That summer, these were qualities the company desperately needed. The company had been established for eight months and it was time for an offensive. IBM's PC/XT and PC/AT were steadily passing through Chinese customs on their way to sale in China. These were the most popular personal computers at the time and were half a grade lower than the later "286." Although still a trickle, their entry into the market would form a tidal wave before long. In the years of "Reform and Opening," Chinese people wanted new things and they were mesmerized by personal computers, despite their lack of a Chinese-operating environment. Chinese-produced computers began in 1985, made by the Great Wall Company, but the quantity was small and the quality was such that they did not inspire trust. The market was in the hands of imported goods. A PC/XT at a Chinese port was valued at RMB 20,000, but the Chinese were willing to pay RMB 40,000 to get one. In two years, Chinese bought more than 110,000 computers at high prices.

The Chinese Academy of Sciences was a focal point of scientific minds in China. These people enjoyed being first, so they were prime buyers of personal computers. In the summer of 1985, 300 PC/XTs and 200 PC/ATs that they had purchased arrived at the Beijing customs port. They waited there for processing, for all the many steps that had to be gone through in admitting them into the country and delivering them safely into customers' hands. Somebody had to check and accept the products, repack them, ship them, train people, do repairs. At the beginning, Lianxiang had no license to import computers, so could not make the full RMB 20,000 margin on each machine. They did have the credentials to enter the latter part of the value chain, though, namely servicing. Liu Chuanzhi asked Li Qin if he could look after this aspect of the business.

Everyone was proud to think of getting a servicing contract. But when Li Qin and Zhang Zuxiang arranged to meet at the Chinese Academy of Sciences, they suddenly found that it was not that simple. People from the Xintong Company had barged ahead of them and were sitting in the office of the Head of the Academy.

Xintong was one of the "Two Tong's and Two Hai's." Its size and reputation were far above those of Lianxiang. The disparity in strength was obvious, along with the fact that the General Manager of Xintong, Jin Yanjing, and the Manager of the Equipment Department of the Academy, Wang Yongle, had a close personal relationship. Wang Yongle had the power to give this business to whomever he chose. He did not know Li Qin or Zhang Zuxiang and he had no knowledge of the company they represented.

Events were to prove that Liu Chuanzhi's faith in Li Qin's abilities was not misplaced. Li Qin was by nature a fighter. He enjoyed a challenge, and he could calculate the strengths and weaknesses of both sides. He knew where to spring from in his attack. Li Qin persuaded Zeng Maochao to use the Computer Institute's name in applying to the Chinese Academy of Sciences. This gave his company a certain official flavor, and made it seem part of a larger family.

Li Qin first gained the trust of Wang Yongle. Wang was an upright and decisive scientist in the Chinese Academy of Sciences who knew that the people behind Li Qin not only had dependable skills but wouldn't use other's ignorance to their own advantage. He eventually handed over the 500 computers to Li Qin. He agreed that as a service fee the company could take 7 percent of the gross price.

Li Qin and Zhang Zuxiang were delighted. They had snatched business out from the hands of Xintong, just as several weeks earlier Liu Chuanzhi had snatched away Ni Guangnan's LX-80 from Xintong. That time he had relied on personal relations and on the organizational standing of the Institute, which could not be considered true market competition. This was their first encounter with a real competitor. From now on, the war was only going to get fiercer. It was going to be a long process: becoming aware of competition and understanding the market, all of which took time.

The 500 computers arrived packed in 2,000 boxes. The twenty employees of the company now took up shoulder poles and began to move the crates. The first work this group performed for the company was hard physical labor. They were so poor they did not have a wheelbarrow—they used themselves. It turned out there wasn't enough space to open the boxes and inspect the machines. Liu Chuanzhi ran over to borrow the office space of Hu Xilan, Director of the Number 757 mainframe. She had an office of 100 square meters where around a dozen people had worked. Everyone had left by now and it was empty. She saw Liu Chuanzhi come in puffing, red-faced, covered with sweat and, without the slightest hesitation, she agreed. Everyone then moved the boxes one by one over to Number 757. The building was equipped with an elevator but it wasn't working. The day was hot.

Then everyone put on the white uniforms that were to be worn when working on mainframes. Before them now were personal computers. Over the course of the next few weeks, the machines were taken out one by one, assembled, tested, and sent on to customers. The training, maintenance and repair work went on for several months. Everyone suddenly felt as though life had some meaning. The company looked pretty good after all. They wouldn't have to put out a stand in front of the Institute's door to sell plastic shoes and watches.

By now, it was time to make a report to Wang Yongle, to ask for payment. Zhang Zuxian had calculated how much money should be made, but Li Qin once again exhibited his brilliance. Standing before Wang Yongle, he described the extreme hardships these 40+ year-olds had just undergone and he relayed the complete satisfaction of all customers. He said that the company still had to do training, maintenance and repair and that this would require a certain amount of funding. In fact, the service fee that they had received would basically not be enough. Wang Yongle expressed his satisfaction at the results, but he was not willing to offer more payment. With even more passionate conviction, Li Qin now brought the company's case to the man under Wang named Tong Xizheng. He showed Tong the receipts detailing what the company had had to spend. Tong began to feel that the company had taken on an unprofitable piece of difficult work, and he could not help but take pity on these scientists. He raised the 7% fee to 9%. This one action resulted in an addition RMB 200,000 for the company.

In 1985, the gross revenue of the company was RMB 3,500,000 and its profit was RMB 2,500,000, which came from the combined income of five different aspects of the business. The income from the service fee on the 500 computers was around one-third of the total.

The success confirmed Liu's confidence in the future of the personal computer—to the extent that he could see into the company's future. It also brought intangibles of great value: as that team of movers ran back and forth in the Institute's compound, they created a marvellous inspirational force among all who saw them. They displayed the persistance, determination and vitality of the company. People who had not yet joined the company watched this from their windows and among those gazing was Hu Xilan. She was Deputy Researcher of the Number 8 Research Lab and Director of the Number 757. In addition, she was the wife of the head of the Institute, Zeng Maochao. She had just left the mainframe project and was wondering what to do. Hu later said: "These people impressed me. They were doing something. I had spent years inside the Institute and I knew the people around me. Some talked but didn't really do anything, others worked away without ever saying anything. Then there were some who both talked and did things but these were becoming fewer and fewer. On that day of the boxes, I could see the fiber in these people. Unfortunately I lacked a historical perspective back then, I didn't know that they would later become Number One in the entire country."

Victory in the first battle
Final testing was completed in June of 1985 on Ni Guangnan's "Lianxiang-type Chinese character system." A report was sent from the Computer Institute to the Development Bureau of the Chinese Academy of Sciences, asking for this product to be designated a "project" in the government Plan. The phrase "Market Economy" was still reviled at the time but one

was allowed to use the phrase "Product Economy". This term had even been written into the formal documents of *Zhongnanhai*. Government officials still took The State Plan as the necessary basis of governing and all products such as computers had to go into the Plan. No company had the power to go its own way. This company of the Institute was not listed among the government's plans, however, and even its qualifications to "send up an application report" were in doubt. The first thing this report did, therefore, was to declare that this technology was researched by the Chinese Academy of Sciences Technology Research Institute, and it was specifically designed to resolve "problems relating to the Sinification of IBM-system computers and IBM compatibles."

The company firmly believed that the Han-card had sufficient merits to attract customers and it was prepared to make it into a saleable product. In the appendix to the report, the company sought permission to use a US$250,000 foreign-exchange quota to import spare parts to improve the Han-card's functioning. This report is preserved to this day among the files of the company, but one cannot find any responding "permission" from the Chinese Academy of Sciences. This was not important: in traditional Chinese style, the company was "acting first and reporting later." More poetically, it was "executing the criminal then telling the Emperor." In this case, the company was reporting at the same time as taking action, the typical mode of operation of all early Chinese enterprises—even if the "Planned Economy System" lacked flexibility, intelligent managers could always find opportunity in its cracks. Liu Chuanzhi was no exception. Production of the Han-card was already proceeding during the month in which the company submitted its request for permission. The first batch of cards was sent out for exhibition at the Beijing Municipal Computer Exhibition on June 25.

The summer of 1985 was ferociously hot in Beijing. At least two battle formations were moving ahead auspiciously for the company: profits from the KT8920 continued to flow in and the assembly and testing of the 500 computers was progressing. Liu Chuanzhi was most delighted, however, with the "Lianxiang Han-card." "Personal Computer" had become a hot topic in the past several months among Chinese, PCs were even being discussed in the slow-reacting government. Beijing was about to open its First Computer Exhibition, and Liu Chuanzhi was planning to open his third battlefield there: the Han-card was the weapon by which he meant to win this battle. It was probably around this time that he told his immediate supervisors that the Lianxiang Han-card would be owned by the company, and it would be sold to the public under the name of the company.

He needed more people to do all this. If he were a string that aligned pearls, right now he needed more pearls. He paced through the Institute's compound, looking this way and that like a hungry lion, and when his eyes lit on someone he liked he said, "Come on over to our company. Come on over!" He was fortunate, for two people were in fact pulled on over to the exhibition hall to help. These were Bi Xianlin and Hu Xilan.

Bi Xianlin had graduated from Jilin University in the early 1960s. He was quick-witted, sometimes irritable and easily excited. Given responsibility for any task, he would throw himself into it wholeheartedly. In the years of the Cultural Revolution, he led various revolutionary incidents, which became the reason for an investigation of him that made him lose all desire to be an activist. He consequently developed a cool and detached approach to life. In the first few weeks of the company, he stood at the window in his own office, watching the Guard Post through a pane of glass. "It's going to be another time of trouble," he remembers thinking. "It won't be a political movement this time, it will be economic, and after the great wind passes the dust will settle down and the smoke will again dissipate." Zhang Zuxian came to ask him to join in, but he said, "My mind's already dead, forget it."

One day, Bi Xianlin attended a study class on computers. He was accosted by Liu Chuanzhi as he walked into the compound. "Help me with an urgent matter," Liu said. "You won't be late for study—help first and then you can go." Bi Xianlin must have been infected with Liu Chuanzhi's enthusiasm because many years later he remembered that moment as if it had just happened: "He asked me to go, so I went. From that day, I felt as though I might actually be of use. I had thought my core died within me, but now it started to live again."

The next person Liu Chuanzhi found was Hu Xilan. As Director of a mainframe project she had a profound understanding of computers. Her first task for the company was to be Explainer of the Han-card at the Beijing Computer Exhibition. The Han-card was primitive when it first came out but it still caused a sensation. Together, Bi Xianlin and Hu Xilan achieved a considerable success for Lianxiang at the Exhibition. A generation of academic scientists were now being trained to be business people, or at the very least were starting to judge their own behavior through commercial standards. The company had spent RMB 1,800 on renting the stand, and RMB 374 on food and drink. After the RMB 3,500 brought back by Bi Xianlin and Hu Xilan, another RMB 550,000 worth of Han-card orders flowed in. This was a drop in the bucket in terms of the total revenue of the Exhibition but to the company it was significant.

Lianxiang personnel in the mid-1980s

It became increasingly apparent that Wang Shuhe was not suited to the position of General Manager—the most important reason being that he had no interest in the affairs of the company. He decided to leave the company and return to an old path that was easy and did not entail any risk. He returned to being Assistant to the Institute's Director, Zeng Maochao. Going full circle, Wang Shuhe returned to the Computer Institute and was known by people at the time as "having twice eaten hardship." There were political overtones in the phrase—not many years before people had used the same words in denouncing class enemies who wanted to pull China back to the way it was before the Communist Party took power in 1949.

Liu Chuanzhi, on the other hand, was charged with enthusiasm for the company and clearly capable of handling it. On July 14, 1986, Liu Chuanzhi was officially appointed General Manager of the company, Li Qin became Deputy General Manager and filled the position left by Wang Shuhe in the Three-man Core Team.

The macro-environment in the mid-1980s was favorable: the call for Reform was particularly strong. The corruption of the scientific establishment, its rigidities and lack of results had become a target of attack. The State Council was beginning to insist that the Chinese Academy of Sciences take conclusive steps. 1986 should have been a celebratory time for the Computer Institute, for in May it would have been established for thirty years. Warning bells were already ringing inside its large compound, however. It was learned that the Computer Institute would be getting rid of at least one third of its personnel and losing its entire budget for scientific research. The Chinese Academy of Sciences intended to adopt the same policies with regard to nineteen other research institutes that were engaged in applied sciences.

Zeng Maochao faced ever-increasing pressure. Ethically, he could not simply get rid of people who had spent half their lives conscientiously contributing to the country. Together with the nineteen other Institute Directors, he wrote a letter to the Premier of the State Council explaining the ethical dilemma he was facing. In pushing forward the strategic agenda for national reform, the Premier was in favor of radical measures. The National Science Commission then convened a meeting to decide how to carry out the mandated policy of Reform. Zeng Maochao was asked to make a report. The Chairman of the Science Commission, Song Jian, asked why Zeng needed to keep so many people on the State payroll and he declared that the decision was still to let one-third of them go. Zeng Maochao responded scornfully; "Didn't you come out of this Institute yourself? Weren't you a Director? Just tell me who brought these 1,500 people into our Institute? We're part of the history of the Communist Party! If you ask me now to let 500 people go, just tell me just how to do it!" It was difficult for Song Jian to respond but he insisted that the Institute must reform, that it needed urgently to find a "doctor," such as Wan Runnan, the Head of Sitong Company. He wondered if Wan Runnan could possibly take the Institute under his jurisdiction. The word Song Jian used is *cheng-bao*, which has a special meaning in the economic reform of China. Companies were allowed to take over State assets if they agreed to pay a certain amount to the State from operating the business. Proceeds made over that amount were theirs to keep. Wan Runnan enjoyed a much greater reputation at ZGC than did Liu Chuanzhi and his ambition was also greater. He heard this statement and immediately said he would be willing to take the Institute on, and to guarantee a return to the State. Someone asked him how he planned to manage it. He said, "Simple. I would get rid of 90% of the people." This put Zeng Maochao in such a rage that he was "steaming smoke from all seven orifices." In a heat of fury, he wrote a letter to the Chinese Academy of Sciences. "What kind of Reform is this? This is the equivalent of sticking a chicken feather into my cap and taking me out on the street to sell me." He then decided to guarantee an amount to the State and assume management of the Institute on a commercial basis himself. He said that he had only two conditions: First, no government-required duties were to be asked of him, second, he refused to fire a single person. "If I went out on the street to fix bicycles, I could make enough to take care of these 1,500 people." At this juncture, it was clear that he would not be able to carry on as before.

The entire country was in a state of upheaval in late 1986 and early 1987. A debate between left and right ideologies raged. In the economic realm, radical and conservative factions contended. In the universities, students protested in the streets. The departure of Hu Yaobang temporarily calmed the situation, but idealistic reformers had the feeling that "if the rabbit was dead the fox was going to be in trouble." Zeng Maochao was trying his best to protect the rice bowls of his subordinates, but he could see that the Institute was not going to be given any responsibilities by which it could justify its existence. No government engineering or military projects were in the pipeline. Even research on the "Milky Way" mainframe had been given to a department under the Ministry of Defense. The country truly had changed. If the "soldier" he had embedded within his ranks, namely Lin Chuanzhi, was not able to succeed, then the Institute, including its 80,000-square-meter piece of land, its 50,000 square meters of building space, and its staff of 1,500, would find it impossible to carry on.

This critical moment opened a new page in the Institute's history, and came thirty years after the Institute's founding. Everyone in its compound felt threatened and scared: they had no idea what might happen. The New Technology Development Company was still small. In the eyes of many people it was not a respectable outfit, yet now it was given new hope. In early January, a man named Zhou Guangzho considered the fact that it had already been established for two years. This well-known physicist was soon to become the Head of the Chinese Academy of Sciences. In his view, the biggest issue he faced was making the 90,000 people in the Academy's research institutes "put their faces towards a market economy." For the past several years he had tried hard to create what he called "One Institute, Two Systems." He had set up a plethora of companies but not many showed as much promise as this one. On January 24, 1987 he wrote the company a letter congratulating them on their hard work over the past two years, and their ability to stand firm on a solid foundation. He pointed out that "your accomplishments and contributions are not merely defined by your operating expenses and your profit, which is in the several millions of RMB. More importantly, you have carried on beneficial experimental work in the process of systems reform in the sciences." Zhou concluded that he wished the company would continue to grow. He urged them to "march onward to becoming the IBM of China!"

The company was indeed growing quickly and more scientists were joining its ranks. By end-1986, it had 104 members. At the beginning of 1987, a man with a reputation on a par with Ni Guangnan came into the company, named Chen Dayou. This was someone Liu Chuanzhi looked up to as his "Teacher." Shortly thereafter, Liu Chuanzhi's wife Gong Guoxing also entered the company, which contravened the standard procedure for families at the time. In the 1980s, a "two-track system" was popular. This generally referred to the macro-economic policy of keeping certain enterprises State-owned and operated while allowing others to move toward a market economy. In terms of family employment, it had a similar rationale. As China "switched tracks" in order to maintain stability while still moving forward, it was believed that one member of the family should stick with a traditional and secure post while the other could "plunge into the sea of commerce." This way the family maintained the necessary ability to advance or retreat as China's policies changed. The fact that Gong Guoxing was also now joining the company was a clear signal to the Institute: all bets were on the company and the two-track system was out.

Many years earlier, the Chinese statesman Sun Yatsen (1866 – 1925), considered the father of modern China, noted, "Megatrends of the world bring with them mighty waves of change. Those who go along with them will win. Those who go against their tide will lose." The mid-1980s in China provided a good example. Four other colleagues worked in the same office with Gong Guoxing: all came over with her to the company.

The troops were increasing in number but, in fact, the operations of the company were dismal. Liu Chuanzhi had planned for the company to break away from the protection of the Institute in 1987, to test the waters of a real free market. He and Li Qin then became involved in a series of transactions that were unsuccessful. The company's wings were not yet fully developed and the complexities of business in China were challenging.

The painful process of being tricked
In China, the interstices between government and commerce can be a beneficial environment for corporations. Liu Chuanzhi never set out to create a "profitable link" in this area, but evidence shows that in the early stages the company and the government did have a rather special relationship. Liu admitted to doing such things as inviting guests over and sending presents in order to "win" favors. In 1987, for example, the company spent RMB 25,570 to buy ten color television sets, two iceboxes and ten bottles of the liquor known as *maotai*, all of which were presents for government officials. The purpose of the gifts was to let these department heads know that the operations of the company needed their help. Liu walked carefully along the line between legal and illegal, and his behavior was reported scrupulously and accurately to his superiors. He wanted to show that he was working on behalf of the company and not for personal gain. When the company was investigated, the Head of the Institute, Zeng Maochao, disclosed that he knew all about it in advance. "Their procedures in giving out presents are complete and proper," he wrote in a testimony. "There are no problems in terms of individual conduct." The

Head of the Chinese Academy of Sciences, Zhou Guangzho, was even more forthright in coming to the company's defense, "They were forced to do this."

The victory of the Lianxiang Han-card in its first battle indicated that commerce and a commercial sense of value were rapidly entering what had been the sole domain of scientific intellectualism. Liu Chuanzhi's role was now labeled "businessman," not "engineer". He hoped to become the agent inside China for IBM's computers. Being an agent for IBM might have been a great opportunity for the company, but there was one problem: the company lacked an import license.

China's system of import licensing was one of Liu Chuanzhi's biggest headaches. At that time, even if one had sufficient funding and paid taxes according to the rules, one could not just go out and import computers. One first had to get governmental permission. This permission system covered more than one hundred kinds of imported items in the 1980s. Larger items included such things as cars and iron and steel and smaller things were items such as watches and jewelry. The scope of items was later reduced, but even today the requirement to have import licenses on certain products is not totally gone. The original idea behind this system was to create a trade barrier, a protective screen that would work along with the customs tax to protect national industries. The effect of the system was to allow import licenses to become a vehicle of corruption. Power over the system was controlled by a small number of people in the government. True importers were often unable to obtain permission to import whereas those who were able to get the licenses often were not true importers: reselling licenses became the best way to earn money. This led to various forms of corruption and endless bribes in order to get anything done.

Liu Chuanzhi was determined to be an agent for foreign computers. Lacking a license, the only way out was to go in search of some person who did have a license. Such a person was found. The computer department of the Hong Kong branch of the Bank of China Group was an IBM computer customer. Based on this credential, the Branch received the right to be an IBM agent and to import machines to China. Liu Chuanzhi found this out and paid a formal call. He announced himself as someone who had a large number of customers inside China, and who had the ability to gather in substantial orders. Moreover, he had plenty of technical talent that could set up a training and repair center.

Both sides came to a tacit agreement. But Liu's company was not well known and also lacked retail distribution channels. In order not to disappoint its very first partner and in order to maintain trust and credibility, the entire company geared itself up to succeed. Several years later, Liu admitted that, "for every piece of business we did, the hardships increased in proportion." In those days, the hardships he encountered had less to do with the laws of economics than with Chinese traditions and the workings of the Chinese system.

The first opportunity for the company's agency business came with a young person named Wang Ke. Wang worked in the Information Department of the State Infrastructure Commission. Wang and Liu met at an Exhibition and it was as though they had known each other forever. Wang said that the Commission was planning to buy twelve IBM computers, and he agreed to sign a contract with Liu Chuanzhi. This was excellent news, but when Liu got to the Commission he found that Wang Ke was indeed a customer for computers but the purchasing of them was not up to him. Purchasing required the permission of the Section Head of the Finance Department. Liu Chuanzhi then worked to open up this second necessary channel but discovered that even more problems lay ahead. The money originally allocated to buy computers had been placed with the China Scientific Instruments Import and Export Company, in whose hands lay an import license.

Liu Chuanzhi and Wang Ke therefore met with the company China Scientific. Liu wanted to sell computers, Wang wanted to buy, and indeed with his own money, yet here they were talking in hushed voices looking for permission from a third party.

"We would like to buy computers from him," said Wang, indicating Liu Chuanzhi.

The China Scientific employee was young, impolite, and disdainful. Staring at Liu Chuanzhi, who stood there respectfully and somewhat formally, he barked, "What's this business to you?"

Liu hurriedly explained. Before he had finished, the young man interrupted him, "So what are you, a foreign businessman? Or a Chinese? Or maybe you're an agent?"

"That's right, I am an agent," Liu said, trying to smile.

"Agents are foreign businessmen. Get out. No foreign businessman can come into this business. Get out of here!"

Gray with shock, Liu Chuanzhi retreated under the eyes of all in the room. Many years later he remembered the incident as an extreme case of humiliation.

Intellectuals were poor at the time, but retained a measure of self-respect. Liu felt that his self-esteem had been trampled upon and he now swore he would get this business. He stopped all other work and went in pursuit of his goal. He first found out more about the young man. He found one of the man's former classmates to act as a go-between. He contained his anger as he devised ways to get close to the man, chat with him, invite him to dinner and make him understand that this business would not bring him any trouble. The young man's face eventually began to soften and smile, and at one point he mentioned that he wanted to go to Hong Kong and that he needed to buy Hong Kong dollars. Liu immediately said, "How much would you like? We have some people there, we can do it for you."

Westerners never understand why Chinese spend so much time and money on eating and drinking. This is because they don't appreciate one of the cardinal rules in China: meals are the oil that grease the economic machine. If you lose this lubrication the entire apparatus stops. By the time Liu Chuanzhi and the young man parted ways, the latter said, "We should be able to do some business together."

"I brought in this piece of business." Liu Chuanzhi was able to say. He had greater confidence now in his abilities. The company's documents do not record this detail, but we can be sure that the meal on that day was the starting point for the company's agency business. Wang Ke's purchase of twelve IBM computers started it all: within several years, Lianxiang was the largest agent for computers in the country.

Having gone through all the hardship and ridicule, Liu Chuanzhi calculated how much profit this business had made and was satisfied. When he got paid, however, the money received was short by US$20,000! Liu Chuanzhi and the Hong Kong branch of the Bank of China had agreed on the profit split, but the agreement had been verbal, there was nothing in black and white. All of the profit from this piece of business was in the account of the Bank of China: Liu could only rely on their honor to respect the deal. This was an enormous amount of money to the company. Liu Chuanzhi's salary in that year was only RMB 1,380. That US$20,000 would have been enough to pay the entire salary of all employees for one year.

Furious, Liu Chuanzhi left immediately for Hong Kong. He couldn't get through immigration there and had to stop in Shenzhen. He needed to save money, so he stayed in a small guest house on Hongling North Road, owned by the Guangdong Provincial Academy of Sciences: one night cost RMB 8. He climbed up to the third floor to spend the night in a room with several strangers.

That night, unable to sleep, he wrote a letter to the head of the Hong Kong branch of the Bank of China, which was a state-owned entity. Liu wrote of all the events that had occurred in the course of setting up the company. What he wrote had an effect: with appropriate apologies, the boss handed over the precise sum of money, and Liu Chuanzhi went home triumphant. He had no time to celebrate, however, for a more serious matter was about to follow.

From the mid-1980s, failing to keep promises, premeditated cheating, helping oneself at the expense of others were common in China. After Liu had become a successful man, he thought back to the process of founding the company, and he described the three things that were hardest: "First: adapting, or as we say in Chinese, "being rubbed to fit the environment." We are not talking about changing your environment—just accommodating to it involves accepting a lot of injustice. Second: creating a common sense of working together with colleagues. Third: taking care of my own body. This was the most perplexing."

The so-called "perplexity of the body" that he referred to happened in the three months between spring and summer of 1987. He began to experience dizzy spells, and to have insomnia. If he did fall asleep he would suddenly awake, startled and full of terror, his heart racing. He checked into the Naval Hospital. The doctor's diagnosis was that he suffered from tremors of the nervous system, perhaps a precursor to Meniere's Disease though it was impossible to explain the cause. Liu Chuanzhi felt he knew the source: he and Li Qin were cheated in a RMB 3,000,000 transaction discussed below. His symptoms started at that time, while Li Qin came down with a fibrillating heart.

The Han-card was now successful, but profits were slim. Selling computers that other people had imported was not a way to make much money, so the two men began to consider directly importing themselves, inserting the Han-card and selling the bundled package. Liu Chuanzhi went to Shenzhen to open up a source of computers, while Li Qin went to the Academy of Sciences to borrow money. After getting the signed approval of the eighteen Leaders, he finally was able to obtain RMB 3,000,000. He wired the money to Shenzhen. No computers appeared. Many telephone calls later, the two finally learned that they had been swindled—the money had been stolen by their "source." Liu Chuanzhi had returned to Beijing but now took a flight to Shenzhen and by the time he entered the city it was late at night. He went straight to the home of the swindler. Nobody was at home, so he waited outside the door till the sun came up and then posted a man to keep watch. Several days later the supplier finally appeared. His eyes were red and he looked depraved. On seeing Liu Chuanzhi, he merely laughed as he said, "I just wanted to use the dough for a few days. You're from a State-owned company too, aren't you? Why in such a hurry?"

Fortunately, that day, the computers they were waiting for finally arrived in Beijing. Tremendously relieved, Li Qin collapsed in a chair, his heart unable to take it. Down south, Liu Chuanzhi too was experiencing a pounding heart and his head was dizzy. This incident happened over eighteen years ago, but the physical ailments of the two men remain basically the same.

Liu Chuanzhi's philosophy became: "Do not cheat others and do not allow yourself to be cheated." In the early period at the company, therefore, he established defense systems everywhere. He constantly warned his subordinates to be careful in their dealings. Liu, along with his company, would long ago have been "buried" in the extreme turbulence of the Chinese system in the 1980s if he had not stuck to his principles, been absolutely determined, and had a good measure of raw toughness about him.

3

IT HAS WHAT YOU WOULD CALL A "ROOT"

You see an oil painting best if you place yourself at a distance. It's hard to read clearly if you are too close, whereas in stepping back you can see the whole effect. The analogy is to remind us to step back and think: we must keep our goal clearly in mind.

Liu Chuanzhi

Z hang Zuxiang arrived in Hong Kong on January 8, 1988, for the first time. He approached this congested and prosperous city with trepidation. He couldn't understand the native Cantonese or the official English but he had a mission: to further Liu Chuanzhi's master plan for taking the company overseas. Zhang was to start implementing the plan in Hong Kong.

Lianxiang's "advance overseas" strategy was part of three-stage plan. Stage One was to set up a Trading Company outside the borders of China, with which to generate capital and experience. Stage Two was to move from trading to manufacturing and to enter the computer industry in earnest. Stage Three was to list the company on the Hong Kong stock market. The timetable for all three stages was to run from June 1988 to February 1994. All three stages were accomplished on schedule.

The plan was called the "Three Marching Songs for the battle plan to advance overseas". The title was martial but the motivation was concrete: to capture more of the 15% margin that the company was currently giving to middlemen. The general rule in buying goods from outside China was that the middleman in the transaction took a minimum of 15% margin. "We always lose out," said Zhang Zuxiang. "If we set up a trading company in Hong Kong we not only can control the purchasing channels but we can take that 15% into our own pockets."

Chinese businessmen have a distinct advantage over foreigners when they make strategic plans. They are able to utilize China's unique situation and national policies, and this advantage now came into play for Lianxiang. In the 1980s, the Chinese government supported a new trend toward "going international" among Chinese companies. Isolation was considered necessary for China in the 1950s, "60s, and "70s, in order to strengthen the country. With no access to outside information, Chinese felt that their lives were supremely fortunate. They believed the government's admonition that "two-thirds of the world's laboring masses are living in a state of desperation, waiting for us to come and liberate them." Only in the 1980s, when China began to open its doors to the outside, did we know that the world was not as we had imagined. Western countries were far out in front; Chinese, in fact, were the ones living in poverty. It then became fashionable to want to enter the mainstream of world affairs, and gradually the government began to be guided by international trends. America's "Star Wars" plan, the Soviet Union's "Development Plan for higher science and technology," and the European "Eureka Plan" all affected the internal policies of the Chinese government. They became a direct factor in the birth of China's own "Strategic Plan for the Development of Science and Technology" of March 1986.

In the fall of 1987, a man named Wang Jian recommended certain policies to the central government. He described the Chinese market and the world market as a unified system, and he called upon China to be a value-added merchant for the world. He recommended that China sell both ends of the spectrum, raw materials and finished products, and that it pump these out to the international market. Wang's ideas resonated with the policy makers in China and particularly with the Premier in the State Council. Premier Zhao Ziyang ordered his Intelligence Group to study Wang's recommendations, and he called the resulting policy "Entering the Great International Circulation." Scholars and journalists broadly embraced the concepts.

Today, thinking back to those times, the Internationalism of the 1980s was as able to incite Chinese passions as the ensuing Nationalism of the 1990s. Liu Chuanzhi was able to ride this Eastern Wind of the 1980s. The national trend gave him tremendous support. It allowed Liu to become famous among business circles, and it gave Zhang Zuxiang the sense that a great national mission had dropped from heaven onto his shoulders.

As one of the Founders of the company and as a colleague of Liu Chuanzhi for years, Zhang Zuxiang was acutely aware of the difficulties that Liu faced. He always did his best to help resolve them, more with an innate sense of integrity than any analytical skills. Zhang was respected in the company for the many occasions on which, in Chinese fashion, he acquiesced. In 1988, Liu Chuanzhi recognized that this was the man to set up the new company in Hong Kong.

Hong Kong had not yet been returned to China, which happened in 1997. Mainland Chinese had to jump through numerous hoops to get into the colony—it was much harder for Chinese to go to Hong Kong than it was to other countries. If Mainland companies wanted to set up a presence in Hong Kong, they had to submit many documents to the Ministry of Foreign Economic Relations and Trade (MOFERT), among which was one that listed the "authorized number of staff sent from inside China." Unless you were on this list, there was no way you could go to Hong Kong. In January 1988, MOFERT's authorization for Lianxiang to set up in Hong Kong noted that "this jointly-managed company could send an authorized strength of six people." This one sentence was particularly valuable. Liu gave the very first "Hong Kong Entry Permit" to Zhang Zuxiang.

Hong Kong Lianxiang

Liu Chuanzhi selected two companies in Hong Kong to be partners of Lianxiang: Hong Kong Daoyuan Computer Systems, Ltd., and China Technology Licensing, Ltd. The first was a little-known company with three investors: Leu Tanping, Wu Liyi, and Zhang Liji. All three had graduated from London University with degrees in Computer Science; all were young men with overseas business experience. They complemented Liu's team of old-school scholars. Liu Chuanzhi later liked to use the analogy of a blind man and a crippled man to explain his choice: he had technical resources but was ignorant of the overseas market, whereas his partners had no technical ability but were highly familiar with the overseas market. Combining the two was like using the feet of a blind man and the eyes of a crippled man to stride forward. This saying was widely used for years and became the definition of the "road to success" in Liu's overseas strategy. His third partner was neither blind nor crippled, however. The China Technology Licensing, Ltd. was a company that was only ever mentioned in internal meetings. On October 10, 1988, Liu Chuanzhi stated at a meeting of employees, "The key thing about China Technology

Licensing is that it can get large amounts of funding. In terms of borrowing money, it has what you would call a "root"."

What Liu Chuanzhi did not mention was that this company was a State-owned Chinese company, the investment arm of the China Council for the Promotion of International Trade (CCPIT) in Hong Kong. He also did not mention that his own father, Liu Gushu, was Chairman of the Board. His father remained Chairman from 1988 until 1993, a critical period for Lianxiang. Lianxiang was then taken public in 1994.

Liu Gushu had been in the banking business his entire life and had built up useful resources in the form of credibility and relationships. At the age of 63, he brought 800,000 Hong Kong dollars' worth of Chinese government funds to Hong Kong and set up the China Technology Licensing Company. Through this vehicle, he took China's patent-licensing industry into world markets. Over the next six years, he made around HK$500 million from the initial investment. In US dollar terms, he started with US$100,000 and turned it into over US$60 million in six years. Liu Gushu's capabilities were highly regarded by both Hong Kong and Chinese businessmen. To Liu Chuanzhi, he was the ultimate model. Years later, after his father had passed away, Liu said that his father had been critically important at key turning points of his life, including his decision to turn away from the Red Guard faction. Without his father's position and help, it is doubtful that Liu Chuanzhi would have had the determination to launch his ambitious long-term strategy in Hong Kong, or that he would ultimately have been successful.

Liu Gushu made good use of his position to help his son obtain significant loans. This became vital financial backing for the company since at the time neither Liu Chuanzhi nor the Daoyuan Company had the reputation to obtain support from the Hong Kong banking community. The assistance did not stop with loans. Liu's father also introduced his son to the Hong Kong business world. Liu Chuanzhi learned proper deportment in this unique community from his father—what to wear, how to talk, how to handle himself in society. Though intangible cultural expressions, these things were extremely useful.

Liu Chuanzhi decided to name the new company "Hong Kong Lianxiang," and nobody objected. The old name had been much too long. The name inside China was later changed to "China Academy of Sciences Computer Institute Company," but that lacked imagination and still did not roll easily off the tongue. The word "Lianxiang" had already been used throughout China in association with the Han-card. In those days, Liu Chuanzhi kept saying, "Let's change our name to the Lianxiang Group!"

The creation of a Hong Kong Lianxiang was an extension of the product name in China, but at the same time it presaged the desire to set up a parallel Beijing Lianxiang.

Liu Chuanzhi and his two partners came to an agreement: each would invest HK$300,000 in the new company, and would then enjoy equal shares as well as equal responsibilities. Leu Tanping became the President of the new company; Liu Chuanzhi became Chairman of the Board. Liu Gushu was not an officer but, in fact, father and son were so connected that Liu Chuanzhi held de facto control over the company.

The company bought an old 80-square-meter apartment in Taikoo City with HK$780,000 or around US$100,000. All of the Beijing people posted to Hong Kong were moved into this space. Ni Guangnan, Liu Chuanzhi, Zhang Zuxian all lived here; since there weren't enough rooms they spread a rug in the hallway to sleep on. Years later, after Hong Kong Lianxiang was powerful and Leu Tanping had become wealthy, some people declared that he didn't deserve it. They said he had been a small shopkeeper who joined ranks with Lianxiang for only HK$300,000, yet was allowed to become a billionaire off it. They said that not only did he live in luxury and drive fancy cars but he had a HK$ twenty-million pleasure boat and Lianxiang shares worth over HK$3.5 billion. They said that without the backing of the Chinese State-owned resources of Lianxiang he would have been nothing. A spate of articles appeared on the Internet about this, saying that Liu Chuanzhi had used Chinese State funds to provide a foreign businessman with "more foreign griddlecakes than he could eat in ten generations." All of this was written from the viewpoint of the year 2004. If we go back to the spring of 1988, however, and the pitiful situation of Hong Kong Lianxiang, the State funds put up by Liu Chuanzhi were exactly the same as the private funds put up by the "small shopkeeper." When Lianxiang bought its apartment in Taikoo City, it even had to borrow HK$180,000 from Leu Tanping in order to make the first payment on the mortgage.

Ten years later, Lianxiang had plenty of resources: its market value was some ten billion Hong Kong dollars. By then, it was hard for the tall tree not to catch some wind. In 1988, when the enterprise started in Hong Kong, it was like a return to 1984 and the days of the Guard Post: everyone was poor. A bus ticket in Hong Kong cost one Hong Kong dollar at that time, but the tramcar price was even cheaper, only 60 cents. Liu Chuanzhi and his group did not take buses or trams, they walked. They did not dare entertain guests where they lived—to keep up appearances, they arranged to meet people in rooms that they rented from hotels.

When negotiations were finished they returned to their primitive quarters. When accepting invitations to other people's functions, they would walk to somewhere nearby and then take a taxi in order to show up in a vehicle.

Poor but determined

Despite financial hardships, Liu Chuanzhi made it look as though they were accomplishing great things. In the late 1980s, "diving into the ocean of commerce" was an astonishing phenomenon in China. Many cast off their government or scholarly positions to become businessmen. All who did so had an acute eye for profit and Liu Chuanzhi was no exception. Unlike many, though, he made extraordinary things happen: one was to engineer a corporate meeting in the Great Hall of the People. The Great Hall of the People was the most important venue in all of China. Every key political event had been launched there since its construction in 1958. China's modern history could be charted through the movements announced there, including "Overthrow Liu Shaoqi" and his later "rehabilitation and exhoneration," "Overthrow Deng Xiaoping" and his later comeback, the funerals of Zhou Enlai, Zhu De, and Mao Zedong, arresting the Gang of Four, disavowing Hua Guofeng as the Illustrious Leader, appointing all new Communist Party Secretaries for the past twenty-five years. State Council Premiers all made their reports to the National People's Congress in this building. On April 18, 1988, the company held a meeting at the Great Hall of the People "to swear in the Troops who are launching the Overseas Advance." In making this place his own stage, it was easy to see that Liu Chuanzhi was consolidating a national identity for the company. He strode into the Great Hall with complete confidence. He delivered a speech that was the greatest celebratory address of the company up to that time. Nobody knew that this great General, "leading his troops overseas," was in fact sleeping on the floor of a tiny apartment in Hong Kong.

Liu Chuanzhi had wanted to make a resounding entry into the public arena, and he succeeded. The event also launched the career of one of his Deputies, a man named Guo Wei. The government had not "opened" the Great Hall of the People in 1988 when Lianxiang held its event there. It was to be two more years before this sacred space was used for commerce. In 1988, if any ordinary citizen wanted to promote himself in this great venue he had to have very senior leaders attend his function. This was a problem for Liu Chuanzhi and his staff. Unknown as the company was, it was useless to think of calling upon the Party Secretary, the Premier, or the Head of the Standing Committee of the National People's Congress. Even the Vice Premiers in the State Council were unreachable. The only thing to do was start lobbying among the Deputy Commission Heads. Liu's staff finally came up with one possibility: a man named Peng Chong. Liu Chuanzhi instructed Guo Wei to accomplish the task of assuring his presence.

Guo Wei was 24 years old at the time. He had just finished a Masters Degree in Management and come straight into the company. This was the first thing he had been asked to do. Taking it seriously, he found out that one of the company drivers' friends knew the son-in-law of this Deputy Chief. Through this slender connection they "felt up the vine to seize the gourd," finally making a connection with the Deputy Chief himself. To everyone's surprise, he agreed to attend, though he could only stay for twenty minutes. On the appointed day, the Deputy Chief did indeed appear at the Great Hall of the People, he heard Liu Chuanzhi's resounding brave words, then left. His presence had been brief but it lit the hall with glory for Liu Chuanzhi. Back then, Chinese entrepreneurs felt inferior to government officials and the more ambitious the Chinese entrepreneur, the more traitorous to the true cause they felt. They therefore put on an attitude of extreme deference. They believed that the government was still a great guarantor and protective force; they also knew that if things went wrong for you, the government could make serious trouble. No matter how far down a future road you aimed to go, you could not afford to turn your face against the existing political system.

Another "Golden Auspicious Day" occurred on June 23, a Thursday. This was the day Hong Kong Lianxiang was to be established. Liu Chuanzhi ran to Taikoo City to receive the newly appointed Head of the Chinese Academy of Sciences, Zhou Guangzho. In the week before the ceremony, Liu had purchased a two-story apartment in Chai Wan on the eastern side of Hong Kong island. The top floor of this apartment was used as an office, the bottom as a warehouse. Before any company started operations in Hong Kong, the custom was to invite a *fengshui* man in to evaluate auspicious directions and procedures. Liu Chuanzhi was not a superstitious man but he was willing to go along with local custom. He paid HK$50,000 for the *fengshui* man. The man said that the company's employees must sit facing the southeast, back to the mountains and facing the water, the furniture must be white, the tables must be eight inches higher than normal. He announced that if everything was done in accordance with his instructions, the company would see wealth flow in: within one year, it would see HK$5 million. Liu Chuanzhi felt that the height of the tables was particularly inconvenient, but he was not willing to go against instructions. He did everything as told. He also burned incense on the auspicious day, and he paid the proper respects to the gods of the four directions. He had a pig roasted for everyone's enjoyment and the company was then "open" and ready to receive great fortune. In point of fact, Hong Kong Lianxiang's profit in that first year greatly exceeded HK$5 million. Things got even better as time went on so that the company kept buying real estate. Each time they bought a property, they would invite a *fengshui* man in to evaluate it, and the price of the services kept going up while the roast pig and other preparations to respect the gods only became more complex!

The "Ribbon-cutting" ceremony in Hong Kong was closely related to the "Troops who are launching the Overseas Advance" meeting in Beijing. The company rented a large hall in a hotel and placed a number of young ladies at the door to receive guests. There was a lion dance; Zhou Guangzho cut the ribbon on behalf of the company. He was the most important guest invited on that day by Liu Chuanzhi and next to him stood a vigorous and and elegant young woman named Ma Xuezheng. Ma was later to become Senior Vice-President of the Lianxiang Group; her English name is Mary Ma. At that time, she was a Department Head in the Chinese Academy of Sciences. The most important of her duties was to arrange the schedule of the Academy's President. Presidents she had worked with included Fang Yi, Li Chang, Lu Jiaxi, and now Zhou Guangzho. Liu Chuanzhi was aware of the importance of her position. He had contacted her weeks in advance and begged her to put this ribbon-cutting ceremony into the President's agenda. That was the first time Ma Xuezheng met Liu Chuanzhi. Years later, she recalled the impression he left on her that day:

"He asked me, no matter what, to arrange time for the President of the Academy and, moreover, to find a way to do it right then and there. The person before me was affable, refined and polite, but that afternoon I learned that Lianxiang people got what they wanted. They could talk from nine in the morning to four in the afternoon and, if you did not agree, they simply would not leave."

Ma Xuezheng later was to have many amusing stories, and one of these related to that Hong Kong Lianxiang Opening Day. The ribbon-cutting was accomplished quickly, and the next few hours brought Ma Xuezheng closer to an understanding of Liu Chuanzhi. Liu insisted on bringing Zhou Guangzho to visit the new office. They drove to the factory district of the eastern part of Hong Kong island, got out of the car and walked into a tall building. Ma Xuezheng had a sense of rampant disorder, "as though I was walking into a dilapidated warehouse." The group detoured around a big delivery truck and entered an elevator—only then did she realize that they really were in a warehouse. Delivery men squeezed in together with them, naked to the waist, sweat pouring down their backs. The visitors were dressed in western suits and leather shoes, and they had just stepped into the elevator when a pushcart piled with goods pushed them into a corner.

Ma Xuezheng had been through Europe and America and was used to the luxury of "Overseas." It was inconceivable to her that this was the face of the grand and glorious "Advance overseas strategy of Lianxiang." Nonetheless, she saw Liu Chuanzhi standing there tall and happy, proud to be showing off his accomplishments, describing the company. He seemed oblivious to the discomfort of his guests.

After emerging from the building, Liu invited his group to sightsee around Hong Kong harbor. As they got on the boat, Ma Xuezheng could see that Liu Chuanzhi was trying to look prosperous, and not succeeding. She knew that there were two kinds of pleasure boats in Hong Kong, one called "Western style," all white, the kind seen in movies, and the local type. What Liu Chuanzhi had obtained was the cheap local type. "Where did you get this old boat?" she laughed. Liu Chuanzhi did not try to hide the price. "I spent several thousand Hong Kong dollars to rent this, just for the purpose of taking you all out for a spin."

He said "out for a spin," but in fact he had business in mind. As soon as all were seated, he began to tell the President of the Academy of Sciences his overseas strategy. He told him his evaluation of trends in the Chinese computer industry, how to get around Chinese restrictions by using the beneficial policies of Hong Kong. He was impassioned and totally at odds with the bleak scene before their eyes. Ma Xuezheng had met Nobel prize winners, American White House advisors, and such in the past. She had never seen anyone who could talk like Liu Chuanzhi. "In such a lousy place, Liu Chuanzhi could still get passionate about his overseas launch. He had more ambition than dozens of people put together, as though he were already wielding the power of "a thousand troops and ten thousand horses." I could see that this was a long ways from "overseas," but I was amazed at the ambition. I had the feeling that this company really was rather interesting." Ten years after Ma Xuezheng's tale of "riding an old boat and talking about ruling the world," Liu Chuanzhi was in fact managing "a thousand troops and ten thousand horses."

New Blood

It seems strange today that no college graduates or outstanding young people were recruited in the first three and one-half years of this so-called "high-tech" company. The staff all came from the Computer Institute.

They were born in the 1940s or even 1930s, and had graduated from college before the Great Cultural Revolution. They were industrious, frugal, tenacious, highly responsible, and self-sacrificing. They represented the best of China's computer scientists; the results of their research came to more than all the other computer company's results put together. Unfortunately, they were simply too old. This became a problem for Liu Chuanzhi and the problems became apparent at his annual "no-agenda meeting". At this meeting, Liu wanted everyone to put down the work in his hands and think strategically, off the map. The idea was to have people consider the major trends in the industry and the general direction of the company. The older generation's field of vision was too narrow. Not only could they not comprehend market strategies required at this new juncture in China's development, they had nothing to contribute in terms of long-term strategic thinking.

In May 1988, therefore, the company put its first employment advertisement in the papers. This was placed in *China Youth News*, on the front page in the right-hand corner. Employment advertisements were rare in China back then. There might be one now and then, badly written and unclear. This ad was put in an eye-catching position, and the wording was compelling: *Come on in and join us, help us make a company together.*

This hit the mark with college graduates who were then moving into their summer vacations. Out of 500 people who responded, the company selected 280 to take a written exam. Out of the results, it selected 120 to be interviewed in person. In the end, there were 58 people that the interviewers felt were appropriate: they could not find any way to reduce this number further. The plan had been to hire only 16 people. They handed the issue over to Liu Chuanzhi to decide and he hired all 58 young people on the spot.

The new recruits represented a new era. They were intelligent, well educated and "moving with the wind" in terms of China's needs and policies. They were excited, but they were inexperienced. They included 18 graduate students, 37 college graduates and 3 students whose education was unconventional. Their average age was not quite twenty-six. They had been born twenty years later than "the old generation," and in the eyes of that generation, they were too young, mere children, like their own sons and daughters. The company now faced a serious generation gap. China's universities had not held entrance exams for twelve years: from 1966 until 1977, not one person had graduated from college. Children who should have gone to school in that period were either on the streets doing what they pleased, working as farm hands in the countryside, or fomenting rebellion. The one thing they were not allowed to do was study. The new generation of college graduates emerged from schools only after 1982 and, because of this, China was faced with the strange juxtaposition of twenty-year-olds and forty-year-olds working together. All of China faced this situation, not just the 58 young people entering Lianxiang. In Lianxiang, as elsewhere, it was to cause problems.

Yang Yuanqing and Guo Wei both appeared on the list of this first group of new recruits and Yang and Guo were later to be called the two Commanders-in-Chief of Lianxiang, and the successors to Liu Chuanzhi. They were to become key players in the history of the company but at that time nobody knew who they were—even those who examined them did not note anything special. Guo Wei came into the company ten weeks before Yang, and he brilliantly handled the April 18 ceremony at the Great Hall of the People, so he was blessed with the trust of Liu Chuanzhi. On the day that ceremony concluded, Liu Chuanzhi called him in to ask what he wanted to do. Guo said he would like to be in sales; Liu instead made him Manager of the Public Relations Department.

Yang Yuanqing and Guo Wei joined Lianxiang in 1988 for similar reasons: they recognized the viability of this small company and they had masters degrees. Other than this, they had almost nothing in common. Yang Yuanqing came from a doctor's family in Hefei City, Anhui province. Guo Wei was the son of a Propaganda Cadre on Qinhuangdao City outside the Great Wall. Yang had a degree in Computer Sciences; while Guo Wei had a degree in Business Management. Guo was an extrovert with dancing eyes and a quick mind, a sociable man who liked to acquaint people with his intelligence and his emotions. Yang Yuanqing's strengths included his ability to hide his intelligence. He was introverted, less sociable, and slower in speech but more nimble in execution. He seemed less accessible than Guo Wei. Yang Yuanqing remained in an obscure position for his first three years, while Guo Wei was made a Manager within his first thirty days.

Guo Wei's first task at the company brought him the taste of success, while Yang Yuanqing's first task brought him failure. Yang was to draft a tender for the company to bid on becoming IBM's agent for PCs. Only after he submitted this did he discover that his bid was double that of his competitors. The business did not come through but it left him with a good sales lesson in the importance of price. Yang was a man of determination. He concealed his emotions and he learned from his mistakes. Guo Wei was able to take the initiative, to "strike first in forestalling the enemy," but Yang was one of those latecomers who surpass the early birds. Now Chairman of the Board of Lenovo, Yang Yuanqing ultimately became far more powerful.

Two Generations

By the summer of 1988, there were more than 100 young people in the company, one of every three employees. They were tremendously energetic, they started a newsletter for inhouse distribution and found an artist named Xu Chude to calligraph the two characters "Lianxiang" for its masthead—final preparation for changing the name of the company. A graduate student from the Journalism Department of the Chinese Academy of Social Sciences became its first editor, a man named Fan Xiaohong, and the first issue was put out on June 17.

Lianxiang began to implement its own principles in the newsletter, in becoming a bridge between old and new. The new generation called people in the older generation "Teacher," as though the young ones were still students in school. A sense of familial solidarity developed, to the extent that a man named Wang Shiying wrote an article called, "The company is really our family." This was published in the newsletter and was the earliest mention of Lianxiang's "Family Culture." It was to become a stark contrast to articles titled "The company is not our family," widely circulated on the Internet fifteen years later.

The cozy emotions in these early days thinly disguised real changes that were occurring. From the summer of 1988, employees diverged into two distinct categories: the older generation that had put its blood and sweat into the company and that did not expect compensation in return, and the younger generation, who were prepared to put their hearts and souls into the business, but who wanted to be paid for it. The older generation had a kind of innocent loyalty to the company. No matter what happened, they could bear up under hard work and criticism. The new generation could bear hard work, but not criticism. They liked to express their own thoughts on the future direction of the company and they hoped to exert their influence. At times they grew impatient. The older generation saw the company being pulled in a new direction and it was impossible for them not to feel alienated. Fan Xiaohong, for example, was a young woman who smoked cigarettes and wore blue jeans to work. She had not been at the company more than two days when she, on her own accord, changed the name of the "Propaganda Group" to the Public Relations Department. These changes were uncomfortable to the oldtimers.

The fact that Guo Wei was appointed head of the Public Relations Department at the age of twenty-four indicated that Liu Chuanzhi was promoting new people. Guo Wei's father had done propaganda his whole life. He knew that propaganda was an assignment that "hurt people and hurt yourself," and Guo Wei was therefore uninterested in this work. Back then, people understood public relations to mean, basically, propaganda.

Soon, though, Guo became aware that he had been given a huge stage on which to operate.

Guo Wei started out with total confidence. His down-to-earth nature enabled him to form a bond with the older generation. He did not realize that the very need to "form a bond" indicated that a gap existed between them. Later events were to draw Guo Wei into a whirlpool of contradictions.

Bringing AST under the thumb of the company

Lianxiang's results looked excellent after the 1988 summer sales season. The Han-card was slowly establishing itself in the Chinese market, selling more than 10,000 sets that season. Some 1,000 customers were distributed nationwide: though few, all of these were State-owned, which hinted at a large potential market. The real strength of Lianxiang was not on the Mainland, though, but in Hong Kong. Hong Kong Lianxiang became successful quickly: in the first four months, the company achieved a monthly sales turnover of HK$9 million and a monthly profit of HK$550,000, yet the company had only thirty employees.

Good news streamed steadily up to the Beijing headquarters, energizing the entire company. On October 7, 1988, several dozen staff worked all day to prepare for a meeting at which they were going to discuss how to raise sales even further. Li Qin, responsible for image promotion of the company, Bi Xianlin, responsible for sales of the company, Liu Chuanzhi and Jia Xufu all attended. This was intended to be a sales meeting that did not involve other departments, but, as it turned out, other departments sent representatives as well.

Three days later, the meeting was still going on. It had been extended to include the entire company. It was being called a meeting to "open up the international market, raise the high tide of sales, and mobilize the troops." Liu Chuanzhi gave a rousing speech. The record of this speech forms one of Lianxiang's most prescient documents. The speech foretold the strategy that was to make Lianxiang succeed.

Liu first reported the good news from Hong Kong to the assembled group. In the 1980s, profits on personal computers sold in China were staggering. All you had to do was obtain a computer, turn it around and sell it, and the gross profit could reach 84%. Hong Kong Lianxiang's greatest virtue was that it was preserving a supply source for the market inside China. In April, May and June, supply had been tight, and capital could not continue to circulate. The loan situation was also not yet resolved: the company could only borrow HK$15 million and depended on the China Technology Licensing Company's good name and relations with banks just to get that. Now, the situation was different. In September, the company had received a loan of HK$50 million from Mitsui Bank, showing that the reputation of the company with banks had improved.

In his speech, Liu Chuanzhi used the new willingness of foreign bankers as a way to describe the rise in the company's prestige, and he used real profit figures to stimulate a fighting will among his staff. His audience became more and more excited. The prescient part of his speech came next.

"You all know perhaps that Lianxiang has signed a ten million US dollar contract with AST company in Hong Kong. We will be buying 3,000 computers, destined for sale both within China and abroad. In one stroke, this is equivalent to controlling all of AST's production in our own hands."

Everyone realized that the situation was really very good. The profit on every AST computer was approximately RMB 10,000. They quickly calculated how much that came to for 3,000 computers. And one could still fit out the 3,000 computers with Han-cards and compatible equipment, bringing in additional profit.

Few know AST today but at the time it was famous. Though an American company, it was started by two people from Hong Kong and a third from Pakistan who used their first initials to form the name. In 1982, they manufactured the first set of computer motherboards for use in IBM computers and also compatible machines and devices that they sold all over the world. Two or three years earlier, they had hired some engineers to develop personal computers. They now began to organize a global sales network for assembled computers. By 1988, the company had more than 1,500 employees scattered around the world, and an annual turnover exceeding US$2 billion. After Liu Chuanzhi narrated the history of AST, he raised his head to announce to his company: "We are going to copy AST and march along the same road that they have travelled."

Even the most unobservant person could see that the age of personal computers had arrived. Liu Chuanzhi was not speaking casually. Several weeks later, he used the first profits garnered from Hong Kong Lianxiang to buy a factory from a Hong Kong businessman. The purchased factory was called the Quantum Company. With this as his manufacturing base, he took the first great stride down the AST road: developing his own computer motherboards.

If AST had had any foresight, its managers would have asked themselves if this partner might be using AST as a springboard to launch its own business. AST might have recognized that it was going to be supplanted, and in fact this is exactly what happened. Unfortunately, AST did not have this foresight and also did not have the capabilities and ambitions of Liu Chuanzhi. Fourteen months later, when Liu Chuanzhi told them that he had started manufacturing his own computers, they simply thought he was bragging.

Liu Chuanzhi's description of the Hong Kong business was not *braggadocio*. All the bad news in the macroeconomic sphere had no effect on the performance of Lianxiang. Since the summer, the financial markets had begun to sound alarms, inflation raised prices and people began to withdraw their savings from banks—quite a few Chinese banks depleted cash reserves. But the trend to buy personal computers continued.

One morning Liu Chuanzhi picked up a newspaper and read the headline, "The Central Politburo of the Party has issued a document on questions regarding cleaning up and rectifying companies. This will address relations between government employees and enterprises, relations between officials and commerce, and the issue of seeking explosively high profits from reselling goods." The background to this announcement was that certain people had been depending on the apron strings of government officials to do business. They made obscene profits, and the whole country was aware of their bad reputation. The government intended to stop this trend. It was clear to Liu Chuanzhi that a mood of retrenchment was blowing across the country. Unavoidably, there was going to be heavy weather.

The winds of "retrenchment" did start blowing. A much stricter financial policy was implemented in thirteen provinces, which raised the amount that had to be held in banks as a reserve against loans. This forced banks to raise the interest offered on their savings accounts and the interest rate on loans to enterprises as well. The government then issued an "urgent notification" that strictly controlled the disbursement of loans made with public funds. It put a tax on employee bonuses, a stamp tax on tobacco, it put a tax on "land" used in cities and towns. Additional taxes extended to virtually everything, even food in restaurants. The taxes were so high that people felt the government was fleecing them. The tax on employee bonuses, for example, could reach 300%.

In the late fall of 1988, the cloud of retrenchment rolled over China. On November 9, the *People's Daily* published an editorial that carried the tone of an official order. It said that the government "must grasp tightly" the process of managing what it called the rectification. The common people must prepare to "go through lean days." The media organs of the Communist Party had not used this editorial tone since the high tide of news reform in the mid-1980s. This was not the worst. After a few days, Premier Li Peng said that in the coming two years there would be "severe management rectifications." This Premier was not like his predecessor. He administered government policies in a low-key manner, as he moved the country inexorably towards more restrictive economic policies. If he used this kind of language, it was obvious that a period of reform was going to give way to a period of "stabilizing transition."

An uneasy atmosphere now prevailed in the company. Nobody knew what tomorrow might bring. The older ones knew exactly what "lean days" meant, and they began to economize on clothes and to store up food. Liu Chuanzhi called all cadres in the company together, hoping that he could calm emotions. He honestly admitted, "if there is to be an economic adjustment, it will influence our company. There are three areas that a rectification, especially a big one, will hit: loans, foreign exchange prices, and customer markets." He also said, however, "the General Manager's office guarantees to everyone that in the process of this "cleaning out and rectification" our company will come through on calm waters. The plans for the company in Hong Kong will continue to go forward."

The bells ringing in the New Year in 1989 sounded bleak. The New Year's message of the Communist Party General Secretary sounded like a layer of frost on top of the snow: "difficult and complicated," "weaknesses, losses and setbacks," "impossible to expect smooth sailing." Chinese had become accustomed to hearing auspicious good wishes on this first day of the New Year. They had never seen the Heads of the Party so pessimistic.

Liu Chuanzhi evaluated the situation and decided to take action. The explosive rise of consumer prices particularly alarmed him. He had been through the years of starvation and he knew that hunger was hard to bear. "If employees don't get enough to eat, there is going to be a major disaster." It was not easy to be an entrepreneur in China, for one had to be concerned about every aspect of employees' lives including eating, drinking, and living arrangements. Liu Chuanzhi spent the day discussing emergency measures and told his secretary not to schedule any appointments. Amongst a million important things, this one thing was paramount. He secretly dispatched a person with RMB 100,000 to Shandong, one of China's great agricultural provinces. Fairly close to Beijing, this province had grain, vegetables, and pork: the money was loaned to farmers and the interest was to be paid back in agricultural goods. If hard times came, at least company employees would be able to eat. His actions can be seen in the context of the fact that at least 30 million people died of starvation in China in the early 1960s.

The "Lianxiang Han-card" gets an award
In early 1989, an event of peculiar significance mobilized the entire company. The Lianxiang Han-card won a key prize from the Chinese government, but not without some behind-the-scenes assistance. A short article in the company files indicates the invigorating nature of this award. It was written by Guo Wei and included the statement, "We made a 5% hope into 100% realization of our goal." This phrase, to make "5% hope into 100% realization" was a succinct expression of Liu Chuanzhi's management philosophy. More than mere philosophy, it could be called a belief: it was simply what one did. In this case, the process had not been easy.

When Liu Chuanzhi and Ni Guangnan applied in 1988 for the National Scientific Advances Number 1 Prize for the Han-card, they did so with high hopes. The software was an astounding technical achievement and also met the needs of the market. The fifty scientists on the judging panel did not feel the same way. After a secret ballot, they gave a Number 2 prize to the Han-card. Liu Chuanzhi was furious. He felt that the panel had not properly understood the value of the Han-card or they could not possibly have come up with this result.

"Take this matter under control," he told Guo Wei. "Unless the Commission changes its decision, "we will not accept the Number 2 award." Guo Wei and a woman named Li Gang took up the challenge. Using a variety of PR measures, they worked the system. The process dealt not only with technology: it fostered key relationships. It dealt with the art of exquisitely calibrating relations between public officials and business leaders in China. Li Gang later became Manager of the Image Promotion Department of the Lianxiang Group, and was also instrumental in getting Lianxiang to be an Olympics Global Partner. "In essence, we were campaigning for votes," she said. "And at the time, campaigning for votes was a very modern concept."

A bombing campaign on the media gets attention from the USA
The process was successful and the Han-card took the Number 1 award. Prior to this, public relations had been considered a joke but now that it had achieved a kind of miracle everyone viewed the department with new respect. The PR Department had prepared well in advance and had a

series of actions ready to roll out. These included mobilizing a kind of intensive bombing campaign on the media. The "bombs" were articles about Lianxiang's Han-card receiving the Number 1 National Scientific Advances Award.

Media participation in this process showed how PR practices were maturing in China. A man named Chen Huixiang joined the Lianxiang team in September 1988, and was assigned to the PR Department. He used the phrase "Enterprise Image Strategy" to describe his work, which had four aspects: product advertising, market promotion, government relations, and cultivation of the overall environment including public policies and public opinion.

The company was careful not to leave traces of manipulating journalists behind in any public place. With consummate ease, though, it was able to influence journalists. The company held an unprecedented press conference to announce its Han-card award to the public and it arranged exclusive interview time with reporters from the *People's Daily*, *Guangming Daily*, *Economic Daily*, *S&T Daily*, and Xinhua News Agency. Advertising clips on CCTV were prepared. The text had only one sentence: "Lianxiang receives the Number 1 Award in National Science Advances." Golden-time ad slots on CCTV, between News and the Weather Forecast, did not require much money back then: RMB 3,000 would buy thirty seconds of broadcast time. Later spending of several hundred million yuan for slots were the bubble creation of clever advertising personnel in cahoots with enterprise managers. Ad people gave kickbacks to enterprise managers, so that the managers were more than willing to spend public funds of their State-owned companies on inflated ad prices. In the early spring of 1989, ad prices of CCTV were still cheap and the content of the ads was uninspiring, but the audience was roughly three times what it is today. Not only that, CCTV also sent reporters to the company to shoot a special news documentary on Lianxiang, without requiring a cent. This was broadcast for 75 seconds during the News broadcast, prime time. CCTV News enjoyed a huge audience at the time since it didn't have Phoenix News as competition. It was watched by essentially everyone in China, from the Leaders in *Zhongnanhai* to the common man in the alleys.

Journalists fastened their attention exclusively on Ni Guangnan. He was the star that summer while all others played supporting roles. Nobody felt this was strange: without Ni Guangnan there would not be any Han-card. Another factor influenced this situation, however, one that could not openly be set out on the table. Liu Chuanzhi had privately instructed staff to focus on Ni Guangnan. "Only one person is allowed to be publicized in our company," he said. Press releases supplied by the company to the media extolled Ni's virtues: "Comrade Ni Guangnan, with his outstanding abilities and stubborn will to succeed, has accomplished astounding results in the realm of computer-science research. He has stood out amongst the millions of scientists in our country." Press releases also noted that Ni Guangnan had "created tremendous wealth for the nation." The company filed an application for Ni Guangnan to be made a Model Worker of Beijing Municipality.

Ni Guangnan was like the sun at high noon. The inner circle at *Zhongnanhai* invited him to meet with them. The Party Secretary General, Politburo members, the Deputy Premier of the State Council, Tian Jiyun, all came forward to shake his hand. In the media, he was described as "a scientist whose talents are overflowing", "a patriot with superlative accomplishments", "a scientist with a reform concept", "a pathbreaker", "the father of the Lianxiang Han-card". Gu Mainan, a senior reporter of Xinhua News Agency and her partner Tang Hua wrote a long article titled "Ni Guangnan and his Liangxiang World." Ni's photograph was published on the overseas cover of a well-known Chinese magazine, making the scientist into a kind of movie star. This attracted instant attention from someone on the other side of the Pacific. This person immediately wrote a letter to Liu Chuanzhi. The result was a tremendous battle over who had invented the Han-card and who owned inventor's patent rights on the product. If it had not been for this article in a magazine, Lan Naigang, living in America, would never have known about the publicity being generated inside China.

Before 1985, Lan Naigang had been a researcher in the Number 6 lab at the Computer Institute. He belonged to the same research team as Ni Guangnan. In administrative terms, he was the Responsible Person for the team, while Ni was only a team member. Both men were talented but Ni was a strong-willed fanatic who hoped that his invention would have an ever-greater influence on China. Lan was easygoing, liked a comfortable life, was not much of a talker; he was not after fame and did not want to be pursued by the media. At the same time, he was unable to accept the fact that Ni Guangnan was getting all the credit for the invention rights.

It was easy for Lan Naigang to discover the article because it was published in the only Chinese-language weekly at that time that was also distributed overseas. The text of the article attributed the invention of Lianxiang's Han-card solely to Ni Guangnan. In his letter to Liu Chuanzhi, Lan objected.

Liu knew Lan Naigang. But he did not know how the Lianxiang Han-card was developed in its early years. Having poured so much energy into the Han-card himself, he realized that he should know the full story. With

Lan Naigang's letter in hand he went to visit some old acquaintances including Zeng Maochao, Cao Zhijiang, Zhang Zuxiang and Liu Jinyi. All read the letter and confirmed the legitimacy of Lan Naigang's claims. Liu Jinyi had been a member of the Han-card system research team. He had been through the entire process of the system's inception and development. "Lan Naigang was the head of the group," Liu said. "He arrived at the Computer Institute five years before Ni Guangnan, and he had a lot more prestige than Ni Guangnan. It was only later that Ni Guangnan became the pick of the crop."

Unsung hero: Lan Naigang
Many contributed to the development of the Lianxiang Han-card system without recognition or fame, but the unsung hero of the process was Lan Naigang.

Developing a Chinese-character system for computers became a key project for the Computer Institute back in 1974, and Lan Naigang was chief architect of the project. Descended from a prestigious family, he was one of the first generation of researchers in the Institute. He headed a group of four people, including Ni Guangnan.

From the beginning, the Lan Naigang group concentrated its efforts on developing equipment by which one could input Chinese characters. The computer industry in China was in very early stages in the 1970s. Input of signals was through "holes." Walking into a so-called computer room in those days one saw an endless rolling stream of paper tape in which were punched a myriad of tiny holes. A hole indicated "1" to the computer; no hole indicated "0". This allowed a binary system of signal input to enter the computer, the early development stage of all computers in the world. What Lan Naigang and his group now wanted to do was allow the computer to recognize other symbols that were faster and more convenient than "holes." Lan called this the "laser signal recognition system."

Research went on for four years and was ultimately successful. It became a part of the input equipment used by China's mainframe computers at the time. Its functions were in fact greater than had been anticipated and the research team also developed a small-scale computer, but it could only recognize the Roman alphabet. At a certain point, one of the members of Lan Naigang's group came across mention of "Chinese-character input" in an imported journal. By Liu Jinyi's recollection, the first Han-character system that he knew of was from Taiwan, but he also heard that Japanese were doing similar research. Lan Naigang was tremendously excited by this news. He understood the "laser signal recognition system" and he wished to direct the research of his group in that direction.

At the time neither Lan Naigang nor Ni Guangnan had any concept of holding rights to inventions. They were simply inventors, they were friends, and they were full of excitement. Lan Naigang was in charge of directing the research and was responsible for the design of new projects, but the importance of Ni Guangnan now clearly rose. He became the chief designer of the "circuit line." His intelligence and his diligence allowed him to surpass the others in the group in terms of influence.

The *modus operandi* of Chinese science at that time was to move forward as a unit with no personal distinctions. The phrase used was to "clasp hands in the forward advance." Many years later, public opinion took Ni Guangnan to be the "father of the Han-card," but some who understood the circumstances at the time tend to feel that Lan Naigang played a more important role. Looking back, it is hard to tell who was the key inventor, who the secondary, indeed one is inclined to feel that there was no single "inventor." The issue is to understand who first put up the core concept for the invention, namely the "lianxiang" or "linked-thinking" function.

This linked-thinking function had tremendous value in the development of China's computer industry. It turns out that Lan Naigang not only created the concept, but started to implement it before he left for the United States. He began with 512 characters. He painstakingly listed the possible compounds linked to these, with the aid of his Xinhua Dictionary. He listed all major two-word and three-word compounds of his core list of 512 characters. He meticulously recorded these, one by one, on sheets of ruled paper.

If the matter had continued in the same direction, there would be no dispute today. Unfortunately, Lan Naigang's work stopped at this point. In 1979, he became a visiting scholar at Stanford University and, when he left, he gave Ni Guangnan an unfinished version of his work. He then remained in America to pursue new research and he never returned to the "linked-thought capability." At this point, the tenacious nature of Ni Guangnan proved its usefulness. After a short stint as a visiting scholar in Canada, Ni returned to his position at the Computer Institute and took up the research again, replacing Lan Naigang as director of the project.

Applied technology has to cross a kind of "bridge" to be realized and within the Computer Institute this bridge was called the process of being "engineered." As Zeng Maochao had said, "For a basic-sciences principle to become a product, it has to travel a different road," and this road included prototype design, materials purchasing, mass production, and sales. In the late 1980s, scientific research in China was not capable of creating wealth. In fact, the entire system lacked any of the requirements of this "engineered" bridge. In the late 1980s, Ni Guangnan became the bridge.

Liu Chuanzhi now realized that the media coverage surrounding Ni Guangnan's sole contribution did not accord with reality. From a purely technical standpoint, there was good reason for Lan Naigang to be upset. But Liu Chuanzhi was not interested in technical issues at this moment. He was concerned about the company's interests and how to maintain the balance of the larger situation. The company needed Ni Guangnan to serve as a standard bearer, and Ni Guangnan was absolutely essential from a technical standpoint as well. The company was researching computers and hoped that before November 16 it could put out a prototype of a new machine. Li Qin had even revealed this news to the media: the "Lianxiang 286" had been included in the list of National Projects for 1989. It had taken years of dreaming and planning for Liu Chuanzhi to reach this point. Ni Guangnan's technical capabilities were an important consideration in making the dream come true. Liu was not going to lose his dream for the lesser issue of giving recognition to Lan Naigang.

In the early spring of 1989, Ni Guangnan was in Hong Kong working night and day to produce a prototype. This was the key to the company's future. The unexpected issues raised by Lan Naigang greatly affected Liu's peace of mind. Emotionally, he was inclined towards Ni Guangnan who persisted in a task to the end, even giving up a chance to work abroad. He had come back to China to finish unfinished work which was in accord with Liu's own work ethic, while Lan Naigang had cast this promising work to the back of his mind and decided to stay in America. This fact helped Liu decide to stand on the side of Ni Guangnan.

After receiving Lan Naigang's letter, Liu Chuanzhi kept it in his own hands. He shelved the issue of right and wrong; with tacit approval and even an accommodating attitude he allowed the media to pursue its exaggerated approach. The company never applied for a patent for the "Lianxiang capability," and the battle over invention rights to the "Lianxiang Han-card system" became an evanescent part of the company's history. This was a quintessentially Chinese method of handling the dispute. It relied not on principle, but on common sense, it related not to the gain or loss of an individual, but to the benefit of the whole. The results of this matter also proved that Liu Chuanzhi was inclined to err on the side of practicality. As he was to prove in a few months, practicality was as important to success as foresight and sagacity.

The "profit curve" and patriotism

Liu Chuanzhi liked to use the analogy of two Chinese wines in discussing his overseas strategy: when you are not famous enough to go up against internationally famous brands, all you can do is make sure that your products are of top quality. Make sure they are the finest *maotai*, although you are only asking the price of a lowly bottle of *erwotou*. He also liked the analogy of a racehorse: the trick was to use your best horse against the other guy's middle horse and to use your middle horse against his lower horse. The trick, in other words, was in knowing how to position your own product.

At the beginning of 1989, Ni Guangnan was working in a tiny laboratory in Hong Kong, designing the "286." Three assistants worked with him late into the night. He hoped that this would be a second great accomplishment worthy of succeeding the Han-card. This was the same conclusion Liu Chuanzhi had arrived at after a trip several weeks earlier to America. Personal computers were like the rising sun: across the globe, all could see the dawning light. At the beginning of the 1980s, personal computer sales were a mere 300,000; by the end of the decade, they had reached some sixty million. This was setting Hong Kong Lianxiang on fire: Liu Chuanzhi began to pick up the pace to have the company enter the world ranks of personal computer companies. He even began to imagine having an "American Lianxiang," even perhaps a "Silicon Valley Lianxiang." On his trip to the States, however, he saw that Italian shoes were arrayed in exquisite perfection in fancy windows, several hundred dollars a pair, while Chinese shoes were cast in a bin, one dollar a pair. The magnificent edifices of American enterprises stood in stark contrast to the small shops of Asians. For the first time he felt that this phrase "Advance Overseas" was perhaps far-fetched. "Lianxiang is still too poor," he admitted. "It would be over-reaching our abilities to think of starting out right away in Silicon Valley as a high-tech company." He reined in his ambitions and hoped that the company would win a decisive victory first on its own doorstep.

He selected Hong Kong to be the initial battleground. The commanding height was to be "motherboards and computer assembly." As noted earlier, the first move in this battle was to buy a Hong Kong company's shares with an outlay of HK$10 million. This company would be the production base. Design and production of motherboards would be the second step. A motherboard is an integrated circuit board composed of many circuit chips. It is complex: it incorporates nearly all the important components inside a computer, including the central processing unit, digital memory unit, display card, and so on. Every computer is composed of many of these integrated circuits, all linked to each other.

The process of early circuit board manufacture was very much like developing a photograph: a flat board of resin was coated with copper foil, on which was painted a layer of sensitization fluid. When the ready-designed circuit was reproduced or printed on the surface, after a certain process the unnecessary copper mold was corroded away. Components were inserted by hand into small holes on the circuit board and welded together, one by one. A motherboard included more than 200 components and 400 welding points and the production process used a considerable amount of human labor: in fact, this constituted the major part of the process. All you needed was good eyesight and nimble hands. In terms of the profit chain of the computer industry, this was not a "commanding height," but rather the lowest level of product. The "Central Processing Unit" and the "Operating System" are at the high point of what in China is known as the "curve of the profit smile." In second place are memory chips, hard drives, and display monitors. Motherboards are at nearly the lowest level with an average profit margin of only 1%. The final assembly of finished computers is at the very lowest level.

Countries with developed computer industries are not willing to invest resources in low-end processes for this reason. They cast this bone out for others. Liu Chuanzhi was a dreamer who believed in realism. He saw this situation and decided to put his most outstanding scientists and all of his financing onto what he saw as a sure thing. This was not only good horse against middle horse, it was good horse against lower horse, or indeed against no horse at all.

Those who study the history of Lianxiang tend to feel that this was the starting point of the computer industry in China. Several State-owned companies within China had already taken initial steps in developing a "286," including the "Great Wall 0520" in Beijing under the Ministry of Electronics, and the "Wave 0520" in Shandong. Production of these was minor, however, measured in the thousands. At the time, total consumption of computers in China was around 200,000, monopolized by IBM and AST. Great Wall and Wave basically assembled ready-made parts: this could not be considered actual creation of computers. What Ni Guangnan's group was now doing was more significant and included, for example, work on the structure of the motherboard, new design of the circuits, and new techniques in welding the components. Although the components were ready-made, they had to be linked together and composed with painstaking care. Along with changes in the central processing unit, the placement and design of motherboards and circuits had to change as well.

Ni Guangnan was a gifted circuit designer. The more complex the structure, the happier he became. A close look at the records of the company reveals that these next few months were a cooperative period that produced good results and brought Ni and Liu closer together. Ni Guangnan was unable to attend the party marking the New Year in 1989, since he was still working in Hong Kong. When he returned to Beijing a few weeks later, carrying an almost-completed "286 motherboard" with him, Liu received him at the airport with a group of employees as though he were a hero returning from war. In the first week of the lunar calendar, Ni Guangnan and seven researchers finished the final details. Liu Chuanzhi came to pay his respects daily, but more importantly he had the Vice-President of the Chinese Academy of Sciences, Hu Qiheng, come to pay her New Year's respects to Ni Guangnan as well.

In the first week of the third month, Liu put Ni Guangnan on an airplane bound for Germany where Ni attended the Hanover Fair, the world's top electronics trade fair. Over 500,000 people from over one hundred countries assembled here with some 3,300 displays exhibiting information and telecommunications technology. Sixteen halls at the fair were full to overflowing. Ni Guangnan brought his "Lianxiang Q286" and motherboard to the event. He stayed for ten days. Liu Chuanzhi waited at home for news. The results were tremendously successful: Lianxiang received orders for 2,073 Lianxiang Q286 computers, and 2,483 motherboards. The orders came from Italy, France, England, Holland, Belgium, Denmark, Finland, and what was then West Germany. These figures did not merely indicate orders. They drew attention: the recognition that the company now enjoyed was extremely useful in terms of support from policy makers, funding sources, and the market itself.

Opposition to Lianxiang's production of computers came from the government in the early days. Specifically, it came from computer factories under the government that had links to government officials. These factories had to obtain "production permits or licenses." Without such "licenses," you were producing illegally, and it was precisely for this reason that Liu Chuanzhi had opened up a "Hong Kong battleground." As Zhang Zuxiang had recommended, he was taking a circuitous route, going the long way around. Producing outside was easier than inside. "When we have succeeded overseas, then they will have to admit us inside China."

Crisis

The success at Hanover put the company into a happy delirium. Liu
Chuanzhi's own delight soon proved short-lived, though, as the company
became embroiled in a corruption case that involved avoiding customs
duties.

Ever since Lianxiang started mass production of Han-cards and began
to serve as agent for AST computers in 1987, it had continuous dealings
with Chinese customs. Illegal importing was common throughout China
at this time: the behavior had become normal social practice. Inside
China, all things were being "reformed" and "made new" but commercial
products were still in short supply. The government maintained its long-
term policy of keeping import taxes high, hoping that it could prevent the
import of Western goods, but this was the source of many problems to
come. Illegal importing, known in Chinese as "private-gain dealings," was
done by a small minority of people at first. It was secret and quiet, but it
quickly grew into a kind of collective behavior. Factories, stores, schools,
organizations, all became party to the practice. There were even cases of
army weapons being sold by government organizations for personal gain.
In the face of cheap prices for products from outside China, and the fact
that one could double or quadruple a product's price once it was inside
China, the government had no influence over this profiteering. In places
near the coastline such as the Pearl River Delta, the Golden Triangle of
southern Fujian (Min-nan), the delta of the Yangtze River, and the two
peninsulas of Liaodong and Jiaodong as well as Hainandao Island, many
local governments joined in the business themselves. The central
government still lacked experience and was not as clever as its successors
in the 1990s. Administrators didn't realize that importing could be a
source of great wealth for the country. If it had not been for the "initial
accumulated capital" derived from this form of private-gain activity, many
regions would never have been able to finance their own construction and
development.

The computer industry naturally was also involved in these activities.
The import tax on assembled computers was 200%. The tax on spare parts
was 30%. The margin between the two left people drooling and became
a most powerful weapon in market competition. An honest, old-fashioned
businessman who paid taxes had no way to compete with businessmen
who paid none.

The Sales Edifice of Lianxiang was constructed on the foundation of
importing. And this edifice enjoyed a brisk growth in the early years. In
1986, sales were RMB 17,100,000, in 1987; RMB 73,450,000, by 1988;

RMB 130,500,000. With regard to import taxes, Liu Chuanzhi had little room to maneuver. If the company did not involve itself in some of these importing activities, it would be a form of commercial suicide. The situation frustrated Liu to the point that he often publicly complained about the deteriorating business environment. He told a fable at the time about how to survive within a tough environment, which was widely repeated:

"The optimum temperature for an egg to produce a little chick is 37 degrees to 39 degrees Centigrade. At 40 to 41 degrees, will the egg produce a chick? I expect that an egg with strong vitality will, but if the temperature goes to 100 degrees, it certainly will not. As for enterprises in China, before 1978 the temperature was just around 100 degrees. By 1984, when we started Lianxiang, it was probably 42 degrees. Today the temperature is around 40 degrees, which is not optimum. Therefore: a smart egg has to study its surroundings and strengthen its vitality in order to turn itself into a little chick."

Legal business could not survive, and illegal business could not be done. Liu Chuanzhi therefore set a policy for the company that found a space between "legal" and "illegal". He was not willing to be implicated in "private profiteering," but he tacitly allowed the General Manager of the import and export department to have communications with others who imported illegally. His staff were allowed to buy the "private products" in these people's hands without any questions about where they came from. In the course of his twenty years in business, there were many matters that went contrary to Liu's convictions, and this was one. He did not like the practice: he characterized this behavior as "eating dead corpses." In addition to ethical self-censure, there was also the issue of legality. As your feet felt for that in-between space, how could you be absolutely certain that your footing was firm? If you slipped, what then? How could you guarantee that your feet were one inch from the edge, no more, no less?

In April 1989, Liu Chuanzhi ran into trouble. The Guangdong Gao'an Ma'an Scientific Instruments Service Company was investigated, closed and sealed by the Bureau of Industry and Commerce. Its General Manager, Song Zhe, was arrested by a sub-bureau of the Guangzhou Public Security Bureau and implicated in private profiteering activity. The police "felt up the vine to seize the gourd" and found that a substantial portion of Song's products had been bought by Liu Chuanzhi's staff. The products appeared to be components of the Lianxiang Han-card and Lianxiang computers. The amount involved exceeded RMB 10 million.

Spring of 1989 turned out to be both euphorically happy and tragic. The day that the Hanover victory was announced was the day that police officials knocked on Liu's door to start their interrogation. Liu Chuanzhi became concerned that he might have to go to jail—in the past he had given gifts to certain parties in order to clear obstacles from the path to successful sales of his products. In order to avoid the control system on China's foreign exchange, he had exchanged RMB for foreign currency on the black market so that employees could be paid in cash and avoid the bonus tax. This time, he knew that he was in more serious trouble.

If Liu had ever felt that transparent dealings and reputation were important to his company and himself, it was now. He had parents, a wife, and two children, he had just moved into a new home, he still had ambitious goals to realize in the company, yet it was possible he would soon be arrested as an accomplice in a profiteering scandal.

He didn't sleep that night. He kept thinking of what it had taken to build the company to this point. He felt that the overall management of the country's economy was hopeless, yet nobody was willing to stand up and make a difference. Anyone who tried would not be supported; not trying meant that one stayed out of jail, but the country suffered. He felt that if he did not raise issues now, he would not have the opportunity to say anything later. In the middle of the night, he went to his desk and wrote a letter to the Heads of the Chinese Academy of Sciences.

The document came to eleven hand-written pages. It expressed his frustration at operating with good conscience in a system that made it impossible to work for the common good. The conflicting emotions were apparent: "I am not a capitalist," versus "I am a capitalist but working for the common good of us all." The letter was addressed to two people in charge of the one hundred and twenty research institutes and hundreds of companies under the auspices of the Chinese Academy of Sciences.

The letter was primarily directed at Hu Qiheng, Vice-President of the Chinese Academy of Sciences. At the same time, she was the younger sister of Hu Qili, then a standing member of the Politburo and later to become Minister of the all-important Ministry of Electronics. Hu Qiheng was highly respected among her colleagues. She read this letter from Liu Chuanzhi and was moved to write the following response:

"Chuanzhi:
Reading your letter, I cried. An open heart is always the most precious thing for our beloved country, our people, and our Party. Despite the turbulent times, people like us harbor eternal hope for this patch of earth.

Since visiting multinational high-tech companies in America in 1978, I have harbored the dream that China too must have its own high-tech industries. Without a doubt, this is a historical need of our nation. President Zhou of the Academy of Sciences has courageously raised this large banner, and on the banner is written the dream of generations of Chinese: China must have, we are determined to establish, high-tech industries. Although several hundred companies have been fostered by the Academy, their motivations are perhaps not absolutely pure. As I read the way you bare your heart to us, I see that your motivation is truly our common dream, our ideal. You took the initiative to walk under this great banner, you were willing to risk torrents of bullets and bombs, what a tremendous support you are to those who raise the banner! We are war comrades who live and die together. Albeit from different positions, we are marching our troops in the same direction."

Hu Qiheng ended on an encouraging note: "Do not be discouraged. Do not retreat. The Chinese people have embarked on a road of no return!" She gave Liu's letter to Zhou Guangzho, Head of the Academy of Sciences. He read it, and returned it with a handwritten note at the top:

"Request that Qiheng pass on the following to Comrade Chuanzhi: We completely trust them. We support them with all our might. We believe that at this turning point in China's history they will, like true members of the Communist Party, struggle to the very end for the sake of the Chinese people. With intelligence and courage, we ask them to go forth and conquer the international market; make a contribution to the true "standing up" of the Chinese nation."

Putting aside the idealism of their generation in the letters of Hu Qiheng and Zhou Guangzho, and the patriotism and strong sense of cause, we can discern some practical content. Obviously, neither of these people felt that Liu Chuanzhi was facing much in the way of trouble. At the very least they did not take him to be a criminal who was about to go to jail. Perhaps the matter was never really that serious, perhaps the law was conscious of the circumstances in the country at that time and was lenient towards him. In the end, Liu Chuanzhi endured a traumatic episode but he did not go to jail. Years later, he was able to walk into *Zhongnanhai* and tell Premier Zhu Rongji how hard it was to manage an enterprise in the Chinese political context. It had been a significant matter to put his personal benefit, honor, and his family's life at risk for the sake of the company. One had to be noble and at the same time have very practical ethical standards. Walking that line in China was no easy task.

Summer 1989

Liu Chuanzhi and his company pulled through this crisis. Their rival, the Xintong Company, did not: it was also investigated for and charged with private profiteering. Meanwhile, the country faced a much larger crisis.

1989 became a watershed in China's modern history. After suffering through a summer of intense heat and tremendous anxiety, oppression, and violent resistance, most Chinese seemed immobilized, sunk in a deep fog. Over twenty Western countries united in refusing to invite Chinese leaders to their countries. They obstructed the investments of businessmen who wanted to come to China. Foreign-invested projects that had already started work were either cancelled or delayed. Even the World Bank stopped making loans to China. The Head of the Foreign Affairs Department of the Chinese Academy of Sciences, Ma Xuezheng, and her young team had little to do. The government now viewed young people, particularly those who had been to college, as "people who have not sufficiently reformed." All students who had recently entered college were required to join the army and be trained. Those who had just graduated from college were required to go to a kind of "bootcamp" for training. One Vice-President, Hua Zhinian, was a cadre in the National Science Commission. He had gone to England to study and not experienced that summer in Beijing. By fall, when he returned, he felt that the environment had changed radically. "It was nothing like as vibrant as before," he said. "It was as though nobody had anything to do." Chen Guodong, who is now the General Manager of a company under Lianxiang called Rongkezhidi Company, was a graduate student at the Chinese People's University at the time and writing his dissertation in the National Planning Commission. After June 4, this organization, meant to be the primary body managing China's economy, was required to spend all day, every day, studying politics.

Any public event became a crossroad: every person who stood at that crossroad had to decide which course to follow. Jobs after graduation were problematic. Many had expressed support for the students during the summer that had just passed, so they were now required to go through a political evaluation before being accepted in any position. Lianxiang's summer recruiting plan was supposed to start on May 16, but it was now stopped altogether. Young people who had already come into the company had thought it was a place with a great future; now they began to worry.

A trend to leave the country swept through research institutes and universities, worrying all those who didn't want to be left behind. Yang Yuanqing completed the requisite English-language Toefl exam and began plans to study abroad. He had little interest in sales, and there were plenty of reasons now for leaving the country. Guo Wei wrote Liu Chuanzhi a letter expressing his desire to study abroad as well. He enrolled in English language courses at the Language Institute. If Liu Chuanzhi had not repeatedly urged both to stay, the history of Lianxiang would have seen no further mention of these two future CEOs.

The only good news was that the company was no longer under a political cloud. Since it was, after all, a State-owned company, it was better suited to the prevailing atmosphere. Doubts about individually-managed enterprises created problems for many who had taken greater risks. When the Chairman of the National Science Commission, Song Jian, and the Mayor of Beijing at the time, Chen Xitong, came to visit ZGC, Lianxiang was shown off as a model to follow. The Chairman of the New Technology Development Region, Hu Zhaoguang, said that the company proved "the Socialist Reform Cause is moving toward Glory." He also said, "This kind of enterprise has real strength: as soon as it brings out the new operating system, it will be calling on technology and production capacity that it has been gestating—even without new investment, it can produce tremendous results." This kind of talk pleased Chen Xitong, (mayor of Beijing until he was put in jail for corruption) but he was more concerned about how many enterprises in ZGC were State-owned. Hu Zhaoguang hurriedly reported, "Among 700 new technology enterprises, 71% are owned by all the people, that is, under state ownership." The Mayor sighed and noted that once the intellectuals were released from their training camps, they would become a tremendous force.

The company Sitong, as an individually-operated as opposed to State-owned enterprise, gave a speech to the Leaders that was not well received. Liu Chuanzhi said that he wished Sitong all success even though it recently had to beg forgiveness for "mistakes". In this new climate of support for State-owned companies, Liu Chuanzhi lost no time in asking the government "to resolve our Import/Export License." He pushed further: "We hope we will be allowed a production license, we hope we will be permitted to sell 70% of our products abroad and 30% within China." It wasn't long before articles began appearing in newspapers about the dangers and problems of individually-managed enterprises. Liu Chuanzhi thanked his lucky stars that he had made sure the profits of the company were still considered "State-owned."

While Liu Chuanzhi's practicality proved useful at times like these, his dreams and long-term vision still led the way into the future. On June 4, the Head of Sitong Company, Wan Runnan, was conscious that the tide had turned and it was time for him to flee the country. Liu Chuanzhi similarly flew down to Hong Kong. The motivations of the two men appeared to be different: Liu ostensibly was going to look into what was happening inside a company he had recently purchased. It had spent the US$1 million loaned to the company and had nothing to show for it.

Before leaving Beijing, he made sure that employees who might encounter difficulties were protected. He ordered that "The company goes to work as usual on June 5". Liu was to remain in Hong Kong without returning to Beijing for several months.

Problems with a perfectionist approach to technology
The Han-card by now had sold 15,000 sets. This was considered a great success, but was still far behind the needs of the public for it only penetrated 5% of Chinese computer users. The problems were not in quality, nor in the conflict over invention rights. They arose because the fanatical nature of the software developers brought them into conflict with the sales staff. Ni Guangnan had been honored as the "Father of the Han-card" in public. Inside the company, a number of people were becoming aware that this Chief Engineer might be a superb circuit designer, but he had a problem: he continually wanted to improve the Han-card by yet another function. As soon as he had inserted one he wanted to add another, which made it hard for the sales force to know which version to try to sell.

The company's leaders had declared that Ni Guangnan was "The most market-oriented scientist in all of China." For a while the media extolled Ni's academic capabilities, though Liu Chuanzhi attempted to guide the discussion in a different direction: "We don't want to emphasize his scholarship. We want to focus on his ideas on economic reform and his sense of practicality: he uses the market to tell him the value of his accomplishments. He has set the model for others to follow in applied research."

At the time, Ni Guangnan was glad to accept the evaluation. In November 1989, he said to a reporter of the *People's Daily*, "Computer science is not a classical science. It must accompany the development of industry, it issues from the needs of the market." He also announced that if China's science and technology could not match industrial development, "it will simply be left behind." In fact, though, Ni had inherited the strong tradition of perfectionism among scientists in China. Measured by this criteria, he felt that the "Hero" in the Lianxiang story should be played by the technology itself—the company was merely the stage for experts working on the technology. As for the sales staff, they were a backup assurance that this marvellous technological thinking would be put to use.

Ni Guangnan headed a group of around thirty people who devoted themselves to the Han-card and who had developed numerous new editions over the past two years. On the one hand Ni would say, "Let the Han-card become a best-seller." On the other, he would gaze critically at the little thing in his hands and think of how it could be improved. New brands were coming out by then, as well as many pirated products and someone else in his position might have applied for a patent. He refused. "I'm not afraid of people copying me," he would say. "I don't need a patent to hold them back: my editions will keep changing and getting better. They can't crawl fast enough to catch me."

This put the Han-card in an awkward position. Company records of meetings reveal the extent of its difficulties. In the past, meetings on Han-cards had revolved around discussions of how the production line was too slow. Now the most troublesome issue was that the pace of putting out new versions was too fast for production and sales people to keep up. Just as salespeople were praising the beauties of Model Three, Model Four would appear with a new ad saying that it was far better than Model Three.

A small group of technical staff appeared to be driving the 200 people in the production and sales teams of the Han-card. Exhausting themselves to keep up, sales people discovered that the results of their efforts were simply to "Conquer yourself." The Lianxiang Han-card was not, as Ni Guangnan kept hoping, "an unwithering best-seller" but rather a "constantly withering bestseller." It was not making enough money.

A slight adjustment at the right time would have brought the situation back on track. However, Liu Chuanzhi could not get back into China. After returning to Hong Kong on June 4, he could not go back to Beijing for months. This period was the peak of what was known as the "Qing-cha Movement" in China. The term means "combing out or ferreting out people." Control of the borders was extremely tight. Liu had to hand all Beijing matters over to Li Qin.

By the winter of 1989, the Han-card problem was serious, for by now it affected not only the company's profits, but the reputation of the Han-card itself. If new software can't operate in a stable environment, bugs start popping up since there has been inadequate time to check everything. In successful companies such as Microsoft, the ratio of software developers to testing personnel is one to one. It takes at least one year to bring a new product to market, and every attempt is made to introduce the product at an opportune time. Ni Guangnan was springing ahead with disregard for any of this. At Lianxiang, the ratio of developers to testing personnel was ten to one and, in fact, there was basically no "testing team" at all. Li Qin asked Chen Dayou to come back to the company. Chen once again became everyone's great hope. Since Chen's scientific abilities were as admirable as Ni Guangnan, bringing him in to work on testing was doing him a great disservice.

Users began to refuse the product. Sales people complained to the developers. The response of Ni's developers was, "The product doesn't have problems. The problem is that you don't know how to use it." While the two sides locked horns, the Han-card did seem to be a strange thing—inserted in the machine at the laboratory it worked fine; inserted in the machine of a salesman, it froze the computer. Li Qin finally set up a "Han-card Coordination Office," and asked Bi Xianlin to resolve the issue.

Bi Xianlin was an old-style scientist, and the only person who dared raise issues about the fast pace of new development to the Chief Engineer. He finally discovered that the two sides were using incompatible computers. Although they were the same brand and the same model, their motherboards contained slight differences: one was a 1.01 version, and another was a 1.01A version. He therefore confirmed that the sales staff was right, there was a compatibility problem with the Han-card. After summing up all the problems, and dismissing the more minor among them, he found that there were still ten issues to be addressed by the developers. He also instituted a plan that mandated that new products could be released only in spring or fall. He controlled the release of new products that were bursting to get out of their cage—he either held them in his own hands or he gave them to users to test for free. He said to testers, "Find any bugs. We will award you RMB 3,000 for any problems you find in the code."

This led to intense conflict with Ni's staff. They criticized him for holding back new technology from the market and for impeding the march of progress. In response he said, "Your technology gets newer by the day but so do the customers' complaints." At an impasse, the two sides finally came to a compromise that may be unique in the history of commerce: the sales staff would only sell the old versions. The developers were allowed to set up a specified sales territory where they themselves could sell their new versions.

Bonus Tax
A number of new recruits arrived in the summer of 1988, and the company held a sales force meeting that autumn. Liu Chuanzhi was quite clear in his own mind that the era of selfless contributions to the company was over. He knew that with the arrival of these new employees he had to

think of how to motivate high performance. At the fall meeting, he took the unprecedented step of initiating a cash bonus system for outstanding sales.

All those who could sell up to RMB 5 million or more were to be in a special class and to receive a cash bonus for their contribution. All those who could sell more than RMB 3 million were to be considered outstanding and were to be considered before others for wage increases and promotions.

The standards were high and the bonus was difficult to get, but this was a tremendous motivator. The following several months were to prove that the word "bonus" had a large impact on sales. In 1989, sales increased 71%, to reach over RMB 223 million. The General Manager's office was delighted and he instructed the accounting department to draw out cash for bonuses. A report submitted shortly after by the accounting department to Liu Chuanzhi was shocking. The report said that if bonuses were issued according to the legally mandated system, the company was obliged to pay the requisite taxes, and therefore the company would have nothing left in the way of profit that year.

The problem arose with the government policy of taxing bonuses at a rate of 300%. If the bonus a company gave an employee exceeded three months' worth of his regular salary, then for every one RMB it gave the employee, it had to pay three RMB to the State. At the time, the government of China ruled that the standard salary of state employees was RMB 60 per month. Much of a salesman's income therefore came from his bonus. The 300% tax was instituted in 1985 and immediately met resistance from enterprises. The government stubbornly persisted. Enterprises could see that their appeals were in vain: they could either decide not to issue bonuses or they could evade taxes. Liu Chuanzhi was not willing to lose the confidence of his staff, so he chose the latter route. He told the accounting department to draw "cash checks," i.e., money orders from the bank, then he had these taken to Guangzhou. Through a friendly company there, he turned the checks into RMB 300,000 in cash. This was packed in a large suitcase and returned on the night train to Beijing where it was used to pay the promised bonuses to employees.

From the company's perspective, this method was believed to be "two legal parts make a legal whole." Each separate part of the procedure was allowable. The procedure raised ripples, however, that nobody had anticipated. Several months later the facts of the matter came out and the tax bureau began to investigate. For the first time, the company's finances were subject to intense scrutiny, which led to another crisis for Liu

Chuanzhi. His actions could be described as the crime of "evading national tax." Although this was not a "severe crime" he could not avoid being punished. After a spate of anxious explanations, of total disclosure, of private and public admission of error, of begging for leniency and going through various mediation channels, the tax bureau finally fined the company RMB 90,000.

The matter did not end there. Certain people inside the company suggested that Liu Chuanzhi had exposed the company to tremendous "political risk" and endangered its standing with the government. It was not so simple. From a broader perspective, behind this matter lay not so much legal issues or even tax issues, but the question of whether or not the entire benefits system of the country should be changed.

At the time, the wage system of China was totally under the control of the government. It was a "fixed and unchangeable graded-scale system." It was composed of four parts: basic wage, seniority pay, position pay, and beneficial-results pay. The name for this pay system was "File Pay." A comparable term for "file" does not exist in English: in Chinese, it means a person's complete dossier, the record of his life, including his political and work record. Everybody has a "file" in China and this travels with him when he changes jobs. The government long ago divided the millions of people in Chinese cities into a number of categories, depending on their line of work. These included, for example: cadres, employees, teachers, factory workers, military personnel, scientific and technical personnel, and so on. The government further divided each category into many classes: a fourteenth-class cadre, a third-class electrician, a second-class deputy researcher, a fourth-class professor. It applied a graduated pay scale to each of these. If you were in a government organization or a State-owned enterprise, on the fifth of every month you would receive a pay packet. A white slip of paper was pasted on each packet describing your total pay and its various components; all this was specific and regulated. This system had persisted for decades. The entire country followed the same rules, which were strict and inflexible. On the rare occasions when there was a revision, the central government would make a unified announcement nation-wide. It would raise the pay level of some one hundred million people, for example, all at the same time. In the 1960s, the concept of "bonus" had been declared a "management style of capitalism" that was forbidden in China. It was unethical and against the people.

As China's economic system changed in the 1980s, it took some time for this mentality to adjust. By the late 1980s, though, the bonus system had made a comeback. Bonus amounts were small at the beginning, and one received them with great trepidation as they were considered unethical. After Lianxiang was established, on the night before Spring Festival in January of 1985 it gave twenty employees RMB 30 each and a bag of cold chicken legs. This was the "bonus." People were advised not to broadcast this, in order to avoid attracting attention and getting in trouble with others. This fear about RMB 30 and a bag of cold chicken legs pretty well expressed the common attitude at the time toward bonuses.

After the mid-1980s, bonuses increased rapidly and with them a disparity in incomes. People began to get vastly different amounts, even within one organization. In 1989, Liu Chuanzhi approved an "Employee-bonus accounting table" that reveals that bonuses received in 1989 equalled around twenty percent of net company profits.

The average bonus per person was RMB 5,492. This was higher than the RMB 3,235 disbursed in 1988, but it was heaven and earth compared to the "RMB 30 and one bag of cold chicken legs" of 1985. The basic principle of this matter was that enterprises held the right to distribute their own profit, leading to a de facto differential in employee income. The prevailing practice was to conceal these bonuses; they quickly became the greater part of one's income. In 1989, they were already twice what the government system allowed as a wage. This challenged the traditional benefits system. The weighting was turned upside down, causing a huge social problem. Nobody would write the amount of bonus into the "pay line" so that bonuses were hidden, the government had no control over them, and they "roamed" outside the system of government finances. They were not taxed. This was unacceptable to any kind of healthy economic system. Those still living under the old traditional system felt wronged, both because they made less and because they paid taxes on it. It became impossible for the government not to stage a counter-attack. The simplest and most effective way to counterattack was to levy a heavy tax on bonuses.

Liu Chuanzhi found it hard to deal with this "bonus tax." His philosophy was that many affairs in this world cannot be put right all at once. To keep the larger situation in balance, he did not want to engage in a battle on the smaller issues, so he chose the course of accepting the punitive fine. Events were to prove, however, that this bonus tax was an adverse government policy. It went against the prevailing trend in China, and even officials of the tax bureau laughed at it in private, saying they were implementing a "legal but irrational policy." Not many months after Liu Chuanzhi paid the fine, the government abolished the tax on bonuses.

The end of the 1980s

Months of anxiety and unrest that permeated China after the summer of 1989 seemed to relax somewhat as the end of the year approached. Jia Xufu and the Jiamusi Agricultural Bureau of Heilongjiang signed the largest piece of business since the summer of 1989: a deal for 130 AST computers with a value of RMB 6.5 million. Sales seemed to be going up. The Lianxiang "286" received a Golden Award at the Beijing International Exhibition, making the older generation in the company feel that their dream of a Chinese personal computer had been realized. Twenty-one new employees were brought into the company and Hu Xilan felt thoroughly encouraged to see them. She told them, "I feel I am looking at the hope of the company when I see so many young people. Everyone says I am like an old mother hen protecting her chicks, and it's true, in my mind you are my children. Without you, there would be no tomorrow for the company."

In November of 1989, the company officially gave itself the name "Lianxiang". The Chinese Academy of Sciences Computer Institute Company now became simply the "Lianxiang Group." The PR Department invited in fifty reporters and asked them to announce this news in all the newspapers; it spent RMB 380,000 on ads on CCTV and in the *People's Daily*. The text of the ads read:

Lianxiang Group celebrates its ideals and aspirations:
together with you, Lianxiang creates a better tomorrow.

The ads were bright red and showed a photograph of a personal computer alongside the text. This implied that the tomorrow of the company was tied to computers.

Part Two

(1990-1994): The Age of Leaders

4

THE SPARTAN FORMATION

Small companies handle business, large companies handle people.

Liu Chuanzhi

The 1990s began in a disjointed way in China. Beijing gradually recovered its equilibrium after the summer of 1989. The Number 5 telecommunications satellite was lifted into space. A television serial called "Intense Hope" brought all of China to TV screens every night in a kind of numb addiction—the story line encouraged goodness and was full of sunshine. Ironically, the reality was not so bright: 50,000 lawsuits brought against the city of Beijing with regard to June 4, the first 146 cases of AIDS reported in Yunnan province, private entrepreneurs in Guangzhou mostly in the process of fleeing China, 2,651 companies declared to be illegal, 18,000 projects ordered to be stopped. Then there were criminal problems, environmental pollution problems, banks' nonperforming-loan problems, currency tightening problems, company debt problems, farmers-coming-into-the-city problems. In the past five years, Lianxiang had been advancing with ferocious speed. After spending four weeks in the company, however, a consultant declared that the company was moving forward with "astonishing speed and astonishing disarray." In actual fact, the entire country was moving ahead with astonishing speed and disarray.

The growth of the company was apparent. Ever since the Hanover Fair in Germany the orders kept coming in, to the point that the company could barely keep up. Producing and selling on a mass scale was difficult. Making a few prototypes was one thing. Large-scale production, sales, and post-sales servicing was another. A production base in Hong Kong was hurriedly set up, called an "assembly line" but in fact it was simply two machines. Most of the work relied on hand labor. The workmanship was poor, slow and substandard. Several dozen workers, housewives with little education, went through a simple training course, then pulled on a pair of gloves and began to work. They inserted the components one by one onto boards, the first person put in the resistor, the second the capacitor, the third the chips. When several hundred parts were inserted, the piece was taken to another machine to be tin-plated. The temperature of the welding depended on subjective feeling alone, control mechanisms were essentially absent. A technically proficient worker welded 160 "legs" onto the central processing unit, then washed the resin off with water and baked it dry. Workers relied on eyesight for quality control and on hands for testing component placement to see if everything was secure. This was workshop-style business, this was not mass production.

Still, the company moved forward. If it had looked backwards two times for every step it took forward, it would never have achieved its goals. The advance was like "storming heavily fortified positions": the front line simply had to keep moving forward. Territory that was secured would gradually be filled in and put in order by those who came later.

Replacing the AST with the Lianxiang computer
Liu Chuanzhi knew that "one day, sooner or later, we will replace AST". To him, this was equivalent to taking a fortified position. He knew this from the year 1987, when IBM and AST selected Lianxiang to be their agent. By January of 1990, Hong Kong Lianxiang relied on importing these computers into China. Subtracting the margin for the importing costs, the tax, and the administrative costs, there was still 24% net profit. An AST computer brought about US$4,200 inside China: the business was lucrative. Although Lianxiang wore the halo of the phrase "advance overseas," in fact it was basically an agent for shipping computers into China. As a result, AST, which had been a second-rate company, rapidly increased its share of the China market and became Number 1. Chinese customers believed the Lianxiang advertising and took the company to be a famous brand overseas.

The early 1990s was a golden era for AST computers. Approximately 80% of the company's products passed through Hong Kong Lianxiang to enter China. Hong Kong Lianxiang in turn passed the business through Beijing Lianxiang. The process was called "collaborate from within with forces from without." AST was content to see Lianxiang insert its own Han-cards into AST's computers and it regarded Lianxiang as a reliable partner. The company was confident that it had made a wise move in agreeing to have Lianxiang serve as its exclusive agent in China, although in so doing it sacrificed other sales channels. As for the monopoly-sourcing behavior of the northern and southern parts of Lianxiang, AST was content to live with the system. The company felt that if Lianxiang could sell AST machines, the system worked well. AST did not recognize that their partner was absolutely quivering with ambition. Lianxiang was using the profits from the AST business to cover losses on its own motherboard production and the company now allocated RMB 13.5 million to develop its own Lianxiang Computer.

From 1990 to 1993, the China Computer Project put the Lianxiang Computer name next to AST computers on the salesmen's price list. Lianxiang let customers make their own choice. The company waited for the right time to supplant AST altogether with their own product. The "Lianxiang 286" now passed inspection and received a government license that allowed the company to produce 5,000 machines in the first year. "The day has arrived," Liu Chuanzhi said. "We are finally going to compete with foreign computers by producing our own."

With control over the marketing of AST computers held firmly in his own hands, Liu Chuanzhi decided to initiate action. He called his sales staff together and declared they were the "Cadres Training Team." Li Qin announced to them, "We have decided that we will no longer promote AST 286 computers. We want our own products to get out to the market." For a while it was unclear what all this actually meant and those in the room broke into excited discussions. Then they heard Li Qin say, "A small group will continue to deal with AST. But we will move the main force of the troops decisively in the direction of Lianxiang Computers. That includes production, purchasing, and sales."

This conference went on for four days—Liu Chuanzhi wanted it to be a real mobilization campaign because he knew that this was not going to be easy. The sales staff was not afraid of selling new products, but they were worried about losing their income. They had become accustomed to eating the "piece of meat" that AST had become and it seemed a shame just to throw it away. "We can see three different scenarios," said Liu Chuanzhi. "The best is that we do a good job with our own machines and we also do not lose AST; the middle scenario is that we do well but we lose AST; and the worst scenario is that we do not do well with our own and we lose AST."

Liu's decision to promote Lianxiang Computers received the support of Li Qin and Ni Guangnan, although at that time the General Manager and the Chief Engineer were at loggerheads. As the conference ended, both developers and sales personnel were equally motivated. They knew that Liu Chuanzhi was ambitious, but were just beginning to realize the scope of his dreams. All outstanding businessmen have strong convictions, while at the same time they are generally transcendent opportunists. The Lianxiang Han-card turned out to be only one step on the road to the company's long-term goals. Producing motherboards was another, and agenting for AST yet another. Liu's true goal was to make Lianxiang Computers. This now became the dream of the entire company.

Small companies handle business, large companies handle people
Liu Chuanzhi focussed his energies on the future of the company. Indeed, he had no control over other, more immediate, problems. One problem refused to go away, however, and he finally had to deal with it in a brutally decisive manner. It related to the management of people.

The plan to sell 5,000 Lianxiang computers and 10,000 sets of Han-cards was entrusted to the company's Business Department and Enterprise Department. The Business Department was responsible for sales throughout the country and was managed by one of the Founders, Jia Xufu. The Enterprise Department was also responsible for nationwide sales, including the seventeen branch companies around the country, and was managed by a young man named Sun Hongbin. Li Qin noted gravely, "The burden on Old Jia and Little Sun's shoulders is extremely heavy." This was true, but the duplication of responsibilities and benefits intensified a growing conflict between the two.

Older people like Jia were accustomed to doing things by the book. They dared not go against rules even if those rules influenced company sales and profits. Younger people, like Sun, were more independent and believed that "all we have to do is get the business and company rules will oblige." Sun Hongbin, for example, perpetually complained about the inflexibility of pricing. With inflexible pricing, Branch offices had less opportunity to benefit, and so were not proactive in support of business. Flexible pricing in China means that salespeople have more leeway in giving kickbacks to purchasing managers, and thereby getting sales. Contradictions between the two sides gradually came to a head. Sun determined that the efficiency rate of channels managed by Old Jia was too low. This lost them opportunities—he recommended finding channels outside the company that could move goods. The two men argued.

Such contradictions can be found throughout China's large organizations. Most companies deal with the disputes in a Chinese fashion: they allow the split to widen until it develops into two different camps and one or the other goes in search of its own separate opportunities. It finds a different "mountain to rely on." Liu Chuanzhi did not want his company to behave in this way and he particularly could not allow cliques to develop around himself. He had to remain impartial.

In the spring of 1989, he decided to deal with the conflict between Jia and Sun with a speed known in Chinese as "thunderclaps that follow lightning so fast you have no time to cover your ears." He told Jia that he was "steadfast but lacked a pioneering spirit and a desire to create new systems." He told Sun that he "had a pioneering spirit and showed he could organize and lead troops," but "had a certain quality of 'self-centeredness' about him." Although not picking sides, Liu's heart was clearly on the side of the young people. He despised work for its own sake; he cared only for results. Since 1987, the company had tried to figure out how to cast a sales network over the entire country. It had tried to set up an "Eighth Route" branch system with a title that harked back to the Eighth Route army of the War of Liberation. This came to nothing since the company was composed of older people at the time who were not willing to spend years in the hinterland outside Beijing. In October 1989, when the Enterprise Department was established, Sun Hongbin quickly set up thirteen independently funded branch offices whose sales activity soon totaled RMB 24 million.

As a result of this success, Liu let everyone understand that in the conflict between old and new he stood on the side of results. Over the ensuing period, he brought every young person in to meet with him individually. Younger people felt that senior management was supporting them and they began to feel less anxious. Sun Hongbin and his Deputy, a man named Chen Hengliu, became the two new stars and Liu Chuanzhi gave them the Enterprise Department to manage. In addition to Guo Wei, this triumvirate then formed the new generation of talent in the company. It became the core of Liu Chuanzhi's succession plan.

Sun Hongbin and Chen Hengliu were a well matched pair. Chen was several years older and regarded Sun as his little brother, while Sun treated Chen as an elder. He was supremely respectful towards him. Colleagues noted that when Chen walked into the office after returning from a trip, Sun would shout for everyone to stand up. Chen was a fluent speaker, his voice was resonant and he had the ability to inspire. Even Liu Chuanzhi, blessed with oratory skills himself, respected this. Unfortunately Chen was less able to take action. Sun Hongbin was the opposite: he was slow in speech but nimble in action. He came from a poor family in Shanxi province, was smart, persistent, and willing to go to any lengths to succeed. He had great vision: he saw the larger picture, he just didn't say it out loud. Liu Chuanzhi was good at arguing and debating, and liked people who could talk. In order to make Sun practice his verbal skills, for a while he asked Sun to tell him a story every day. Spending this kind of time on Sun showed that he had high hopes for the young man.

One early morning in March 1990, Liu Chuanzhi found a newsletter set on his table. It was titled Lianxiang, but clearly was not the newsletter for which he had calligraphed the masthead. Opening it, he realized it was the work of Sun Hongbin's Enterprise Department. This made him uncomfortable. The first issue published the "Program of the Enterprise Department", which made him even more uneasy. The first line read, "The welfare of the Enterprise Department stands above all else," and declared that the Enterprise Department was totally authorized to manage the branch company managers. What Sun Hongbin was doing and what Liu Chuanzhi had expected were two different things. Sun wanted to make the Enterprise Department into his own fiefdom. It looked as though he might even want to split off from Lianxiang.

Liu Chuanzhi had always been able to see how things could develop by catching a glimpse of their beginnings. This newsletter was sufficient to open his eyes to the situation. He knew that he had to fly back to Beijing to deal with the issue in person. He had been pressing to find intelligent young people who could take over from older cadres that couldn't keep up with the times. He now feared that he had made a mistake in placing his hopes on Sun. "Selecting the right young people was the hardest engineering problem of the company," Liu was later to say. What happened in Beijing Liangxiang in the spring of 1990 had a supremely Chinese quality to it. Only by understanding it can one appreciate the full implications of Liu's statement.

Liu met with senior management of the company in Beijing in March, 1990. He told them that he had seen things in the Lianxiang Enterprise Newsletter that shocked him. The Enterprise Department could not have its own bylaws and it could not have its own paper. "If branch managers only read this Enterprise News and not our Lianxiang News, if all they are seeing is an Enterprise Department and Sun Hongbin, that is absolutely disadvantageous to Headquarter's concept of setting up a unified structure of branch offices. It cannot be allowed."

Liu Chuanzhi had not yet formed a final opinion of Sun. He planned to observe him. In the meantime, he said that Sun was "endowed with substantial organizational abilities and a zealous approach that is fully capable of leading people." As Deputy, Li Qin added in the meeting, "Young people have their virtues. They can go all over the country, they can live outside Beijing, whereas older comrades simply can't be on the road for months at a time doing sales." He spoke directly to the older Jia

Xufu. He said that he "had interfered." It could even be said that in some respects he "destroyed the strategic deployment we set up for the company around China." After the conference, all could see that Jia Xufu was mortally wounded. He resigned from his position and no longer had anything to do with Sun Hongbin.

Liu Chuanzhi hoped that everyone would draw a lesson from this event. He wanted the company to work together as one unit, with each part responsible for a unified "Lianxiang Culture." During this March meeting in Beijing, he used the structure of a ship to illustrate the concept. He felt that it was helpful in ridding the company of factions and divisive cliques: "The company is like a large ship moving in a direction determined by the President's Office: this is the unified principle of the ship's structure. The purpose of each part of the ship, and the position of each person is clear: this is the position principle of the ship's structure. The division of labor and cooperation among all parts are key: this is the cooperative principle of the ship's structure. What we want to emphasize today are the unified principle and the cooperative principle."

The March meeting came to an end without anybody fully realizing that the matter of Sun Hongbin had just begun. Two weeks after Jia Xufu was forced to give up much of his authority, Sun Hongbin faced total disaster. Some later said that this was engineered by Liu Chuanzhi. They implied that Liu Chuanzhi had used deception to catch Sun Hongbin, and many alleged that Liu Chuanzhi excelled in being devious. Yet on March 19, at the conference, Liu spoke in front of everyone of Sun's "self-centeredness" and his "secret-society type behavior." He said that Sun had the capacity to be either "a trainable genius" or "a dangerous person in the company." Sun himself was in the audience and heard this.

In the end, nobody gained from the conflict. Sun was sent to jail for five years for corruption. Liu lost the person on whom he had placed tremendous hopes and was forced to defer his succession plan for years. The sequence of events transpired as follows.

The Sun Hongbin Affair

Once the obstacle in the form of Jia Xufu had been resolved, Sun Hongbin became smug. He clearly did not comprehend the gravity of the warning from his boss. Managers of the thirteen branch offices as well as young people in the Enterprise Department now gathered around him in close support, as though they had found their true leader.

The influence of these young people quickly pervaded the rest of the company. More and more fault was found with the older generation. The Founding Cadres appeared to occupy all important positions in the company while young ones did the work and only got criticized. Liu Chuanzhi was seen as sitting alone at the top without capable people next to him who could carry on: young people were the golden hope of the future and needed to be given more responsibility. This sort of thing was said in the interests of the company, but it disregarded the hardships and trauma endured by the Founders.

Liu Chuanzhi received regular reports from his subordinates and was kept informed as to what was happening. The Founders too were writing him letters, saying that Sun was behaving as though there were no constraints on him at all. What worried people was that Sun was capable of "winning an inch and taking a mile": he now claimed for himself territory that originally belonged to the Human Resources part of the President's Office. He transferred three people into his own sphere of influence to serve as his reliable agents. These men now copied Liu Chuanzhi's "cadre training plan" and began to hold training sessions for new recruits. In the course of these, it was made clear that staff should express total loyalty to Sun Hongbin. Everyone began to say that Sun was their "leader." The talk began to put Sun together in the same breath as Wan Runnan and Liu Chuanzhi, the two most famous names in ZGC. Sun's subordinates now concluded that: "Sun is Number 1, Wan is Number 2, and Liu is Number 3." This was because "Sun uses capable people and gives them a stage on which to accomplish things, while Liu Chuanzhi has only mediocre people next to him. He holds onto power and won't let go."

The talk solidified into a rule: "Employees of the Enterprise Department must be responsible to Sun alone." All new employees of the Enterprise Department had to answer such questions as, "What relationship does our direct boss have with the boss of the company? If you produce 200 components one day, and your direct boss reports to the big boss that in fact 300 pieces have been produced, if you are asked about it, how will you answer?" The correct answer was, "With one voice, in unison, we will say 300." Another example had to do with this concept of the "ship structure" of the company. Enterprise Department employees puzzled this over and in the end concluded: Lianxiang Company is a big ship. The Enterprise Department is a small ship. If the big ship sinks, and the small ship floats, then it will become the big ship.

Sun did nothing to conceal this thinking. He even asked Li Qin to participate in the meetings. While Liu Chuanzhi was busy managing affairs in Hong Kong, Li Qin administered Lianxiang in Beijing. Many people in the company later came to the conclusion that the egregious behavior of Sun was made possible by the latitude given to him by Li. The assumption was that Sun was, intentionally or not, using Li as the "mountain to lean against," using him as protective backdrop. All these views failed to take into account the entire picture. From a purely administrative standpoint, Li Qin needed young people to go out and sell product, capture the national market. He shielded Sun in the split between Sun and Jia, but he could not condone Sun's outrageous behavior.

Liu Chuanzhi began to see that Sun was going further and further along a separate path. If he allowed this to continue it would end in disaster for the company. He hurried back to Beijing from Hong Kong and "cross-checked accounts" with Li Qin. This "cross-checking" was a commonly used phrase among employees in the company; it is used to this day and means to harmonize or bring steps into unison. Li Qin could see which way the wind was blowing: without hesitation, he agreed with Liu's judgment. The two men decided to transfer Sun out of the Enterprise Department and move him over to occupy the position vacated by Old Jia in the Business Department. Liu Chuanzhi admonished Sun to "come in with a humble attitude." "You are not allowed to set up a new unit or bring anyone else with you," he said. He hoped that the young man could be reined in at the brink of the precipice, that the company would then be able to make use of his capabilities. This was undeniably a huge blow to Sun. He would be distanced from his power base, surrounded and scrutinized by the Founders, and the young people in the Enterprise Group would be like a pod of dragons without a chief. When Liu Chuanzhi announced this decision on April 4, open conflict erupted.

What happened next came to be called the Shaoyuan Debacle, since it occurred at a meeting of the Enterprise Department held in the Shaoyuan Building of Peking University. Liu Chuanzhi later said that this meeting was the watershed: from the day of this meeting, Liu knew that Sun and his "Small Group" were not saveable. A series of unavoidable struggles was to follow.

According to records of the Shaoyuan meeting taken at the time, Sun Hongbin told his audience, which included Liu Chuanzhi, that his subordinates could not understand the company's decision. An employee named Bai Quen spoke next. Bai was editor of the newsletter that had first come to Liu's attention. He asked, "What exactly is wrong with the Enterprise Department?" Bai's deputy poured oil on the flames, "Since the company's newsletter is lousy, why can't we publish one that is better?" Liu Chuanzhi just sat there, listening, but when Sun Hongbin commented, "Their newsletter is a low-class little rag," he could restrain his anger no longer. He stood up to castigate the presumptive arrogance of the young people. He said that they somehow felt their own self-assurance would be able to save the situation. To his surprise, his audience "was in the midst of a kind of trance," as he later said. "People who are sleepwalking hear nothing, no matter how you shout at them. I suddenly realized it was impossible to try to talk reason into them."

The meeting ended badly. "Your attitude demonstrates that you know only about the Enterprise Department. You don't know anything about the Lianxiang Group!" said Liu Chuanzhi. "I hope you are not just pretending to be asleep, for if you are I have the means to bring you wide awake." He then strode offstage like a character in Peking Opera, but before he went out the door he flung back one last word, "You will find out who the boss of Lianxiang is."

His method of waking them up was severe. The two most active participants of the Shaoyuan Debacle were fired. The company's accounts were sealed and public security personnel were dispatched to protect the security of the company. Liu Chuanzhi personally assumed the position of Head of the Enterprise Department while Li Qin managed the Business Department. Sun was removed from his position and transferred to the Business Department to be Li Qin's assistant.

On the afternoon of April 7, Liu Chuanzhi called together all personnel of the Enterprise Department to make an announcement. The atmosphere of the meeting was cold. All sat absolutely straight in their chairs. The two people who had already been fired were still in their midst. When Liu walked into the room, all members of the Department immediately and in unison crossed their arms over their chests and faced him with a belligerent posture. When Sun Hongbin walked in, all instantly dropped their hands respectfully to their sides. The room was dense with cigarette smoke and Liu couldn't help but squint his eyes. Sun barked out an order, "put out your cigarettes" and everyone obliged. Sun again barked out, "Stand up," and all stood in unison. The secretary that Liu had brought with him, Ying Qi, sat down beside Liu, but Sun shouted, "That is not your place." Sun was commanding his Enterprise Department to show disrespect for Liu Chuanzhi. Liu first said to Ying Qi, "You may stay there." Then he quietly announced that all employees of the Enterprise Department must comply with his decisions. He said that forming factions was not allowed. Intimidating anyone was not allowed. "Any offenders, no matter who they are, will face severe punishment including being expelled from the company."

Sun Hongbin began to realize that the game was up. That night he called his subordinates to the Changchun Garden to discuss counter-measures, not realizing that this was a big mistake. The young people around him were highly indignant and unrestrained in what they said.

Some wanted him to stand up to Liu Chuanzhi, others wanted him to recognize the dangers and retreat, while some recommended disappearing with the funds. They were unaware that a person loyal to Liu Chuanzhi was planted among them. Liu Chuanzhi received the report immediately: the final decision of the Changchun Garden gathering was to appear to accept the company's decision while secretly transferring funds. This became the immediate reason for Sun's incarceration.

Sun Hongbin never admitted to the charges. He later said that someone might have said this about moving funds, but that it had not been a "conclusion" and, especially, that there had been no such action. Unfortunately, the situation was not so clear-cut. That very night an accountant reported that someone in the Enterprise Department intended to draw money to "outside". The next day was Sunday, and five more of Sun's subordinates came to Liu to "expose" the fact that people intended to withdraw funds and disappear. They warned the company to be on its guard. Liu Chuanzhi had no irrefutable facts that proved the claim to be true. From his experience over the course of many years, however, when a personal dispute intensified to this point, one or the other of the parties had to go. In fact, until recently in modern Chinese history, one or the other parties often had to die.

From the company's standpoint, Liu had to take preventive action. The branches that Sun was in charge of had at least RMB 17 million in their accounts, over US$2 million. If someone really "rolled up funds and escaped," it would lead the company into financial crisis and also a crisis of confidence in the shares.

Both Sun and Liu Chuanzhi were busy that weekend. Sun was asking Chen Hengliu, in Hong Kong, for advice on what to do. Liu was writing a report to the Security Bureau of the Chinese Academy of Sciences. This dispute was no longer within the confines of the company: it touched upon criminal activity, so he also reported the case to the National Public Security Bureau and the Department of Investigation. At the same time, he dispatched twenty people to all parts of the country to review and seal the company's accounts. He asked a man named Wang Yong to be his personal bodyguard and not leave his side.

Meetings continued on Monday morning. Sun Hongbin continued to argue his own defense but Liu Chuanzhi had decided not to waste any more time. He told Sun he was to "stop work and self-reflect." Sun was then led out of the company and taken to an apartment building owned by the Lianxiang Production Base in the northern suburbs of Beijing, at a place called Dongbeiwang. He was placed under the surveillance of at least two people at all times. All those around Liu Chuanzhi had upheld his decision, but he later candidly admitted that the "detaining of Sun Hongbin on that day was not unassailable in terms of legal proceedings. If problems had arisen and someone came forth to put counter-charges against me, I would certainly have been held accountable. This company is not my personal wealth. When State-owned companies are plundered and left empty, generally nobody stands up to deal with the matter. Why? Because nobody is willing to take responsibility. I was willing to play with my own life for sake of the company, and that's why I did it. After this thing was over, I made a report to the Academy. People say there is plenty of this asset plundering going on in ZGC but there aren't many who take action."

The results of the later investigation proved that Liu Chuanzhi was correct in his action. Sun Hongbin had indeed already moved company funds to another company and the amount was not minor. Sun Hongbin explained this by saying that he had no plan to "use public for private means," it was just that the company's financial system was so rigid, the procedures were so complicated, that he kept back a portion of operating capital in order to run the business smoothly. In fact, the investigation did not uncover any evidence that he had "corrupt tendencies." Even so, using public funds without authorization constituted a legal issue.

The company brought all of Sun's former subordinates to the northern suburbs of Beijing in Huairou County for a disciplinary meeting. A person from the Department of Investigation came to speak to them. His name was Xiang Ming and he was a Deputy Investigation Chief. He talked about the law, about what constituted "economic crimes," what constituted "corruption." He said that, "Corruption involving RMB 2,000 can be punished as a criminal offense, while corruption involving more than RMB 50,000 goes above the line of allowing a death penalty." This so shocked the group that there was not a sound in the room. One young man named Lu was still unwilling to submit, however. Privately, he declared that he was going to break the arms of the traitors in their midst. Then he commandeered a car from the company's pool of vehicles and had the driver take him to the apartment where Sun was locked up, prepared to beat up the guards and rescue the prisoner. Sun Hongbin begged him to go home. He said he himself did not intend to sever relations completely with the company, by which he prevented an even greater problem.

Lu returned to the company but his behavior was reported to Liu Chuanzhi. The next day, Liu Chuanzhi blocked him on the side of a street in ZGC. Liu said to him, "You had better understand that you can't win, evil cannot triumph over good. From now on, if something happens to any employee at the company, I will consider it your responsibility." Lu was prepared to argue back until he heard Liu Chuanzhi say, "Don't give me all that secret-society talk. Who do you think I am? Let me ask you, if you are walking along the street and suddenly a bike runs into you…might that be possible?"

"Sure."

"And after you get run into, the two of you start to argue. You're sent to the local police station. The one who ran into you is allowed to go. You are kept locked up there, to get roughed up for a while. Is that possible?"

"Yes, it's possible."

"Or you're walking along the street and you find out that three men keep following you. They tail you all day, all night….scared?"

Lu had already turned white at this exchange. He said on the spot that he intended to leave Lianxiang and that he would not interfere with the company in any way.

On April 22, Liu Chuanzhi told every employee in the company about this affair. At the time, he said that Sun Hongbin had been "pursuing criminal activity with both an organization and a program." Fifteen years later, he looked on it a little differently. "Actually when I think back on it today, when Sun Hongbin came into the company he never said he was setting up against anyone. He just wanted to form his own system; he felt that this would be his own kingdom. He didn't want anyone ruling over him. His methods and mine were different, that's all."

Sun Hongbin was handcuffed by police authorities on May 28, 1990 and was put into jail on June 5. He then began a long period of incarceration, with no visits by family or friends. After more than twelve months, the Haidian District Court publicly heard the case on July 10, 1991. The prosecutor charged him with "accepting bribes and diverting public funds." Another thirteen months went by before there was a verdict. The Lower Court had not found evidence for the charge of "accepting bribes" but it had determined that the crime of diverting public funds did occur and it sentenced Sun to five years. The Court's decision was Case Number 172 in the Haidian Court Records.

"Rectifying" the company

Liu Chuanzhi returned to Hong Kong on May 5, but was unable to put his mind at ease regarding the Beijing problems. Those who know Chinese organizations, with their human complexities and conflicts, know that it was not uncommon to handle events in the way the Sun Hongbin case was handled. The matter was a blow to Liu Chuanzhi, nonetheless, and he knew it would have ramifications for some time. Opinions of employees of the thirteen branch companies vacillated. Day to day business was paralyzed. If the branch companies remained in disarray, the 1990 sales plan for all of Lianxiang would burst like a bubble and all the efforts put into the Lianxiang Computer would be for nothing.

Even more importantly, Liu's plan to cultivate a new generation of successors was seriously compromised. Among the three young people he most appreciated and hoped to lean upon, one, Sun Hongbin "had explosively revealed his true self", another, Chen Hengliu, had been implicated to a substantial degree, and the company's Founders started having serious doubts about the third, Guo Wei. Guo Wei had never communicated much with the older generation in the company, and he weathered this event somewhat shakily. Liu Chuanzhi still placed his trust in the man, however. He set up an "Investigation and Surveillance Department" and appointed Guo Wei as its Chief Commissioner. Guo Wei became the connection between the company and the Public Security Investigation Court. In order to give Guo Wei a further chance to prove his capabilities, Liu Chuanzhi asked him to take over Sun Hongbin's position and address the chaotic situation within the branch companies. Guo Wei promptly left Beijing and led a Group of Five that, in one fell swoop, visited all branch offices.

This task that Guo Wei had accepted was an extremely difficult matter. His first mandate was to deal with urgent financial issues, to scrutinize the accounts, to control the uncontrolled spending behavior of various branch Heads, and to look into any improper conduct. No other person could have accomplished this mission in the Lianxiang Group at the time. Young people generally had the spirit and the will but insufficient experience. The older generation had a wealth of experience but were unwilling to get involved. They knew that the branches were in chaos, their finances lacked transparency and it would be an unmitigated disaster if the matter was poorly handled.

Guo Wei had always felt that "when the company is in trouble, we take responsibility." He also hoped that by grasping this opportunity he could restore his own image in the eyes of his boss. "The situation was a cesspool of contradictions and the risk was extremely great," he said later. He knew that people with "economic problems" would be gambling for their lives with him if they were exposed. The term "economic problems" in China refers to corruption of one kind or another. In fact, he did indeed encounter threats from people with "problems" and, as a result, he went armed.

When faced with danger, Guo Wei's instinct was to move forward, and the more he faced adversity the more his spirits soared. This was precisely the kind of person needed at this time. Guo Wei and his Group of Five went from branch to branch, from northeast China to the northwest, then from south to southeast, and by the end of the year they had secured the branch offices in Taiyuan, Xi'an, Chengdu, Chongqing, Guangzhou, Changsha, Wuhan, Nanjing, Shandong, and Shanghai. The results showed that the branch companies were not totally without merit. In the past year, they had created RMB 10.38 million in profit, and returned 75.4% on investment. However, they owed the company RMB 18.69 million in inventory goods. Guo Wei stripped the General Manager in the Chengdu Company of his position. He closed the branch company in Chongqing, he recruited new Managers for the branches Wuhan and Changsha. The Xi'an Company also had problems but these were less severe. He said to that General Manager, "I use the approach of the Communist Party: if you are open and above board you'll be treated with leniency, if you resist, you'll have trouble." That General Manager obligingly revealed everything.

The business of the branch companies rapidly recovered and, in the course of the next year, they sold half of the personal computers sold by the entire company. From that time onward, Guo Wei was judged to be a man who "blocked the bullet" for his boss.

"Heavenly rules" and "Entering the mold"

Despite Guo Wei's success, it was not sufficient to mend the fences after the sheep were gone. All Chinese companies have to grow in the midst of chaotic conditions. If the chaos is perpetual, however, growth stops and even the entrepreneurs cannot protect themselves. The "overturned carts of the 1980s" served as examples: companies and individuals that "bit the dust". Lianxiang had to do something of lasting value to set its house in order and, in the remaining months of 1990, these things were done by a man named Tang Dandong. If Guo Wei could be called the "Hero of a Chaotic World", Tang Dandong was the one who set up a system of order.

Tang Dandong is a member of the Miao nationality. He graduated with a Diploma in Law from the Central Minorities University. He is introspective in character and meticulous in work habits. He has a clear mind and is a prime example of the kind of person who is not on the inside what he seems on the outside. Before coming to Lianxiang, he was a cadre in the Policy Bureau of the Chinese Academy of Sciences. His work experience and academic credentials made him a natural candidate for setting up the Legal Affairs Department of the company.

Tang arrived in the company just as the Sun Hongbin case erupted. He had a low-level position, but his legal knowledge brought him to the fore. He knew little about managing enterprises, for his own way of thinking had emerged from his profession, but he realized that there was a need within the company for people to understand the concepts of "institution" and "systems". This thinking was in alignment with the ideas of Liu Chuanzhi.

In 1990, the rules and regulations of the company were haphazard at best. For example, when a man named Wang Pingsheng entered the company in 1990, he asked the Head of the Human Resources Department how many people the company employed: the Head of the Department didn't know. He asked the Head of the Finance Department how much money the company had: the Head of the Finance Department did not know. He asked the Warehouse Manager how much they had in inventory: the Warehouse Manager did not know.

The company had been operating for years under what were called "heavenly rules," and it had a fine reputation in the industry. Tang Dandong knew that those who engaged in certain practices, related essentially to kickbacks and bribes, would be severely punished. Tang discovered, however, that these "heavenly rules" were all verbal. There was not a single black letter on a white sheet of paper to give employees guidance in the matter. He was shocked. He believed that "Any system has to have a "vehicle," a medium through which to operate, rules have to be understood without the shadow of a doubt, otherwise employees will have no basis on which to proceed and managers will have no basis for administering rewards and punishments." He drafted the first set of written rules for the company:

1. In business activities, it is forbidden to take any kind of kickback for any kind of reason and in any form. Those who break this regulation will be expelled from the company.
2. It is forbidden to operate a second business; anyone who breaks this regulation will be expelled.
3. It is forbidden to use company or work privileges to seek personal profit; those who break this regulation will have confiscated what they have received illegally, and will be fined an appropriate amount in addition.
4. Compensation for any work done outside the company must first be reported to the responsible Head of the department (or General Manager), and the compensation must be handed over to the manager for handling. All those who break this regulation will have twice the amount of what they have received deducted from their compensation.

5.   Receiving presents in the course of business activities must be reported to the Department Manager. Any presents under a value of RMB 50 are to be managed by the Department Manager; from RMB 50 to 100 the Manager should hand over to the General Manager or Responsible Manager, over RMB 100 should be handed over to the Human Resources Department. All those who break this regulation will have twice the value of gifts they have received deducted from their bonuses.

6.   It is forbidden to ask others about their bonuses or their benefits. All those who break this regulation will have that month's bonus deducted.

7.   These regulations apply to all employees in the company, including regular employees and part-time employees.

Tang Dandong's efforts to "Regularize the income system of the company" were supported by the President's Office. Liu Chuanzhi specifically set up a group to draft all the needed procedures and a man named Zhou Lingxiu became its commander. The work of the committee progressed rapidly so that 1990 became famous within the company for being the Year of Setting up Systems. As 1990 ended, the company completed its first rendition of the process. The message emerging from thousands of items was a strong one: the "Big Ship Culture" related not only to political and economic values but also legal and systemic values. These values impacted each and every person. As they were understood and incorporated in the business, the company's culture was formed.

Liu Chuanzhi knew that many things in a person's mental framework cannot be restrained by systems or laws, however. To emphasize the unified nature of Lianxiang, he gave countless speeches. The President's Office compiled these into a booklet and distributed it to all employees. One notable speech was delivered on October 6, 1990, in which Liu said, "We have to create a true Spartan formation. If one part of the company has problems, the whole will not be destroyed." Known for particular courage and skill in warfare, Spartans relied on centralized military authority in establishing their autocratic power in southern Greece. By using "Spartan spirit" to describe the core culture of the company, Liu emphasized the aspects of marching in step, consolidating efforts, motivating troops, and so on. He was not content with mere words. The company began to organize employee training sessions. The term for the sessions was "entering the mold." According to Liu Chuanzhi, the company should become a kind of firm "mold" made up of the ideals of Lianxiang, the beliefs, the values, the system, the rules, and the etiquette. The process of "entering the mold" was carried out mostly in lovely locations. It was an intense process, more rigorous than normal work. "We would get up to do exercises in early morning, before it was light," said one graduate of the program. "It was like army training. Later we would loudly sing the Lianxiang song, then begin the day's lesson."

Liu Chuanzhi is a management maestro who is also endowed with "Chinese qualities": schooled in the traditions and peculiarities of the Chinese system, he developed the ability to deal with its difficulties. In the 1990s, he brought what was essentially a paramilitary management style of highly centralized command into a high-tech industry. On the other side of the Pacific, entrepreneurs like Bill Gates were practicing a kind of free-rein management style in the information industries. In China, Liu Chuanzhi insisted on having the company become a Spartan battle structure with each person and each department taking its proper place as one component of the whole.

Opening up a "grievance market"

As Tang Dandong was energetically setting up rules, Wang Pingsheng was assigned to be Manager of Human Resources. Wang was formerly in the Policy Bureau of the Chinese Academy of Sciences, and belonged to the generation between Liu Chuanzhi and Tang Dandong. He had been through the whole process of the Cultural Revolution, from 1966: the sending of young people to the countryside in 1969, the Workers Farmers and Soldiers schools in 1974, the death in rapid succession of Zhou Enlai, Zhu De and Mao Zedong in 1976, up to the April 5th Incident in which the Gang of Four fell from power. He even had a clear memory of the great famine in the early 1960s. Throughout the 1980s, he excelled in his duties at the Chinese Academy of Sciences. He had been Deputy Chair of the Research Office, Secretary of the Party structure, and Chief Engineer of the Policy Bureau: his official career had been smooth. The extreme social changes of the late 1980s left him rethinking his own path in life, however. Under the encouragement of Liu Chuanzhi, he left his official position and entered Lianxiang.

By inviting Wang Pingsheng to join Lianxiang, Liu Chuanzhi was setting up a second line of command in the company. He knew that the computer industry was a world that belonged to young people. Computer companies were proliferating in China, and the most successful were being managed by people under forty. Liu Chuanzhi and his fellow Founders had stumbled on this stage just at the right time and were able to be amateur players, but the faster the business was turned over to young people, the better. Liu's most urgent task was to find someone who was capable and trustworthy, someone who could handle the company's human resources issues and thereby become his right hand man.

Liu had been in frequent contact with Wang Pingsheng and he recognized that this was not a frivolous man: his conduct and deportment were "upright," he had definite views, he had a sense of the bigger picture and he dared to speak his mind to members of the State Council, the nine-man group that is at the top of the power structure in China. In discussing national affairs, Liu had the impression that here was a man much like himself. In terms of knowledge or personal magnetism, Wang Pingsheng was at least on a par with Chen Hengliu. Liu and Li Qin went together to ask him to join their team. They invited Wang to come into the President's Office of the company, and they gave him a badge that read "Number 00011." Wang had recently been in a car accident in which his entire body was injured and he had not yet fully recovered. So they assigned him a car for his own use and bought him a rotating chair so that his movements were not too painful.

Like Tang Dandong, the first impression Wang Pingsheng had of Lianxiang was that the damage done by Sun Hongbin to the company was severe. He began to evaluate the company from the perspective of people's psychology. Employee morale was bad. Older people doubted the loyalty of younger people. Younger people resented the repressive system imposed by older people. The rift between the two generations was apparent, and everyone in the company had grievances with regard to the company's leaders. Before, the company seemed to have a heart and employees had no reservations about their leadership. Now, Wang Pingsheng could see that the trust of employees had changed. "The economic loss of several million was something you could see," he later said. "What you couldn't see was the psychological damage."

"You have problems," Wang told Liu Chuanzhi. "The company is like a pot bubbling over the fire with steam building up inside. Its lid is on tightly and the fire is burning away underneath. Without an escape valve, I'm afraid the pot will explode."

Liu understood what Wang was trying to tell him: he was linking the greater situation of China to the situation inside the company. "If it were up to you, what would you do?" Liu asked

"If it were up to me, I would hold a "grievance fair.""

He explained his idea to Liu Chuanqhi. Holding a grievance fair had to be composed of three steps. ONE: Hold a seminar for employees. Sort out the ideas of everyone: which problems have to be resolved immediately, which cannot be resolved but have to be clearly explained. TWO: Indicate exactly what employees should do. THREE: Counter-attack the people who have bad intentions and are capable of damage.

Wang Pingsheng agreed that he was following the artfulness of Mao Zedong. "If they don't say anything when you allow them to complain, you can counter them after they bring up issues when you've closed the grievance fair. Without doing this, it will be impossible to unify the energies of the majority of people."

Liu Chuanzhi decided to go along with his recommendations. He said that he would personally conduct a seminar. The seminar went on for six days. People talked about the leaders' bureaucratic manner, the failures in supervising people, the lack of clarity between what was right and wrong, the lack of a rigorous operating system. They talked of training young people, of whether the company was set up to make money or start a new industry, they talked about employee transport problems, eating hall problems, quality of employee problems, air conditioning and heating problems, telephone problems, natural gas cannister problems.

Humans are complex beings: the more people are kept from expressing themselves, the more resentful they get. If they are given opportunities to talk, they become mellow and compliant. The psychology of employees at Lianxiang in 1990 went through this process. By the time the meetings had finished, Liu Chuanzhi stood before all employees and performed a self-criticism. Then, one by one, he answered everyone's questions. The anxious atmosphere at all levels of the company relaxed and it was possible to move forward under a lighter burden.

Spring 1991: Belief in the Lianxiang Computer
Ma Xuezheng moved to Hong Kong at the beginning of 1991. Directors of the Academy of Sciences had spent seven months using a variety of tactics to try to persuade her to join Lianxiang, and she finally agreed. Mary Ma, as she is known outside China, is now Chief Financial Officer of the New Lianxiang, the company that is combined with IBM-PC.

In 1991, Liu Chuanzhi first asked Ma Xuezheng to go to the front line and work as a factory worker. Then he sent her to the sales counters to be a salesperson. After a tough six months, he allowed her to take over the position of Chen Hengliu and become his Executive Assistant in Hong Kong. Ma Xuezheng was already familiar with the etiquette of any occasion and she spoke fluent English. Hong Kong people sometimes intimidated Lianxiang employees with their English, and the company felt fortified with Ma Xuezheng in their midst. She was 37 years old at the time.

Lianxiang was in some ways typical of Chinese enterprises in the 1990s. China's first batch of entrepreneurs established themselves in this period. They relied on scientists, salesmen, market researchers, PR people, agents and lawyers, but they relied particularly on close relations with public officials, journalists, and key retired older people.

In the spring of 1991, the company enjoyed close relations with such key people. Its outstanding achievements had created a lucrative tax base for the government. Sales had been rising every year for the past five years and in 1990 had reached RMB 326.8 million. Taxes paid on that amount came to RMB 9.4 million. This appeared to be a money tree. Another practical reason for official attention was that people began to recognize the success of ZGC. This high-tech development district in Beijing had been prospering for three years and many Leaders came to make a public appearance and applaud it. The Chairman of the National Science Commission, Song Jian, appealed to everyone "to revitalize the Chinese people. Prepare to put forth your total strength, intelligence and your passion." The President of the Chinese Academy of Sciences, Zhou Guangzho, felt that no one need discuss any more whether or not Lianxiang would survive: the company was bound to become "one of the leading high-tech enterprises in the world." The Secretary of the Beijing Municipal Commission, Chen Xitong, wanted to know if the Lianxiang Group lacked for anything. He guaranteed that the Beijing Municipal Government "would take all measures to resolve any problems the company might have". The Chairman of the Development Region, Hu Zhaoguang, declared, "Lianxiang is not big enough. It is ranked Number Two here and it should be Number One. We are confident you can change that." Even Liu Huaqing, the Vice-Chairman of the Central Military Commission came to visit the company. After he had seen the Lianxiang Computer, he wrote a commendation, "Roam abroad, in serving the national defense." This showed that Lianxiang not only had the government's approval but was now in harmony with the military as well. Yuan Mu, of the State Council, solemnly stated, "I ask Comrades to think from a broader perspective for a moment, from the historical imperative of two kinds of social systems: to think of the important needs of high-technology, of its superior standing in the competition, comparison, and confrontations of the two kinds of social systems."

This was somewhat abstruse, but no matter how you looked at the company, it was clear that it combined traditional logic and an unknown high-tech future. As a hybrid animal, half-Chinese government, half-that mysterious other economic system, it was something that both government and military representatives admired. The true hero of the company had to be the Lianxiang Computer. Liu Chuanzhi's brilliance was that he recognized this and used belief in a "national computer, the Lianxiang Computer," to unite all forces.

Problems with mass production
For a while, all seemed to be going smoothly. The company was back on track, there were now two research centers, one in Beijing, one in Hong Kong, there were three production bases, Beijing's Dongbeiwang, Shenzhen's Baguailing and Hong Kong's Chaiwan. There were loans from banks: RMB 40 million on the Mainland, HK$1.2 billion in Hong Kong. Every month, 8,000 motherboards were being sold to North America and Europe. Within the China market, more and more computer manufacturers were buying Han-card users' rights, including AST, IBM, Great Wall, and Wave. In 1989 the company sold 4,552 Han-cards; in 1991, the figure was 22,000. Money flowed in. By supplying services, the company expanded its client base and brought in potential Lianxiang Computer users. In May 1990, the company exhibited two hundred "Lianxiang 286" computers at a National Exhibition, to tremendous acclaim. One week later, it exhibited at the Beijing Computer Fair and won orders worth over RMB 12 million, highest among the 200 computer enterprises participating. Afterwards, Liu Chuanzhi met with the Vice-President of America's DEC Company, and proudly listened to him praise Lianxiang's accomplishments over the past six years.

All this was a prelude to starting mass production of computers. Unfortunately the symphony was not as well orchestrated. As soon as the company went into mass production, quality control became a problem. The company had been licensed to produce 5,000 computers at the beginning of 1990 and it had set its sales targets accordingly. In fact, Lianxiang sold only 2,131 machines in 1990. Liu Chuanzhi became aware that, in his optimism, he had not anticipated the difference between mass production and small batch production. He thought that sample orders from the exhibition could be extrapolated into regular orders and thereby transform company profits.

This time, the problems were not technical. To a certain degree, they were caused by the company's production methods. These were the same as methods used to make color television sets in China in the 1980s and also cars in the 1990s: basically all of the components were imported. In 1990, China's computer production capacity reached a level of 85,000 machines, in 1991 it was 200,000, with Wave and Great Wall being the most famous brands. Regarded as "national brands", in fact these were made of imported components that were then adorned with a Chinese brand. China was familiar with the phrase "screwdriver factory": such factories bought in spare parts from a variety of suppliers, compiled them into computers and sold them to customers.

Lianxiang Computers followed the same practice. Motherboards were made in its production base in Hong Kong, but all other parts were purchased from outside China's borders. The supply of components therefore became the first link in the production process. The pioneer in setting up the company's importing channels was Jia Xufu, General Manager of the Import Department. Years later, when he had retired and Lianxiang Computers had reached sales of several million machines a year, he recalled the circumstances of the "screwdriver period." A computer had eight primary components, so he dubbed the process the "Eight-nation Alliance." "The central processing unit came from Intel in America, the internal chips were Japanese, the hard drive came from Singapore, the display screen came from Korea, the monitor card came from Taiwan, the case and keyboard also came from Taiwan, the motherboard came from Hong Kong Lianxiang. Only the electric plug was actually produced on the Mainland."

Purchasing channels were therefore highly fragmented. Since the company did not have the right to import, it had to go through middlemen in China. This was a complicated business. A third party with an import license had to sign all contracts with suppliers of the goods, even though Lianxiang was the true buyer. The phrase in the trade for this extra loop was to "turn foreign trade into internal trade." The key was to make sure that "one hand handed over the money while the other took the goods". Otherwise goods and money could part ways—one could easily slip into the tricks of wily profiteers. Jia Xufu called the successful implementation of this extra loop a "firewall", meaning a safeguard that confirmed one complied with Chinese law.

All of these extra loops lowered the efficiency of the use of money, however, and they increased the likelihood of unforeseen problems. Even worse, though Lianxiang sales were increasing rapidly in 1991, they still totaled only a few thousand machines. To have such a complex and elaborate supply chain serve such a minor production quantity resulted in fluctuating quality problems and high-priced components.

Liu Chuanzhi realized that if problems were not resolved there would be no need for a hundred-year plan for the company. Indeed, the company's immediate existence would be in doubt. He issued orders: "Hong Kong must immediately find a new supply source for the keyboards. Hong Kong must ask for guidance from experienced structural design personnel and must take any and all reinforcing measures to meet the emergency." He then flew from Hong Kong to Beijing and told management, "If the quality issues are not resolved, I am resigning from the company." He issued a report to all employees, "there are a hundred interlinked connections that must be made properly from start to finish. It is unacceptable for any one of those links to have any mistakes. If you are the one who makes a mistake, you will be considered a criminal within this company!"

Quality issues now became priority for the company. The President's Office issued 1,899 letters in a market research poll. It received 867 replies. A consolidated report handed over on March 8, 1991 showed that 41% of respondees were dissatisfied with or non-committal about product quality. The good news was that another 59% expressed approval and listed the "Lianxiang 286" ahead of the AST computer. In 1991, these customers had bought 8,582 Lianxiang Computers, bringing some degree of comfort to Liu Chuanzhi and his President's Office.

The Romantic Ads of the early 1990s

In the early 1990s, the image of the company was enhanced by an advertising approach that spread the corporate message throughout the country. The reform process in the 1980s had begun to release tremendous creativity in China. Capitalizing on this psychology, the PR Department began to use ads that stimulated people's emotions. Use of the two words "lian" and "xiang" had long been recognized as a brilliant move in terms of corporate image. The next step, led by Chen Huixiang, was to create ads that caught the spirit of the times.

Chen Huixiang came up with a phrase that resounds through the company to this day: "If humanity loses Lianxiang, what will become of the world." This bold and poetic statement utilized the original meaning of the name of the company, Lianxiang. It implied, "if humanity loses the ability to think in a logical and linked way, what will become of the world." It drew on the rich heritage of several thousand years of Chinese characters, while at the same time playing to people's yearning for a kind of modern consciousness. This aptly met a trend in China and tapped into latent ambitions of the entire society.

Chen was a young man who did not like to be restrained. He was one of the few people in the company who had an interest in literature. His creative inspiration came from the experience of having been repressed and isolated in earlier years. He published a novel in 1988 describing this experience: he had worked in a factory belonging to the Ministry of Electronic Industries located in the eastern suburbs of Beijing at a place called Da Shanzi. Like all industries related to the military at the time in China, this factory was described only with a roman numeral. The compound was surrounded by a high wall and there was no sign at the gate, just a guard post for armed soldiers. "Along the wall were several dozen cannons covered by protective sheathing, from the street it was easy to see their barrels pointed up to the sky." Six enterprises inside the compound employed more than ten thousand people. All of these were highly regimented and totally unlike those on Electronics Street in ZGC. In 1988, a new factory began to be built on the far side of the wall, a joint venture for making kinescopes with the Japanese company Matsushita. The large compound was no longer quiet and peaceful: every day, someone would resign from his position and run across the street to get a new job. One day, at a meeting in the factory, Chen declared, "We're not a business here, we're like some kind of labor reform camp. We don't even have a name for this outfit." He went on, "Why don't we put a name on top of one of our buildings, like Matsushita? Why don't we tear down the walls to the streets and let customers come on inside?" Nine out of every ten Chinese at the time had the same inclination, and were trying in various ways to make a living that conformed to their hopes and dreams.

The phrase, "If humanity loses Lianxiang, what will become of the world" was not created solely by Chen Huixiang. It had gestated many days inside the PR Department. According to Guo Wei, Manager of the Department at the time, the source could be traced back to An Zijie, a famous person in Hong Kong. An knew that this name "lianxiang" was much admired. He said, "Lianxiang is the source of all of humanity's science and technology." According to Guo Wei, "An Zijie took this phrase from the famous Chinese dictionary called "Cihai," "ocean of words."" Guo Wei's memory may not be correct, however, for there is no such phrase in Cihai, just an explanation of the meaning of Lianxiang: "the mental process of linking one thing with another."

Nonetheless, this description hit the mark with the PR Department. They wanted to write this sentence into the ads they were planning. All ads came from people within the Department—the company still was not using outside ad agencies. They brought in a student who had just graduated from the Zhejiang Arts Academy and a scriptwriter from the Film Academy. Everyone sat around to mull over the company's very first TV ad. One person said that while An's phrase was a good one, it was not poetic enough and was too long to say easily. Everyone tried to articulate the real meaning of the phrase till Chen Huixiang said, "If humanity loses Lianxiang, what will become of the world." Everyone said, "That's it!"

Company ads had previously been very concrete. The PR Department was influenced by the prevailing wisdom in the business which said that an ad had to contain a "basic message" and any vagueness about that core message was unacceptable. The budget for advertising was RMB 2,253,900, all spent on content that was realistic and concrete. This budget went into ads in twenty-five newspapers and six television stations, and into brochures, posters, calendars. This new phrase indicated a change in approach: for the first time, the company created a style that was poetic. At the same time, the message was serious and nothing like as extravagant and exaggerated as later ads became.

The final version of the television ad was thirty seconds long. A chimpanzee played the leading role. He came toward the audience and, after turning 360 degrees, took the pose of "The Thinker" in Rodin's statue. A bright moon rose in stark contrast to the dark sky. Symphonic music washed over the scene, full of passion and longing. A window then opened on the screen and a line floated before the audience: "If humanity loses Lianxiang, what will become of the world."

The company spent RMB 35,000 on creating this ad. It spent another RMB 260,000 to buy golden-time slots on the evening news of Beijing TV. Several weeks later the ad was moved to CCTV where a thirty-second slot after the News Broadcast cost RMB 166.66 per second. All these figures are ridiculously low by today's standards. Two hundred million people saw the phrase. It contained none of the key elements of a traditional ad, product description and price, for example, yet to the amazement of all ad companies at the time, it was supremely successful. According to a research poll in 1991, 12.6% of customers knew about the Lianxiang Group from this ad and 7.6% felt that the ad had a decisive effect on getting them to buy Lianxiang products.

This piece of ad copy went on to become a popular phrase throughout China, a kind of hip thing to say. It migrated from the realm of advertising to the realm of popular culture and evolved into a kind of belief. This was and remains a rare phenomenon in China.

The global "black storm" and Intel

In the fall of 1991, Liu Chuanzhi announced that Intel was increasing the number of chips it wanted to sell through Lianxiang. 1991 was a disastrous year for the computer industry throughout the world. Intel was the only exception. Several hundred computer-integrating factories had closed or gone bankrupt. IBM was of course "venerable" and could not be swayed by any passing breeze, yet even this company of 300,000 employees cut its forces by 40,000 in order to maintain its 1% profit margin. Compaq's computer sales were first in the world that year, yet its president was fired and the reason was simple: company shares plummeted by 70%. In Hong Kong, at least forty companies that produced motherboards and products similar to Lianxiang's went down like an avalanche.

Lianxiang's assembly line was still in motion. Its factories were still taking in parts and sending out products, but the company had been losing money every month since April. As the summer ended, cash flow became a problem. With years of accumulated good repute, the company tried to increase its loans but banks refused. People used the term "black storm" to describe the times, as though nobody could avoid its force. It came with a suddenness that nobody expected, and it came from Intel.

Intel's headquarters are in Silicon Valley in the United States. The company is the largest producer of central processing units in the world. In the early 1990s, its CPUs were 80% of the approximately sixty million computers in the world. In order to keep its monopoly share of the market, Intel always kept chip production lower than normal demand, then it would distribute quota to various computer assemblers. This method of "quota" and "fixed price" resembled the period of scarce supply in China before the 1980s. The difference was that China had nothing to sell at the time whereas Intel did, and Intel painstakingly maintained a balance in order to keep its own profits stable. One only need observe how happy Liu Chuanzhi was to announce that he had received "chip quota" from Intel to know that this thing was important. In the spring of 1991, the "quota price" of the chips for the 386SX CPU was US$95 for one chip. Lianxiang, lacking quota, had to pay US$195 per chip when it placed an order for ten thousand chips on the black market.

Although Lianxiang was losing money on its CPUs, it needed to make a profit on its assembled computers. Unexpectedly, a company called AMD now threw its own "386SX chips" on the market. The capabilities of this chip were better and its price was cheaper. AMD was a small-scale chip manufacturer that had always followed closely on the heels of Intel. Intel naturally could not allow AMD to edge ahead of it so it announced a price drop on its own products. A price war ensued. Liu Chuanzhi and his employees prayed that they would be able to get their already-purchased batch of expensive black-market chips off their hands quickly. This was not to happen. Customers were already waiting for a change in the market, wanting to buy in a rising market, not in a falling one. The stalemate continued throughout the summer. One could see chip prices slip daily until they were selling for only US$50 by July. The value of the goods in Lianxiang's warehouse fell by 70%.

In mid-summer, Liu Chuanzhi and all members of his Board of Directors held a meeting in Thailand. The Finance personnel reported that the loss in company accounts had reached HK$17 million. In 1991, the company was far from the size it is now, and the entire production value of Hong Kong Lianxiang products came to only HK$30 million. They had lost half their lifeblood in just a few months. Liu Chuanzhi was distressed and hurried back to Hong Kong. Before leaving Bangkok, however, a friend recommended that he go pray to the four-faced Buddha. He was told that this Buddha was particularly efficacious, but after one's wish was satisfied, it was important to give something back in return. Disaster would follow if one did not. Liu Chuanzhi did not believe all this but he was anxious about the company's affairs. He went to the Buddha to pray for the company's safety.

Hong Kong Lianxiang was in a mess. If things did not turn around within two months, the only course of action was to close down. Like the general of a defeated army exhorting his soldiers not to retreat, Liu Chuanzhi raised the cry, "Stand up to it, hold firm!" Then he began to slash company expenditures. A more important measure that pulled the company through the crisis, though, was changing the Hong Kong company's *modus operandi*. Its production line was removed from Hong Kong to Shenzhen which reduced blue-collar staff in Hong Kong by one hundred people and lowered company expenditures each month by HK$1.2 million.

This first staff reduction in the company's history was accomplished in the course of two hours. On the day that Ying Qi received the order to manage the reduction process, he spent all night preparing checks for workers who would be leaving. The next day in the morning he arrived at the factory, met with the workers, and announced the decision. Then he handed over the checks and explained how much of each check was salary and how much was bonus. Most of the one hundred workers were women who inserted components into computers. Most had only graduated from middle school, some only from grade school, which meant that it was going to be very hard for them to find work in the future. Yet nobody argued with him. All silently returned to their workstations to pick up their belongings, then under the eyes of security personnel walked out of the factory, one by one. Ying Qi was left with a heavy heart.

China should have its own IBM

In January of 1992, the PR Department applauded ten great events in the company in 1991. Surviving the "black storm" was among them. In December of 1991, sales of "board cards" reached 100,000, and in the same month revenues totalled HK$132 million, the highest recorded amount since establishing the company.

The "Retreat to the Mainland" policy appeared to have been effective. The Shenzhen Lianxiang factories entered production just as 1991 was ending and accomplished the aim of bringing Lianxiang computer production back into the National Plan. At the end of 1991, Liu Chuanzhi held a joint birthday party in Hong Kong. Facing officials from the computer industry, colleagues, government and banking circles, he delivered a speech on the subject of "What it took for us to ride through the Black Storm of '91." "Not only have we weathered the storm, we have greatly exceeded our sales targets. By our original plan, in fiscal year 1991 we should have turnover of HK$550 million, but in fact we achieved HK$950 million, with an increase over last year of 88.2%. Not only did we cover the previous loss of HK$17 million, but we took in HK$10 million in profit." He noted that, "Hong Kong Lianxiang's production and sales of motherboards and expansion slots amount to around 2% and 8% respectively of the world's market share."

After this speech, Liu flew back to Beijing where he waited for the distinguished visit of the last in line of the Deputy Ministers of the Ministry of Electronics, Hu Qili. Hu was a rather colorful figure in China. He was made Secretary of the Communist Youth League at a very young age, and he rose to become a standing member of the Communist Party's Politburo. After the tumult of the summer of 1989, he was stripped of a large part of his powers. He took up a post at the Electronics Ministry with the hope that divisions between state-managed and people-managed companies in the electronics industry would soon be a thing of the past. After Chinese New Year in 1992, Hu Qili came to visit Lianxiang and said to its senior management: "China should have its own IBM. It should have its own multinational companies. We at the Ministry intend to adhere to this policy."

It looked as though the black storm had not buried Lianxiang, and the future looked bright. Liu Chuanzhi did not tell the Deputy Minister that the salvation of the company had been to sell products imported from non-Chinese companies. These included 26,000 AST computers that brought in more than HK$200 million. The company had also sold 3000 inkjet printers, 1200 laser printers, 558 charting instruments, 330 scanners and 100 workstations, sourced from Hewlett-Packard, Sun, and IBM. Profits from agenting these foreign products made good the losses of the company and even brought in profit. During the storm, Liu Chuanzhi had engaged in a campaign to "fill in the breach" by deploying troops and resources to "expand trade revenue from other things." When the storm had passed, he was able to say that the "losses in the internal dyke were filled from the outside."

Early spring was particularly brilliant in Beijing in 1992. Having survived the crisis Liu Chuanzhi was able to relax. One day, when he was in the midst of joking with someone, his head spun and he fainted. When he woke up, he was lying in a hospital bed. The doctor said that his old illness had not only returned but evolved into a serious case of Meniere's Disease. In that moment, he remembered the four-headed Buddha in Thailand and the fact that he had never gone back to repay the favor.

5

EAT MY DUST

This is a race. The guy in front says to those behind, "Eat my dust." He runs faster and, yes, I eat his dust. Right now that's the way it is: we have to stay calm and keeping on eating dust. Inside, though, we hold the plan to beat them.

Liu Chuanzhi

In the summer of 1992, when Deng Xiaoping was gathering activist reformers around him in southern China, Liu Chuanzhi was similarly urging his staff on in Beijing. He encouraged them to be warriors who swept through all fortifications in how they managed business. For the preceding thirty-six months, Beijing had been divided into two camps by an ideological struggle. The key question was, "Do you call it Socialist or do you call it Capitalist?" Corollaries included, "Do you call it a Planned Economy, or a Market Economy?" and "Do you take Peaceful Evolution as Number 1, or do you take Economic Construction as the core?"

These issues were hotly debated in the media. Leftists and Rightists argued pros and cons, while government officials merely equivocated. Even the *People's Daily*, always the one to give the clear signal of government policy at times like this, waited for instructions from the new leaders in *Zhongnanhai*. All of China was hearing the approaching footsteps of a new era. In the last week of January 1992, a farmer in Shunde City of Guangdong province declared, "I don't care what kind of "ism" you call it, things are good right now. If you call this socialism, it's socialism. If you call it capitalism, so be it." If this had been said quietly, in private, it wouldn't have meant much, but the radical statement was openly published in newspapers. What surprised people even more was that the farmer said this while surrounded by a group of high-level Party officials. They clustered around this old man, who had already been retired for twenty-six months. His name was Deng Xiaoping.

Deng Xiaoping's inspection tour through Guangdong, Wuhan, and Shanghai became a key event in China. The National Chairman, Yang Shangkun, was also ready to take the country in the direction of economic takeoff. One week later, the Ministry of Electronics held an internal conference for its senior officers. Those attending expressed disbelief that Lianxiang could be selling 100,000 motherboards every month to overseas markets. Officials who dealt in foreign trade at the time had no concept of how to sell. They invited Liu Chuanzhi to come over and tell them the story of "*maotai* quality and *erwotou* price."

In February, the price of real estate in Shenzhen doubled. In order to bring Hong Kong production back into China, Lianxiang had bought half a hectare of land there as its production base and now everyone regretted not buying more. At this same time, the Ministry of Finance extended a benefit to Lianxiang that had long eluded the company: lowered taxes. Lianxiang could now avoid the imposition of production tax, it could reduce its income tax by half, it could write off 10% of sales revenues as Research and Development expenses, and it could avoid import taxes for certain major items.

Government policies regarding computer development seemed contradictory. On February 20, the purchase of computers with public funds was curtailed and put into a list of "controlled projects." This would reduce computer sales by 5% at the very least. At the same time, the Ministry of Electronics submitted a plan to *Zhongnanhai* that aimed to realize extensive use of computers within three years by such industries as banking, construction, electric power, metallurgy, science and technology design, telecommunications, meteorology, finance and accounting, the postal service, information management systems, and the army. The Ministry also wanted to implement computerization in 13 provincial and 434 municipal governments, as well as 12,000 large- and medium-sized enterprises and ten million commercial sales networks. If this plan was realized, the Chinese market for computers would not fall by 5%, but would increase annually by over 50%.

Another barrier to international trade in China was dismantled in the spring of 1992. The central government announced an immediate cancellation of the so-called "adjustment tax" on imported computers. It decided to stop requiring import licenses for computers within two years. This so alarmed computer manufacturers and sellers inside China that officials from the State Council immediately came forward with promises that the State Council would approve various policies to protect "national-brand computers", and would extend a relatively large amount of investment in support of production bases for computers. When Lianxiang began to ask which "famous brands" and "production bases" were included and whether or not the policy would include Lianxiang, the company was told that the precise list of names had not yet been decided. One week later, when the list became public, the Great Wall Computer Company, under the Ministry of Electronics, the Yang-tse Company and Langchao (Wave) were on it. Lianxiang was not. The Ministry's report went on to say that the country would invest RMB three million in these three companies over the coming five years, bringing their production capacity to more than 350,000 machines in total. Obviously, Lianxiang had been tossed to one side. What Hu Qili said didn't count—he was only a Deputy Minister.

This government cold-shoulder to Lianxiang was not done intentionally. Lianxiang held the position of Number 2 in sales, but most of this derived from selling overseas products. People looked on the company as an agent; its name was not among the top ten computer brands. A research study at the time indicated that the four Chinese names in the top-ten list were all State-owned enterprises. All of them enjoyed government investment and various kinds of State-planning benefits: IBM 22.80%, Great Wall 14.52%, AST 12.24%, Super 4.66%, Apple 4.45%, Compaq 2.85%, Sun 2.19%, Langchao (Wave) 2.07%, Donghai 1.52%, Yanshan 1.14%

Liu Chuanzhi and Li Qin met to discuss this situation at the Lianxiang headquarters in ZGC. China's computer industry had already been in existence for thirty-six years. It covered the entire spectrum from small-scale machines, computers, externals, software, information processing, to servicing. Its market totaled around RMB 7 billion. Compared to overseas companies, however, Chinese computer manufacturers were at least twelve months behind. The assets of two hundred Chinese computer enterprises added together did not come up to the strength of just one large foreign company. There were hundred-fold differences in sales—others planned in terms of millions whereas Chinese companies planned in terms of ten thousand.

"Trying to take over their market is like trying to snatch food from a tiger's mouth," Li Qin said. Liu Chuanzhi responded, "I figure the best defense is an attack!"

The wolf arrives

Everyone knew that this was going to be a battle of widely disparate strengths. In the first few months of 1992, Liu Chuanzhi already had strong intimations that the Chinese market would become an international market: he believed that a crisis among Chinese makers was imminent. He relayed his thinking to all employees and candidly admitted that he was worried. It seemed the "black storm" of 1991 had not abated—it was still brewing up from America, Europe and Asia. It was bringing the world's largest computer manufacturers and dealers in droves to the Chinese market and they were digging in and preparing for a fight.

The first clear indication appeared at a purchasing forum with the banking industry. Banks had always been major customers: Lianxiang had to get that business. It raised the capabilities of the 386/33 to become 386/40 and it dropped the unit price from RMB 25,000 to RMB 20,500. Liu thought that this would deal with the smaller contenders for the market, but this time it was not the "little nuisances" that were the problem but the "big troubles." When Zhou Xiaolan led the company's salespeople into the purchasing forum hall, he immediately saw the problem: they were surrounded by computers from foreign countries and Taiwan: IBM, AST, Compaq, also Hongji and Shentong. Worst of all was that Liu Chuanzhi's "competitive price" was a joke.

Bad news travels in packs. In February of 1992, the computer industry's profits inside China dropped by 26%. Although sales of the largest company, Great Wall, rose, its profit dropped by 53%. Li Qin thought back to one year earlier when company discussions had led to the feeling that Lianxiang's competitors were Great Wall and Langchao (Wave). Now these contenders were insignificant compared to the new threat. "The chief competition comes from Taiwanese-made products," he said. "Behind Taiwan comes America."

The average price of computers on the market fell by RMB 4,000 in one week. Lianxiang's computers had to preserve a gross margin of at least 15% in order to break even. On top of production costs, they had to add regional agenting fees, repair fees, training fees, advertising fees, daily expenditures, and tax. "The wolf has arrived," said Li Qin. "If we don't kill it, we are going to be eaten by it. We can only resolve to do what we can and go up against it."

Agenda-less Meeting

Under intense pressure, ten of Lianxiang's senior managers met at the Dragon-springs Hotel on the outskirts of Beijing to hold a twelve-day meeting. The Communist Party of China is fond of recalling its "Zunyi Conference" and its "Lushan Conference." This crucial meeting of Lianxiang was similarly pivotal in its consequences.

The company generally held two meetings at the beginning of each spring. One was for policy-level people to discuss future goals of the company, as well as the sales strategy and annual plan. The other was for all employees to "send out the old and receive the new" and to sing out the marching call of the New Year. Liu Chuanzhi had observed that these two meetings came to define the character of the company. They set the direction, raised the flag.

According to records of the time, the Dragon-springs Conference set a sales target for 1992 of 25,000 computers and 35,000 Han-cards. Participants also decided that before the end of the year they would put two new products on the market, household computers, and Chinese laser printers. The plan seemed concrete and practical, perhaps overly so. The concept of "no agenda" was popular at the time in China, known to all, from the lowest level of officials to leaders in the Politburo. Its basic purpose was to unify the thinking of those who participated in a meeting. The point was not to encourage debate, and certainly not to be concerned with technical issues. The practice left a colorful record in the annals of the Party, and was sometimes applied to corporate life as well.

If Lianxiang really was a Big Ship plowing through distant oceans, then Liu Chuanzhi now intended to set the ship's course. Though the topics at the Dragon-springs Conference were concrete, he wanted to use the "no agenda" method to make managers see what was happening before their very eyes. "This is a meeting that decides the fate of the company," he said. "If we don't get through this pass, we are going to die."

This brought the managers to full attention. Lying in wait for the Chinese market were not only Taiwanese Chinese, but also Americans, Japanese, Singaporeans and Koreans. During the course of the meeting they were inundated with information. The PR Department had essentially become an "information department" that focussed its energies on printing an internal paper called the *S&T Information Journal*. This collected the latest information and distributed it to managers. These reports helped shape the discussion.

Liu Chuanzhi motivated people by using a war analogy. Everyone talked about how to fight a war. Everyone took the frontline of sales to be the battlefield and the concept of "sales are King" arose at this time. After tremendous discussion, the final resolution was that Lianxiang would have to lower its price to win this battle. Since the Taiwanese makers were already using price as a weapon, this was hard. The public had to feel that Lianxiang was the most generous supplier. Li Qin declared, "Put the margin down to the absolute lowest, and sell out three times as many machines."

By the time the meeting was in its final day, all were inspired and ready for action. They had been careful to set up a system of rewards and punishments. Salespeople who made special contributions were to be sent abroad for training—the company said it could pull enough money out of its pocket to send them. As for managers, they would receive double in bonus what they got as normal salary if they met their targets. If they completed a "very good target", they would get four times, if they completed an "outstanding target", they would get five times.

Everyone left Dragon-springs in high spirits. Just as they had defeated the international market during the "black storm," they would, in 1992, defeat the "black storm" in the internal market. As the Lianxiang journal was later to report to all employees, "We've cast off a defeatist attitude. Previous obstacles have been swept away. This year really is the moment when we will rely on individual's talents." And it quoted Liu Chuanzhi: "We hope we will see goldfish leaping through the Dragon-Gate to become dragons. We hope that next year at this time we will have passed through a hard patch, that we will be able to sit back, pour some wine, and celebrate our work."

Seventy-two apartments shake up Beijing

One day in March, as Liu Chuanzhi was trying to find the path forward in his sales attack, he received a document that galvanized him with new energy. The document sketched out a plan for the distribution of housing. This was to be the first "apartment distribution" of the company since its establishment. Liu still remembered the excitement with which he had been allocated an apartment six years earlier. He knew that the allocation of living quarters was the most sensitive subject in China and had the power to mobilize employees' passion, intelligence and hopes. Several months earlier when he asked Wang Pingsheng to formulate this document, Wang Pingsheng had suggested to him, "We want a breakthrough. When young colts have their greatest vitality you should feed them the best hay. When they are old, to reward employees with a three-room apartment is meaningless." Liu agreed, but he had his doubts: how could Wang Pingsheng work it so that older people were willing and even glad to let younger people stand ahead of them in line? Reading this document, he found that Wang Pingsheng had found the way.

Before the 1990s, housing was considered part of an employee's "benefits" and was allocated on the basis of seniority. As a consequence, it was impossible to avoid endless struggles inside any organization. The company now announced that whoever wanted to get new housing simply had to take out a loan. The company would use its own resources as guarantor of the loan, but the employee himself had to go to the bank to get the funding, and the employee had to pay the loan back in instalments. Nowadays this kind of arrangement is common, but in the early 1990s it was met with great excitement. Lianxiang's was the very first case in Beijing of allowing employees to buy their own apartments. It was also a precedent for the first contract by which a common person borrowed money from a state-owned bank not for "investment" but for "personal consumption." This allowed most employees to withdraw their names from the list of applicants. They no longer felt cheated if they were not the ones to receive their share of housing.

Lianxiang changed distribution of housing into selling of housing. The total loan amount for seventy-two new homes for employees was RMB 6 million. This was not a large figure, but the company, the banks and also the Chinese government were tremendously excited at this new approach. All felt there should be a noteworthy contract-signing ceremony. On the morning of March 14, 1992, the borrowers and officials from the State-owned China Construction Bank came to the conference hall of the Beijing branch. Beijing municipal government officials and Chinese Academy of Sciences officials also arrived. It was clear that everyone wanted to witness this extraordinary moment. The first two people to walk up to the signing table were Branch Director Chang Zheng of the Haidian branch and Lianxiang employee Chen Xiaoming. Li Qin represented the company in signing as guarantor. This Vice-President had signed numerous loan agreements on behalf of the company over the past seven years, for sums of over RMB 500 million, but he had never attracted such attention as on this day. In front of a barrage of flashbulbs, bank officials said with some emotion, "This is the first time in history we have ever granted long-term low-interest loans to any individual." When the China Construction Bank decided it wanted to participate in this business, it looked through its bylaws and could not find a single line that could be used as reference. The only thing to do was send a petition to the People's Bank of China to ask permission for this unique event and to get approval for the requisite margin. Since nothing like this had never been done before, people at the Beijing Municipal Housing Reform Office were not quite sure if it should be permitted or not. They "showed resourcefulness in the emergency," however, and were able to think their way through it: they drew up a red-lettered document and sent it on down with their blessing.

This became a hot topic for the Beijing media in 1992. More than thirty newspapers wrote up the event as headline news. The *Beijing News* raised an intriguing question: "How can young people live in three whole rooms?" The *Beijing Youth Journal* adopted a different approach and published a large photograph on the front page in the most prominent spot. The backdrop was the newly constructed apartment building. The 72 proud owners stood before it on the rubble, everyone's faces glowing with excitement.

Resolving the problem of "having money but nowhere to spend it"

One of the basic principles by which Liu Chuanzhi administered the company was the belief that people naturally pursued their own interests. A good compensation system would tie that self-interest to a feeling of responsibility towards the company. In a meeting for all employees in 1990, he had said that by the end of the century each employee would have his own home. None of the audience sitting below reacted, which Liu Chuanzhi found strange. "Why didn't you applaud that?" he later asked. The response was that the government had made promises before in this regard and none had been realized. The "seventy-two homes" of 1992 was only one of the compensation reforms instituted by Lianxiang. It was not the end of the story.

Lianxiang maintained a strict policy of secrecy with regard to its compensation. This is one of the western traits in a company that otherwise has a strong Chinese flavor to it. Compensation is one of the company's "heavenly rules" and employees are forbidden to talk about it. This regulation has continued to this day and is engraved in people's minds to the extent that even among employees there is no discussion of how much one makes. The compensation of an employee is decided by the Human Resources Department. The Finance Department is involved only in paying out the wages or amount of the bonus: it does not know details about an employee's full income. The managers only know the incomes of employees directly under their supervision, they know nothing about incomes in other departments. They are not, moreover, allowed to ask.

From a purely economic standpoint, company employees' income is a reflection of a company's production and sales. But in China, ideological issues and government control or surveillance turn this matter into something more complex. The "bonus tax" mentioned before is an example.

Throughout the 1990s, Lianxiang's compensation system was undergoing continuous changes. The process started in 1992, and ended only in 2001, when employees were finally authorized to own their own shares.

The wages of Lianxiang employees were no different from work units throughout China before 1992, in terms of the system used and the amounts. What were different were the bonuses and benefits that lay outside the system. Since enterprises were not allowed to modify wage scales at the time, they inflated the portion attributable to a "bonus." The government then imposed an exorbitant tax on bonuses. Enterprises then found ways to evade the tax, through various legal and illegal ways, also through ways that seemed to be what they were not. One of the most commonly used measures was to keep the cash bonus amount at a minimum and to buy actual goods or physical objects for employees instead. These could be anything from soap and toothpaste to food, all listed as expenses in the "cost-of-doing-business" accounts. A popular phrase at the time was "courtyard economy," which meant that, in the several days surrounding New Years or holidays, every courtyard would allocate all kinds of things to its employee-residents. This measure hollowed out the coffers of the "bonus tax."

The government knew what was going on. From the late 1980s, it began to decrease the rate of the bonus tax to a point where it was simply abolished. Instead, it now added a "personal income adjustment tax." In an Experimental District such as ZGC, the government went a step further in relaxing controls: the new policy was summarized in the phrase "five three two," which meant that an enterprise must plow 50% of its profits back into production, 30% was to be used on a benefits fund, and bonuses must now not exceed 20%. This was the first time the government had made a distinction, in terms of its actual system, between "benefits" and "bonuses."

Benefits and bonuses were both income to employees that lay outside their regular salary. The distinction was that the latter depended on a work evaluation and was paid in cash. The former was for "group use," and it was issued in the form of actual goods and services. Examples could include employee housing, medical and health benefits, nursery school, cafeteria, etc. All of these were "benefits." Abuses of the system derived from the hidden nature of the items, which made employees unclear about exactly what profit they derived. Secondly, benefit levels were established on the basis of "qualifications and record of service" and "job or duties," and this was the source of endless conflict. People felt that it was useless to be given things they did not urgently need. Young people, simply because they were junior, could not get what they felt rightfully belonged to them. It was apparent that collectivism as a system, no matter how meticulously well constructed, was unable to restrain personal desires.

The government was now handing over to an enterprise the right to allocate benefit funds and this was a tremendous motivation to the creative powers of company managers. They decided to allocate the funds and put them under the name of employees. At the end of the year, each employee would receive a sheet of paper on which was written the value of any benefits an employee could receive. Employees were not allowed to receive cash, but they could use the funds to purchase housing, to have pension plans, insurance, communications equipment such as telephones, children's education funds or even vacation funds. "This personalized the benefits funds," as Tang Dandong said by way of explaining this. For the first time, an employee could use this portion of his income in a manner according to his own needs. He no longer needed to worry that his money would be used by others.

The new system also allowed the company to end a situation of "having money without the ability to use it." Employees' total compensation greatly increased as a result. In 1992, the average benefit fund of an employee was around RMB 10,000, around two times the amount of his or her fixed wages. This period was known in the annals of the company as the time of "low wages, high benefits." This again, however, attracted attention from the government. Several officials from the tax bureau visited the company and requested all documents regarding the benefits fund. They suspected that this method of doing things evaded the personal income adjustment tax. This time, the company decided to fight back and several weeks followed of stalemate with the tax authorities.

Tang Dandong declared to tax authorities that its "reform policies" were confidential company information and that nobody had the power to divulge them. He candidly admitted that the company was "trying to play edgeball with government policies," "edgeball" being that term of art in pingpong when you hit the ball to the very edge of the table. He said that they did indeed want to avoid the adjustment tax, but at the same time he told the story of the "seventy-two homes" in vivid terms, and defended the company's practice. "If a company as a collective unit buys an apartment and, without anything in return, allocates it to an employee, or, say, opens a nursery school and lets employee children go there for free, this is not counted as employee income. Employees have no obligation to pay tax on it. Right now, all we are doing is distributing benefits to employees and asking them to make the choice of whether housing or nursery school is what they really need. That is the only difference."

The tax authorities admitted that this had some logic behind it. They countered, however, with the distinction that the right of the company to distribute the benefit of housing was a collective property right, whereas giving individuals the "benefit" and having them buy their own housing was an individual property right.

"Well then," said Tang Dandong, "when they sell the property and get their profits, you can collect tax on that private income." He continued, "If you are not willing to let this one horse go for me, then all I can do is make these seventy-two homes the property right of the whole enterprise. We'll pay the debt under the name of a company loan—but this has nothing to recommend it to anyone, individuals or the company, and it has nothing in it for the country either."

Tang later admitted that this was "quibbling," but to his surprise the tax authorities accepted this line of reasoning. They even said that Lianxiang had come up with "a new creation".

Mobilizing a "New Person Strategy" once again

Another memorable event occurred in the few months between spring and summer of 1992. On April 5, an opening ceremony was held for the production base that had been built on Ba-gua Road in Shenzhen. Eight months earlier the call had gone out to "retreat to hold the line at Shenzhen." The call was now sounding again, to announce the entering armies. The President of the Chinese Academy of Sciences, Zhou Guangzho, attended, as well as a large group of government officials. These came from the Export Department of the State Council, the Ministry of Electronics, the Bank of China, the Hong Kong branch of Xinhua News Agency, but what most amazed people was that Hu Qili had been invited by the company to perform the ribbon cutting. Since the summer of 1989, he had not much been in the public eye. Now there he was, smiling at the press, happily gazing into the lenses of television cameras. The importance of this smiling face extended not just to economics: in the minds of most Chinese it extended to politics. Given Hu Qili's presence, Liu Chuanzhi's political star seemed to be rising.

At the beginning of summer, a class of new recruits came into the company. Ever since the first group of university graduates came in, in 1988, it had become the custom to recruit new employees twice a year, every spring and fall. The company was expanding: 100 people came in

1990, 150 in 1991, and still every department needed more people. Li Qin was worried that the pace of adding new employees was too fast, that the company couldn't handle it. He wrote a report to the Human Resources Department ordering that it restrict the total headcount to 650 people. He led a fourteen-person recruiting team, planning to do a rigorous sifting-through in the selection process. Nevertheless new employees continued to increase at a fast rate. By June of 1992, the number already exceeded the prescribed headcount and reached 670. This was only for Beijing. There were another 500 distributed throughout the country in all the branch companies, and another 400 overseas.

A company is like a person's body: it loses vitality if you don't get rid of the old and bring in new. In China, however, the exchange of new for old is a vexing problem. It is so difficult and so complex that most companies resolve it simply by taking in people and never getting rid of them. This method has one prerequisite, however, which is that the company's business must continue to grow. The stage must get bigger every day. If business slows down or stops, and the intake is not adjusted accordingly, a bloated organization will result and people will be floating around with little to do. Mired in this situation, the easiest solution is to stop "taking in the new." As Liu Chuanzhi once said, the exchange of new and old was the most difficult problem the company faced in its twenty years.

In the summer of 1992, Liu decided to mobilize another "new recruits strategy." He gave a speech in which he told a humorous story aimed at the older generation. Liu then said to them, "We all have to step down at some point. The company will reward the hard times we went through in founding it. It will guarantee that we have more than sufficient means to live on." The Founders were all highly educated people and they knew that the reasoning behind his humorous story was right. Cai Shuyong heard the speech and resigned his position at the production base of the company. He had seen the production line go from absolutely nothing to an annual production of 20,000 computers. He had put in a tremendous amount of his own blood, sweat, and tears, and now he was turning around and leaving, though he hated to do so. Rationally, he knew the production line would just get faster and produce not 20,000 but 100,000 and even perhaps 1,000,000. He felt daunted at the prospect.

On April 20, 1992, Liu Chuanzhi announced new appointments. Guo Wei and Wang Pingsheng became Vice-Presidents, their tasks divided between managing the Enterprise Planning Department and the Group Office. Liu promoted Chen Jianren as Chief Manager in charge of the

Research and Development (R&D) Center. In announcing these appointments, Liu Chuanzhi took pains to mention that none of the three on the team managing the R&D Center was yet thirty years old.

The names list had one more appointment that, at the time, did not stir up any great attention: Yang Yuanqing. He became the Computer Aided Design (CAD) Department's General Manager. Later events were to prove the significance of this appointment. To a certain degree, this could be considered the prelude to the abrupt rise of the Lianxiang computer. It was therefore one of the key links in the history of the company. Yang Yuanqing took this as his platform: he transcended old disputes in the company and made this platform succeed.

Retail: the "new sales concepts" in China
In the next two years, Yang Yuanqing took the annual revenues of the CAD department from RMB 30 million to RMB 300 million.

He was the last to rise as a star among that early group of young people who joined the company. When Sun Hongbin stirred up a hornet's nest, Chen Hengliu ascended to Senior Counsellor and Guo Wei entered the President's Office. When Wang Pingsheng was managing affairs of the Human Resources Department, Yang was just a salesperson whose responsibility was to sell servers for the American company Sun Microsystems. His daily work was simple and boring. Yang did not like sales and considered going abroad to study. Nonetheless, he was one of those people who put all his energy into the immediate task and his sales accomplishments were therefore superlative. In 1991, the Lianxiang computer was the company's new hope, but this did not make the sales personnel content. The company rearranged its troops, reassigned people, putting its finest into the computer efforts. Yang Yuanqing was not within the sights of Liu Chuanzhi at that time. Liu had the General Manager of the CAD Department, the forty-year-old Chen Xiaoming transferred to be commander of the Computer Department. Yang Yuanqing received the baton passed by Chen, and moved into a mid-level management position in the company.

The CAD Department's most important business was selling drafting equipment for Hewlett-Packard (HP). Lianxiang had become HP's agent, but until 1992 the profits from this business only came to half the profits of agenting for AST. The AST computer was the first product in the course of Lianxiang's agenting experience. Lianxiang made that formerly unknown brand a star in China's market, which also brought Lianxiang considerable profits. It was Hewlett-Packard, however, that brought a new form of sales method to Yang Yuanqing's attention. This was a vital development, both for Yang himself and for Lianxiang.

In the decades before 1992, China did not have the concepts of "agenting" or of "distribution". These terms are not in the main Chinese dictionaries published in the 1980s and it is hard to translate them accurately into concepts at the time. Only two forms of selling existed in the market: one was called *pi-fa*, translated as "wholesale" in English, in which something bought by one party was then sold to another commercial entity. The other kind was called *ling-shou*, or "retail" in English, in which an entity sold directly to the consumer. If one went into any computer store in ZGC in the early 1990s, the first question out of the mouth of the person behind the counter would be, "pifa or lingshou," wholesale or retail? This was because retail generally had to bear a higher tax rate, so every store put two different prices on exactly the same product. Needless to say, the buyer would generally buy at "wholesale" what was in fact a piece of retail business.

Whether it was retail or wholesale, however, both had a common characteristic: both were called "sitting business" in Chinese, or "sitting commerce." The seller would sit in a store waiting for customers to come to him. He had no specialized sales channels and he had no prescribed group of customers or customer base. It is on this point that *fen-xiao* or, literally, "distributed selling" exhibits its differences. Distributed selling was like wholesale, but not exactly the same. Its essence was in having predetermined agents or sales channels: linking these together, distributed selling structurally formed a huge sales network.

A close study of the distributed selling history of the Chinese computer industry reveals that Hewlett-Packard was the first to introduce this concept to China. Its starting point was in 1992 when Yang Yuanqing was in charge of Lianxiang's CAD Department. Before that, when he was peddling Sun servers, he had not yet formed a complete concept of the distinctions between "agenting" and "distributed selling." Right now, spread before Yang was the Hewlett-Packard selling network. The CAD Department was one part of the network. Yang saw the complete nature of a huge network and was mesmerized by it: if HP could establish an agency system that stretched to the ends of the world, with itself in the center, then why not Lianxiang?

In April of 1992, the CAD Department and a small company in ZGC called Ludao signed an agency agreement. According to its terms, Ludao would take on the responsibility of "distributed selling" of Hewlett-Packard drafting instruments; Lianxiang would receive a return of 3% of the volume of business. The drafter of this contract was a man named Lin Yang, at the time the Deputy General Manager under Yang Yuanqing. He had graduated from the Electrical Engineering Institute of Xi'an and joined Lianxiang in the summer of 1990. He is now Vice-President of Digital China. He believes that the contract he drafted that year was the first significant agency agreement in ZGC. "I took the agency agreement that HP had given us," he said, "and painted a dipper by looking at a gourd. That is, I copied it."

The zeal with which the young people set up the agency system was similar to the way the older generation set up the direct sales system. Yang Yuanqing led a group of people to the main intersection of ZGC. Four teams faced north, south, east, and west. They called out "one two three!" then started walking. Each team went down the road, looking right and left. If they saw a shop selling computers they would go inside, introduce themselves by saying they were from Lianxiang, say that they had a lot of products, low priced but superior quality, then explain what they meant by "agent." They would ask if the shop was willing or not to do this business. Shop by shop they went on down, sometimes returning empty-handed but sometimes coming home after a day's work with numerous contracts. Soon after this, the company held its first conference on the agency business in a hotel in western Beijing. It was a small conference, with only a dozen or so people attending, and there is no record of this in the company's annals of great events, but this presaged a completely new form of selling model. As a result of this, Lianxiang also was able to elevate its position in the entire global network of Hewlett-Packard.

Hewlett-Packard was quite happy to see this development. The company quickly brought out a raft of new products for Lianxiang to sell, such as the first-generation of inkjet printers. They changed the word in their authorization contracts from "dealer" to "wholesaler". In a gesture of trust, Hewlett-Packard said to Lin Yang that Lianxiang was Hewlett-Packard's Number 1 Wholesaler in China. Lin Yang looked at this word in the contract and thought, "If "dealer" means *daili* in Chinese, then "wholesaler" must certainly mean *zong-daili*." It was an honest mistake. Lin Yang put an ad in the *Computer World* magazine. In large characters, the first line said, "Warm Congratulations to the CAD for becoming Hewlett-Packard's exclusive Chinese agent." Nobody expected the trouble that ensued. Another agent for Hewlett-Packard immediately wrote a letter to *Computer World* magazine as well as to the Hewlett-Packard Company, charging that the advertisement misrepresented the truth, for Lianxiang was fundamentally not an exclusive agent.

At that time, most Chinese put their energies into getting things pretty much right, they weren't worried about being too precise. They had just come to a sufficient understanding of the differences between a "planned economy" and a "market economy." Chairman Jiang Zemin had in June of this year announced that China's economy was "a Socialist Market Economy" and that distinction alone was enough to make officials, scholars, journalists and salespeople shout for joy. But when it came to more specific concepts of how to sell in a market, everyone was more than a little fuzzy. As to the distinctions between *zongdaili* and *daili*, or between *fen xiao* and *jing xiao* they were in the dark.

Although Hewlett-Packard brought these terms into China, they were under no obligation to give the Chinese people lessons in what the terms meant. "Dealer" and "wholesaler" were simply two different terms used in their authorization agreements to distinguish between two different kinds of agents. If the rights you were receiving were dealer rights, it meant you had to sell the product directly to the customer. If what you were receiving was wholesaling rights, it meant that you could sell to another intermediary. This was the same all over the world. As to what the Chinese should call it, even Hewlett-Packard could not say for sure. The two agents now found themselves entangled in a dispute that went from 1992 all the way till, in the end, the President of the Hewlett-Packard China Company was required to mediate the issue. His name was Cheng Tianzong and he said: "Now that people have brought this up, let's make a name for it in Chinese."

Several people then discussed the naming. The result was that they agreed to translate the term "wholesaler" into the Chinese term *fen-xiao*. Lin Yang then again put an advertisement in the magazine. This time he said, "Warm congratulations to Lianxiang for becoming the sole wholesaler in China for Hewlett-Packard." The advertisement also put the word "Wholesaler" in English, in brackets. Below, in smaller letters, was the note: "Previous mistaken translation was Exclusive Agent, should have been translated as Wholesaler."

From that day onward, the computer industry in China had a new concept. In 1992, the CAD Department's business doubled. In 1993, it again doubled again, to RMB 230 million. Going on like this, it would not take many years for Lianxiang to become the largest agent of foreign goods sold into the Chinese market.

That is in fact what happened. After Yang Yuanqing left the department in 1994, it kept achieving an average annual growth rate of 83% in sales for the next four years. Meanwhile, the Hewlett-Packard selling methods that Yang had learned at the CAD Department went on to impact the entire computer industry, not just the company.

Ni Guangnan's period of supremacy and the downfall of the Han-card
Chief Engineer Ni Guangnan was putting more and more of his energies into computers. As for the Han-card, for three years he had tried unremittingly to improve its properties and strengthen its functions. In 1990, he rolled out the Han-card Model 7, which hit a new record in sales. Although Ni Guangnan hoped that the Han-card would become a perpetual money tree, he did not intend to take out a company patent on this technology. He knew better than anyone that it was impossible to monopolize the technology. Han-character systems were proliferating, with more than fifteen of them now sold on the market. Each pursued a different logic and different standards and naturally they all plagiarized each other.

Ni Guangnan's subordinates were concerned about this large group of contenders coming right behind Lianxiang. He told them, "They're not important, we will keep putting out new editions, they can't keep up." Before 1992, the Chief Engineer's approach was successful. Lianxiang Han-card sales kept rising at an average annual rate of more than 70%. By October 1992, the combined sales of Han-cards had surpassed 60,000 sets indicating that for every ten computers in China, one was fitted with a Lianxiang Han-card.

1992 appeared to be the apogee of the Lianxiang Han-card. One notable indication was that on May 15, Chairman Jiang Zemin and Premier Li Peng went on an inspection tour of ZGC and were transfixed by the Lianxiang Han-card system. Western reporters noted that: "This is another powerful policy expression of Chinese senior leaders, ever since Deng Xiaoping spurred the pace of Reform and Opening on his Investigation Trip in the south." Chinese journalists, on the other hand, felt that this was "The first time the creators of the Lianxiang Han-character system could present all eight years of their hard-earned results."

The Han-card had already reached its ninth model by the time of this important visit. The company displayed a large graph that illustrated the process from Model 1 to Model 9. The Chairman of the Country and the Premier stopped in front of this impressive graph, while Liu Chuanzhi and Ni Guangnan hurried forward to greet them. That night, 200 million Chinese saw the full scene on CCTV Nightly News: they saw the graph symbolizing the march of progress, with the country's Chairman and Premier nearly dwarfed in front of it. The leaders seemed to serve as tiny foils, putting the dimensions of real progress into perspective.

The Model 9 Han-card seemed to epitomize a new age. Journalists were infatuated with its tremendous capacities. They did not realize that the Lianxiang Han-card was on the verge of disappearing from the market. For sixteen continuous weeks the company had not hit its sales targets. By August of 1992, the Head of the sales leadership team, Liu Jinyi, described a bleak picture to assembled salespeople. At this meeting, people learned that after reaching a breakthrough record of 1,701 sets of Han-card sales in December, 1991, sales had been slipping. In the first four months of fiscal year 1992, only 5,555 sets had been sold, amounting to only 67% of the sales target.

The technically perfect Model 9 Han-card had unequivocally become a market catastrophe. Customers did not care about perfection, they cared about their own needs. The functions of the new product undoubtedly were tremendous, but what their designers were after was a technical goal, not the needs of customers. For example, the new Han-card brought the functions of Han characters together with display capabilities, but the Han-card had to be put into a computer in order to use it and standard equipment of all computers at the time included display cards.

The media continued to praise the card, however. On December 19, 1992, the Chinese Academy of Sciences awarded a prize to Ni Guangnan together with RMB 500,000. He had also recently been appointed a representative to the Eighth National People's Congress and a member of the National People's Political Consultative Committee (NPPCC). It was general practice in China for a scientist with outstanding accomplishments to be made a member of one of these bodies, or to be given a government position. The same is true today. For one person to be appointed to these two positions at the same time was, and is still, extremely rare. The honors did not end there, however. In 1994, Ni Guangnan became one of the first 96 Academicians in the Chinese Engineering Academy. To Chinese scientists this lifelong position is a rare honor.

Liu Chuanzhi spared no energy in promoting Ni Guangnan as an Academician. He asked Liu Jinyi to lobby at the Beijing Municipal Commission and the Chinese Academy of Sciences, confirming that the engineer's record was glorious and that his background was spotless. He also had the older generation in the company put their weighty reputations behind the effort, had them say good things about the Chief Engineer to senior people in order for him to be chosen as one of the first group of

Academicians. At that time, many regarded Ni Guangnan's technology as outstanding, but felt that there were plenty of other scientists in the Computer Institute who were outstanding too. Liu Chuanzhi knew the full situation, but he also knew that, in China, just because you have the truth in hand does not mean that the truth prevails. One must handle matters in accord with actual circumstances and expediency.

All senior managers in the company participated in promoting Ni Guangnan. In a speech in 1992, Li Qin even mentioned Ni Guangnan and Nobel Laureats in the same breath. Liu Chuanzhi had determined that the company needed the banner of Ni Guangnan; he made Ni Guangnan into a kind of idol that was not in accord with reality. Liu, for example, instructed Cao Zhijiang to describe Ni Guangnan as his own teacher in front of a group of senior personnel. Cao was the company's Deputy Chief Engineer. He was modest and polite, but he felt that Liu's request was a little too much. "Ni Guangnan's technology is terrific, that's true," he complained, "But we come from the same generation, we're the same age. He never was my teacher." Since Liu and Cao not only had the same background, but shared a deep friendship, how could Liu not have known Cao's feelings on this? He was thinking not of fairness towards one or the other man at the time, but rather of the company's larger benefit. He persisted in his request until Cao agreed.

Chinese affairs are sometimes strange. When a person's contributions are most striking he often gets no credit. Once a reputation is broadcast to the world, a person often has a name but nothing much to back it up. Around this time, a Peking University Professor named Wang Xuang noted, "We can see the same sort of thing in Ni Guangnan. 1992 was the peak year of his accomplishments though he himself was aware that the thing for which he was famous, the Liangxiang Han-card, had already started on the downward path." According to Hu Xilan, after 1990, the Han-card met three years of declining sales. She later criticized the sales force, but in all fairness, reasons for the decline of the Han-card were to be found outside the company, not inside.

The world market for computers was going precisely along the trendline indicated by Moore: the capacity of computer chips was doubling every eighteen months while the price was falling by half. In the 1980s, memory chip capacity was insufficient and chip prices were expensive, so "soft Han-characters" were the solution. The Chinese-character system was realized completely through software. This software was unable to resolve certain issues: either one met up with the limitations of the chip and could not perfect the functions of the characters, or one had to expand the hardware, which led to raising the price. It became necessary to accommodate the Han-character system outside the standard configuration of a hardware structure. The Han-card got its development rationale from this, and was soon substituted for the soft Han-characters. History moves forward, however: by 1992, the "486" was already the main computer model and one year later came the Pentium. Every six months, Intel put out a new generation of central processing units. Chip capacity kept rising and the price kept going down, with irresistibly seductive appeal to creative technical people. They began to utilize chip technology in researching the soft Han-characters once again. In the early 1990s, the dead ashes of the soft Han-characters were rekindled to flames with the representative work at the time being the popular WPS Chinese handling system. This was packed in a five-inch floppy disk. All customers had to do was tap on the keyboard and they could set up a complete Chinese-character handling system in their own computers.

The entire country now showed a strong demand for soft Han-characters, which could be substituted for the Han-card functions, and the price was cheap. What's more, it was supremely convenient for those who did not care about pirated copies. At one point Lianxiang considered creating its own soft Han-character system. The development program was underway, but the long-term viability was questionable and the effort was stopped. Zeng Maochao determined that "mistakes on the road of technology led to the eventual closing down of the Han-card." He pointed to Ni Guangnan as being "a person from the Academy of Sciences with a certain kind of thinking and a certain culture. What he sought was invention. He sought unlimited technical capacity. He did not even remotely consider the market."

Ni Guangnan did not agree with Zeng Maochao's criticism. He said, "any product has a life cycle. Whether you are talking about the Model 6 or the Model 9, the Soft Han-card or the Hard Han-card, in the end they have to retreat from the marketplace. This is not something one decides and it isn't the fault of the Lianxiang Company. This is the common fate of all companies engaged in Han-character systems."

The last month of 1992 was a final moment of glory for the Han-card. It sold 2,664 sets, 164 over target, but this was accomplished through intense efforts by salespeople, using year-end funds that the government had suddenly released. The President's Office issued bonuses of RMB 5,000 to sales personnel, and on the commendation notices wrote "hoping that the Han-card Division continues its good work." At the same time, the company came to an agreement with Microsoft to jointly develop a Chinese version of Works™. The media noted, "This is the first cooperation between the Mainland and the largest software company on earth. It is a sign that software development on the Mainland is coming in line with world standards." Ni Guangnan attended the signing ceremony. To him, this ceremony revealed a powerful message: the Lianxiang Han-card had lost the advantage of being first. It had essentially reached the end of the line.

1+1

The best entrepreneurs have firm convictions, but they also take advantage of prevailing trends. As the days of the Han-card drew to an end, sales of motherboards, though large, were unprofitable. Liu Chuanzhi was able to find another way to survive, by promoting a line of home-use computers.

From the establishment of the Home-use Computer Department in May of 1992, up to May of 1994, Yang Yuanqing promoted the so-called E-series to households as the main sales target. The gestation period for this product had been around 24 months, both for Lianxiang and the country at large. If this period is ever written into the history of China's computer industry, several names deserve to be mentioned. First is Xu Zhiping, the first Manager of the Department, who came up with the concept of home-use computers. Next is Li Qin, who believed that computers would move from businesses and offices into people's homes. This was not apparent to people at the time. Li Qin understood the contribution that home computers would make to social development in general and he strongly promoted their production at Lianxiang. Nowadays the idea seems apparent. Back then, using a computer at home was an epoch-defining concept. Before this, nobody had put any high hopes on personal computers. To distinguish smaller computers from mainframes, Chinese use the word "micro-computer."

As a concept, "home-use computers" was developed sometime in 1992. Xu Zhiping's idea was that computers in homes and those in offices would be different. This instantly attracted criticism, to the point that debate was stirred up in ZGC. Many people fundamentally did not believe that computers would move into people's homes. There were also some, for example people in Great Wall Computer, Number 1 in China at the time in terms of China-brand computers, who did not deny that people might take office computers home to use but who ridiculed the idea that a computer for use at home was different from an office computer. Xu Zhiping was only 29-years-old at the time. He had no authority to command the development of the entire computer industry, but he believed that home-use computers and computers for use at home were two separate things. He thought that the company's resources should be focussed on developing this different home-use computer. His proposal to set up a Home-use Computer Department was supported by the President's Office of the company.

A good idea will not necessarily get quick results in the world of computers. Xu Zhiping was an outstanding engineer but he had no way of knowing that for "computers for use at home" to move to "home-use computers" would take a full twenty-four months.

Xu Zhiping completed the first prototype for a home-use computer. The PR Department hoped to find a good name to entice customers, and announced a Naming Contest in the Lianxiang Journal. All employees in the company were invited to contribute their ideas. The Department received over 100 entries, among which they chose three: "Golden Key," "Little Sun," and "1+1." After a vote, the last was the winner, a name thought up by an engineer in the Production Technology Department.

On October 24, 1992 the *Lianxiang Journal* announced: "The new product has a fine-sounding name: "1+1" has come out of its shell and become a new brand name for education and home-use computers."

Linking these two concepts showed how limited their creators' understanding was of how the machines would be used. At the time, it was believed that computers would mainly be used for parents to help teach children at home. Computers were not yet using multi-media software, one could not watch movies, listen to music, see photos, play games, not to mention manage family affairs. All these were unthinkable at the time. The only direction that home-use computers might conceivably take, it was felt, was towards education. China had 7,081 middle schools that were in the process of developing computer education. In the preceding five years this number had increased 114% and the number of middle schools that actually had computers went from 33,950 to 76,862. At the very least three million middle school students had contact with personal computers, and in a few years they would be growing into adults. This was good news to computer manufacturers. They lost no time in promoting computers that were appropriate for family consumption. These included, for example, simplified versions of the "PC/XT" and the "PC8088." These machines generally had a 5-inch floppy disk drive, and an orangy or greenish-colored single-color monitor. Their price was around RMB 3000.

Lianxiang's 1+1 brand now entered the fray. Ads at the time noted its user friendliness and appropriate price. According to Liu Jun, in fact Lianxiang "had just added a Chinese-environment chip, so that it became a Chinese-ified computer, then we sold it to customers who had education in mind, including households." The name "1+1" was intriguing to the market. The intentionally vague answer of the company as to what it meant was that it allowed people to unleash their creativity: however they wanted to think of it was fine.

Xu Zhiping said, 1+1 indicates education computer + household computer. Others said it implied buy one and give another to a friend. University students said it implied a passport to the 21st century and a visa that can be used anywhere. Grade school students said: 1+1 implies simple and easy to learn.

Company reporters published all of these in the 1992 annual year-end edition of *Lianxiang Journal*. It included a little story: A five-year-old was happy to see his father and mother buying a 1+1 computer. The salesman asked the little boy: what does 1+1 mean? He said, 1+1 = 2. His mother laughed and said, "1+1 probably means one child, one computer."

The company sent the very first 1+1 to the young man who came up with the name. He had come into the company three months earlier and he said, "It's the character for king, *wang* written sideways. China's home-use computers should be King."

Buyers' market

The sellers' market for computers in China gradually turned into a buyers' market. The turning point came in the slow season between the winter of 1992 and the spring of 1993.

The terms buyers' and sellers' market appeared in Chinese only later, in 1995. Sellers' market referred to that era when China was in product-scarcity mode, and no matter what you had to sell, it sold and the seller had the last word. Products became greatly more available in the mid-1990s and in certain sectors were in over-supply. Buyers then had the opportunity to make their own choices. The "Customer is King" became a fashionable slogan. In the computer market, however, this entire process appeared at least three years earlier than for other products.

In 1992, Lianxiang's new product listings were plentiful yet the listing did not seem to satisfy potential customers. The only things sold were 13,874 Lianxiang computers and 21,291 Han-cards. This came in far below the targets set at the Dragon-springs conference. Lianxiang's records note that the company for the first time failed to complete its sales obligations in 1993, although this phenomenon had already begun in 1992. If the company truly was a golden carp, then in 1992 it failed to leap through the dragon gate and was still failing in 1993.

Quality was no longer the issue. Information from all sides showed that Lianxiang's computer quality already had the approval of customers, and random checks in the market proved that 100% met product requirements. The problem was also not that Lianxiang's machines were backwards: computers produced inside China were rapidly approaching international market standards. In 1987, the birth of the "286" computer was five years behind the comparable machine in the rest of the world, the "386" was two years behind. In 1991, the first batch of "486" machines was six months behind the world market; by 1993 when the first-generation Pentiums appeared, China was only behind by three months.

Price tactics also did not seem to be a problem, for example the price of the Lianxiang computer was comparative to that of the AST—it was always set a little cheaper, but not a lot cheaper, usually around 10%. Yet the AST sold at least 80,000 machines in this year while Lianxiang computer sales were on a plateau.

The supply chain was moving smoothly and also not at issue. Liu Chuanzhi and Li Qin both based themselves in Hong Kong in this year and shortened the supply time for machines from 90 days down to 45 days. This brought about an adverse reaction: as batches of computers flowed unceasingly into Beijing, salespeople couldn't keep up and warehouse incomings exceeded the outgoings. Inventory piled up.

Although Liu Chuanzhi had already predicted that another black storm was on its way, he underestimated its scope and ferocity. At that time, he and Li Qin believed that the greatest danger came from Taiwan but facts were to prove that all of the computer manufacturers in the world were on their way. Experts predicted that the import tax on all imported computers would fall to 9% within twelve months. This greatly encouraged the ambitions of foreign manufacturers as they vied for the China market.

When spring began, the trend was even more apparent. Reporters of the company's internal publication, the *S&T Information*, even began to use terms like "ZGC is facing a life-and-death battle" in their headlines. According to their investigations, 98% of computers sold on Electronics Street in ZGC came from Compaq in America, IBM, AST, Hewlett-Packard and such companies, while computers manufactured within China came to less than 1%. In addition, foreign products held more than 50%

of the market for monitors, 80% for copiers, 90% for software and floppy disks, 100% of the printers, 100% of fax machines, 100% of hard drives, and 100% of mainframe boards.

This bad news alarmed ZGC. On March 3 of 1993, *Reference News* consolidated the trends of the past two years and announced that, "International computer companies are attacking ZGC". The President of Sitong, Duan Yongji, was so alarmed that he passed this article to the Chairman of the National Science Commission, Song Jian. In an attached letter, he said, "I hope to bring your attention to this grave matter." The greatest pressure was coming from Compaq. This company had lowered the net profit on its personal computers to between 1 and 3% in selling into the China market. The most eye-opening part of their ads read, "Compaq pushes out low-price computers." IBM quickly responded and computers around the entire globe began to drop in price. Yet according to a price list of March 1993, Lianxiang's 486/33 was RMB 6,800 more expensive than the comparable AST machine.

Manufacturers in Taiwan such as Hongji, Shenda, Renbao, and Lantian followed the rest of the world in the trend. A journalist named Tan Zhongmin from the *Taiwan Industry and Commerce Report* investigated the market and discovered that Hongji was maintaining a price that was 10% below that of Compaq, while Shenda was meeting demand with a price 15% below. He noted that this price war would only intensify as time went on. The statement soon had collateral evidence. The President of Great Wall Company, Wang Zhi, met up unexpectedly with the Vice-President of Compaq and the latter said, "if you want to defeat your opponent you have to think of how to deal with the price issue." He said this with some satisfaction since Compaq machines were doing well at the time: in 1992 they constituted only 5.2% of the market, still behind Lianxiang, but by 1993 they were 17.5%. Wang Zhi returned to Beijing and immediately instructed his staff to lower the price of Great Wall computers by 38%. He also reduced his R&D personnel by 50% in order to maintain the balance between profit and loss of that product.

The market situation was initially ignited by Compaq. By lowering prices, all the other manufacturers added oil to the flames until it burned indiscriminately, turning the computer market into a real buyers' market. The media noted that, in 1993, computer sales in China would increase to 300,000 machines, while total sales value would drop. Twenty-two companies were producing computers on the Mainland at that time, and all had the same problem. According to a report on the Chinese computer market, in the first two months of 1993 they had produced 8,232 computers but still had 16,875 in warehouses. By May, the number in inventory had increased to 26,851.

Computer Ads fill the skies

The intense competition in the computer industry spurred the development of media, as ads fattened the coffers of this secondary industry. Historians who research Chinese commercial history in the future will discover that the fortunes of media and enterprises were joined as ineluctably as husband and wife. Corporate enterprises used the power of media to create their reputations while media profited whether the situation was going well for industry or poorly. When enterprises were full sail in the right direction, media enjoyed a full cup; when things were hard, media simply ran after the firetrucks. All over the world, the media industry employs the same *modus vivendi*. In 1993, during computer makers' worst times, advertising enjoyed a golden era. Promotion Fairs were held everywhere, Exhibitions, Forums, Sales conventions, meetings for tendering bids. These were the front line of the battle. Chinese computer makers and huge western companies went into hand-to-hand combat. Chinese began to learn western advertising concepts and tactics; they copied western ways in hiring professional agents, signing contracts with ad companies, putting large sums into product advertising. Advertising became a rapidly growing industry. Ten years earlier, there had been only 184 advertising companies in China. By 1993, there were 11,044. In 1993, these did ninety-three times in business what they had done ten years earlier.

In 1992, Lianxiang put 1.5% of its income from sales directly into ads. The highest sum on record for the company to date was spent on this budget item: RMB 6,600,000. As 1993 started, the company found itself an advertising agency, the New Century Advertising Company. All product advertising was put through this company for both ad production and placement. Ten percent was fixed as a rebate of total advertising expense. The President's Office and the Enterprise Planning Department raised the budget for advertising to RMB 7,790,000, but under the pressure of the market and the encouragement of the advertising agency, in the first quarter they spent RMB 2,310,000, in the second they spent 3,420,000, and by the end of the year they had spent RMB 10,270,000 on advertising. This was 2.1% of total revenue.

Media relished this situation. All publications got on the bandwagon. The *China Computer News* expanded its pages from 32 to 64. *Computer World* now had 128 pages in each issue. Other papers that originally had little to do with computers, such as *Liberation Daily*, *New People Evening News*, *Beijing Evening News*, *Beijing Youth Journal*, all began to put out computer sections. The reputation of media was better then than it is today and media advertising personnel had the respect of enterprises. They had the prestige of government officials, and enterprises wanting to put ads in their pages lined up at the door. If you wanted to place an ad in a newspaper such as the *People's Daily*, a Communist Party organization, you had to wait for several weeks. All companies wanted to gain strategic advantage and get their ads in first, so they either depended on personal relations with the publisher or they paid more: often 30% to 100% over the standard fee. The person in charge of advertising at Lianxiang was Li Gang who experienced plenty of cold treatment that year: "If you said you wanted to place an ad, you had to go begging. The guys wouldn't even talk to you. It wasn't like today." Li Gang learned the phrase "buying media" from that time: as she said, "They have their price."

Placing ads was like buying things in another respect: you had to pay attention to the value of the purchased product. According to a market research report on advertising results for the computer market in 1993: ads in general newspapers constituted 30% of the total, ads in professional newspapers and journals constituted 33%, television advertising was highest and totaled 48%. Television advertising was also the most expensive. Even though the auction was not to appear for another two years, ad fees were already soaring. Television ad fees were raised on March 1, 1993 by 20%. On July 1 they were again raised by 25%. The Head of the Advertising Department, Tan Xisong, shook his head as he said, "Under market economy conditions, things should be done according to the laws of pricing." Many companies spent large sums of money on the "golden time" just before and after the Weather Report on nightly television: companies such as Lianxiang, Peking University's Founder, Matsushita Television, Wahaha, and the Huaguang Group. Buying golden time was calculated by the second: for the beginning segment, each second of a five-second slot cost RMB 3,836; for the end segment, each second of a five-second slot cost RMB 3,068. The slots at 7pm were somewhat cheaper, but every second was still RMB 1,315.

Lianxiang also spent large sums daily on ads in such professional computer publications such as *Computer World*, *Reference News*, and *China Finance Computers*. The company set up a large outdoor signboard on Jianguomen Street in central Beijing that cost RMB 602.73 per day. During the twelve days of the Seventh National Sports Event they spent RMB 420,000 on broadcasting ads, 360 seconds each, split into twelve broadcasts. Putting the two words "Lian Xiang" onto a program at Beijing Television Station as sponsor cost them RMB 10,000. TV stations outside Beijing had not yet raised prices so drastically. Average prices among ten provincial and municipal stations was RMB 33.33 per second, even cheaper than ads on the Central People's Radio station. On this radio station, time before the "News and Selections from Newspapers" cost RMB 38.93 per second.

TV Dramas had become a way to pass time after meals in China. Fueled by ad revenue, they penetrated millions of family homes. The most popular TV drama in 1993 was "A Beijinger in New York," with Jiang Wen and Wang Ji in the lead roles. Everyone shared the tribulations of a Chinese person's fate in a faraway city in a strange land. The series was divided into twenty-one episodes. Computer companies hired professional companies to design ads and insert them in the broadcasts: the television station naturally took the opportunity to raise prices. Lianxiang took thirty seconds in each episode, and paid CCTV RMB 1.2 million.

Profit-sharing rights

Liu Chuanzhi woke up on the morning of August 16, 1993 to the news that Sitong Company had raised capital by taking the company public on the Hong Kong stock market. The day before, Sitong had raised HK$ one hundred and eighty-nine million. The Head of Sitong, Duan Yongji, told a reporter that employees would be receiving 10% of the shares, and that employees need only pay 10% of the face value of these shares. The other 90% would be covered by the employee benefit fund stored up over years by the company.

Stock markets were set up in two places on the Mainland in 1991, Shanghai and Shenzhen. After a difficult initial twelve months, these markets took off once Deng Xiaoping had made his 1992 inspection tour to the South. The two places began to produce instant millionaires. This Sitong news was particularly noteworthy, however, since it heralded the first people-managed S&T enterprise from the Chinese Mainland to be listed on the Hong Kong stock market. Sitong told the media that the tortuous path to listing had been like fighting the "Huaihai Campaign," a famous battle in Chinese Communist Party history. This phrase galvanized Liu Chuanzhi. In 1988, he determined to "advance overseas" as part of a three-stage plan. The third stage was to list the company on the Hong Kong stock market in 1993. Over the course of five years of hard work he had kept this in mind, but he had not expected to be beaten by his good friend and competitor Duan Yongji.

Liu Chuanzhi now urged the company to pick up the pace of the listing project. He had never worked in the field of securities and he was an outsider to the stock market. It was not easy to push this matter forward, but Liu's ability to serve as a string to link pearls came into play once again. This time, the pearl being put on the string was not just any old person but the President of the Chinese Academy of Sciences, Zhou Guangzho. On August 26, Zhou Guangzho wrote a letter to the Chairman of the Securities Exchange in Hong Kong, a man named Liu Hongru, asking him to lend guidance and support to Lianxiang. He also invited Liu Hongru to Beijing to take a look at the company.

This letter from Zhou Guangzho proved useful. Lianxiang's plans to list on the stock market moved forward briskly. By February 14, 1994, Lianxiang had put its name on the board of the Hong Kong exchange. To investors, this was just another addition to the many other listed companies, nothing earth-shattering. To Lianxiang, and to China, it had particular meaning. Assets of the company at that time belonged to the State. Liu Chuanzhi had separated out a portion of shares, however, that were to belong to the Founders of the enterprise and to employees. Before listing, he asked his subordinates to present two detailed plans to him. These were called the "case for reforming the share system." Liu passed them to his superiors and asked them to choose between them.

The key aspect of the plan that was eventually approved was that 55% of Lianxiang's assets were to belong to the State, while 45% were to belong to employees. Many managers of State-owned enterprises had dreamed of similar arrangements, but they had been unable to find any legal and reasonable method of implementing their plans. Either they would be creating tremendous wealth for others, while remaining poor themselves, or they would be "turning public assets into private benefit" with the attendant risk of being locked up as criminals. Liu Chuanzhi did not aspire to either of these results. He wanted to find a path that was both legal and ethical and that all agreed would be in the State's interests as well as those of employees.

One can imagine the latent dangers and complexities of this process. In January 1992, Liu applied for permission to allow the company to leave the Computer Institute and to reside under the name of the Chinese Academy of Sciences. Permission was granted within three days. Under the Academy, it was still difficult to avoid a miscarriage of the "case for reforming the share system." Theoretically, the rights to State-owned assets in China belonged to the entire body of citizens, whose representative was not the Computer Institute, and also not the Chinese Academy of

Sciences, but rather the Ministry of Finance and the State-owned Assets Management Bureau. Officials of these two Ministries were nothing like as easy to talk to as Zhou Guangzho.

Liu Chuanzhi did not lack ways and means. As the sole shareholder, the Chinese Academy of Sciences possessed the right to manage the profits of the enterprise. It used this power to allocate profits of the company: 65% were retained for its own use, the other 35% went under the name of Lianxiang employees, and the company itself decided how to divide the proceeds. They were split among Founders and employees who entered the company after the Founders.

Liu's efforts were rewarded. He made the following theoretical distribution of the "profit distribution right": Founders who had entered in the year 1984 took 35%. Employees who entered the company after 1984 but before 1986 took 25%. Employees who entered the company after 1986 took 40%.

At the time, these were only numbers on paper. Since they were not realized benefits, nobody felt any of this was a big deal. To leaders of the Chinese Academy of Sciences and employees of the company, this was like "painting a picture of a pancake to appease your hunger." Liu Chuanzhi was one of the few people to see the value in this staged process. He believed this was a first step towards "ownership of wealth." Since he had been able to take that first step, he was now confident that nothing would prevent him from reaching his goal. He was to spend another seven years before he took the second step. In the year 2000, he was able to exchange the 35% of "the right to divide profits" into a right to hold 35% of shares. This block of shares would be segregated as belonging to employees. In the process, it would make him and the colleagues with whom he founded the company millionaires overnight. This accomplishment is the best proof that Liu Chuanzhi is a consummate businessman. He had sufficient determination and patience to allow the currently operating economic system of China to evolve until it could realize his own goals. This all came later, however. Let us return to 1993, which was soon to be ending, and see what was happening in the computer market.

Fudging the figures

Li Qin had been repeatedly warning company employees that the slogan of "jumping through the dragon gate" was not a request, it was an order. In 1992, the company was not jumping well, however. It looked as though things would be equally tough in 1993. In the beginning of the year, a reporter named Liu Keli reported in *Computer World* that "warning signs were circulating in 1992 and one could not be optimistic at all about 1993." Unfortunately, this hit the mark.

The Head of the Sales Leadership Team, Liu Jinyi, publicly voiced encouragement to the company's sales staff. Privately, he anxiously exhorted Liu Chuanzhi and Li Qin to adopt urgent measures to resolve various corrupt practices in the company's sales system. Each department in the company administered itself. The entire computer business was controlled by three Vice-Presidents and one Assistant to the President. Jia Xufu handled the import of components, Bi Xianlin handled production, Guo Wei handled finance and so came up with the cost of goods. Liu Jinyi himself was responsible for selling the goods, but he had no control over the cost of the goods, their capabilities, or their quality. He had only one power in his hands: after getting the cost of goods from Guo Wei, he could add a 15% gross margin and then try to sell them. "Every day that this situation goes on," he said, "means another day's worth of computers piling up in the warehouse." In the summer of 1993, Liu Jinyi made a two-hour presentation. He said, "In the past twelve months, we have lowered the price three times in succession. We have done our best to assure that the price is closely aligned with the market, but it's hard to keep going when the price has gone down 40%."

Liu Chuanzhi knew that Liu Jinyi was right—the company had to adopt radical measures. He had not yet been able to figure out what he should do. He had always believed that "you shouldn't rush into doing things that aren't clear, you should stop and think. Once you truly understand, then you pick up your feet and run like mad." This might be one of those times. He said to Liu Jinyi, "I will allow you to lose RMB 3 million in the last few months of 1993. If you just sell out more computers, I'll consider that a success." At the same time, he transferred Yang Yuanqing to become Deputy Head of the Sales Leadership Team. Superficially Yang was becoming assistant to Liu Jinyi, but in fact he was there to learn the entire business of computers. When the time was ripe, Liu would have to dismiss some of his cavalrymen.

As per the plan to lose RMB 3 million, Liu Jinyi again lowered his computer prices. Strangely enough, Lianxiang computers still could not gain a price advantage. They sold in a halting fashion in November and Liu Jinyi began to feel more and more strongly that something was wrong. He went to the finance department to review the accounting. The results were shocking: the company in fact was enjoying a 24% gross margin and a 9% net profit. The problem all along had been the separate nature and self-interest of departments. Each link in the chain wanted to preserve its own profit: each, to varying degrees, raised the numbers on its cost of goods. The result was that the cost of goods in the books was much higher than it really was. While all other computer manufacturers were lowering prices, Lianxiang was still in fact preserving a respectable profit margin.

Profit margin and market share generally represent the two ends of a balance: when one goes up, the other goes down. The important thing for any company facing intense competition is to find the right balancing point. In 1993, Lianxiang's computers earned profits of RMB 7 million, but the company only sold 25,669 machines—still not achieving the mandated target. This did not tally with the wishes of the people setting company policies, and it became the despair of Liu Jinyi. Many years later he was still brooding over this: "At the very least I could have sold another 4,000 computers if I had known the right figures."

Birthplace of Lenovo: the company was founded in this small building in 1984. Originally the Guard Post of the Computer Institute, this space was granted to Liu Chuanzhi and ten other "founders" to serve as the company's first office.

Proud owners of seventy-two new apartments, in the summer of 1992. Lenovo was the first company in China that provided "apartment distribution" for its employees. Individuals were given the right to take out loans from banks to "buy" their own homes. Before this time, homes were public property, owned by the State.

Lianxiang's very first PC-586, and the very first Pentium-PC made in China. Production began in 1994.

The Lianxiang Han-card. In the late 1980s, thousands of Chinese who understood no English were able to enter the computer age through this device. It allowed input of Chinese characters via stroke order. Though large at the beginning—a box connected to the computer by cable—the card was later inserted into the computer itself. This photo shows a later version.

The new building of the Lianxiang Group in Shangdi, Zhongguancun. Yang Yuanqing's spacious sixty-square-meter office was located on the third floor in the southeast corner. The building was constructed in 2000.

Twentieth-anniversary celebration of Lenovo, in the winter of 2004. This massive celebratory event was attended by about 20,000 people.

The Kaitian M4000 computer, launched by Lianxiang in July 2004.

Liu Chuanzhi of Lianxiang (center left) and John Joyce of IBM (center right) shaking hands at the signing ceremony for Lianxiang's purchase of the global PC business of IBM.

6

1994 —Turning Point

Our goal is to get to the other side of the river. Everyone knows
that. The hard part is knowing how to do it: do we build a bridge,
or make a boat, or learn to swim. Since we don't know how to
swim, jumping in the water will just whip up bubbles and create
an amusing tragedy. Lianxiang doesn't want that. Lianxiang wants
to be a hero who can get things done.

Liu Chuanzhi

L iu Chuanzhi spent Chinese New Year of 1994 in Beijing. The
company spent RMB 1.3 million to buy him a Benz 320. This
sleek black car impressed everyone in the company except him.
The status symbol sat quietly in a garage; it was only used when
drivers took it out to make sure it still ran.

Lianxiang employees liked to tell this story for it epitomized the
unmaterialistic nature of their boss. One has only to look at the larger
picture in 1994 to understand the story's deeper implications.

The winter season was always a peak time for buying goods with public
funds; it was also the golden season for computer sales. This year,
government controls over the public outlays were severe, however.
Zhongnanhai's macro-economic policy adjustments were entering their
seventh month and there was not any noticeable loosening of the reins.
Company contracts for computers were being cancelled. An order for
3 million computers by the Bank of Industry and Commerce was suddenly
cancelled; Dagang Oilfield negotiations to buy computers were delayed.
Several months earlier, salespeople could sign contracts that included the
phrase "delivery of goods can precede receipt of funds." Finance personnel

now prohibited any such practice. Bad accounts had been on the increase. Inflation was increasing, banks had raised their interest rates on deposits seven times in succession, which led to a three-fold increase in the cost of loans to enterprises. The banks were beginning to "take in" only, not to "give out." Vice Premier Zhu Rongji of the State Council dismissed the Head of the People's Bank of China, Li Guixian, and took over the responsibility himself. He ordered the bank to call in loans at the prescribed times. Fearing the fate of their boss, bank employees tightened their hold on funds. Soon enterprises dared not send any money to banks, they bought safeboxes. This led to the invention of a new term to describe this phenomenon: "external circulation," meaning circulation of funds outside any official entity.

In 1978, one had to pay RMB 1.7 to buy one US dollar. In 1991, it was RMB 4, in 1992, RMB 5.8, and in 1994 it was up to RMB 8.89. This was the official rate promulgated by the State Foreign Currency Management Bureau, but the black market price in 1994 was more like RMB 11. This black market price implied that the RMB was rapidly depreciating, which in turn meant that the cost of components that computer manufacturers had to import increased by the day. It also implied that the value of the inventory in Lianxiang's warehouses decreased by the week. At the same time, the import tax on foreign-brand computers entering China continued to decline. Looking at all these things together, it is not surprising to see the following snapshot of changes in the computer market in China:

Percentage of Chinese-produced to foreign-produced computers		
Year	**Chinese Produced**	**Foreign Produced**
1989:	67%	33%
1990:	60%	40%
1991:	49.5%	50.5%
1992:	28.3%	71.7%
1993:	22%	78%

Foreign computers were winning every battle. China's policy makers seemed to be standing back while the country's "open economic zones" became dominoes for western companies. The situation in the computer market in 1990 was a repeat of the home-use computer market in the 1980s. Ironically, the foreign goods changed the lives of Chinese people for the better just as nationalistic "buy-China" sentiments were sweeping across the country. One can imagine how this tormented Liu Chuanzhi and his company.

A pessimistic mood began to pervade the company. Once red-hot, the Han-card could no longer evade its fate. Personal computers had been unprofitable for two years in a row, disappointing everyone and increasing contradictions within the company. In the first month after New Year's Day, the head of the Computer Institute, Zeng Maochao, and two officials from the High-Technology Enterprise Bureau of the Academy of Sciences visited the company. As representatives of the majority shareholder, they called a high-level meeting to amend the company's bylaws and form a new Board of Directors. Zeng Maochao and Wang Shuhe were put on the Board as representatives of shareholders. Zeng, as Chairman of the Board, held two voting rights. The remaining three directors were Liu Chuanzhi, Li Qin, and Ni Guangnan. This had been long-established operating procedure of the Hong Kong-listed company, it was nothing new. After this, however, Ni Guangnang began to challenge the authority of Li Qin.

Ni Guangnang had always insisted that he was a scientist and not an official, but he now began to express strong political opinions. He told Liu Chuanzhi that Li Qin's manner was autocratic, that he was corrupt and self-serving, that his leadership of the company in Beijing was disadvantageous during Liu Chuanzhi's six-month stay in Hong Kong, and that Li Qin should take primary responsibility for the company's losses in 1993. Ni planned to persuade Zeng Maochao to dismiss Li Qin from the position of Standing Vice-President. Zeng indicated that the matter could not be dealt with in this way: "Our principle is that the Board of Directors selects the President and the President recommends the Vice-President. If you want to fire him, you have to ask Liu Chuanzhi's opinion." Ni Guangnan thereby tried to persuade Liu Chuanzhi and Zhang Zuxiang to stand behind him. Zhang refused politely, and begged him to give up this line of thinking. Liu Chuanzhi was more emphatic, saying that he did not stand with Ni Guangnan on this issue at all. Ni's views might not be wholly ungrounded, but Liu believed that it was unfair to blame Li Qin alone for the company's setbacks. Liu told Ni Guangnan that Ni's outspoken opinions would create a schism in the company.

The schism had already developed. Ni Guangnan and Li Qin disagreed over how to manage many aspects of the company and, on a more personal level, they lost faith in each others' honest intentions. They began to contradict one another in meetings. In private, there was no hope of their seeing eye to eye. When this kind of ill will appears among leaders of an organization, and is not immediately dealt with, subordinates will naturally follow suit and divide into factions. Each will want the security of "a strong mountain" behind them.

Liu Chuanzhi was aware of the risks of this matter but he could not transcend reality. He found himself in an awkward position. For many years he had supported Ni Guangnan and he had successfully shaped Ni Guangnan into becoming the standard bearer of the company. Now it became evident that he could no longer restrain this man.

Old sickness, new pain

Two inspirational events occurred after the Spring Festival of 1994. Firstly, on February 14, Hong Kong Lianxiang was listed on the Hong Kong stock market. The company sold 168 million shares, each at RMB 1.33. The price-to-earnings ratio was 13.8 and the issue was oversubscribed by 409 times. Once listed, the company's share price jumped rapidly to a market capitalization of HK$828 million. Secondly, the Ministry of Electronics sponsored a "Ranking of National Electronics Enterprises," and twenty-one computer enterprises were included: Lianxiang's revenues came in first place. At RMB 3,015,200,000, they exceeded those of Shenzhen Saige, Changcheng (Great Wall), Peking University's Founder, Wave, Sitong, Changjiang, Kehai and Fujian Shida.

The first of these two events indicated that Liu Chuanzhi's three-stage policy was being realized. The latter had great symbolic value and should have been something to celebrate, but Liu Chuanzhi had no heart for such things. Every evening his head ached and he couldn't sleep. A number of meetings were held in March at which scientists and managers fell into endless bickering. Factions behind them joined in to the extent that the meetings could not proceed. Liu could not control his intense anxiety and he began to feel that he was soon going to collapse.

He finally admitted himself to the Naval Hospital, as the Meniere's Disease surfaced again. He remained there for seventy days. During this period, a number of issues were resolved by bringing in people from the company and effectively holding agenda-less meetings in the hospital.

To resolve the senior leadership conflict that was becoming more apparent by the day, Liu came to a decision. He promoted Yang Yuanqing. He transfered Guo Wei and Wang Pingsheng out of Beijing: one was to go to Shenzhen to manage production base operations, the other to Huizhou to save the nearly defunct Daya Bay S&T Park. Liu Chuanzhi now determined that Yang Yuanqing could be relied upon. Yang not only was capable of raising a Department's annual revenue from RMB 30 to 300 million, he never let himself get embroiled in personal disputes. Liu therefore positioned Yang Yuanqing as the General Manager of a newly established Computer Enterprise Department. He handed the entire process of the making and selling of computers over to Yang.

Every day in hospital he lay in bed thinking over the company's future; every evening he failed to sleep. At dawn, he would take walks by the August First Lake beside the hospital. Here he found a world completely unlike the one he was embroiled in. To most people in Beijing, the sight was common: only a person like Liu Chuanzhi could think of it as new and fresh. A group of older men and women would dance together daily by the side of the lake. All were retired. He sat down to watch until an older lady offered to teach him the steps and he accepted.

Liu Chuanzhi began to recover. He stopped taking medicine. Every day he took a jog with Dr. Li beside the lake. His mental condition started to improve and he gradually found he could sleep.

The agenda-less meetings continued in the hospital. The most important question among senior managers was: do we really want to continue to make our own computers? Lianxiang's computers were facing stiff competition so that staff doubted that they had the strength. Letting go would mean the company was just an agent of overseas products, and this was not acceptable to Liu Chuanzhi. Liu Chuanzhi and Ni Guangnan had at least two meetings during this time. Ni Guangnan supported his determination never to let go of the Lianxiang computer, and also supported his decision to promote Yang Yuanqing.

Sun Hongbin

At noon on a day in early March 1994, Sun Hongbin suddenly appeared before Liu Chuanzhi as though he had dropped from the skies. Liu had not seen him since their parting in 1990. It turned out Sun's behavior in prison had been exemplary and he had written many articles for the magazine of the Labor Reform Bureau, called *Beijing New Life*. Since prisoners were allowed no compensation, what he earned from this were "credit" points. His points added up, and Sun was able to shorten his prison sentence by one year and two months. When he was close to leaving prison, Sun said that the person he most wanted to see was Liu Chuanzhi. He had always said to those around him that he had great respect for this man, despite everything that had happened. During a brief time in Beijing when he was buying supplies for the prison, he took the opportunity to telephone Liu Chuanzhi. The two men agreed to meet in a restaurant. Liu paid the bill. Sun expressed his deep regret for what had happened, and described his great awakening while in jail.

Sun had received the notice that he was expelled from the company in September of 1992. Two weeks prior to this, on August 22, 1992, he was read the verdict of the court. By this time, he had already been in custody for twenty-eight months at a location near Yuanmingyuan, the Summer Palace to the northwest of Beijing. Incarcerated with him were criminals sentenced to death: he watched some two dozen of these being "dragged out to be shot."

When the verdict was read and he was sentenced, Sun was finally able to leave the custody prison. He was transferred to a prison on the outskirts of Tianjin to serve his sentence. This time he was on a farm, now forced to do labor, which was better than when he had been in prison—at least he could get out into the sunshine and his wife could come see him. He particularly thought of his child but he did not want the child to see what state his father was in.

In fact, in the years to come he rarely mentioned this period of hardship to anyone. His conduct was exemplary, so he was "appointed" to be "troop leader." This meant he became Convict Chief in the prison surveillance system. He still had plenty of time to sit facing a wall and think. In an interview for this book, he stated, "At the beginning I felt a kind of hatred towards Boss Liu. Later that slowly went away and my whole thinking about the matter changed. If I had been in Liu's shoes, I might have done the same. If things had not been handled the way he handled them, where would it have led? So I eventually accepted all that happened. A lot of things in themselves are neither right nor wrong. They depend on the time, place, sense of the situation. That's the way it is. If you put some things into one environment, they're good. If you put them in a different environment, they're a mess. You have to clarify what environment you are working in—if you don't, and you really want to do things, you'll be in trouble. In fact, you will die. If I had the opportunity to go back and start again, I wouldn't do things the way I did."

Ten years later, Sun Hongbin realized his own two goals: to start one of the outstanding real estate firms in the Tianjin region, and to have the Court erase his original verdict. The first objective was described in its entirety to Liu Chuanzhi when they had lunch together in March of 1994. Sun said he wanted to create a real estate business and he said that he hoped he would be able to stand up, start a new life, move down the right track. He wanted to leave the past behind. Liu Chuanzhi looked at the young man before him and knew that it had not been easy for him to emerge from prison with a positive attitude. Liu then said something that Sun would never forget:

Liu said, "You can tell others, "Liu Chuanzhi is your friend.""

Gambling on one throw of the dice

On March 19, 1994, Lianxiang Company established a Computer Administration Department. Yang Yuanqing accepted Liu's request to manage this department. Liu gave all aspects related to computers to Yang Yuanqing: development, production, sales, inventory, supply, and finance. This was power that had previously been shared among four Vice-Presidents and the action came to be regarded as gambling on one throw of the dice. In the years to come, Liu Chuanzhi used a kind of philosophical approach in guiding the company to make sure it was in accord with Chinese realities; while Yang Yuanqing used the experience gained from administering the CAD Department to reform the company's structure. This team—one old, one young—became partners that complemented each other, though de facto power remained in the hands of Liu Chuanzhi.

The Computer Administration Department was set up in haste. Competition in the computer industry was increasing rapidly. Most China-produced computers had already been routed and now China makers looked to foreign companies to cooperate with them, Great Wall with IBM, Founder with DEC, Sitong with Compaq. AST had not entered ZGC but it set up a production base in Tianjin from which it was said that the production capacity would in future exceed all China-produced computers.

Liu Chuanzhi placed his last hope of a Computer Administration Department on Yang Yuanqing. Later, when people talked about the situation at the time, they said that the establishment of the Department and the appearance of Yang Yuanqing were the turning point in Lianxiang's computers, and the turning point as well in all of the Chinese computer industry. But at the time, everyone looked at Yang Yuanqing with highly doubtful eyes. Liu Chuanzhi had told employees that the river was at their backs and there was no retreat, and he gave Yang Yuanqing full rein, but in fact he kept a back way out. Sales of computers occupied only 12% of total sales of the company back then. If they had lost everything, the entire game was not up unless they retreated all the way to being an agent.

Yang Yuanqing gladly took the assignment but that did not mean he was confident. He was the kind of person who wants to see the endpoint, the goal on the other side of the river, and then row for his life. Even if he knew the boat might sink he was not going to let go of the oars.

Yang Yuanqing

Yang Yuanqing, destined to take up the "Lianxiang Computer Revolution," was neither a highly qualified scientist nor one of the older generation. In 1994, he was not yet thirty years old. His entire experience had been in agenting foreign products.

Yang was born in the transistor age—he was a "new-age" person. People had a deep impression on first meeting him. His character was sharp but also introspective, tough and decisive but also reserved. He was acutely intelligent but not very good at communicating with people. When he took action, he adopted a fairly autocratic approach. When he disagreed, even with Liu Chuanzhi, he was stubborn and uncompromising, but when he expressed his own thoughts, he had a sense of humility. There may have been young people around Liu Chuanzhi who were smarter, more acute, better at expressing themselves, and who had entered the core team of the company earlier. Without doubt, though, Yang was the manager with the most outstanding accomplishments in the company.

Liu Chuanzhi is known for recognizing talent. Many experiences molded his approach to people over the years. One of his inclinations is well known in the company: "If one person is dependable but not capable, while another is very capable but not so honest, which should I choose? I would use the latter. I would find another person to come watch over him. And I would find ways to put his talents to work."

Yang Yuanqing was born in Hefei city, Anhui Province, in 1964. His ancestral home is Dinghai, in Zhejiang province, which is known to be China's great land of fish farming. The practice of fishing for a living stopped with Yang's grandfather. His father was taken to Shanghai as a young boy of four years old, where he grew up. Yang stayed in Anhui until he was seventeen, then was admitted into Shanghai's Jiaotong University. After graduating, he returned to Anhui where he entered the Chinese Science & Technology University as a graduate student. His education provides a key to his character: "I studied in two schools, and in both I studied computer science. Jiaotong University was more rigorous, relatively speaking. I believe it emphasizes logical thinking and fundamental knowledge, and students are more disciplined and obedient since they want to get good grades. Science & Technology University, on the other hand, is more open. The students there are highly individualistic and they have their own point of view. I personally think you need both methods, both were useful for me." Taking charge of the computer aspects of Lianxiang was a rare opportunity and a major challenge. "I like challenges," he noted. "I like difficult questions. They make me happy."

His first action was to reform the structure of the company. He knew that going up against multinationals in competing for the China market was going to be tricky. Over the past four years, power in the company had become decentralized. The more than 400 people in the company related to computers were scattered over five departments. Large and cumbersome, the organization was already fertile ground for a bureaucratic approach to business. The Managers of Departments were like "Men of the Green Woods," each protecting his own turf and at the same time arrogantly looking down on the authority of the President's Office. When a sales question required a concerted approach, Yang found that each person had his own benefit in mind and pulled in a different direction.

The new Department was characterized by centralized control. Yang Yuanqing took all powers having anything to do with computers and concentrated them in one body. Then he reduced the number of people that were directly under him by two-thirds so that only 112 people out of over 300 were left. Yang was supported by young people in the company, but the most important thing was that he also had the support of two of the Founders—Cao Zhijiang and Yuan Baoji. They were from a generation of outstanding technical people, and they were a bridge connecting the newer generation to the older one. In the first two years in which Yang Yuanqing led the Computer Department, the support of these two was critical. Yang delegated many responsibilities to them, including the most important: product R&D and product quality. He focussed on setting up the new selling system.

The E-series: China's first economy computer

Yang Yuanqing moved the organization under his control to ZGC, bringing it around three kilometers closer to the center of Beijing. He bought a 1,000 square meter floor in the S&T Trade Center Building near the National Library, and opened the first office space dedicated to the computer business. On the day the office opened, everyone wanted to broadcast the news but there was no budget for ads. Yang Yuanqing sat in the room and looked outside the windows, thinking. He saw streets full of people and activity and he had an idea. He had his staff write the characters "Computer Administration Department" on large sheets of paper and paste it in the windows. They also wrote "Lianxiang 386," "Lianxiang 486," and "Lianxiang 586," all of which could be seen through the glass. When evening came, he sent down a person to make a spotlight so that anyone could see the characters at night as well. "There's our ad," he said proudly to his subordinates.

That spring saw the same kind of feverish activity as in the early days of setting up the company. Industrious, and excited, staff worked with tremendous creativity. The Home-use Computer Administration Department now was also under the command of Yang Yuanqing. Two years earlier, Xu Zhiping had invented this concept and given it the mysterious name of 1+1, but in terms of market penetration he had not been successful. The home-use computer sold a few thousand machines in total. Yang Yuanqing now took over the process.

Electric typewriters were still first choice in office equipment at the time, the Windows™ operating system of Microsoft had not yet become popular. Sitong Company with its M2401 electric typewriter was much more popular than Lianxiang. Despite this, the computer market had been increasing over the past two years and the plan was to use the schools as a springboard in penetrating the home market after successfully occupying the office market. Computer education, more common by the day, was stimulating a home-use computer market; all parents imagined the day when they could carry a computer home to their only child. More and more professors, scientists, journalists, and authors were wanting to use computers in their work. In a market research report put out at the beginning of the year, Intelligence Commercial Networks pointed out that in large cities such as Beijing, 42.41% of households planned to buy a computer in 1994 and another 47.02% were planning to buy one within the next two years. Clearly the home market was no longer merely potential: it represented real buying power.

The majority of Chinese understood what a personal computer implied. But getting computers into homes was still a far cry from the deep market penetration of color television sets. The number of people who could use computers at all was, after all, small, and those who used computers at home was even smaller. TV sets were by now indispensable, but computers were not. Incomes, moreover, were, and still are, low: the average monthly wage in large cities is not yet RMB 4,000. Although the functions, capabilities, and craftsmanship of Apple, HP, and IBM computers are outstanding, these machines are simply too expensive. From the very beginning, therefore, Chinese households have placed their sights on peripherals and have assembled their own computers. All that is needed is a 386 CPU with an 8MB memory card and a 200MB high-speed hard drive, add an SVGA color monitor, and you have a machine that is adequate. The price is one-third of the standard name brands.

Some brave entrepreneurs saw this situation and couldn't wait to take computers down the path of home-use electronics, but facts were to prove that this was a mistaken path. A home-use computer may be different from one used for business, but both of them are distinctly different from home appliances. Everyone knows this now, but at that time only Yang Yuanqing and his group of people understood its implications.

"Since we are a Chinese brand, we don't want to position ourselves as a kind of Cadillac," Yang Yuanqing said. "If you are going to be making computers for China's 300 million households, then you have to make them appropriate to the purchasing power." The first thing he did after taking up his position was to change the market positioning of the Lianxiang Computer. The new generation of computers was christened the "Economy," and thus began the "E-series," which simply meant economy-model computer. Yang explained: "Put a little less poetically, this "economy model" is basically just a bunch of compatibles put together."

This was the first time the term "economy model" had been used in Lianxiang and also perhaps in China. Later Yang Yuanqing said that the campaign to block foreign brands in China with Chinese-produced machines began with this E-series. If true, this is one of the most important events in the history of Chinese computers in the mid-1990s. The General Manager of the Technology Department, Li Zhiwen was the point person on the E-series, and a man under him named Liu Jun became the main technology wizard. He entered Lianxiang after getting a graduate degree at Qinghua University and later became one of the Group's most powerful Vice-Presidents. Li Zhiwen once spent 40 days in succession at the company, sleeping there overnight, in order to design a particular model of the E-series. The process of creating an economy-model computer was deeply satisfying to Liu Jun. "The strategic positioning of this computer could be fixed very specifically," he said. "Before this, we had tried to think of how to make computers cheaper but we were then targeting a commercial market. Foremost in our minds now were millions of households, so we really were able to drop the cost of production by half."

Several suppliers who were competing with each other supplied components and integrated parts, keyboard, disk, driver, mouse. Yang further pushed down the price by ordering in bulk. Lianxiang's competitive strength in the market for this E-series relied on this key element—price.

In the first week of May, the E-series was placed in thousands of computer stores around China. At that time a computer cost around RMB 30,000; this one cost only RMB 16,000. Newspapers broadcast prices for standard components of the Lianxiang E-series.

Although the Lianxiang computer had been termed a "national product" in the early days, in fact only the trademark was its own. All other parts were imported: even the case and the packing cartons were produced in Taiwan. Liu Jun now had to spend more sleepless nights redesigning these, and at the same time finding new manufacturers. His team had to select new materials, and to find ways to lower the price of the yellow cardboard and white plastic bubbles. New computer cases were soon found: the rolled steel was very thin, the worksmanship was rough, but the cost of production was a mere RMB 200, one-eighth the cost of the imported cases. Fortunately Chinese had just passed through severe deprivation and were not picky about what they bought: if it was cheap, it was fine.

Computer engineers at that time felt they could do anything, and indeed they got to do a lot of things that computer engineers had never done before. Liu Jun designed computers, and the packing carton, and he wanted to design a new mold for the foam packing inside the crates. When all of this was done properly, he began to design the characters that would be printed on the paper boxes. The characters "Lianxiang E-system Computer" on top of the boxes were calligraphed by himself. He had no training in the arts, but he neither hired an ad company nor asked for advice from artists. With no hesitation at all he chose a bright blue for the main color for the packaging that later became the main color for the Lianxiang computer itself. It has been used ever since.

On May 10, 1994, the day a large batch of E-series machines hit the market, Yang Yuanqing was in Beijing holding his first press conference since taking over the computers of the company. It was common among computer companies to initiate a new product by holding a press conference and Yang Yuanqing was to hold countless similar events in the years to come.

Thirty days later, for the first time in two years the numbers released by the Finance Department were optimistic: 5,500 assembled Lianxiang computers had already been sold. At the same time, Liu Chuanzhi got a report showing that the first-quarter sales target for computers for the 1994 fiscal year had been accomplished fifteen days ahead of schedule.

Liu Chuanzhi and Ni Guangnan part ways

The final parting of ways between Liu Chuanzhi and Ni Guangnan started with a minor matter, involving Ni Guangnan's driver. This created a schism between the two and indeed within the company. The Chief Engineer may have been using a pretext to stir up a larger issue. He succeeded. Chinese have an entrenched culture of "struggling against people," perhaps as a result of a long period of class struggle. We are adept at finding unlimited causation in the details of human disputes—a person's words, one act, one smile, one frown, all can hold tremendous meaning.

In ancient days, this practice was called, "a gale-force wind blowing over the tip-ends of duckweed." Nowadays, it is called "class struggle all the way along the route of the campaign." Ni Guangnan's motives may have incorporated emotional elements deriving from this tradition.

This loss of trust between the two men appeared to bring great damage to the company in the summer of 1994. This seems slightly contradictory— Liu Chuanzhi could handle with equanimity someone who had brought him extreme trouble, namely Sun Hongbin, but could not do the same for Ni Guangnan, a man whose influence was deeply inscribed on the company. Yet these two men were arguing over such a small thing. The crux of the matter is that trust is the most important bond between one human and another. It incorporates strong emotions and contains absolute belief. If it is once lost, then any small fissure can develop into an unbridgeable chasm.

In this instance, the strategic issue of Chinese integrated circuit chips evolved into a decisive personal dispute. On the day that Yang Yuanqing launched the E-series in Beijing, Ni Guangnan flew to Shanghai to expedite his new dream. He was accompanied by Leu Tanping and Wu Liyi from the Hong Kong company, also Vice-President Zhang Zuxiang from China. They spent three days together in Shanghai where they signed an agreement with Fudan University and with the Yangtse River Computer Company with the intent to set up a "Lianhai Computer Design Center." The name *lian-hai* implies a united strategy between Hong Kong and the Mainland.

The goal of the Design Center was to develop "integrated circuits," the specialized chips used in computers. This belonged to the high end of the product curve, and the upper end of profit margins in the computer industry. Ni Guangnan had been pouring his energies into it for months, believing that the technical personnel in Beijing and Hong Kong were inadequate to take on this responsibility. He had instructed the Hong Kong Lianxiang company to hire at least another fifteen scientists, and he intended to hire a chip design expert from the United States. These two things had not progressed in the last few months, however, so he had come to Shanghai to build a new platform for his own operations.

There is conflicting evidence about corporate support for this endeavor. On April 23, in the course of a President's Office meeting, Ni Guangnan reported his "Shanghai Plan" to Liu Chuanzhi and Zeng Maochao. Records from that meeting show that Liu Chuanzhi and other comrades expressed approval. Other evidence, however, indicates that Liu Chuanzhi was still considering the pros and cons in the balance of power and that the Presidents' Office meeting did not in fact form a resolution.

Ni Guangnan's desire to focus all of his own energy and intelligence on integrated circuits was understandable. The situation of the Lianxiang Han-card was beyond repair; the establishment of the Computer Administration Department with Yang Yuanqing as its sole commander also meant that Ni Guangnan would not be able to rule over Lianxiang computers in the future as he had over the Lianxiang Han-card in the past. To a Chief Engineer, not to have a seat at the table in guiding the company's most important product was unacceptable. If the company's technology leader was not actually guiding the direction of technology, his prestige and position were shaky.

Broader issues also came into play. In the 1990s, China was greatly in favor of removing barriers to trade. The cry to join the World Trade Organization resounded on all sides. The irony of this was that in the process of opening China's doors, a "nationalistic trend" was also ignited within the country. Foreign companies were entering in droves, bringing a latent social schism in the country to the surface. Public debate on the issue erupted in 1994.

This was a national debate, with serious consequences for China's future. Yang Yuanqing and Ni Guangnan were representative of the two different technological approaches. They were a reflection of trends in Chinese society at large. In terms of pure technology, two key initiatives at Lianxiang were planned as offensive campaigns against foreign computers in 1994: Yang Yuanqing's release of the E-series and Ni Guangnan's plans for a "Chinese Chip." These campaigns were aimed in two opposite directions, however. Yang Yuanqing's efforts aimed at the low end while Ni Guangnan's aimed at the high end. Yang Yuanqing's strategy had the flavor of Mao Zedong's guerilla warfare in a national campaign: it avoided frontal attack and hit where the opposition was least prepared. Ni Guangnan's approach prepared an assault on the strongest fortifications of the enemy.

The call "to take the high point in technology" had a thrilling and almost moral imperative behind it. The phrase "Chinese Chip" had particular allure. The Chinese term for "Chinese Chip" sounds the same as the words for "Chinese heart," so the term had an embedded sense of nationalism. In English, the term's implications are purely technical and economic, whereas in Chinese the term reinforced an emotion. Bill Gates had come to China in March and held a press conference for both Chinese and foreign reporters. He was entertained by the Chairman of the country, Jiang Zemin and he spoke before a group of one thousand people. His visit touched a sensitive nerve in Chinese society. A journalist asked Wang Xuan, the founder of a major computer company, to give his views on the subject. He responded: "The most important factor determining the success or failure of China's computer industry in the coming international competition will be a battle of wills. That means a competition of national spirit and national self-confidence." Clearly, Yang Yuanqing was engaging in a struggle of intelligence while Ni Guangnan was employing sheer willpower.

As the debate continued, the enthusiasm of the Chinese people for a "Chinese Chip" increased. By summer it had reached its zenith. People had only to think of the way Intel monopolized 80% of CPUs to feel that this was unacceptable, that if they did not take the high ground now, the Chinese people as a race might as well consider it all over. The Chinese government warmly promoted this line of thinking. It encouraged the strongest computer enterprises to strengthen their research and even developed a subsidy plan. Minister Hu Qili and the President of the Chinese Academy of Sciences, Zhou Guangzho, told Liu Chuanzhi of their hopes for a Chinese Chip. They hoped that Lianxiang would come into the fold and participate in this effort.

Ni Guangnan's "Shanghai Plan" was aligned with the prevailing trend. Liu Chuanzhi calculated the investment required for chips, and the prospects of sales, and the results came to a shocking loss. On June 5, he wrote Leu Tanping and Ni Guangnan a letter in which he expressed his opposition to the Shanghai Plan:

"Regarding the establishment of a Design Center in Shanghai, I have already expressed my opinion to Ni-zong and I summarize it here:

1. Production of motherboards is the long-term direction of our business so that setting up a chip-design development center should be actively promoted under sufficiently prepared conditions.
2. Since we are an enterprise, not a research institute, engaging in this would require the following conditions:
   a. It would require a market to which to sell. Since we sell motherboards ourselves, this item is ready.
   b. It would require bringing in the most modern technology. I feel that we don't have a handle on this item at the current time.
   c. It would require sufficiently capable managers and a well-honed form of management. At present we lack an effective resolution of this issue.

   d. It would require sufficient investment capital and high-calibre developers. This would be possible if we applied ourselves with enough energy.

3. Not one of the above four factors can be omitted. Right now conditions are not sufficient, especially the third. This affair is the responsibility of Hong Kong Lianxiang so I ask Leu-zong to take it under serious and responsible consideration. I personally do not agree with setting up a joint venture in Shanghai. Only after there is a clear understanding of how all issues could be resolved can we think of forming a close partnership with Shanghai."

Choices dictated by a market and choices made in a pure-research environment are fundamentally different. This is key to understanding Liu Chuanzhi's approach. In a research lab you can pursue perfection, which is why the terms "high" or "great" are always applied to the palaces of science. In the marketplace, the best things may not be what the customer wants: the "best" are instead those most appropriate to consumer use. An excellent manager hopes to change the world's dreams, and in this regard is the same as a superlative scientist. The difference is that he cannot allow those dreams to lead him around by the nose. He has to have sufficient intelligence to distinguish what is possible for him to change and what is not possible.

Liu Chuanzhi realized that China's whole setup was not yet capable of changing the world's computer industry, in terms of technological background, industrial infrastructure, investment capital, managerial capacity, and the ability to sell to a market. He therefore had the company stop its offensive short of the high ground of "integrated circuits." Bravely going to your death against the high ground was not as good as staying clear of the enemy and striking at weak points, taking territory in the low ground of technology. From an operations standpoint, Liu's action may have been too abrupt. Leu Tanping had already announced that Lianxiang was going ahead with chip development, and newspapers in Hong Kong had already created a whirlwind out of it. Four days before this letter, *Computer World* in Beijing had also reported in first-page news: "Lianxiang, Changjiang, and Fudan join hands to develop a Professional Chip Design Center." For two weeks, the idea of an Integrated Circuit Design Center had already been in the public eye. The President of Fudan University, Yang Fujia, made a speech on it, the Shanghai Municipal officials were already setting Ni Guangnan up as a pioneer. Now, with these few lines, Liu Chuanzhi had put a stop to all of this. This was unacceptable to many people, including Ni Guangnan. "This is the first time Liu Chuanzhi had said no to me," Ni was later to say. Ni could not imagine that Liu

Chuanzhi would turn his back on him with regard to such an important matter.

It is not uncommon for senior management to have differences of opinion on strategy, but the split between Liu Chuanzhi and Ni Guangnan had a special flavor. Many years later this affair was to be seen as a necessary phenomenon in China as the country moved forward in its modernization. Some felt it came down to the issue of whether capital determines the allocation of knowledge, or knowledge determines the allocation of capital. In fact, the matter may not have been so abstruse. It may only have been a uniquely Chinese form of tragedy. If this kind of conflict had developed in the West, those involved would have talked it over, frankly expressed their own views and listened to others, then made a judgment and adjusted the situation with a view to arriving at concrete results. One side would not have demanded ultimate surrender by the other. If simple measures could not harmonize results, then one side or the other would have walked away without carrying on an interminable dispute. Western culture does not include the trait called in Chinese, "I live, you die," or, in other words, one or the other of us has to die. Chinese, moreover, are a people who are accustomed to the word "yes," they do not like "no." They don't like to say it, and they don't like to hear it. This has been true for eons. If a "no" suddenly comes across between two people, it causes tremendous disruption. Participants as well as onlookers will be inclined to make the matter into a personal conflict, while the merits of the issue itself will take second place. Liu Chuanzhi said that this affair brought on a complete schism between himself and Ni Guangnan. Ni did not deny it. Tracing back, it is hard to say if personal antipathies led to the disagreement of these two, or if the disagreement itself brought on their inability to change the course of events.

The split in strategic direction led to the rendering of their partnership. Ni Guangnan could not hold back his anger because, from now on, this "no" was not going to turn into a "yes." Meetings in the President's Office turned into arguments between Ni Guangnan and Liu Chuanzhi. Every difference of opinion regarding work turned into personal accusations. Liu Chuanzhi began to declare that Ni Guangnan was engaging in "harrassment with unreasonable demands," while Ni Guangnan, in a public speech, warned Liu, "I will never be done with you." On the occasion of a public speech, he said, "Liu Chuanzhi, your actions are breaking company laws." On a third occasion, he said, "I will go against you to the end."

The Chief Engineer did what he said he would do: he "took it to the end" against the President. He brought a suit against Liu Chuanzhi for autocratic behavior, and followed that with the accusation that Liu had severe economic problems, meaning corruption. By this time, the situation had reached a point of "one or the other of us has to die."

A key case of intellectual property rights in China

The intractable nature of the Chief Engineer's dispute with Liu Chuanzhi meant that it was to persist for some time longer, but this was not the only problem the company was facing in 1994. An even more pressing issue was the Wangma Computer Company.

In the summer of 1994, Wangma filed a series of lawsuits against Lianxiang regarding the "five-stroke Chinese character method." It appeared to be winning. On June 6, 1994, the Wangma company brought suit in the Beijing Municipal Intermediate People's Court, claiming that Lianxiang's use of the "five-stroke method" was illegal. Just as Lianxiang was mobilizing its troops to revitalize China's computer industry, it suddenly discovered that it had to contend with a serious opponent. This opponent demanded that Lianxiang admit it had infringed rights, and that it compensate the company for RMB 8.4 million.

The Head of the Wangma Company at the time was an extremely gifted inventor named Wang Yongmin. His five-stroke method was the most popular method of inputting Chinese characters into computers in the 1980s. By the 1990s, there were over 400 types of inputting methods that could be divided into two main types: one used the sound of the character and the other used the shape of the character. The former used the traditional *pinyin* spelling of the sound and this was the easier method for all those people schooled in *pinyin* from grade school. Since there are many Chinese characters with the same sound, however, one wasted time on finding the right character and this slowed things down. The latter method used the shape of the character. One analyzed the strokes of the character's "radical" or lead-element and applied different keystrokes accordingly. The five-stroke method was the best of this latter inputting method.

Most Chinese characters are divided into two parts, a "radical" that often relates to the meaning of the word, and a secondary part that often relates to the sound. There are a total of 227 such radicals in Chinese; all Chinese characters can be found in a dictionary by first looking up its "radical" and then looking through a list of characters under that radical. Since the logic of the "five-stroke" way to look up a character on a computer only relates to a character's form and not its sound or its meaning, it presents difficulties when one is just beginning to learn it. The system avoids duplication to a large degree once it is learned, though, so is much faster in the end. The five-stroke method is generally used by professionals today.

This method coexisted with Ni Guangnan's Lianxiang Han-card invention for a long time—it can also be traced back to the 1970s. A small group in the Science & Technology Bureau of the Nanyang District of Henan Province did the research on it; the circumstances were similar to early research on the Han-card. In the mid-1980s, the five-stroke method developed briskly and was even awarded a first prize by the Henan Science & Technology Bureau. There were ongoing disputes about its authors' rights, however. Funding for the research came from the Science Commission of Nanyang District in Henan and from the Science Commission of Henan Province itself. At least twenty scientists participated. On the Award Certificate issued by the Provincial Government, five people were listed as "inventors." In the following order, they were Wang Yongmin, Zhang Daozheng, Xu Shiying, Chang Shengmin, and Hua Yunshan. Wang Yongmin was the de facto organizer and the "Number 1 Inventor."

The Number 2 man in the list, Zhang Daozheng, wanted rights to this invention but never received permission from Wang Yongmin. He angrily left the group and independently started his own research. Shortly after the two cooperators parted ways, Wang, under his own name, applied for patents from both the United States and England for the five-stroke method, first edition. He was awarded the rights in 1986 from the United States and in 1987 from England. From this, Wang Yongmin received numerous awards from both domestic and international information technology organizations. Within China, he was regarded as a "young professional with outstanding contributions," "a National Labor Hero," and as "an outstanding Communist Party member of Beijing." His creation of the five-stroke method was described by the press as a kind of "scientific epic," and he was regarded as a national hero for resolving the difficult task of inputting Chinese characters in computers. An internal report of the Xinhua News Agency to *Zhongnanhai* declared that "as a scientific accomplishment, the five-stroke method has epoch-making significance in the history of writing technology." A famous scientist named Professor Yan Jici declared that "the difficult problem of inputting Chinese characters into computers has fundamentally been resolved." All of the publicity implicitly gave full credit for the invention to Wang Yongmin. This disturbed many people who understood the full situation.

Research on the five-stroke method continued in the hands of the two now-separated men. Zhang Daozheng and his eighth edition were awarded patents in America in September of 1992 and China in October of 1993. Zhang developed a new edition every year. Wang Yongmin then brought suit against Zhang for plagiarizing his results, and published official notices saying that Zhang was the "false inventor." At the same time, he applied for a Chinese patent, as an individual, for his third edition.

Since the third edition was completely based on the earlier research, as soon as Wang's application was announced it met with opposition. First in line was the province of Henan, which pointed out that the patent should belong to the Science Commission of the Nanyang District, and moreover that other people were involved, not just Wang Yongmin. Three others then came forward to declare that they held rights to the invention. These included a professor at the Beijing Normal University named Li Jin, and the early cooperators with Wang Yongmin, Zhang Daozheng and Hua Yuanshan. Two other people raised dissenting objections, saying that the contents of this third edition were already public knowledge.

The resolution of all this was that Wang Yongmin retracted his original application. He changed his "non-occupational invention" to an "occupational invention", he admitted that patent rights should belong to four entities including the Science Commission of the Nanyang District, the Computer Center of Henan Province, the Chinese Information Research Society of Henan Province, and the Wangma Company. He was authorized by these four parties to be the "Representative for all Rights." The four parties were delighted at this and held a signing ceremony sponsored by the Henan Provincial Patent Office. As though distributing shareholders rights in an enterprise, they allocated patent rights according to percentages. They totally disregarded the rights of the other inventors. In February of 1992, the patent was authorized, however, under the name "Superior five-stroke method coding and its keyboard." In common parlance this was simplified to the "third edition." As he wanted, Wang Yongmin became the sole "applicant" for this patent as well as the "inventor." The twenty-four patent rights that he had requested for the third edition were reduced to seven, however, among which most were already recognized as publicly held technology. All of these details foreshadowed the struggle that was to come.

The Wangma Company, led by Wang Yongmin, lost no time in putting the five-stroke method out on the market. At least twelve companies from abroad signed agreements with him to use the technology. His educational material regarding the method was widely distributed. Fame and money flowed in. Suddenly a new edition came on the market, the "five-stroke character model". This clearly incorporated new efforts and had better functionality than the third edition, however nobody applied for a patent on it. Users quickly abandoned Wang Yongmin's patented method, and turned to this new edition. They refused to pay Wangma Company any usage fees. Wang Yongmin felt that this brazen behavior infringed his patent rights. The way he saw it, the new edition was no different from his old edition. After a series of surprise attacks, investigators working under him announced that at least sixteen companies that had not been given authorization were making use of the patent, and in addition had illegally published some 800,000 copies of his five-stroke method materials. This enraged Wang and he wrote to these companies telling them to stop their infringement. He said he would proceed with lawsuits if they did not sign patent agreements.

Wang Yongmin put himself forward as a Guardian of Intellectual Property Rights. He listed the "infringers" in an accusatory list of names, and Lianxiang was among them. Under the guidance of a team of lawyers, he planned to start off with suing the smaller companies to serve as an example to the larger companies like Lianxiang. In Chinese, the process is known as "killing a chicken to frighten the monkey". He initiated lawsuits against infringement in several places, including computer factories in Hunan and the China Southeast Trading Company. In 1993, the Changsha Municipal Intermediate Court upheld the patent infringement case against the Hunan Computer Factory, while in Beijing, the Municipal Intermediate Court in a separate case similarly determined against the Southeast Company. The two defendants immediately raised appeals to the Supreme People's Court.

The unpatented fourth edition five-stroke method was widely used in many different applications. As a result, its defenders were numerous. If the Southeast Trading Company were to fail, as "the lips are in immediate proximity to the teeth," it was clear that everyone would have to start paying money to Wangma Company. A large group of enterprises in the computer industry now consolidated their efforts; they had always resented Wang Yongmin for appropriating the results of collective research as his own property. It was now even more in their interest to act in unison and they therefore stood on the side of Southeast. A spate of lawsuits ensued. All of ZGC had been provoked into action.

The three largest computer manufacturers in China were Great Wall, Sitong, and Lianxiang. Competitors in the marketplace, these three were now united in a common cause. They called together a research forum in

Beijing which superficially was meant to "develop Chinese character input technology and to protect intellectual property rights." In fact, it was called in support of Southeast Trading Company. This forum received the support of quite famous and influential scholars, legal professionals and government officials. These disparate voices declared in unison that it was imperative that intellectual property rights be protected "accurately" and "effectively". It was not acceptable to protect old technology while not protecting developed new technology, to protect a certain rights-holder and not protect the rights of other rights-holders. This all was directed at Wang Yongmin and the third edition. This forum was recognized as a declaration of war against Wang Yongmin and the Wangma Company.

Liu Chuanzhi instructed his staff to settle outside the courts, if it came to that, and he was even willing to give in some respects, for example by funding some of Wangma's research. Wang Yongmin was not willing to compromise. He wanted reparations, even if it was the symbolic sum of one RMB, and he wanted Lianxiang to admit to infringement. Having been through two lawsuits that came out in his favor, he thought that he would triumph this time as well. To a certain extent, he had to win since this lawsuit determined his future and that of his company. If he succeeded he would be wealthy: every one of several hundred computer companies would have to pay him retroactive patent-use fees. If he lost, it was very likely he would never recover. Few people were now using his third edition patent and it would soon lose commercial value.

More importantly, after several months of observation, Wang realized that an antipathy against him had built up in ZGC. According to what he told a reporter at the time, he had received anonymous letters, and threatening telephone calls. One call ordered Wangma Company to drop its suit against Southeast or someone would engineer the collapse of Wangma. Another said they would pay RMB 50,000 to buy one of Wang Yongmin's eyeballs and either a forearm or a leg. A third said they were putting out one million RMB for his life, and that they could manufacture a car accident for the purpose. The attack-style anonymous letters came in three batches: on January 10, he received 500, on January 15, he got 3,000, and on July 10, he got 500. In the summer of 1994, most companies in ZGC also received a small booklet ridiculing and castigating Wang Yongmin. Countless small-character posters were pasted all over the streets attacking the Wangma Company. All of this proved that there was a sinister "Club to Knock Down Wang" in ZGC and that it was organized and dangerous. Wang told reporters that this was testing the strength of those who protected intellectual property rights and those who were against them. He invited reporters to transmit his appeal to the government: he asked them to offer protection for his personal safety and protection for the inventor's patent rights to the five-stroke method.

Two battles now waged inside and outside the courts. Both defenders and plaintiffs had experience in using reporters to influence public opinion. Reporters therefore also divided into two opposing camps. At the beginning, Wang Yongmin's manipulation of public opinion clearly had the upper hand. Wang is an outstanding speaker with the ability to inflame people and his declarations convinced most reporters. In the first few months of 1994, public opinion was emphatically in favor of him and his company.

Only one journalist was conscious of the fact that the situation was not that simple. Tao Guofeng was a reporter for the Legal Page of the *Economic Daily*. After exhaustive research, he decided that he stood on the side of the defendant. He published a series of articles in his newspaper and not only pointed out why Wang Yongmin's suit did not hold water, he hinted that the original granting of patent rights for the five-stroke method to Wang Yongmin was questionable, that the background of this inventor was basically a "myth". This infuriated Wang Yongmin who mobilized more reporters on his behalf and prepared to launch a counter-attack. He wrote a strongly worded letter to the Editor-in-Chief of the *Economic Daily*. This not only declared that Tao's article, "overlooked and distorted objective reality," but that it "recklessly attacked and slandered" the National Labor Hero Wang Yongmin, that it "manipulated public opinion and obstructed legal proceedings". He also now accused Tao of being a core member, perhaps even ringleader, of the "Knock Down Wang Club". He demanded that the *Economic Daily* conduct a thorough investigation into this reporter. Wangma Company now also, under the name of a Communist party branch, published an article saying that the reporter Tao Guofeng "needed to be looked into". This was then passed up to the Secretary of the National Disciplinary Investigation Commission, to a man named Hou Zongbin, together with a letter respectfully requesting that the secretary "give it his considered attention in the midst of his busy duties."

The situation thereby expanded till all were drawn into the fray, company managers, technology inventors, patent holders, reporters, members of the legal community and government officials. Whether or not what Wang Yongmin said was true, one can imagine that the mood in ZGC was decidedly bad. Both sides of the litigation appeared to be contributing to the hostile atmosphere. Wang Yongmin pointed out that the supposed membership of the "Knock Down Wang Club" did not include Lianxiang, but since he regarded all his opponents as being a kind of "black society or mafia," there was no hope of resolution from that quarter.

After two months of unresolved mediation, Liu Chuanzhi decided to engage the battle. Although Lianxiang had been to court on numerous occasions, this was generally to resolve contractual disputes and in almost every case the verdict had resulted in victory for Lianxiang and the case had been quashed. This time was different. Infringement of intellectual property rights had become a national concern. The Chinese government was feeling tremendous international pressure and, since both plaintiff and defendant were famous personages in ZGC, this litigation had overwhelming influence the moment it began. It was being called the "Precedent Case for Chinese Intellectual Property."

Liu Chuanzhi knew that Lianxiang's future depended on winning this lawsuit. The situation looked highly unfavorable. Superficially, Wang Yongmin did possess legal as well as ethical right to the five-stroke method, and he had on his side the precedents of winning cases against the Southeast Company and the Hunan Computer Company. Liu Chuanzhi had no option but to bring his entire force to bear on putting up a defense. He asked Tang Dandong to give him a report on what chance Lianxiang had of winning the case from a legal perspective.

After meticulous study, Tang and his team of lawyers determined that Wang Yongmin's thinking did not have any legal standing. The central issue was that protection of intellectual property rights was not equivalent to excessive reliance on the pretext of intellectual property rights. In the course of its gradual evolution, the five-stroke method had engaged the intelligence and labor of many people so that the majority of its contents were already public technology. The third edition patent held by Wang Yongmin only applied to the part dealing with the method's concrete application, not to its underlying principle or the pioneering invention. What Lianxiang and other companies were using was the fourth edition of the five-stroke method, which had never been applied for as a patent by anyone. The fourth edition involved publicly-held technology. Neither the Wangma Company nor Wang Yongmin personally had any right to receive payment for publicly-held technology. The defendants claimed that Wang's demands used the pretext of intellectual property rights to commandeer commercial rights to things that did not belong to him.

On August 12, 1994, Tang Dandong and his team of lawyers submitted a document to the Court that totalled 7,781 characters and was called Civil Case Response. It pointed out that Wang's patent rights to the third edition were an example of the results of "illegally splitting up a gourd." It described in detail Lianxiang's reasons for claiming non-infringement. It said that if the Court's determination did not accord with reality and found that the third edition could cover the fourth edition," it would be equivalent to taking public intellectual property and putting it into private pockets. That would, it said, be a huge mistake. All fourth edition users as well as the patent-holder to the Eighth edition, Zhang Daozheng, would then be embroiled in endless lawsuits.

The Intermediate as well as the High Court now faced the same issues. The Intermediate Court suspended the case between Wangma and Lianxiang, pending the final determination of the Higher Court regarding the Southeast Company case. Judges of the Beijing Municipal High People's Court issued consultancy letters to various expert organizations asking for assistance with the technological issues of the case. According to the case documentation, at least five of the professional organizations issued statements that were unfavorable to Wang Yongmin and his company. All of these felt that the critical technological aspects of the third edition could not "cover" the unpatented fourth edition. The Ministry of Electronics Industries issued a statement: "If there is no appropriate broadening of the concept of intellectual property rights "protection" of the third edition patent for the five-stroke method, not only will it prevent the advancement of our country's computerized Chinese-character input technology but it will severely influence the normal development of the many computer enterprises in our country." When the defendants said this at the beginning, the courts felt they were merely using scare tactics in their own interests. There was no room for doubt when all of these professional organizations and government ministries said the same thing.

The balance of scales gradually shifted. After three years of deliberation, the case was concluded in a decisive manner: the original verdict against the Southeast Company was completely overturned, meaning that Lianxiang was also a victor.

The Banner of Nationalism of the mid-1990s

In the years of the opening of China, everyone worked "towards making the country stronger". Not only did they hope to gain from the modernizing trends of the world, but they hoped to tap the wellsprings of their own patriotic feelings as a nation. "Patriotic brands" increased as a result.

Liu Chuanzhi had courageously rejected the concept of a "Chinese Chip," but this did not mean that he did not want to promote a national computer industry. In the past ten years, many of his strategic decisions had been imbued with a patriotic flavor: promoting the Han-card, setting up a Hong Kong base, advancing into the global market with motherboards, developing a China-produced computer and so on.

Liu Chuanzhi felt that a national brand could not be created with integrated chips. He believed that it was likely to be created on the computer assembly production lines being set up by Yang Yuanqing. In the first 160 days of Yang Yuanqing's administration, Lianxiang computers sold 15,000 machines, a 159% increase over the same period in 1993. The sales also made a respectable profit. Everyone's spirit was galvanized, so Liu Chuanzhi decided to use prevailing trends to "push the wave and assist the billows." On September 13, he led all members of the Presidents Office on a formal visit to the Minister of Electronics Industries, Hu Qili. Hu had been promoted to head the Ministry. This company visit was therefore noted in company records as "Making a Report to the Minister." Liu Chuanzhi's private way of describing it was to "tell him what we've decided."

The meeting was quite formal. In addition to Hu Qili from the Ministry, there were the Deputy Ministers Zhang Jinqiang and Qu Weizhi, as well as four Department Heads. This was the first time Lianxiang had had this kind of face-to-face meeting with high-ranking government officials. Liu Chuanzhi knew it was a rare opportunity for the company and that, if he were not able to win the sympathy and support of these people, then Lianxiang would have problems in the days to come. He spoke directly. "We want to maintain the capacity to produce a national brand of computers." He admitted that in the past year Lianxiang computers had not achieved its goals, but said that this was the first such instance since starting the company. "Several large companies have basically given up their own brands and gone in with foreign companies on various cooperative methods to produce new brands. We are an enterprise, so we understand the behavior of these companies. If we too were to give up the Lianxiang brand of computers, then it is very likely no China-made computers would survive."

This speech echoed through powerful government halls. It alarmed and stimulated all who heard it. Liu Chuanzhi now described how Lianxiang had reformed its company structure, and how it was able to "sprint with small steps." New purchasing methods had shortened production times and lowered capital requirements. All of this sounded promising:

"Last year, annual revenues were RMB 200 million, requiring loans of RMB 120 million. Money circulated 1.66 times over the course of the year. This year revenues were RMB 300 million, loans were RMB 60

million and the rate of circulation was five times over the course of the
year. From this increased rate, we will save more than RMB 10 million on
interest alone. The cost of assembling one computer has been lowered
from RMB 150 to RMB 38. Last year the price of Lianxiang's computers
were equally matched with those of AST. If we had lowered more we
would have lost money. This year our LX 486/40 is an equivalent machine
to AST's, but ours is cheaper by RMB 1,200. Our LX 486/25 is the same
as a Compaq machine but ours is cheaper by RMB 2,100, and we still are
able to enjoy a profit margin."

Liu Chuanzhi proceeded with a statement of purpose:

"Our specific thinking is the following:
1. We ask that the government take careful note of us and when we
    do well, that it declare we have done well. Merely to emphasize
    "national industries" can lead to an adverse reaction. People want
    good products, not national products. We hope that the Ministry
    of Electronics will send personnel from propaganda and public
    opinion departments to inspect our quality, inspect our service; if
    we do not perform well, we hope it will issue us a warning so that
    we can immediately take steps to reform.
2. We hope to have industry purchasing policies established that are
    of benefit to the national industrial development. This would
    mean that nationally produced products have priority in purchasing
    plans, under the premise of similar functionality and price.

It all sounded reasonable and acceptable. The Chinese Electronics
Industries over which Hu Qili presided were entering their most flourishing
era, but the figures obscured numerous latent crises. Hu Qili said that
among Lianxiang's issues were many that he had long considered. "There
are only a few large enterprises in the computer industry, and Lianxiang is
the largest group among them. I would like to join with you in discussing
exactly how to support the development of our national products, in order
to strengthen our competitiveness."

Liu Chuanzhi liked to "pour water off a steep roof," meaning he liked
to operate from a position that was strategically advantageous. He was
adept at using overall social trends in China to advantage. His current
goal was to remove all intangible obstacles from the path of Yang Yuanqing
and it looked as though he had been successful. Today, looking back on
the history of China-made computers, 1994 can be regarded as the toughest
year, but also one in which unprecedented national spirit came to the
fore.

Copying the Hewlett-Packard model

Winning over the market was not going to depend solely on pouring water off a steep roof. The process required painstaking management, and strategy. In the fall of 1994, the most significant thing that happened at Lianxiang, even as the company was espousing national sentiments, was the quiet copying of the Hewlett-Packard selling model. Nothing could better indicate how a successful manager stands on the bridge between idealism and reality, profiting from both sides.

While Liu Chuanzhi was speaking with great assurance to officials in the Ministry of Electronics Industries, Yang Yuanqing was traveling around the country setting up a new structure for selling computers. Before leaving Beijing, he laid off more than one hundred sales people in the Department, leaving only eighteen. These were then dubbed the "eighteen young pine trees." This analogy was particularly compelling since it came from a modern Peking Opera in which men were hiding in the reeds but emerged at the opportune moment. Yang Yuanqing was not so romantic. His comment at the time was that "if you don't get rid of the old, there's no room to deploy the new."

Yang Yuanqing explained the new selling system in terms of what he called its main points. First, he abolished the old direct sales system and set up an agenting structure. Then he established a set of policies for the agents. He called the new plan the "1994 Lianxiang partner plan." This "partner" concept was different from the way Lianxiang had viewed partners for the past ten years. To the older generation, partners were customers. To Yang Yuanqing, they were agency firms. In his words, the point was to set up policies that let the channels win. "You must open the channels," he said, "use the strength of agents to raise the market share of Lianxiang computers in the Chinese market."

Selling computers is a specialized industry, since there are always more than a dozen different models contending on the market, with several hundred kinds of software applications potentially bundled inside. If the consumer wants particular applications, one has to be able to advise him. The change from direct selling to "distributed selling" or using agents was crucial to the rise of Lianxiang. As Yang Yuanqing said, "It was an extremely important decision." It was one that was made possible by the macro-economic policies of the country. Ever since "setting up a market economy system" became the guiding policy of *Zhongnanhai*, market structures grew rapidly in China.

For many years preceding this change, middlemen had been looked upon as "speculators and profiteers" who operated outside the law. They were illegal. Now, they were not only upright citizens, but something many people and organizations aspired to be. Yang Yuanqing's ideas on agenting channels came from Hewlett-Packard. Hewlett-Packard was founded in Silicon Valley in 1939, and at the beginning was a typical "garage company." By now, more than forty of its products were regarded as first in the world, including the personal computer, inkjet-printers and color printers. It had become the second largest computer company in America, second only to IBM. In 1993, while computer industries around the globe were operating in dismal mode, Hewlett-Packard raised its annual turnover by 24% to US$20.3 billion. For the past thirty months, Yang Yuanqing had been the most important agent of Hewlett-Packard in China. Hewlett-Packard had dozens of China agents including many that were successful, but Yang Yuanqing was different from the rest: he not only successfully promoted HP's products, he recognized the strengths of HP's system and the value of agents in the entire business chain.

Yang knew what products customers needed, and he knew how to utilize HP skills in organizing its sales teams. He was on very good terms with senior HP managers, and he absorbed those things from the HP culture that were of use to him. He used HP's Ten-step planning process to set up planning procedures for his company. He used lessons of senior HP management for Lianxiang managers. While Liu Chuanzhi was trumpeting "raise the flag of China-made brands," he was also saying, "Hewlett-Packard is Lianxiang's teacher." Both were equally true. Even the first Lianxiang employee badge was modeled after HP's: HP did not mind Lianxiang's mimicking them—they were proud to say that Yang Yuanqing and Guo Wei were their students. Yang Yuanqing frankly admitted all of this. He said, "they don't have to tell us, we just watch them and then do it ourselves."

Lianxiang sales for the past ten years had been outstanding, but Yang Yuanqing knew that there was a tremendous amount of corruption in the system. He had come from the ranks of salesmen. In the early days, once he had completed a piece of business he would write out the sales slip and hand deliver it to the Finance Department, then he would monitor the account and only once the funds had arrived would he take the evidence to the warehouse to get the goods. He would then personally handle the computers—he would open up the packaging, test the machines, supervise the shipping. He would then send the shipping notice to the customer and help facilitate delivery. Once the goods arrived, if there were problems he would personally go to resolve them. At the same time he observed the "distributed-selling system" of Hewlett-Packard. HP's salespeople only handled customer relations. After signing the purchase order, the rest of the process was the task of the agent: how to deliver the goods, receive the money, evaluate customer creditworthiness.

This seemed a more rational procedure. Yang Yuanqing essentially brought the HP selling method intact over to Lianxiang. He used an overlapping structure used by all large companies in the world to extend Lianxiang's exposure into every corner of China. He eliminated the direct sales system his elders had spent ten years creating. This was an enormous risk and was a tribute to his determination. Quite a few in the older generation opposed what they saw as sheer recklessness. If the old system was smashed and the new one didn't work, they knew that the company was finished. This concern was not without reason, for at that time 80% of Lianxiang's computer sales relied on direct selling.

Yang Yuanqing did not look back, though, and Liu Chuanzhi supported him. Yang used the concept of channels to describe agents, something completely new to China at the time. "Channels" were like a water pipe attached to the main spigot. You could conduct the water to wherever it was needed. The water pipe did not itself have any inherent pressure, the pressure inside was determined by the force of the flow of water. The flow was the manufacturer: if your products compared favorably and your sales policies were good, then the channel would be wide open and flowing well. After he formulated this concept in 1994, it stayed basically the same, and it was extremely successful.

The southern battlefield

Guo Wei spent 1994 trying to set up a new production base in Huizhou, Guangdong province. The Huizhou production base was given a pretty name: "Lianxiang S&T Park." It was meant to be the product of the confluence of two profit streams, real estate and computer manufacture. Ever since the company brought its production line from Hong Kong back into Shenzhen and established a new factory in "Sai-ge Industrial Park," that city had expanded rapidly. Over the course of two years, what had been outskirts became the center, land prices rose dramatically and the cost of operating also doubled. It became necessary to retreat into China's interior. Since 1993, China had seen a tremendous rise in large-scale building construction. This led to the formation of a great army of real estate businesses. Huizhou had originally been a poor and secluded village, but its geographic position was favorable: it was equidistant from Shenzhen and Guangzhou and so formed the third leg of a triangle. A foreign automobile finance group was said to be investing US$1 billion here to create a "Panda Auto Group," so Huizhou in Guangdong and Beihai in Guangxi became "two Hot Spots in China." Lianxiang bought a 500,000-square-meter patch of land at the foot of a small mountain in western Huizhou for RMB 120 per square meter. The company hoped that this would "shoot two hawks with one arrow," that it would attract industries related to the computer manufacturing to form a complete manufacturing system at the location, and at the same time that it would benefit from rising land prices.

Unfortunately, the concept did not proceed according to plan. Not only did land prices drop precipitously due to a tightening policy announced by the central government, but the imagined computer manufacturers were not willing to come. In the spring of 1994, Guo Wei gladly accepted orders to come here; he wanted to win the southern campaign in the same way that Yang Yuanqing seemed to be winning in the north. On the first day he could see that the situation was chaotic. Four-fifths of the land was still vacant, its price had tumbled by 70%, the 80,000-square-meter factory under construction was a mess, there was no quality control over the construction and no control over the costs.

Guo went to Liu Chuanzhi hoping for guidance. Liu Chuanzhi was busy supporting Yang Yuanqing, however, and contending with the challenge from Ni Guangnan. There was no way he could deal with this vacant and wasted piece of land.

Guo Wei's good fortune was that he then asked a person named Chen Guodong to assist him with policy planning. Chen was a professor at the Chinese People's University at the time. He exceled in economic analysis and forecasting, but he was not fond of academics. He had an acute understanding of the market. Chen was to contribute substantially to the opening of the Huizhou battlefield, and then to become the General Manager of a company called Rongke Zhidi, under the Lianxiang Group. When he was called in by Guo Wei, he immediately saw that the situation at Huizhou was dreadful. The government was adopting a stance of "big-slaughter big-chopdown," letting people sink or swim on their own. They had also run up against the "iron bowl premier'—Zhu Rongji—which instantly cooled off the real estate market. Chen said, "we have to weave a story" in order to turn the crisis around.

This term, "weave a story," should have a place in the history of Chinese business in the 1990s. It combines a shameless braggadocio-style of trickery, and a legitimate form of commercial planning. The results of a discussion between Chen and Guo belonged to the second set of circumstances. When they said Science and Technology Park, they actually meant to move the entire production line from Shenzhen's Sai-ge Industrial Park over to Huizhou. They announced to the media that Lianxiang had established "Asia's largest production base for motherboard production." This was not untrue, for Lianxiang's production of motherboards already had a ten percent share of the world computer market. Even if there were no Huizhou, it could still be considered "first in Asia."

Chen invited personnel from the State Council's research center to write feasibility reports. This allowed him to get local government support. On June 18, 1994, the Lianxiang Science & Technology Park's second-phase engineering held a ceremony to celebrate a new motherboard factory. Guo Wei invited several hundred people, among whom were at least one hundred reporters. As the Manager of the Lianxiang S&T Park, Guo Wei received their interviews and spoke with great confidence. He said that phase-one engineering had begun in May of 1993 for the Lianxiang Science & Technology Park, and that it had already been completed. It included three factories, each fitted with elevators for goods, living quarters for the employees, an employee cafeteria, a health and recreation center, and a 72-room senior employee apartment building. He also announced that the already-begun second phase of engineering would be finished in 1995, at which time the Lianxiang Science and Technology Park would have doubled in size.

What had formerly been considered a broken-down project was thereby given some PR spin and turned into "Asia's largest motherboard production base." Reporters wrote, "This continues Lianxiang's investment in the Pearl River Delta and represents another massive high-tech project, following on the company's creation of the Shenzhen Lianxiang Computer production base."

Guo Wei later said proudly, "This story was woven rather well. Officials like to hear things like "largest."" At the same time, he set about fixing the problems. He ordered the workers to tear down all of the construction that had been done with earth mixed into the reinforced concrete. He made the engineering specifications come up to standards.

A major battle is finally won

1994 was about to end and all felt it had been extraordinary. The first bullet had been fired in the blocking action for China's computer industry:

China-brand computers began to reverse the trend of foreign domination. Two senior leaders of the company "turned the bridles of their horses in opposite directions" and parted ways. Lianxiang made a patriotic appeal to the central government. The company rejected a China Chip. Guo Wei turned the tide in the battle on the southern front, Yang Yuanqing reproduced the selling method of Hewlett-Packard on the northern front. The company now had at least two agents around the country, headquarters in Beijing no longer sold computers, but sales figures for computers kept going up. In 1994, sales increased by 100%, to 45,000 machines.

In addition to these events, the central government promulgated and began its new reform policies with regard to government, enterprises, the tax system, finance system, investment system, housing system and price system. Banks put their printing equipment into high gear for the printing of money, leading to an inflation rate of 21.7%. The exchange rate of RMB against the dollar, which had dropped for a consecutive fifteen years, stabilized at RMB 8.7 to US$1. Intel dropped the price of its chips: from US$1,000 for a pentium 100MHz CPU the price dropped to US$750, leading to a drop in the price of all personal computers in the world market just at the Christmas period. Inside China, sales of computers rose 68.1% to 650,000 machines. Money spent on advertising by computer manufacturers inside China doubled. China-brand makers slightly increased their share but foreign brands and Taiwan brands still occupied 69% of the market. At least 27% of consumers were still loyal to AST, but this company faced a US$40 million loss, a loss of US$1.25 per share, which led to the company's closure of production lines and firing of more than 10% of its employees. Yet Lianxiang's computer market share rose by 3% to hold 8% of the market, putting it in first place among China-brand machines. Statistics of the Ministry of Electronics Industries showed that behind Lianxiang were the old brands and some new ones: Great Wall Group, Langchao (Wave) Group, Changjiang Group, Nantian Group, Chang'an Group, Changbai Group, Huaguang Group, and Zijin Group.

The Third Ring Road project was finally completed in northwest Beijing, and a large interchange was now constructed over the ZGC intersection. The company applied to the government for permission to name this bridge the "Lianxiang Bridge." It said this would help the expansion of Electronics Street—that it was easy to say and from an aesthetics standpoint would be a lovely name for a bridge. The Sitong Company put out the same request, however, which led to a sponsorship battle. Fortunately three other new bridges were just in the process of being built nearby so that this was resolved in a compromise. Sitong took one of those bridges. Perpetual rights to name the other two were bought

by Lianxiang for RMB 500,000: one is Lianxiang Bridge and the other
Lianxiang East Bridge.

Almost every company has a kind of pioneering energy at the outset.
The hard thing is to keep that energy from dissipating. One thing the
battles over the past year had shown was that Lianxiang was not willing
to be declared a loser. Another was that Lianxiang, unlike most companies,
dared to make courageous decisions. Though Liu Chuanzhi announced
the end of a major battle, it was not over for Yang Yuanqing. His work was
just beginning.

Part Three

(1995-1999): The Age of the Market

7

WE'RE JUST A DRAGONETTE

Running a company is a question of systems design. All parts have
to be considered for the entire system to function. If you dispatch
an attack force to resolve something, one issue may be settled, but
you've messed up all the rest.

Liu Chuanzhi

Ll those close to Liu Chuanzhi in the spring of 1995 could feel
that he was more relaxed. For the past three years, he had
talked about the "goldfish jumping through the dragon gate
to become a dragon." Finally he could say, "We did it."
"Naturally," he added modestly, "we can't be called a real dragon.
We're just a dragonette." The company decided to have a fifteen-day
vacation over Chinese New Year, which was twice the amount allowed by
law. Liu told his employees, "It's time to let everyone have a good rest."

February 8 fell on a weekend, and the company spent RMB 20,000 to
rent the Poly Theater in eastern Beijing to hold an evening of
entertainment. The underlying purpose was to commemorate the fiftieth
anniversary of the first computer of the century, the ENIAC. Computer
technology had changed the life of mankind in the last decades of the
20th century. Its influence surpassed that of war, religion, ethnic differences,
and ideological disputes. Unfortunately, as the century drew to a close,
two-thirds of the globe's people were still unaware of what a computer
was. Even in China, which had declared that it was now in step with the
world, the penetration rate of computers was less than 1%. In the vast
central and western parts of the country, seventy million people were still
struggling for enough food to eat while five hundred million people had

never seen a computer. They were waiting for someone to come and open
the door to the computer age for them.

A strange tale from the western regions

After the New Year vacation, a young man named Chen Shaopeng came
to Xi'an to do preparatory work in setting up the first distributed selling or
agency structure for the Computer Administration Department. To extend
the reach of computer sales, Yang Yuanqing first had to set up a stable
connection between the company and its agents. In the past eight months,
agency efforts had developed briskly and there were already more than
100 agencies, a number to be doubled in the upcoming twelve months.
These were scattered throughout China, like a rootless floating waterlily.
Although Lianxiang's trademark symbolized a new force in the computer
market, nobody knew if the company really had any long-term prospects.
Yang Yuanqing dispatched his best salesmen to all major cities to establish
offices. The first were set up in Shanghai, Wuhan and Xi'an. It was a small
number, but enough to prove that he intended to wrap the entire country
in one package, from east to west. "Yuanqing was very clever," Chen
Shaopeng said, "he knew that if he didn't do this the agencies would feel
as though they couldn't "find their way home," that they didn't have
direct contact with the company."

In 1995, Chen Shaopeng was 26-years-old. He was a generation
younger than Yang Yuanqing and Guo Wei. Like all good salespeople, his
manner made people trust him right away. He had a natural gift for
communicating. His colleagues said that he "could sell ice cream at the
North Pole." He revelled in invading other people's turf and occupying
their territory.

Chen's brief was to be the "Manager of the Xi'an Office." Using a more
professional term, he was "Business Representative." At that time,
Lianxiang had eighteen such Representatives, who, as mentioned earlier,
were called the "eighteen young pine trees". Two other young people
named Liu Haifeng and Gao Wenping were managing the Eastern and
South-central regions, while Chen Shaopeng's territory was southwest
and northwest. This included Yunnan, Guizhou, Sichuan, Shaanxi, Gansu,
Ningxia, Xinjiang, and Tibet: eight provinces and regions and many
hundreds of millions of people. This young man had obviously taken to
heart Mao Zedong's strategy of the early years: win over the strong with
the weak. His method of expanding the market for Lianxiang was "to
surround the cities by using villages".

At the beginning, breaking into the market was tough. Most large
companies paid no attention to him. One person named Du Ting was

different. Du Ting was born in the Nanchong region in the northern part of Sichuan, and was raised in Chengdu. He was heading a company that had three employees. Du was adept at fostering relationships with total strangers: seeing that someone from Lianxiang's headquarters had come all the way out to Chengdu, he made sure to get to know him. He accompanied Chen everywhere and soon he recognized that here was a man with a sense of responsibility and also great enthusiasm. Tremendously excited, he said, "Let's work together!" He had no idea at the time that this was to be the turning point of his life.

Chen Shaopeng founded ten agencies in the southwest region in this year, and he increased sales of Lianxiang computers by 150%. Du Ting received an award for being "Number 1 in the Lianxiang Agency system." Chen Shaopeng told him that there had been irregularities in the distribution system in the past, but that now Lianxiang could extend a key policy to him: his agent's fee and bonus would be calculated every quarter and would be paid on the spot. The reward for sales above RMB 800,000 would be 3%, for 1,500,000 and above it would be 4%. There would be a one-to-one matching sum for advertising, which meant that if the agent took out one RMB's worth of advertising, Lianxiang would add to that one RMB. Du Ting calculated the difference between incoming and outgoing and realized that he would be making 18% gross profit.

Chen proceeded to immerse himself in the daily work with Du Ting, and they shared joys and tribulations. If the car broke down on their travels, they pushed it, if they had nothing to eat at times, they went hungry, if there were orders, they'd take them in together. "It was like being brothers." In the following three years, Du took the annual sales revenue of Lianxiang computers from 600 machines to 60,000 machines, more than the sales of foreign brands by the largest state-owner retailer in Chengdu. His shop on Xinpeng Road got bigger and bigger, his employees increased to over one hundred. He bought himself a BMW and travelled daily between Chengdu and the surrounding towns with the car stuffed with Lianxiang ads and order forms.

The strange story of the opening of the western region for Lianxiang in 1995 was to a large degree written by Chen Shaopeng and the agent Du Ting. The interesting thing is that their activities at the time did not attract the attention of sales professionals of other computers in the market. Agents for western-brand computers paid no attention to ads for brands like Lianxiang and Great Wall on the television, for they had been steeped for years in their own success. They all overlooked one thing: the deep desire for "foreign goods" was a trend that stayed along the China coastline. In the southwest, the northwest, in the northeast and the central regions, that is to say in 500 medium-sized cities and more than 3,000 small cities, things were different. China-made products held that market, while "Western Goods" basically had no foothold. Foreign manufacturers and their Chinese agency structures apparently had not realized that, although these were China's poorest regions, they still needed to use computers. Yang Yuanqing and his sales personnel saw this: they decided to be first in snatching this morsel that dangled at the very frontiers of the market.

The needs of poor people were a kind of turning point for Lianxiang. The Chinese Communist Party army had set up its base in the regions of weakest control by the Kuomintang, and in the same manner Lianxiang penetrated "the rear". Chen Shaopeng's accomplishment in the southwest proved that this strategy was effective.

By spring of 1995, Chen Shaopeng turned his efforts from the southwest to the northwest and discovered that this was almost virgin territory: Shaanxi, Gansu, and Ningxia provinces and regions had only two agents, and in the city of Xi'an, Lianxiang had sold only 231 machines in the past twelve months. Chen was amazed to discover that even in such poor places as Gansu and Ningxia, the reception of Lianxiang computers was better than it was in Xi'an. National defense industries were concentrated in these places, so they had Science and Technology Centers.

Chen Shaopeng's arrival was like a stone being tossed into still waters. He rented a building in the Youth Palace and held a display of the Second-generation Multimedia Home-use Computers that had just been put out by the company. Multimedia was a hot concept in computers in 1995 in China. The fact that a computer could handle not just text documents, but sound, pictures, and animated graphics truly astonished people. What's more, these computers came with names, depending on what peripherals were attached: the Precious Vase had an optical disk drive, the Troops added a video card, the Golden Ox had a special sound card.

It rained on the first day of the exhibition. City streets were wet and cold, but the Youth Palace was crammed with officials, academics, businessmen, reporters and ordinary citizens. Local people had never seen such an array of computers. All items on display carried the same China-brand, they looked good, and they were cheap.

Every product in the display was sold out, though this had not been Chen Shaopeng's goal. As "Business Representative," he had meant to hold the exhibit to let businesses in the city see that people actually bought Lianxiang computers. He wanted them to come willingly to

Lianxiang to be agents, and this goal was achieved. After this campaign, all people in the computer business in Xi'an knew about Lianxiang. They knew that the company had someone named Chen, and that the machines were easy to sell.

Chen Shaopeng still had no office, however. He borrowed a room, moved in a few tables and chairs, then invited a teacher from the Arts Institute to design a sign for him: "The Xi'an Office of the Computer Administration Department of the Lianxiang Group." He was Manager at the time, but under him was exactly one staff member. The two men hung the sign outside the door that day, and admired it: "We now had a presence."

The two then rented a car and made exploratory trips around the perimeter of Shaanxi. Their target was middle-sized cities. As soon as they got to a place they would check it out, see which stores sold computers, pay a call on them. They would then hold a small exhibition at the person's own shop. This exhibition really meant suspending a banner from an electricity pole, setting up a table, putting out some ads, then with one hand selling a sample computer while signing an agency agreement with the other.

Anyone wanting to buy a computer in Xi'an this spring discovered that the stores selling "Lianxiang" had greatly increased. Swallow Tower Road at the center of Xi'an was a famous "Electronics Street," formerly full of AST, Compaq, and IBM brands. Now one store put up a wall inset with frosted glass on which was written the characters "Lianxiang Computers." All passersby could see it. In the following few weeks, such signs increased. Corporate colors had not been standardized at that time so there was a rainbow of hues. Chen Shaopeng recommended that everyone use a yellow background and blue characters. "Yellow is more vivid," he said. Springtime had not yet ended when there were already five such signs, then more than ten on Swallow Tower Road. Under each "yellow background with blue characters" was a new Lianxiang Agent. They sold 1,111 Lianxiang computers that year, almost five times the amount in the previous year.

Linking hands with the government

In Beijing, it was increasingly clear that Liu Chuanzhi's consolidation of power was helped by his close friendships with senior government officials. Just as his sales people excelled at spreading their wares before customers, he was good at selling the company to the top echelons. In early 1995, when the Ministry of Electronics Industries selected "key companies qualifying for support," Lianxiang was one of the six companies listed. The other five were famous home appliance manufacturers, and they were State-owned companies under the jurisdiction of the Ministry so this was not surprising. Only the sixth company, Lianxiang, had no relationship with the Ministry in terms of financial or administrative ties. This raised eyebrows in the computer industry. Only a few years earlier, Lianxiang had been considered a "privately born son", or bastard, outside the planning system. It was hard to place Lianxiang among the ranks of favored sons while excluding State-owned computer manufacturers such as Great Wall and Langchao (Wave). Minister Hu Qili faced tremendous pressure as a result. Some influential elders went about canvassing on behalf of the State-owned companies.

Hu Qili lived up to his promise. He did not allow special interests to influence the government's relations with industry—ownership of assets was not the determining factor even if privileged parties were powerful.

In February of 1995, Liu Chuanzhi had the opportunity to be a guest of the Beijing Mayor, Li Qiyan. Also attending the function were Vice Mayor Hu Zhaoguang, and the Chairman of the Science Commission, Song Jian. A memorandum from that period is full of terms of endearment between Lianxiang and the Beijing municipal government. The Mayor asked how big he felt Lianxiang could become. Liu Chuanzhi said, "US$1.6 billion." The Mayor appeared to want to hear a greater degree of confidence. He laughed, saying, "That might do it if you're building something that can withstand an eight-degree earthquake, but don't you want to withstand a twelve-degree earthquake? Aren't you too conservative?" Liu Chuanzhi smiled and replied, "We never say things we don't have absolute control over. If we can do better than that, I'll come see you again." This statement carried strong intent but "did not leak a drop of water." The Mayor indicated then that the government would offer all the material support it could.

Liu Chuanzhi grabbed the opportunity. He said, "Can you give us a patch of land? We would like to build an apartment building for housing our employees." The Mayor nodded approval, then asked what else. Liu Chuanzhi, "getting an inch, advanced a mile": "I hope that the Beijing Municipal Adult Education Bureau can promote the widespread use of home-use computers." This was rather a large request. If realized, it would open a vast market for Lianxiang's home-use computer strategy. "All right," the Vice Mayor Hu Zhaoguang replied. "We'll go together to see the Bureau Chief of the Adult Education Bureau." He went on to explain the significance of this: "From now on, our policy is that government employees won't be promoted if they can't use computers. They can't move up in rank. And if you want to be able to use one, naturally you have to buy one and take it home." Liu Chuanzhi smiled. "And what brand?" he joked. "Best to buy Lianxiang. Naturally this last part is something I alone can say."

Looking back, the months at the end of 1994 and early 1995 were a "honeymoon" between Lianxiang and the government. Not only did the government treat Lianxiang as a "true son", it invited Liu Chuanzhi to a variety of important meetings. For example, the central government discovered that only 8% of GNP came from high-level science and technology. Of one hundred billion dollars worth of exports, only 5% was derived from sale of science and technology products. The rest of the 95%, in the words of the Chairman of the Science Commission, Song Jian, was "all Mainland goods." The government therefore decided to set up an investigative committee, the "Super 863 Software topic working committee." It prepared to invest RMB 10 billion over the next five years to promote high-tech industries. In the spring of 1995, the working committee held its first meeting and virtually all of the most powerful people in China's science and technology fields attended. These included the President and Vice-President of the Chinese Academy of Sciences, the Chairman and Vice-Chairman of the Science Commission, the National Education Commission Chairman and the Ministers of the State Council. They also included Liu Chuanzhi. Scientists and professors argued that government investment in scientific research was inadequate. They called upon statistics to illustrate how much foreign governments invested in science compared to their GNPs, how many times greater that ratio was than China's. Everyone had a say. Liu Chuanzhi discovered that the scientists at the meeting all overlooked one fact. Only when Song Jian gave him the opportunity to make a speech did he bring it up. He said, "Are we not doing applied science? Shouldn't it make money? If you're not making money, yet perpetually asking the government for more, is that going to persuade anyone? Why have Chinese companies been looked down upon up to now? Isn't it because all we do is spend money, till it's gone, and then come to the government to ask for more?" He saw the abashed faces before him. He went on to say, "Since this is applied technology, from the country's standpoint are we doing it for prestige? Or are we doing it for profit? I personally feel that we need to start with profit as our primary goal."

Liu Chuanzhi knew that many government officials had been upset by his refusal to endorse a China Chip. Many even said he had no core technology but was stuck in the lowest level of computer-assembly workshop-style business. Now came his chance to refute them. He said what was on his mind: "Some high-tech products are not necessarily saleable. And only when products are sold is there any return on investment. Let me give you an example from abroad: In the entire world there are approximately fifty million personal computers, Apple holds not quite 10% of the market, all the rest are IBM or IBM-compatible. Apple's functionality is far better than IBM-compatible machines but Apple promotes its products badly. This is because Apple's underlying strength is insufficient. Which is to say, if your ability to sell is inadequate, you're not going to make it, even if your product's functionality and price are relatively good.

"If the Lianxiang Group wanted to mass produce integrated chips, the first question would be to whom to sell them. Everyone knows that only when the quantity produced is large can the cost per unit of goods be low. But if you don't know how many you can sell, you don't dare produce in quantity. If you produce only a few, your acceptance rate is low and your cost of goods so high that no matter how good your chips are, you will find you can't make money. This becomes a vicious circle. My point is that if you do not clearly consider your sales channels, you will not be able to accomplish this business."

After the meeting, he went to pay annual New Year's respects to the Head of the Computer Division of the Ministry of Electronics, Zhang Qi. He expressed his appreciation to the government, and he also said, "It is necessary to give face to the leaders and comrades who support us." Zhang Qi reminded him that he should not consider only his own welfare, he should remember to take care of his neighbors. He hinted that Lianxiang had "run into some trouble."

The company had boasted about its own accomplishments but had forgotten the ancient lesson of knowing when to stop. One day the *People's Daily* ran an article that was signed with the name of Liu Chuanzhi. The text implied that Great Wall and Langchao (Wave) were companies that were no longer producing their own computers. Liu Chuanzhi had indeed said this before, but in an internal speech at the company. These words made a few people unhappy when they became public. The gist of the matter was that the Head of Great Wall Company was offended by advertising tactics used by the ad agency of Lianxiang that slighted Great Wall's Han-card at the expense of Lianxiang's and that made factual mistakes. As a government official, Zhang Qi brought this to Liu Chuanzhi's attention, showing how delicate the balancing act of government and corporate personnel could be. Liu Chuanzhi immediately took remedial action. He wrote a letter to Wang Zhi, the Head of Great Wall, begging forgiveness. Liu then warned his subordinates: "You must be supremely careful in whatever you do. If anything is handled badly, there will be hell to pay for it."

On February 16, 1995, the 62-year-old Head of the Computer Institute, Zeng Maochao, retired. In the past sixteen years he had led the Institute to glory, receiving forty national-level accomplishments in science and technology. He had brought along an outstanding team of computer scientists, but he was most proud of his role in turning technology into actual products. Now he was leaving. To Liu Chuanzhi, this came just when the company needed him most. Lianxiang would not have survived many crises if Zeng Maochao had not been there to help. Liu Chuanzhi therefore decided to persuade the leaders of the Academy of Sciences to let Zeng Maochao continue on as Chairman of the Board of Lianxiang Company. He succeeded and on the fifth day after Zeng retired from the Institute, the Chinese Academy of Sciences announced that it had decided to adjust the Lianxiang Group's Board: the new Board would be composed of six people including Zeng Maochao, Liu Chuanzhi, Li Zhijiao, Li Qin, Ni Guangnan, and Zhang Zuxian. Each would have a tenure of four years. Zeng Maochao was to be Chairman of the Board, and to hold "double voting power."

This kind of arrangement was not uncommon, however strange it may seem. The stranger thing was that the Chinese Academy of Sciences decided that Liu Chuanzhi would now assume the position that Zeng Maochao had left. Liu became President of the Computer Institute, with Lianxiang's former Vice-President, Li Chuyi, as his Vice-President. The official explanation for this was that the Academy of Sciences hoped to bring Lianxiang's management philosophy into the Research Institute. Many were opposed to this. In their eyes, the Academy of Sciences was "Grand-dad," the Computer Institute was "Daddy," and Lianxiang Company was merely "son." A saying went round the compound at Number 2 Academy of Sciences South Road: "Grand-dad gives an order, telling son to manage Daddy."

In fact this "son" did not want to manage "Daddy." He just did not want to be managed by Daddy. It was clear that nobody could accept an administrative structure that had any possibility of bringing trouble to Lianxiang. The Institute had already started more than a dozen companies but up to now only Lianxiang could be considered successful. Lianxiang had turned RMB 200,000 worth of investment into RMB 137.89 million worth of assets, and its annual revenues were RMB 4.7 billion. If Lianxiang ran into unexpected problems, this would be unacceptable not only from the standpoint of propriety, but from a profit perspective. Details were insignificant: the good health of Lianxiang stood above all.

Driving the "Lianxiang Express" across the country

In the mid-1990s, as patriotic sentiment swept into the field of commerce, the 100,000th computer rolled off Lianxiang's production lines and was set up with great fanfare on the cultural soil of the Chinese nation.

Lianxiang reported the arrival of the 100,000th computer in advance, saying it had "milepost" significance. Although the Great Wall Company, its most important competitor, had already announced its 200,000th computer eight days earlier, Lianxiang's ad department still felt that their own milepost was worth celebrating and was an opportunity to broadcast the Lianxiang brand. On April 1, well in advance of the date of the event, the department figured out a gimmick to get people to take note. They created ad copy that said, "The customer is "god" to Lianxiang: Lianxiang requests guidance from god: where should the 100,000th Lianxiang computer go?" This copy appeared in the *Reference News*, *Computer World*, and *China Computer Journal*, the established professional media in the computer field, as well as the so-called mainstream papers of the *People's Daily* and *Guangming Daily*. The significance of this computer then began to transcend the computer itself. As Li Qin said, "From the day that Lianxiang was born it was a "Lianxiang" not only for Lianxiang people but for society, for all people." There was some truth in this: the company received 21,648 letters and at least 1,000 telephone calls. The common thread amongst responses was that all felt united under the banner of this "National Brand".

Quite a few people were already assembled under this flag. Lianxiang was seen as different: since the establishment of the country, there had not been an enterprise that, without asking for State investment, was able to break out into the international market. The media began to talk about the Lianxiang Spirit. It determined that two aspects were most important, unyielding beliefs and persevering human spirit. One journalist from the *Beijing Youth Journal* went so far as to put out a call to "Protect and Defend Lianxiang," taking people back to fifty years earlier when the KMT armies surrounded the Communist Party base in the mountains of northern Shaanxi and the call went out, "Protect and Defend Yan'an." Responses of common people to the ad copy can perhaps be taken as representative of the sentiment in society at large. Two among them proposed:

"Send the computer to the President of IBM. Let him see that China's computers aren't inferior to theirs." "Send it to Badaling at the Great Wall, let "old outsiders" (foreigners) use it as backdrop for their photographs."

On April 16, the machine so infused with national pride rolled off the assembly line. It was a "Precious Vase II Model," with a serial number of 196007, a 486/66 processing unit, 270M hard disk, 16M of memory, and a 1.44M floppy disk drive. The question of "where shall it go" was finally decided. The company decided to send it to Chen Jingrun, a solitary mathematician who had spent his life researching a mathematical theorem. This man had become famous throughout the country as a symbol of patriotic spirit. Before this, he had never had any contact with computers, so this "Precious Vase" accompanied him in the later years of his life.

The bestowing ceremony had a thrilling title: "Ten years of glorious pioneering progress, millions of superb products fill our sacred land." In front of several hundreds of guests and reporters, Li Qin grandly said, "we feel we have arrived". In the course of five years, from the first Lianxiang slogan, "If mankind loses Lianxiang, what will the world do," to this one, "millions of superb products fill our sacred land," China had experienced considerable change in social sentiment.

These were acutely understood and utilized by a lady named Qiao Jian, Head of Lianxiang's public relations. Qiao Jian had graduated in 1990 from Shanghai's Fudan University and then joined Lianxiang. Her first assignment was to sell Lianxiang computers. In 1994, when Yang Yuanqing took charge of the Computer Administration Department and began to promote the "home-use computer," he also began to elevate the importance of relationships with the public and officialdom. Outlay on company advertising in 1994 reached RMB 19,320,000, 88% more than in 1993. Qiao Jian came to the Department at just this time and began to work in the fields of public relations, promotion, advertising, and media. She came at the right time.

By nature she was smart and full of enthusiasm, but unfortunately she was inexperienced. The "birth and bestowing of the 100,000th computer" was her first large promotion activity. She started out with the basics, creating a planning sheet, making a schedule, issuing invitations, making ads, doing promotion, arranging the ceremony, and she was tremendously excited by it all. Only on the actual evening of the event did she discover that she lacked a speech for the host. The standard procedure was to invite some famous person to make a keynote speech and generally the organizer of the event provided the text. Qiao Jian had no ready speech at hand and she had no concept of what should be said. Fortunately professionals are adept at such things. She found one, the thing was done in a second, and the show went on.

This kind of event was new to the company, not just to Qiao Jian. Lianxiang had issued a tremendous amount of publicity over the past ten years but everyone had been fixated on the "Father of the Han-card, Ni Guangnan." He was made into a great scientist, put on a pedestal and lauded for his integrity. Now, all were focusing on the 100,000th computer. The "heroes" behind the computer had become unimportant. The China of the 1990s was no longer an era of heroes. Among the changes in China was an intangible but very clear transformation: people no longer worshipped the power of spirit and things high and mighty, they thought about the needs of ordinary folk. Companies with the best understanding of the market were first to realize this and quickly modified their public image. Qiao Jian later described the event as successful, for she had learned the concept of "Market Promotion."

The Department had gone from the pre-1980s "Propaganda Department" to the "Public Relations Department" of the early 1990s. It was now the "Market Image Promotion Department" of the mid-1990s. The evolution of the name matched the trajectory of the times. Lianxiang now realized that the image of a product was more important than the product itself, was even more important than the inventor of the product. This spurred Qiao Jian to change the company's image promotion: she aimed more directly at the market and she picked up the pace.

On May 12, an even larger event began. The "1995 Lianxiang Express" headed out across China from a starting point at the Municipal Government of Beijing. That morning a large vehicle emerged from the Lianxiang Company, drove down Chang'an Street, across Tiananmen, then into Taijichang Street where armed sentries stood stiffly at attention. It drove into the large courtyard of the Beijing Municipal Government, where its contents were inspected by senior officials. The Vice Mayor of the City, Hu Zhaoguang, warmly welcomed its arrival. He remembered his promise of several months earlier to Liu Chuanzhi; he expressed the hope that this vehicle would go throughout the country promoting the widespread use of computers.

"We want it to head across the land, north to south," he said. Picking up on those words, Qiao Jian reported them to several dozen reporters. "We are not going out to sell computers," she said. "We are taking this opportunity to popularize knowledge about computers. We will be going to every city to give lectures and we will answer any questions from anyone."

In the next three months, the Lianxiang Express went throughout China and the Lianxiang banner flew in at least 300 cities. Events were organized in S&T Halls, Culture Palaces, organizations, stores, arenas, even in the streets. On the banner was written, " Computer knowledge is a passport to the 21st century." Added to this was the Lianxiang logo, that circle in a square with its trademark azure blue. Hundreds of millions of Chinese saw it. They also read the Lianxiang series of "lessons" in the *Economic Daily* and the *Guangming Daily*. They saw new ads in fifteen-second spots on CCTV.

Over two hundred million people saw the TV ads since they were inserted after the News Summary, during the golden-time slot. In one ad, a "1+1" flies past a warm and united family of three, while the lilting voice of a child says: One family, one "1+1." Helps Daddy figure out problems. One family, one "1+1." Helps Mommy manage the household. One family, one "1+1." Helps me study."

Lianxiang was not delivering philosophy or some mighty statement in this ad. It was letting ordinary people understand that a personal computer could be used in an ordinary person's home to teach children, and plenty more: it could make your family life happier, more harmonious, more efficient. It could make your life different from what it was before. Qiao Jian was by now a pro at the company's market promotion. She said, "Our strategy is to find the best meeting point between the company's profit and the needs of the customer. Right now, in the 1990s, this meeting point is the popularization of computer knowledge. Once every normal household feels that computers are useful, this market will become mature."

The mid-1990s were the end of an era of scarcity of goods in China. The year when China went from being a "seller's market" to being a "buyer's market" can be dated precisely to 1995. Commodities were plentiful and inventories increased; the rationing system and all kinds of coupons of the period of "extreme scarcity" had been abolished. Buyers began to "select fat and reject lean." Firms hurried to say their brands were "famous," they talked about their superior products and also the "intangible value of brands." As Qiao Jian saw it, it was more important to let hundreds of millions of people become aware of their own needs. "If everyone thinks computers are no use to them," she said, "then how are you going to sell computers?" To her, opening up a market and promoting products were two different things. Liu Chuanzhi may have influenced her in this regard, for this young woman also liked military analogies in describing commercial competition. "Opening up a market is like aerial bombardment," she said, "whereas promoting products is like an infantry charge. You first have to create a need, then you make everyone recognize the helpfulness of your brand."

What she was hoping for did in fact come about. After three years of gestation and preparatory steps, Chinese people became quite clear about what personal computers meant to their families. The turning point came in 1995: after this, sales of personal computers increased at a rate of 50% per year. Among families who bought computers, 40 of every 100 bought the Lianxiang "1+1."

Ni Guangnan loses

Ni Guangnan, newly made an academician in the Chinese Engineering Academy, wished to restore his influence over the company. As described earlier, he and Liu Chuanzhi split in 1994 over the direction of technology in the company, and he sowed the seeds for a power struggle.

The increasing problems eventually ignited. Ni Guangnan sent a letter to the Chinese Academy of Sciences, accusing Liu Chuanzhi of autocratic behavior in terms of corporate investment decisions, and of presumptuously changing the "Han-card Administrative Department" into the "Software Administrative Department", which effectively cancelled the Han-card. He implied that Liu Chuanzhi had serious "economic problems", in other words Liu was guilty of corrupt practices. He said that Liu had siphoned bank loans, to the extent that considerable State-owned funds were missing. He said that the property rights to the Huizhou Science & Technology Park were murky, that financial movements were irregular and there were many things about which he as a Board member had not been properly informed. As for Liu Chuanzhi's sudden dismissal of the former Finance Director, Hu Qingyu, Ni Guangnan declared there must be serious "facts one wishes to hide" behind this. Ni said he held important evidence in his hands: in 1994, Liu Chuanzhi loaned US$5,525,000 of company funds to Hong Kong's Leu Tanping and others to increase their own share ownership from 33.3% to 43.3%.

When the Chairman of the Board Zeng Maochao received this letter informing against Liu Chuanzhi, he was appalled. If true, the accusations would be the end of Liu Chuanzhi.

When Ni Guangnan first presented his accusations, many senior and experienced people doubted if Liu Chuanzhi could make a total disclosure. Since the 1980s in China, in the course of chaotic and disorderly development, many people had essentially profited at others' expense. A popular phrase was, "First arrest the most wealthy bosses, investigate later," the implication being that these people must have been engaging in unlawful activity. There were also many who knew the inside story on Lianxiang and who had misgivings about Ni Guangnan's motivation. For him to come forth with disclosures now was a tactic to maintain his own authority.

The Head of the High-tech Industries Bureau of the Chinese Academy of Sciences, a man named Li Zhijie, led an investigative committee to look into the company. This was already a second investigation: the first came to investigate Liu Chuanzhi's "management style," and it raised such issues as "is he too autocratic within the company?", "what is the hiring and firing procedure for employees?", "has he ever inserted his own relatives into the company?", and so on. This time was considerably more severe. It was looking into economic crimes, and the ultimate question the investigators had to answer was, "would this company survive without Liu Chuanzhi?" The understanding in ZGC was that Liu Chuanzhi might very well be going to jail.

Of all the crises that Liu Chuanzhi had met with in his life, none caused him as much pain and anxiety as this one. He felt wronged, but there was no way he could avoid focussing his entire attention on dealing with this nuisance. When he heard that the senior leaders of the Chinese Academy of Sciences were going to hold a meeting to discuss Lianxiang issues, he immediately wrote a letter asking that he be allowed to submit a written statement. After defending his own behavior and actions, in this statement he described the opposing attitudes of himself and Ni Guangnan. "The contradictions between us are irreconcilable," he wrote. "I no longer am able to work with him. As President, I therefore propose to the Board of Directors that he be removed from the position of Chief Engineer. At the same time, I ask the leaders of the Academy to consider removing him from the posts of the Board of the Lianxiang Group and Hong Kong Lianxiang."

In his written statement, Liu also asked that the investigative committee give him the opportunity to appeal. Later he got his wish. Excerpts of his rebuttal to the committee follow.

Regarding the issue of why Beijing Lianxiang Computer New Technology Development Company lent US$5 million to Leu Tanping and others; there were three main issues:

1. There were originally three shareholders in Hong Kong Lianxiang: Beijing Lianxiang, Hong Kong Daoyuan, that is, Leu Tanping and

others, and the China Technology Licensing Company. The share ownership of the three was the same, 33.33% each. At that time, Beijing Lianxiang and Hong Kong Daoyuan were on equal footing, and there was no issue of our side being the majority shareholder and their side being the minority shareholder.

2. In 1993, Hong Kong Lianxiang issued another HK$100 million worth of stock. The Technology Licensing Company did not plan to participate. They gave up 30% so their share capital went from 33.33% to 3.33%. If both Beijing Lianxiang and Hong Kong Daoyuan had been willing to take the 30% in equal measure, each would then have held 48.33% of total shares, 33.33 + 15. If Leu Tanping and others had trouble finding the funds to increase their shares to this level, Beijing Lianxiang said it was willing to help them resolve it. However, the Beijing Lianxiang share ratio would as a result have to be larger, it would move up to 20% of the 30% while Hong Kong Daoyuan would hold 10%. Leu Tanping agreed to this. Beijing Lianxiang then held around 53.33% while Hong Kong Daoyuan held about 43.33%. Beijing Lianxiang became the majority shareholder. That is to say, there were preconditions for Beijing Lianxiang's becoming the majority shareholder with 53.33%: the precondition was that Beijing Lianxiang would make a loan to Leu Tanping, otherwise everyone would stay at an equal ratio.

3. If Beijing Lianxiang was not willing to make a loan to Hong Kong Daoyuan, then Daoyuan could put up 5% of shares to any bank or any investment company to get the funds to increase their shareholding. Based on Lianxiang's reputation at the time, this was an extremely easy thing to do. If that had been the case, the share ratio would be Beijing Lianxiang 48.33%, Hong Kong Daoyuan 43.33%, some other third party investor 5%, China Technology Licensing 3.33%. What use, however, would this have been to Beijing Lianxiang?

As for the issue of undemocratic decision making, and the feeling that major issues had not been discussed at the President's Office meetings: Liu Chuanzhi responded that if items had not been discussed with Ni Guangnan they had been discussed with one of his assistants. Liu said, however, that this method of doing things was improper and disregarded prior consultation before the matter at hand. After the bylaws of the Board of Directors were established, the Board should then establish decision-making procedures for the President's Office. These should call for greater consultation, in order to increase the effectiveness of the President's Office. Orders from the Office could then carry more weight.

As for the issue of inappropriate use of people: Liu Chuanzhi said that four or five people out of several hundred cadres had not worked out. He asked, "Is this such a bad record?"

As for the issue of overly centralized power: Liu Chuanzhi said that he was someone who could take advice, that if many people felt this way he should take it under consideration.

Senior managers in the company all stood on the side of Liu Chuanzhi. This contributed to the eventual acceptance of Liu Chuanzhi's explanation by the investigation committee, and their conclusion that the nature of this incident was a split in the leadership team of the Lianxiang Group. The committee determined that the suspicion of economic crimes had been made intangible by the nature of the response. An Investigative Report was deliberated upon and passed by the Communist Party organization of the Chinese Academy of Sciences. Key points in this Report are put for reference below:

1. When Hong Kong Lianxiang shares were listed on the market, Lianxiang used an increase in investment to raise the share ratio of Beijing Lianxiang and adjust the share relations of the other two parties: no problems exist.
2. Property ownership relations of the Daya Bay property are clear, no problems exist.
3. Regarding decisions about major investments of Lianxiang, these were verbally relayed to the Chairman of the Board, and were discussed at the President's Office.
4. Liu Chuanzhi did not recommend the name change of the "Han-card Administrative Department," it was brought up jointly by a person in the original Han-card Administrative Department and a person from the Group Office. This was done in order to enhance Lianxiang's software business and in line with the actual circumstances of the Han-card system in the marketplace. There is no question of "attack" in this.
5. No material was found to prove that Comrade Liu Chuanzhi had any personal economic problems.

After the investigation committee came out with this conclusion, it expressed its stand on more comprehensive issues as follows:

"We feel that scientific personnel cannot have the ultimate word on how research and development is carried out in a company, and how that R&D determines the funding of products. Key responsible people must make decisions based on the market and the situation of the company. In this instance, Liu Chuanzhi should have greater rights as spokesman and as decision-maker.

The split between Comrade Ni Guangnan and leadership of Lianxiang can be traced back to personal qualities of Comrade Liu Chuanzhi. We feel that this way of evaluating problems is frivolous and irresponsible. Comrade Ni Guangnan adopted methods that allowed him to carry out investigations and propose theories on his own. As a result, the opinions he raised were mainly without reliable evidence and were not in accord with the facts."

The Head of the Academy of Sciences at the time, Zhou Guangzho, attempted to ameliorate the relationship between the two men, but failed. Years later, he described the situation. "It could not go on, for Liu Chuanzhi would have quit. We had to choose between the two of them, one or the other. I figured there were many more scientists than entrepreneurs at the time. Entrepreneurs were an extremely scarce resource in China. No matter what else you might say about Liu Chuanzhi, he has the ability to grow a business. Out of the two, he had to be the one I would choose. Ni Guangnan is a pretty good scientist—that is undeniable. But there are far more scientists on a par with him than there are entrepreneurs the calibre of Liu Chuanzhi."

Ni Guangnan was now in a highly unfavorable position. He had lost this battle, and he had lost badly. On the morning of June 30, 1995, the Board of Directors asked 200 cadres to gather in the conference room on the sixth floor. Zhou Guangzho asked Li Zhijie to announce the conclusion of the investigation by the Chinese Academy of Sciences. In his new position as Chairman of the Board, Zeng Maochao read the decision of the Board of Directors. The decision was entered into the company files with a registration number of "Lian Board (95)001". It said, "With regard to the request put forward to the Board of Directors by Liangxiang Group President Liu Chuanzhi to rescind the title of Chief Engineer of the Lianxiang Group for Comrade Ni Guangnan: after consideration by the Board of Directors, we agree to remove Comrade Ni Guangnan from the post of Chief Engineer of the Lianxiang Group."

Liu Chuanzhi and Ni Guangnan sat on opposite ends of the first row of seats, their eyes avoiding one another. Li Qin stood up to say, "I feel tremendous sorrow and regret that the company has come to this pass." Zeng Maochao then expressed support for the way the Academy of Sciences had handled the matter. He also said, "This is the result of a necessary choice, it is the resolution that none of us would have wanted to see. But under the current situation, this choice is without doubt the only correct solution for the smooth development of the Lianxiang Group in the future."

Liu Chuanzhi had been told of the decision before the meeting, and so was able to prepare his thoughts and emotions appropriately. Asked to make some remarks, his speech was both passionate and individualistic. One of the most affecting parts of it was the following:

"I thank the Investigation Committee of the Academy for the tremendous amount of time and energy they have had to spend on my problems. I thank them for carrying on a multi-faceted investigation that in the end rewarded me with a pure-white verdict. Since starting the company in 1984, we have been through numerous storms. The Founders should be gratified that the Lianxiang edifice has been built with so much blood, sweat, and tears. They also should feel proud of the mutual friendship and trust that has developed in the company. As the company moves into fast-paced growth, it needs an extraordinary degree of sincerity and unity. The appearance of this kind of problem only turns people's thoughts in a painful direction.

"In March of last year when the President's Office held a working committee meeting, I wrote Comrade Ni Guangnan a letter about what I saw as intensifying contradictions. In it, I said that our mutual trust and solidarity formed the foundation of the Lianxiang structure. I hoped that he could respect the unity of the President's Office for the sake of Lianxiang's future. I spent an entire day and night writing this letter, at a time when there truly were a thousand other issues to handle. Old times came before me as I wrote.

"I remembered the extreme hardships we surmounted. I recalled how our Han-card was given the Number 1 Prize for National Scientific Advances and the entire company went crazy with joy. I thought of New Years Day of 1989 when I led the staff of Beijing Lianxiang south to Hong Kong to congratulate Ni-zong on the success of the development of the 286 motherboard, a staff that had the devotion almost of disciples towards him. I don't know if Lao Ni still remembers or not the Spring Festival company celebration in 1988 when all members of the President's Office made everyone laugh up on the stage?" Liu went on to recall other events and said, "All of this is engraved in my heart."

As he reached this point, Liu Chuanzhi began to cry. Everyone in the audience stared at him, their mouths open. Their boss was the epitome of a tough guy. They had never seen him break down.

Liu Chuanzhi wiped his eyes with a handkerchief and then continued. "Leu Tanping is a dedicated Hong Kong capitalist. He puts 120% of his being into his work. He and Ni Guangnan are totally different, though. They have lived in completely different environments. Their cultural backgrounds, worldview, management methods are different. If we talk about advantages filling in for defects, this would be one example: either the crippled would have to be willing to guide the blind man or the blind man willing to guide the cripple … and neither one is that easy. In resolving problems, one has to be fair and even-handed. As Chairman of the Board of Hong Kong Lianxiang, I must take as my starting point the benefit of Hong Kong Lianxiang while at the same time guaranteeing the benefit of Beijing Lianxiang. One must truthfully and fairly consider the benefits of both partners. I was careful to communicate frequently and effectively and as a result I gained the trust and respect of the Hong Kong partner. I thought that with a straightforward approach and a spirit of self-sacrifice, as well as a decisive and resolute way of handling problems, we could make things work. I discussed almost every aspect of Hong Kong Lianxiang in advance with Zeng Maochao and Li Qin, two board members; at that time Ni was not yet a board member. I also brought all major matters, in advance, to the attention of the President's Office in Beijing. I knew that it was very difficult for the Beijing comrades to comprehend just how hard it was to further every matter overseas. They would say, "first make the cake big, then consider how to divide it up:" this is easy to say but extremely hard to do. Ni Guangnan and Leu Tanping had conflicting ideas about the guiding philosophy of the R&D Center of Hong Kong Lianxiang. The contradictions expanded to every arena. Comrade Ni Guangnan saw my work in Hong Kong; we communicated on everything, from work to matters that were outside the scope of work. I believe that Ni Guangnan understands me. I cannot believe that Comrade Ni Guangnan could have made such accusations about me as a result of objective issues.

"From the end of last year, when Comrade Ni Guangnan and I had sharp differences of opinion about work, he began to accuse me of economic crimes before leaders of the Academy. As one issue was investigated, explained and rejected, another would be brought up. He was not going to rest until he had sent me to jail. The investigation committee from the Academy assumed that his doubts were the result of objective factors, while I felt he was intentionally out to harm me.

"Comrade Ni Guangnan and I have different views on the direction and course of the company's technology as well as certain management methods. For a President and a Chief Engineer not to agree is common—it is not irregular for an enterprise—but when the Chief Engineer cannot listen to the President's decisions, and uses violent methods in opposition, then that is not regular. This affair turned into a model example of methods used during the Cultural Revolution. It led to a vicious attack on a person's character, with the intent to "knock down" or destroy the opposition. Such methods are sickening. They turn resolvable problems into total opposition, into a situation that cannot be managed through compromise.

"As the legal representative of the company, the hardest thing I do is to take risks that are both economic and political. If I come through the risks happily on the other side, everyone shares in enjoying the benefits. If things do not go well, then as the legal representative I represent everyone else in tasting the bitter results. The political risk arises because our country's laws and policies are in a state of constant evolution and improvement. Enterprises have to understand the looseness, the lack of stringent laws and policies, during this transition period. The government has to understand what companies are confronting and allow them some room to maneuver in the face of immature policies. All of this has to go through a process of actual experimentation. A difference in interpretation, the angle from which one views things, can lead to absolutely different results. Even though we might approach sensitive issues with tremendous caution and trepidation, our actions can lead to a prison sentence all the same. If someone is sitting there fixing you with intense scrutiny, picking out issues and "criticizing from the higher plane of principle," then the leader of an enterprise has two possible courses: one is to resign, the other is to decline to take action. The second course means you sit there together with the enterprise, waiting for the final bullet.

"This year when the Academy's Committee again started investigating me based on Comrade Ni Guangnan's accusations, I was fairly passive for a while. This was a passivity that came after pain and anger. Pain because I had not been able to receive the understanding of someone I truly respected, pain because I was afraid that a lack of unity would influence Lianxiang's development. Anger due to being attacked beyond imagination. The passivity was because, yet again, I was being subjected to an accusatory investigation. I couldn't comprehend it, I felt wronged, I couldn't figure out whom I was really working for and whether or not it was worth carrying on. The leaders of the Academy and Comrades in the Investigation Committe did a lot of work. In the end, they definitely expressed their trust in me. Comrades of the President's Office also actively supported my work. I want to state very clearly that the cause of Lianxiang is the cause of the Academy of Sciences, and also the cause of the country.

"My speech today has been totally unlike that of a President. After eleven years, please permit my tears to flow freely for once. Please forgive me!"

Ni Guangnan sat unmoved while watching Liu Chuanzhi's unrestrained emotion. He clearly did not feel the matter justified Liu Chuanzhi's trauma. "It was pure acting," he later told a reporter. "As for removing me from my position, I'm glad, that's all." He had asked the Board of Directors not to hold this meeting; he had said he would be willing to resign on the basis of poor health. However, the Board of Directors wanted employees to have an opportunity to understand the entire affair. They resolved to go through with the event in order to disperse some of the cloud that had hovered over the company.

It was now Ni Guangnan's turn to speak. He rose slowly to his feet. With an impassive face, no script in his hands, he spoke in a voice that was soft and even. It was as though the results of the investigation that had just been announced, the decision to strip him of his position, the speech of Liu Chuanzhi, had nothing to do with him.

"Leaders, Comrades:
When I first started working, I focused on hardware since I originally studied computers and also wireless radio. Later, circumstances changed and I was able to study abroad. There I found that every person had his own terminal. Because of this I was able to learn a lot of things about software on my terminal and, coming back to China, I gradually moved in the direction of software. Changes in one's work environment are, so far as I am concerned, an opportunity to learn. Since I am being removed from my administrative position, I will have more time to do research. I feel I am still able to do a little something. Perhaps I can even do something of help to everyone.

Right now, I feel that the great goal of our new era is to raise the country through scientific teaching. Although responsibilities are different, positions are different, capabilities are different, just think of it: what we all can do is wholeheartedly work towards this goal. Each of us can do his own part. For this great purpose, our Lianxiang Group bears a particular responsibility. It can help in developing the people's computer industry. No matter what position we are in, as individuals we should not forget this greater purpose. Working wholeheartedly for this great purpose, we can be considered the most fortunate of people."

Those in the audience were waiting for him to do a "self-criticism" or else to counter-attack the President. Only in the last few sentences did he seem to respond to Liu Chuanzhi's speech:

> "Some things have come up in the company recently that led to my being asked about my role. I answered with three points: first, Ni Guangnan is still at Lianxiang. This is a fact. Second, I am still working. This too is a fact. Third, I ask the Chairman of the Board to transmit my comments back to the Academy since it is said that the Academy leaders are considering the question of allocating work. I would like for my opinion to be taken into consideration: so long as I can still work, I will work forever for Lianxiang."

Although the Board of Directors did not believe in broadcasting "family problems," and did not want this affair to get out, reporters could see that things were not right in the company. In the end, the affair was summed up by the media as a battle between the "market faction" and the "technology faction." As one of the more lively commentators of the latter 1990s, Geng Qiping, said, "it was a conflict between knowledge and capital." A group of young people had appointed themselves as critics of successful large computer enterprises and he was one of them. They were not willing to let this kind of thing go without comment—in their view, this was a necessary conflict as China moved towards a modern market economy.

Ni Guangnan was already an Academician in the Chinese Engineering Academy. This was no small matter, and behind him a large group of Academicians now declared that he had been treated unfairly. Worried that the matter would get out of hand and go beyond the ability of the Board of Directors to control, Li Zhijie and Zeng Maochao felt that that there was a need for greater political support. On July 20, the two men went to the State Science Commission where they presented a report on the course of events to two Deputy Chairpersons, Zhu Lilan and Hui Yongzheng. The record of the meeting makes clear that in the end the discussion returned to the issue of who had the final say in a Chinese enterprise, the CEO or the Chief Technical Officer. Hui Yongzheng stated that scientific personnel must obey the President. He added that the reason a lot of scientific results cannot be realized and made into products is that the inventor keeps all decision-making power to himself. Zhu Lilan tried to transcend the material nature of the dispute. She said to Zeng Maochao, "The responsibilities of a President and a Chief Engineer have to be clearly delineated. Who has the right to decide on what issues? When you have a group of high-level intellectuals you need some kind of organizational structure." She also noted, "You all must be scared, so scared that you come talk to us. I support neither Liu Chuanzhi nor Ni Guangnan: you yourselves have to adopt measures to resolve this. You must remind Liu Chuanzhi to assimilate the lessons learned. To a certain degree, Liu Chuanzhi is also responsible."

The implications of the issue itself were not, perhaps, so serious. Conflict among senior management is common in any country. The unique thing about China is not the controversial issues themselves but the method of resolving them, which has peculiarly Chinese qualities.

With the deposing of Ni Guangnan, Liu now modified a key management concept: "technology-engineering-trade." In the years before 1995, Liu used these words to describe the company's path of development. On March 19, 1990, for example, he described the two necessary preconditions for Lianxiang's success in a speech. The first was, "a market base both inside and outside China." The second was, "the three-dimensional structure that we are creating, formed of the integration of technology, engineering, and trade." He described this concept repeatedly over the following years. In the summer of 1995, however, for the first time he changed the order from "technology, engineering and trade" to "trade, engineering, and technology." This change was significant.

Liu Chuanzhi was later to spend considerable time explaining this modification to people inside and outside the company. The core of the idea could easily be explained as the relative weighting of "technology" and "trade". From this one can extrapolate to various issues touched upon already such as whose contributions were more important, those of Ni Guangnan or Liu Chuanzhi. Some people quite unabashedly said that the modification implied that Liu Chuanzhi was trying to cast off the influence of Ni Guangnan. When asked, Liu Chuanzhi said that this modification did not imply issues of who was first or last, who was to be emphasized and who was to be diminished. It had to do with the practical allocation of resources. Since the winter of 1993, the R&D Center of the company had been experiencing difficulties. It was steeped in a super-technical atmosphere and soaked up money, yet results could seldom be turned into products. If scientific results were eventually made into products, they were rarely successful. Liu Chuanzhi believed that no matter how good the technology might be, it was useless if there was not a clear channel for selling products.

Ni Guangnan naturally believed that the order should be "technology, engineering, trade." He pointed out that, "Lianxiang is a prime example of a company that relies on technology for its development. The greatest evidence of this is the Lianxiang Han-card."

Liu Chuanzhi had never denied the tremendous utility of the Han-card in the company's early history. At the same time he maintained that the company's biggest accomplishment was not in the technology per se, but in turning technology into money. "One of the tasks of a high-tech enterprise is to complete the process of turning products into money," he said. "It's a systems engineering issue." Scientific research was an important link in the chain but it was not the whole story. Under many circumstances it could not even be considered the most crucial link. Liu commented at one point, "A superb technology is marvelous but it's harder to find good managers. If you've got good technology but not a good CEO, you won't be able to make the thing work."

The "technology faction" disliked this statement. They said he must have forgotten those early hungry years when he came begging to Ni Guangnan to "come down from the mountain." The personal issues surrounding this debate in the 1990s gradually faded. What remains in the record are issues that have less to do with individuals than with structural change in systems. Although the emergence of new technologies is always exciting, in the early years of Lianxiang scientific personnel were stimulated by the results of sales, not the marvels of new design. Technology propelled the computer age forward, but if one relied only on technology, nothing would get done. As a journalist named Jeffrey Yang said in *Fortune* Magazine, "After a new invention comes out, it quickly loses its mysteries. What really changes the world is the ability to promote the technology." Yang used examples from the development of computers in the 1960s to prove that "science only provides the fuel, commerce is the real generator."

Fall of 1995: A rare moment of stability in the history of the company
The company's internal problems temporarily abated and waters were calm once again. Ni Guangnan had undeniably lost, but it was hard for Liu Chuanzhi to turn this personal victory into a victory for the entire company. A great rift had appeared in the spirit of the company. Relations between scientific staff and management were strained. Ni Guangnan continued to have his own office and a secretary within the company; his salary and all other benefits continued as before, but he no longer had the position of a Chief Engineer. Fortunately, a generation of younger people had already matured to the point that they could rely on their own intelligence and efforts. They began to fill in the trench between the two

sides. Eventually, the entire incident was regarded as a kind of tale from long ago in the company.

The fall of 1995 was a rare period of smooth sailing for Beijing Lianxiang. Management of the Computer Technology Research Institute was finally resolved. The heads of the forty-five other research institutes within the Chinese Academy of Sciences were amazed that everyone was focussing so much attention on Lianxiang. Revised by-laws of the Lianxiang Group were passed. For the first time, the investment ratio of partners was put into writing: Chinese Academy of Sciences Computer Institute 45%, Chinese Academy of Sciences 20%, employee shareholder group 35%. The first Lianxiang Pentium was born, based on the "Pentium Second CPU." This was the first time Chinese computers marched in step with the world in terms of new models. More than one hundred academics from the Central Communist Party School paid a visit to Lianxiang, all of whom were high-level government officials. Liu Chuanzhi made good on his promise to Sun Hongbin and invested RMB 5 million in Sun's real estate company after Sun emerged from prison. Other matters included the Year 2000 Plan, the bid for a Third-phase Japanese yen-denominated loan for Five Big Information Systems, the ribbon-cutting ceremony for the establishment of the Daya Bay S&T Park, the awarding of a prize to Lianxiang for being one of China's Famous Brands. Liu Chuanzhi became an "outstanding entrepreneur" in the Beijing Municipal electronics industries, Beijing Lianxiang received the Golden Horse Award, the highest honor of National Outstanding Industries in 1994, Hong Kong Lianxiang's was awarded ISO 9001 quality certification. The Computer Administration Department, after that drastic personnel reduction in the first year, began a major recruiting drive so that Lianxiang employees reached a headcount of 820 people. The first training sessions for new recruits and core employees were held. A new set of basic regulations for company cadres was set down, and a new set of standards for hiring new employees was formulated.

Liu Chuanzhi had asked the government to "make investigations any time" and this was now put into play. Yang Yuanqing announced that he had sufficient confidence in the quality of his computers, at which the Head of Quality Control, Li Zhiwen, drafted a "random sample document" and submitted it to the National Bureau of Technology Supervision, the organization directly responsible for product quality within the central government. Past experience of this body had indicated that enterprises generally evaded quality control supervision. Here was a company that was facilitating the process—the Bureau was naturally delighted, but its personnel was careful not to be deceived by appearances. They kept the times and places of surprise checks strictly secret as per their regulations regarding "sudden sampling." Lianxiang gladly agreed to this, only putting forth one condition: if the results of the investigation proved that computer quality was good, it wanted the government, in the name of the Bureau, to "applaud Lianxiang and say "well done"."

The Bureau was not going to declare something "well done" lightly, so it was quite rigorous. Checkers descended on the Beijing markets three times in July and August, randomly selecting three groups of Lianxiang computers, with three machines in each group. They tested these machines for 26 criteria in eight main categories including crate opening, exterior structure, function, safety, power supply adaptability, noise level, environmental adaptability, and electromagnetic compatibility. Parameters included working temperature, humidity allowances, shaking, jarring, dropping. Electromagnetic compatibility looked at magnetic field sensitivity, power source voltage, electric pressure, peak signal susceptibility, radiation, interference susceptibility and radiation interference. This inspection went on for twenty days and the results were kept secret: Liu Chuanzhi and Yang Yuanqing could not help but worry.

On September 14, a group of investigators suddenly appeared at the Lianxiang production base. They took 43 out of a batch of 141 486/66 computers. They repeated all tests on three machines, and put the other 40 through reliability tests. Nine days later, they declared that the four sudden-attack investigations proved that, in all respects, Lianxiang computers had passed with outstanding marks.

"Responsible Accountant"

Modern accounting was another of the disciplines that Lianxiang now began to impose on itself. A lady named Wang Lijie was one of the regular accountants in the Finance Department, but in 1995 she was given the task of holding financial training courses for the company. Through this, she was able to disseminate new financial concepts among its senior management.

Wang came to Lianxiang in 1993 after graduating with a degree in finance from the People's University. She had imagined that Lianxiang would have a sophisticated level of financial management and that the people around her would have a higher academic background than she did. She quickly discovered she was wrong. Overstressed and busy, company staff were lax in many respects and followed no regular systems. For a long time, she assumed the role of helping out when any area needed more attention. In order to get into Lianxiang she had taken a course in applied computer science. Once in the company, she discovered to her amazement that many finance people in this computer company were still using abacusses and, moreover, were keeping accounts by hand. She had used an abacus till 1994 and was not afraid of the device—in school she had become adept at pushing the beads. But as she later said, "to my way of thinking, a high-tech company really shouldn't be operating in this fashion."

Computers had just entered the management systems of the company and still were not awarded to all positions. More than a dozen people in the finance department shared two "286" machines. These were not networked so that information had to be sent from one computer to another by use of a 5" floppy disk. One of Wang Lijie's responsibilities before leaving work every day was to take a floppy, go up to the warehouse on the second floor and copy data, then take it up to the finance department on the third floor and insert it into a floppy disk drive there. The biggest problem was not that the technological measures were backward, but that the financial way of thinking had problems. The company mistakenly felt that the responsibilities of accountants and what in China are called *chu-na*, or people who "give out money and take it in," were limited to recording accounts and producing forms. In fact, the significance of accounting to a company goes far beyond these tasks.

One of the most significant events of 1995 was the renovation of the company's financial system. As Wang Lijie later explained to people, "The financial system of a company should be able to increase the efficiency of a company's utilization of capital. This in turn lowers the company's financial risk." Beijing Lianxiang's loans from banks had reached a level of RMB 250 million, while Hong Kong Lianxiang's remaining loans were RMB 1.4 billion. These loans were secured on the basis of "trust" and did not require any collateral, indicating that the company's finances were regarded as fairly mature. This situation was in stark contrast to the financial "trust crisis" facing the country as a whole. The company's by-laws stipulated: The fiscal year will start from March 26 of the western calendar and go to March 25 of the following year. In the first month of every fiscal year, the company's Finance Department will prepare a statement of assets and liabilities and a statement of profit and loss." This was to accommodate the regulations of Hong Kong's stock market authorities.

Conscious of how financial regulations could have a major influence on company profits, management began to encourage the Finance Department to implement greater supervision. Guo Wei was General

Manager of the Finance Department at the time and the Chief Accountant was a man named Sun Zhanming. These two were in charge of a set of fairly strict, but somewhat trivial regulations. Their basic principle was that any given product was not allowed to stay in the warehouse for more than 90 days.

The company now established a set of new positions called Responsible Accountant. The implication was that responsibilities for financial accounting were to be distributed throughout the company: each Department was to have its own Responsible Accountant. The system embodied an important concept: although all Departments were integrated under the umbrella of the company, each now became both a profit center and an accounting unit. Wang Lijie was the Responsible Accountant for the Computer Administration Department. This constituted an independent profit center, and Wang Lijie now had to clarify and make transparent all of the Department's "internal savings," its accounts receivable, its bad accounts, its inventory, which pieces of business made money, which lost money, and so on. She represented the company in this effort, not Yang Yuanqing.

The new accounting system allowed the company as a whole to make more accurate forecasts, but needless to say it also put greater pressure on everyone. One of the first tasks of each Responsible Accountant was to explain the new system clearly to each manager. This was done through training. The point of this training was not to impose constraints on people but to institute a whole new concept of how a system works. The first training session was held on September 14, 1995.

The entire company was being transformed through the implementation of the new system. Financial conditions of the company began to turn around, overstocking declined and payments were faster. Unfortunately, the new system allowed contradictions that had been building up within the company to explode once again, something Wang had not anticipated. The word for contradiction in Chinese is composed of the two terms "sword" and "shield": these were again pointed at each other, as described below.

Yuan Yuanqing learns how to compromise
Yang Yuanqing was becoming more self-confident. He had charged onto the stage, grabbing territory from his competitors, taking Lianxiang market penetration from 4% to 6%. He was still young, though, and neglected a cardinal rule in China, which is that when you are happy, you need to be careful not to make others unhappy. Right now, quite a few people were

unhappy. Many were his colleagues. Some were young and felt it unfair to see him promoted above them; they left the company to do other things. Older colleagues didn't like the way Yang seemed to be implementing new systems. Although he still politely called them "Teacher," the problems were reaching a point of violent conflict.

If psychological barriers between the two generations had been carefully managed by accommodations on both sides, the situation might have been defused. In ancient Chinese wisdom, this was known as practicing a kind of Tai Chi Chuan of management: going with the flow, accommodating nature, taking retreat as advance, overcoming hard with soft. Yang Yuanqing had never been this kind of person, however, and the computer market also did not allow time for such things. The contradictions erupted in 1994, when the older generation wanted to pass on to him responsibility for several thousand computers stuck in the warehouse. Yang Yuanqing knew he could not sell these computers. He refused to accept them as his responsibility. Yang Yuanqing had been doing everything he could to set up the agenting distributed-sales system and he didn't care about losing old customers in the process. At issue with some of the older generation was the fact that old relations would be severed, and with them long-established financial benefits.

Everyone was concerned about the profits of the company but the methods different people wanted to employ were not the same. The older generation rushed to Liu Chuanzhi to complain. Liu Chuanzhi supported Yang Yuanqing in the important issues. He was willing to put everything into setting up this new distribution system, and he was willing to allow Yang to increase the incomes of his subordinates. He even turned to the older generation of Vice-Presidents and said, "we have to let a few people wear leather shoes now, while most of the people will have to continue to wear straw sandals. Do your best to support Yang Yuanqing because he's out there playing hardball right now." At the same time, Liu Chuanzhi hoped that Yang could understand and forgive the bitterness of the older generation. At the very least, he wanted him to iron out those "bad accounts" that had been caused by warehoused goods. This was in line with a Chinese approach to common decency. Liu Chuanzhi went in person to persuade Yang Yuanqing. No matter what he said, though, the young man was not willing to accept the warehoused goods unless he was permitted to sell them at an extremely low price and have the loss be the responsibility of the previous administration.

Yang was a believer in what was fair and just. He was not flexible. He would not compromise on this. As a result, his relations with those around him became extremely stressful. Yang resolved to take back some of the privileges given to salespeople in setting the company's selling price—this was opposed, since price flexibility is often where a salesman can "give" benefits to the buyer in order to get a sale. Yang wanted to standardize prices with all of the agents. In 1995, towards the end of the year, the conflict among senior leadership reached a peak. Yang Yuanqing, with solitary power, opposed his older-generation predecessors, while Liu Chuanzhi "sat on the fence". "I sided with neither group," he said, "which meant that pressure from both came down on me."

In truth, Liu Chuanzhi very much appreciated the way Yang Yuanqing took control. These two company commanders, one old, one young, were and are very similar. Both are firm, rigid, unselfish and unafraid, undeterred by adversity, and full of passion. Both have the righteous cause of the nation in mind, and they treat the welfare of the company as if it were their own life. If one were to analyze the differences between the two, the younger man, Yang Yuanqing, had a quality of absolute steeliness. He failed to realize that what could be an outstanding quality in some ways, if pushed to extremes, could be harmful to others. Liu Chuanzhi, on the other hand, was a master of compromise. He was schooled in uncommon sensitivities due to his life experiences. The most acute and deeply significant of Liu's intellectual qualities was his ability to compromise. While he stubbornly set himself to changing those things he had the ability to change, he also accomodated those things he could not change. Most importantly, he had sufficient intelligence to distinguish between them.

Liu Chuanzhi does not like the word "compromise." He has noted that the term implies too much passivity. It often allows one to do things against one's own conscience. Before employees, he much preferred to say, "If you find there is a wall in the direction in which you wish to go, then you have to blow a hole in the wall to get through. However, you then have a wall with a hole in it. Why not just walk a little ways down the wall and find a doorway through which you can pass?"

In China, though, compromise, endurance, concealment, tolerating ridicule and bearing a load are often magic weapons for defeating the enemy. In an interview with the American magazine *Fortune*, Liu Chuanzhi once admitted that he only used 30% of his energies in actually managing the enterprise, that the other 70% was used to handle outside matters. "You have to sacrifice some of your individual leadership rights and freedom, do more accepting and compromising," he told this perplexed American journalist. "Go with the flow, in order to add some lubrication or sliding room with the outside environment. Make sure that you are not just increasing problems for a company already facing ferocious competition in the marketplace."

Absolute justice is not necessarily the wisest choice under most circumstances. When to compromise versus when to insist on what is just and right is something that only highly intelligent people who have been through hard times, and have trained themselves to the utmost, are able to get just right.

The unending conflicts in the company led Liu Chuanzhi to make a decision: he would teach the young people how to compromise. In early 1996, Yang Yuanqing and all senior managers under him received an order to come to Number 505. For many years this has been the most important room in the company; all important decisions are made here. Yang and his people sat along one side of the long table and were laughing and smiling when the door opened and Liu Chuanzhi, Li Qin and Zeng Maochao marched in. Their expressions were grim, their eyes looked straight ahead. Liu Chuanzhi chose a seat directly opposite Yang. He proceeded to deliver a stream of reprimands right into the young man's face. He said that although the Computer Administration Department was not at all easy and its contributions were great, it had utterly disregarded the feelings of people around it. Liu allowed his gaze to rest on Yang Yuanqing as he said, without the slightest give in his voice, "Don't think that it was a sure thing that you received this position. We faced tremendous pressure in giving this stage of operations to you. Faced with contradictions among many kinds of forces, you really should work together with one heart, establish your position gradually, strive for an even larger stage. You can't just pay attention to what is in front of your nose. Everyone has been coming to me, asking me to do what's fair. If you don't compromise at all, how do you expect me to resolve things?"

Liu Chuanzhi announced two decisions on the spot: first, within one year, Yang Yuanqing must make several compromises. Second, Liu Xiaolin was immediately being transferred to a position in the Planning Department.

Traumatized, Yang Yuanqing stayed awake the entire night. The next day, the first thing he saw on his desk when he got to his office was a long letter from Liu Chuanzhi. Ever after, he was to keep this letter nearby: it became an enduring inspiration to him both in terms of work and his own character. Later he was to receive ultimate control of the company. When Liu had his 60th birthday, Yang Yuanqing and a group of young people went to pay their respects. While there, Yang asked Liu Chuanzhi: "That day when that meeting ended, just as you were leaving you told me you wanted to clear accounts with me. Do you still remember those accounts?" Liu Chuanzhi smiled without replying, for he knew that Yang Yuanqing was referring to the following letter:

"Yuanqing:

Since coming to Hong Kong, my own tasks have been absorbing and I haven't had much time, but I have not felt easy about how you are doing. Once I looked into it, I realized that my communication with you over these years has been inadequate. All we have talked about have been specific issues that needed resolving. Objective reasons for this have been that you and I are both busy. Subjective reasons are that I did not place enough importance on our communications. I want to use a little leisure time right now to write you. Written communication is rather cold but I don't want to seem formal, I'm just taking up my pen and writing wherever the spirit moves me. This is a casual record of my feelings, not necessarily logical. If it is too incomplete and I don't finish in one sitting I'll write more later.

I like young people who are capable. The reason the boss of a privately-administered company likes capable people is that they can help him make money. That one aspect is enough. A boss of a state-administered company naturally hopes that there is also some emotional match within the company. Nobody wants a successor who can expand the business but whose relations are bad with the previous administration. Here's a joke to illustrate the point: in finding a mate, if the lady is simply pretty, something like highly capable, that is, but doesn't love me, what's the use?

Lianxiang is already a fair-sized business. According to the plan it is going to get even bigger. If the core leadership is not cultivated right now, then all of this is empty talk.

In my mind's eye, what sort of young person should core leadership include? First, ethical. This term includes several meanings: first, he must be loyal to Lianxiang's cause, which is to say that his personal benefit submits to Lianxiang's benefit. Speaking publicly, this is the most important principle. Speaking off the record, there is another principle: he must be able to handle the previous generation of Founders with true heart and true mind. I feel that this should be included as one of the meanings of "ethical". In a purely commercial society, after the Founders of an enterprise grow it and then hand it over to the next team, they get a well-deserved material as well as emotional reward. In our society, since the system is different, neither of these can necessarily be guaranteed. This makes the older generation hang onto power all the harder. They would rather delay real business than hand over to the next team. My responsibility is to get the older cadres to pass the baton peacefully and smoothly, but at the same time to guarantee their interests. Moreover, my task is to select core leadership from among the new layers of talent that lie under older layers of ossified personnel.

Around the boundaries of such issues as "talented" and "ethical" lie other factors. Young leaders have to be unselfish. They have to make severe demands on themselves, while being lenient and expansive toward their colleagues. They have to exhibit outstanding leadership ability, while still being humble in recognizing the strong points in others. They have to go over their own shortcomings in their own minds constantly and cultivate qualities that make others follow them. You know my theory about the "big chicken" and the "little chicken." Only when you have trained yourself to be as big as a rooster will little chickens be willing to admit that you are bigger than they are and only when you are as big as an ostrich will they happily follow you. When you have won this "happily follow" status, you have prepared the conditions within your own generation but not necessarily in the one above you. Naturally in state-owned enterprises, people lower down mostly follow senior management unwillingly: the leadership team is hard to unite. If I don't consider this problem in advance, if I just simply appoint someone as they do in the usual state-owned company, it may bring disaster to our Lianxiang team.

I want to train you in this direction. When you were transferred to the Computer Administration Department from the CADF Department, and then in that same year accomplished such wonderful things, I was delighted. I was glad at the success of the business but even happier to have uncovered this talent. Not long after you had started work, though, various contradictions emerged. I am against trying to make someone perfect. If I simply try to slap all of my own experience on you, it may make things hard for you. But we want to try to unify our thinking, do our utmost to guarantee that the environment for the Computer Department is supportive. Facts have proven your capabilities and also your unwillingness to stop till you've reached your goal. You have that kind of spirit.

When problems began to develop, I should have supported conditions that would aid in your growth, while at the same time pointing out your inadequacies. I should have paid attention to how you might rise to a higher stage. And you, at this time, what should you be thinking of? I feel you might perhaps start by summarizing both your better aspects and your weaknesses. Think about what support Lianxiang has given you in achieving what you've been able to do—this might make you able to evaluate your accomplishments more accurately. What do you have to be careful of in rising to a higher stage?

When I am clear in my own mind that you satisfy conditions for core leadership, things that I want to do for you are: 1. Improve my understanding of you in all respects. You should grab every opportunity to discuss all manner of things with me, not just things related to work. 2. Improve my lines of communication with you. I want you to understand my own good side and my failings, the weaker points in my character. Only then can we have a true communication. 3. Help each other out. I want to use methods you can accept in guiding you to improve shortcomings, in moving toward goals.

I wrote the above in an hour on Saturday and an hour on Sunday. Right now, I have to go out and so I'm just going to finish up. Below are items that I want to hear from you on: 1. Are you truly of a mind to be able to "eat hardship," to be able to bear injustice, as you climb to a higher peak? 2. After having thought it over, if you do intend to advance toward this goal, what do you lack that will hold you back?

When you have responded with a letter to me, I will write again. That's it for now. Wishing you all the best!
Liu Chuanzhi"

Prelude to a battle of life or death

Problems that Liu Chuanzhi encountered in the mid-1990s were similar to those that the Vice-Premier of the country, Zhu Rongji, was confronting. Although purchasing power of Chinese had risen rapidly, an appetite for consumption had not kept pace. This was a more pressing issue than that of new technology revolutions. The Sixteen Articles that Zhu Rongji had promulgated in 1993 put the rapidly advancing Chinese economy on a certain path along which it could be controlled. In 1994, his revolutionary steps in promulgating the "Great Program" were widely supported. Before taking over the post of Premier, he had to "hand over" to the bosses of Chinese enterprises one important thing: an understanding of what means they could use in selling the things that they had produced.

The country was transitioning from being a seller's market to being a buyer's market. Commodities in certain markets saw greater supply than demand and this applied to the computer industry. As mentioned, the mid-1990s marked the historical starting point for computers entering Chinese homes. Lianxiang now declared that competition in the computer market had risen to such a level that it would soon become a life-or-death battle for the company.

Bill Gates introduced his Windows '95™ with a US$500 million promotion budget. In March 1996, Gates brought the Windows '95™ Chinese version into the Chinese market. The biggest Chinese computer manufacturers seemed to like IBM better. For its newest generation of Pentium computers and the "Wang-quan server," Lianxiang chose IBM's OS/2Warp operating system. Unfortunately, this system soon proved to be a disaster and by September of 1996 even IBM had to buy licenses for Windows '95™.

In addition to hand-to-hand combat between operating systems, 1996 saw the appearance of more applications in software and multimedia technology. Multimedia had been declared the "future direction of the world" at China's National Computer Exhibition in the summer of 1995. The year also saw the rise of the Internet in China, already stimulating great excitement in America. Bill Gates's reaction was initially slow but he saw the potential in December and wrote a letter to all Microsoft employees called "The Great Wave of the Internet." In China, the government did not at all understand the Internet's implications, so did not prohibit it in any way. University students were already secretly using computers in classrooms to get on the Net. Like addicts, they became China's first net-people and were as excited as if they had eaten the apple in the Garden of Eden. A company called Yinghaiwei was born this year, and became China's first Internet company. It hung out an ad at the Baishiqiao intersection that read, "Enter the new Internet era 1,000 meters to the north." Yinghaiwei started the first Internet Discussion group, where a young employee explained for the benefit of participants what the Internet was all about. He declared, "the idea of a global village is about to become reality."

Lianxiang commissioned a market report from the Beijing Commercial Information Consulting Center. The report came out on July 20, 1995, and its conclusions showed that only one Chinese manufacturer appeared among the top ten personal computer brands being bought in China. That was Lianxiang, which came in at Number 5. Lianxiang held 6.6% of the market. Ahead of it were Compaq (27.3%), AST (13.6%), IBM (11.5%), and Hewlett-Packard (7.3%). Behind it were DEC, DELL and Taiwan Hongji. This report also listed in detail the prices of each company's computers, the amount of their inventory, and their sales methods. All indications were that competition was intense. IBM claimed to help solve all problems but in point of fact Compaq was the star of the year with its computer sales rising 30% for two years in a row. In 1994, it surpassed the world sales of IBM. In 1995, it beat AST in the China market. As expected, AST continued along its declining path. Losing US$98.7 million in 1996, its output of computers fell 19%, its CEO resigned, and its Board of Directors decided to sell its shares to Korea's Samsung for US$250 million. It began procedures for leaving the China market. For years, Lianxiang had been lying in wait for the market share to be given up by AST—this largest share of the China cake now looked as though it would be eaten by bigger, craftier wolves trotting alongside.

These wolves included the State-owned computer companies, and various new brands that had appeared on the market such as Peking University Founder, and Xi'an Haixing [Seastar]. Founder announced that, in the first month of 1995, it had already sold 3,000 sets, and that next year it was aiming for third in the country. Xi'an Haixing called itself "the most competitive to Founder's computers in terms of price." All of these computers were termed "trash brands" by consumers at the time. In truth, the most flourishing brands at the time in ZGC were not the famous international brands, and they were not the "trash brands," but rather the "assembled machines." Components were bought from suppliers and, with a screwdriver in one hand and boxes in the other, companies would go door to door and assemble right then and there. One hand took the money as the other delivered the goods. There was absolutely no quality control procedure, and there was no production license. Once this business started in the mid-1990s it continued to flourish until it held 10% of market share.

More than a market phenomenon, this could be called a kind of social phenomenon. Manufacturers that proudly held official production licenses from the government could no nothing about it. The total number of companies in ZGC declined for the first time in ten years: those that died in 1995 far exceeded the number that came in fresh to the market. According to the *Beijing S&T* Newspaper, in 1995, 30% of the companies in ZGC suffered a loss, while 50% were only able to maintain a flat income. They had 20% profit, but considering that inflation that year reached 18%, there clearly was too much duplication among companies. The question was really, "What is the Future of Electronics Street in ZGC?" At that point, nobody knew.

The Han-card that had made Lianxiang famous stopped production in 1995. Inventory was sold off cheaply. At the same time, Lianxiang computers were shining like the rising sun. Lianxiang produced 105,780 computers in 1995 and for the first time surpassed the production of Great Wall to rank first in the country. From the beginning, it was clear that computers would come up against more tribulations than Han-cards, for China had started to move from an "era of explosive profits" to an "era of tiny profits." Some even said that the computer market provided "no profit but a lot of glory," although this was an exaggeration. It was a fact that the computer industry in China contained a group of highly intelligent and talented people competing for coolie wages. Profits kept declining. Three years earlier, the average gross profit of the world's computer industry was 40%; now it stood at around 20%. Eight years earlier, you could make RMB 20,000 profit by selling one computer in ZGC, now a RMB 200 profit would make a salesman happy.

Notebook computers packed with a Pentium chip began to appear on the Chinese market for the first time in 1995. Unfortunately these were expensive and there were few takers; the competition was still in the desktop models. Lowering prices had once been a reflection of being able to lower production costs; now it became a powerful weapon in killing the opponent. Within the space of one year, Compaq dropped the price of its series by between 11% and 23%. Lianxiang was surrounded by a group of foreign makers—solitary and helpless, it was forced to react. After the E, G, and P series prices were set in October of 1994, prices did not move for six months but eventually the company could not avoid announcing a new policy: it dropped prices for the entire line of products from 4.8% to 21.5%. Unfortunately this still did not keep up with changes in the world market. As the fall of 1995 began, Compaq repeatedly announced it was dropping its desktop models by 13 to 25%. IBM reacted within two weeks and dropped its series price by 20%, Hewlett-Packard's response was slightly slower and on November 1 it announced new prices for the entire globe. Foreign manufacturers advertised that their computers were cheaper. They clearly did not know that the Chinese custom has always been to "buy into a rising market, not a falling market." The situation was exacerbated by some so-called computer experts advising: "hold on tight to your purse, for a new PC price war is about to start again."

1995 ended as a reporter from the American *Wall Street Journal* came to Beijing and spent several hours in the reception room on the sixth floor of the Lianxiang Group. What he wanted to know was, "How could a Chinese brand named Lianxiang be among the first ten in the Chinese computer market?" He asked this question since he knew even better than Lianxiang just how powerful its opponents were.

Liu Chuanzhi did not meet with the reporter. He was in Hong Kong preparing his speech for the company's Christmas Party. Liu's speeches were all written by himself, and he did not use a computer in drafting them but wrote by hand on paper. On this day there was no drafting paper at hand, so he grabbed an Apple Computer envelope that happened to be nearby and wrote his thoughts in tiny characters.

On Christmas Eve, he told the Hong Kong audience the story of his experiences in founding the company, he talked of the storms that computers had weathered over the years, he told of the development strategy he had formulated for the company. Naturally, he did not forget to thank the government, the banks, the media, and Lianxiang suppliers, as well as its hundreds of thousands of customers. He made it sound as though everything was going smoothly. One year later he publicly confessed that the speech had been the most difficult and awkward he had ever made. The company was actually facing an immense crisis. It was fighting a "war on two fronts".

8

FROM PIG-RAISING FOR EVERYONE TO COMPUTERS FOR EVERYONE

What factors are on our side if we're fighting a war in China? We have the local topography of our Chinese system. Our costs are low, our government and people are supportive. If we go abroad, do we still have those?

Liu Chuanzhi

L iu Chuanzhi liked war stories and often used battles as analogies in explaining the road to market success. Everyone knows that fighting a battle on two fronts is a soldiers' nightmare, which is what Liu was facing in the spring of 1996. On the northern front, Beijing Lianxiang had to break through the encirclement of western countries' computers; on the southern front, Hong Kong Lianxiang had lost HK$190 million in the past twelve months and, if the outflow did not stop, the company would soon be bankrupt. A close read of Lianxiang's history up to now makes it clear that this was the most dangerous and also the most exciting step along the whole road.

Liu Chuanzhi positioned himself on the "southern front," trying to prevent total defeat for Hong Kong. At the same time, he ordered Yang Yuanqing to assume personal command in Beijing, to use his courage, strategizing, and also his resolute trust in Moore's Law, to begin a "scorched-earth" counterattack.

The decisive moment of the war

Yang Yuanqing had determined that by early 1996 at the very latest, Lianxiang should become First in the Chinese Market, surpassing Compaq, IBM, AST and Hewlett-Packard. Under his administration, sales of computers had tripled, but still only accounted for 12% of total company revenue. In terms of market share, Lianxiang machines did not even come close to Compaq's one-third of the market. When Yang Yuanqing told his ambition to Liu Xiaolin, who was just then compiling a Three-year Plan, Liu replied, "Yuanqing, have you gone crazy? What makes you think we can be Number One within three years?"

"I've figured it out," said Yang. "It's true the others are ahead of us, but we'll use marathon methods. They're sprinting. If we can make sure our pace is consistent then sooner or later there will be a day when we put on the gas and overtake them."

Yuan Yuanqing told Liu Xiaolin to put this into his plan. Then he went in search of Ying Qi, in charge of production. He asked him to figure out how much assembly-line production capacity would be needed to meet this plan, exactly how much they would have to expand the plant, how much increased investment it would require, how many experienced workers they lacked. Then he ordered the person responsible for materials supply, Qiao Song, to figure out purchasing quantities required for the Number One plan, to look at whether or not he wanted to change the purchasing process, find new suppliers, and so on. He instructed Liu Xiaolin to write all the results into the Three-year Plan, he put it in a plastic folder, and bound it into a booklet so that, with proper ceremony, it could be submitted to the President's Office as well as employees. "All employees in the company should be clear about this goal," he said. "Then we put our face toward Number 1 and march in that direction." Some asked him how he planned to do it. He answered, "All day long I'll keep looking at the costs of materials, for one. I'll get a clear idea of what yesterday was like, what today is like, what tomorrow is going to be like."

He knew that the company's future depended on winning this battle. He called it, "a matter of life and death". Yang Yuanqing was extremely meticulous: if he did not have full command of something he didn't begin it. For several weeks, he compared price information on Intel processors. He had an acute understanding of pricing and he paid specific attention to the chip manufacturers arrayed behind Intel, including the American companies CYRIX, AMD, and TI. The market share of smaller companies added together was only 30%, but they were in hot pursuit of the giant ahead of them. They kept putting out similar products to Intel's, while setting their prices slightly lower. Their tech-follower strategy appeared to be successful, so that Intel did not dare slow down. The resulting price declines benefited all downstream computer manufacturers.

On February 1, 1996, Yuang Yuanqing received a report saying that Intel had announced that the price of its mainstream product, the Pentium 100MHz Chip, would be lowered from US$278 to US$195. One week later, further information came in: market experts predicted that in the next three months the Pentium 150 MHz Chip would drop from US$804 to US$600, and the 100MHz chip would drop further to US$130. Intel appeared to be placing all bets on the Pentium, hoping that this one throw of the dice would cast off the followers behind it.

"We always follow foreign brands," said Yang, "but they bring their most backward products to China, things that have been old inventory in the warehouse. We all know this, but we've never had the power to change it because our own brand is too weak. Customers just buy what foreigners send them. Now, however, things are beginning to be different." They were quite different. Lianxiang's brand was rising, and China had reached the key turning point of substituting Pentiums for the "486."

Yang Yuanqing saw that he could profit from the decline in CPU prices. A Pentium 75MHz originally priced at RMB 15,000 was now priced at RMB 9,999: buying it for his machines, he could still be profitable. He tested the plan with just a few of his agencies: lowering the price but not diminishing the package of components, and the new products were well received. Foreign computer companies were advertising all over China, but to Chinese customers it was a wiser choice to spend half the money to buy the same computer. Yang Yuanqing then ordered an increase in production from 300 machines a day to 1000. He told sales personnel to prepare to send a stream of computers all over China.

March 15, 1996 deserves mention, whether in Lianxiang's own history or the history of the Chinese computer industry. After countless setbacks, Lianxiang computers for the first time appeared on the marketplace as a strong contender. Compaq and IBM were indisputably Kings of the Computer World, but now they discovered that they had to face a young and vigorous opponent. The Lianxiang Group announced on this day that all Pentium Series under their own banner had lowered prices. The entry-level model, the 75MHz, was selling at RMB 9,999. This was the first time in the global computer industry that a Pentium had been sold for less than RMB 10,000.

When the new price appeared on the market it stirred tremendous unease among other computer manufacturers. Foreign manufacturers had always been sensitive to price wars, but this time it was Chinese makers who made the first response. On April 10, Tongchuang announced that its Pentium 75 would be selling at RMB 9,700. On April 12, Founder announced that it would drop its Pentium 75 to RMB 10,000. On April 15, Langchao announced that it would drop its entire Pentium series by 20% to 30%.

Yang Yuanqing scrutinized reports sent to him daily by salespeople from all regions of China. He had placed his bet and was waiting for customers to flock behind him, and he couldn't help but be anxious. After all, a batch of 486s still stood in his warehouse: he was forcing himself to accept the loss and just get rid of them. "If the Pentium is below 10,000," he told salespeople, "how much can the 486 be worth?" His plan was to compensate for the loss on the 486 with the success of the Pentium.

In the end, Yang was successful. Orders began to flow in like running water, so that people in the company had little time to rest. In the first month, Lianxiang's daily output of computers exceeded 1,000, and the 486s that had caused so much trouble were sold at the same time, so there was no inventory. Not only did the gains cover the losses, but the gamble had made RMB 5 million of net profit. The triumph exceeded everyone's wildest dreams.

When spring ended, the foreign manufacturers still had not responded. They watched the great counterattack of the "united army of Chinese computers" but they held back their soldiers and didn't move. They still sold their own 486s at RMB 15,000 and Pentiums at a price of more than 20,000. Even Yang Yuanqing was puzzled. For the first time, he began to think, "The decision-making of foreign companies is not all that nimble. They seem pretty slow to respond. It also could be that they belittle the strength of their enemy. They take Lianxiang's carefully planned campaign to be some kind of fluke."

If foreigners felt that they could go back to their old ways after the spring market, they were wrong. The "final battle" in Yang Yuanqing's plan turned out to be a continuous series of actions. What he wanted was not merely a bull's eye, he wanted to change the rules of the game. March 15, 1996 was just the beginning of this story. Yang Yuanqing had a substantial force behind him, namely the prevailing mood of the people. The reason he was able to deliver such a resounding cannonball was that he capitalized on the timing and the general mood of the times in China.

1996: the Year of National Industries
As Yang Yuanqing and his subordinates were secretly deploying their armies for a campaign to be Number One, a similar movement was

appearing throughout China in other fields. An economic movement galvanized by Chinese patriotism was building.

The World Trade Organization (WTO) officially supplanted the General Agreement on Trade and Tariffs at the end of 1995. This contributed to the process of "opening up" China. Chairman Jiang Zemin announced in Osaka, Japan, that the Chinese government had decided to lower import taxes by at least 30%, which would affect more than 4,000 of the 6,000 kinds of imported commodities. He announced that the government was also getting rid of the quota and licensing system for 174 kinds of products. Implementation of all of this was to be started in 1996. Pressure on the Chinese government to speed up its "opening" was brought to bear from two different directions. On the one hand, the Americans haggled endlessly with Minister Wu Yi, Head of the Chinese Ministry of Foreign Relations and Trade. On the other hand, a pent-up patriotism in China's economic circles burst forth. A nationalistic TV documentary was broadcast on CCTV in March of 1996. The editors chose exactly the right time, for this was when both the National People's Congress and the National People's Political Consultative Committee meetings were being held. In Shanghai, China's most important industrialized city, a popular slogan circulated: "Take back lost territory." As if in response, the government brought back a brand that had been sold off to foreigners, a kind of toothpaste. China paid a high price for this and the media clamored about it for days. Much of the news was not good, however. In Beijing, a journalist named Duan Gang published an article in the *Beijing Youth Journal* with the headline, "How much longer can Lianxiang survive?" Two reporters of the *S&T Daily*, Sun Danhong and Leng Wensheng, interviewed the President of the Haier Group, Zhang Ruimin. The journalists knew that Haier had just received acclaim for being "China's most valuable brand." They hoped to hear some inspiring words. Instead, Zhang Ruimin lamented, "Does the country really want its own national industries? If not, then we should take advantage of the fact that our enterprise is still young and pretty and just sell her off." Reporters asked, "What is the direction of national industries?" knowing that the term "national" in Chinese incorporates the words for "people" or even "tribe of people," which reinforces its patriotic appeal. Zhang replied, "If the external environment for national enterprise development is good, then I can make Haier very big. If not, then I will try to be the last one to die." By "external environment" he meant support from Chinese consumers.

Public opinion is like a big wave. One of those standing at the top of the wave was the Editor-in-Chief of the *Economic Daily*, Ai Feng. He put together a conference on Chinese Famous Brands in Hefei, Anhui Province.

Hoping to pump some spirit into Chinese enterprises, he refused to allow foreign enterprises to participate. In the industries already open to foreign competition, one or two Chinese enterprises were all that remained. These industries included home electronics, beverages, cosmetics, value-added foodstuffs, and beer. Foreign giants beseiged Chinese brands, which a reporter from CCTV, Zhang Xi, now called, "The last ramparts." Lianxiang's Chen Huixiang was writing a book called "Why Liangxiang" at the time, and he wrote details of the conference into this book. "On the world economic stage," he wrote, "the real representatives of countries are their enterprises, just as athletes are a nation's representatives in the Olympics. Competition between enterprises is quite self-interested; national competition is just as self-interested. No country will struggle for the sake of some hypothetical greater good, for another country's benefit. That won't happen. No matter how the world flows increasingly into one channel, it will not channelize to the point that "they" and "we" are indistinguishable."

From 1994, a call to "Raise high the banner of national brands" sounded throughout China. China-brand computers had encountered quality and pricing problems in the past. Now, every time consumers voiced dissatisfaction, they were reminded that they were contributing to their own interests in buying China-made machines. One reporter asked Liu Chuanzhi, "If China loses its own "national industries," in point of fact, so what?" "So what?!" Liu Chuanzhi opened his eyes wide in answer. "Nothing at all, it just allows our people to be slaughtered!"

The Northern Front
When spring was over, a company named Yuanliu Consulting and Research Company, Ltd., put out a stimulating report. It found that many more people were using computers than those who had one at home. Among those using computers, the Lianxiang brand was "most liked," Great Wall was second, and IBM third.

After mobilizing the Spring Offensive, 10,000 Lianxiang computers were sold in the first month, while 18,000 were sold in the second month. These were twice the figures for 1995, and at the same time the profit was RMB 9.3 million. Liu Chuanzhi did not quite believe it. He had always considered market share and profit to be something you could not get at the same time, like fish and bear's paws. So he asked the finance personnel if these profit figures included any funds "left over from before." The results proved that there was nothing murky about the figure, it was just one month's profit. Liu quickly relayed this news to the entire company. "This is a manifestation of real power. What real power? Lianxiang's computers can compete with others"." He praised Yang Yuanqing for discerning foreign companies' pricing tactics and using their own lance to attack their own shield.

Yang Yuanqing now began implementing the "second attack" in his plan. On May 23, he announced a second adjustment downward in pricing, and this time his weapon was the "Pentium 120MHz." He dropped his selling price by 20%—each machine cost RMB 9,888. This day marked the opening of the Seventeenth National Computer Products Exhibition Fair in Beijing. Great Wall reduced its Pentium/100 price to RMB 9,980. As you walked into the Exhibition Hall you could see bold banners to right and left. On one side was "9980, Golden Great Wall Pentium My Home", on the other was "9,888, Lianxiang Pentium/120."

This time, however, the weight of public opinion did not rest entirely on the side of the "attacker." Chinese critics worried about winning and at the same time about losing. When China-brand prices were high, people said this would prevent the nation's industries from developing; now that China-brand prices were declining precipitously, they said it would damage national industries. Others criticized what was happening as a "vicious price war." First among these was a color television producer called Changhong. This maker had initiated a price war in the color TV market this year, unintentionally at the same time as Lianxiang, in March. When people criticized Changhong they also dragged in Lianxiang, saying that the only weapon in the Pentium War was price and this would not necessarily be advantageous to Chinese computer makers.

Yang Yuanqing had embarked on a course of no return, but he could not guarantee that he would not get hit. Six months later, Lianxiang's computers passed the certification for ISO 9001 and Yang regarded this pedigree as a rebuff to those who had believed that China-made computers were of inferior quality. The ISO 9001 was a quality standard system used by more than one hundred countries, after all. Then Yang called a group of reporters to the Beijing Media Center and told them that Lianxiang had developed what he called the Rainbow Plan. The Plan went across all seven links in the value chain, namely production, repair, training, commerce, industry public relations, market promotion, and market management. This delighted those who supported Lianxiang and they put the headline in various newspapers: "The Rainblow Plan stretches across the universe." Those who had been criticizing Lianxiang's price war now fell silent.

The first quarter of the financial year brought good news: Lianxiang sold 42,000 computers, a 220% increase over the same period the previous year. The market then entered the high-sales summer season as Yang

Yuanqing's Third Attack began. This time the activities were not in the public eye, but rather "took advantage of darkness to cross the river." Anyone who bought a Lianxiang Pentium would get "special compensation" in return.

Newspapers in all large cities in China carried an ad that said, "The Lianxiang 1+1 sends warm regards to you this summer," which enticed people into shops wanting to know exactly what the "special compensation" and the "warm regards" involved. On July 18, all computer retailers hung a sign outside their doorway that revealed the secret. There would be a discount on a foreign-brand item if you bought a Lianxiang machine: if you bought a "Lion Pentium 100," for example, and paid only RMB 200 more, you could get an HP DJ200 inkjet printer worth RMB 1,858.

The Southern Front: still hard-pressed

As the northern front was progressing, the southern front was still hard-pressed. Moore's Law was a two-edged sword that was particularly cutting in 1996. The computer market went through a cycle of elation to despair and back again, though few companies did it in such a dramatic way as Lianxiang.

Hong Kong Lianxiang was already one of the largest motherboard manufacturers in the world by the early 1990s. 1994 was the peak of its business: its motherboard card sales reached 3,751,966 pieces, which was 10% of the world's market. Although misunderstandings frequently occurred in terms of management, the product still brought in more than HK$80 million of profit to the company, roughly US$10 million. Things were not rosy on the northern front: the entry of foreign computers into China as well as the split with Ni Guangnan had left Liu Chuanzhi feeling he was being hit on all sides. He began to feel he had best leave management of Hong Kong Lianxiang to Leu Tanping and return to Beijing to protect that threatened turf.

Leu Tanping was a novice when it came to enterprise management, however. He was the quintessential Hong Kong man—smart, industrious, full of energy and enthusiasm, with a superb educational background and with an outsider's disdain for the Mainland. He had low regard for anyone sent from Beijing Lianxiang to be a manager together with him. The only person he respected was Liu Chuanzhi.

But Liu Chuanzhi had now gone. He was in Beijing, getting reports from Hong Kong and fretting. Everyone knew that in fighting this war on two fronts the company was like the two ends of a seesaw. One went up as the other went down. Whichever end the Boss assumed control over would see smooth sailing, while the other end would have trouble. Just now the seesaw issue asserted itself: not many months after Liu Chuanzhi left Hong Kong, that business was in a mess.

The trouble started in 1995. Leu Tanping's style was to attend to matters personally. He often made major decisions based on his own feelings. As a result, he was in frequent conflict with senior management directly under his jurisdiction. In calm times, this could be papered over and things would move forward; when a battle erupted, however, it resulted in disaster for Lianxiang.

In 1995, Microsoft put out its Windows '95™, making the Pentium computer the standard and bringing on the swift demise of the 486. Hong Kong Lianxiang began purchasing large batches of Pentium microprocessors while it also bought in large batches of low-priced AST486s. It planned to sell the mainstream motherboards to the world market while selling the out-of-date computers into China. There was a strong flavor of opportunism in this plan. Its foundations were shaky to begin with and the minute discord arose among the commanders, the plan was poorly managed and, in brief, led to disaster.

Leu Tanping was confident that success was in hand, however. He bought 660,000 Intel Pentium chips at a price of US$16 per chip. He planned to do tremendous business with these but suddenly discovered that his production capacity to handle the load was inadequate—so he rushed out to buy equipment. The entire purchasing process was based on a spur of the minute decision since there was no time for meticulous planning. The production line only required five of a particular piece of equipment, but he bought ten. His managers pleaded with him to be more careful but he would not listen. Just at this time, Intel's Pentium microprocessors began declining in price. Every three months they dropped 30%, leading eventually to a price of US$4 for memory chips throughout the world. Each minute in the world market meant financial loss or gain, yet Leu Tanping and the General Manager of the Hong Kong factory were engaged in an argument that did not get resolved for two months. The company was chaotic to the point that nobody was managing the accumulating chips in the warehouse, or motherboard production, or sales. According to Liu Chuanzhi's calculations, "they argued away HK$100 million during the course of those wasted two months."

Fiscal year 1995 ended in this fashion. At its beginning, Leu Tanping had meant to kill two hawks with one arrow, but one of the hawks had already brought on calamity. In twelve months, Hong Kong Lianxiang lost HK$195 million and the profits of the previous three years were totally gone. Leu Tanping was apoplectic. This company held not only his personal wealth but also his "heart blood." He was a workaholic to begin with. Now he did not sleep for days on end. He flung himself back and forth between Asia and America, Asia and Europe, getting a few naps in on the airplane. Unfortunately, all of this was for naught.

By February 12, 1996, the company's Board of Directors held an emergency meeting in Beijing. Liu Chuanzhi finally was aware that the situation was dire, for banks were refusing to loan Hong Kong Lianxiang any more money. Faced with an inability to make ends meet, if banks completely cut the line of credit, the company would be headed to its demise.

Fortunately the trouble in Beijing had come to an end. Liu Chuanzhi hurried to Hong Kong to "look into causes," and he asked for mercy from his old friends in banks, hoping that he could, as in the past, rely on his reputation in getting loans. Over the past ten years, he had consistently promoted the company's reputation in the banking community. The reputation of Hong Kong Lianxiang was now in doubt, however. All he could do was put up the company stock as collateral. At the beginning of the year, the share price had been more than HK$2; by now it had tumbled to near HK$1. Banks suspected that even this price was too high and wanted the shares to be depreciated by three quarters before they were willing to accept them as collateral, meaning that if the shares were valued at HK$1, they would only lend HK$0.25 cents. Liu Chuanzhi put all 53% majority ownership of Beijing down as collateral.

The bad news did not end there. The price of a Pentium computer was by now under HK$10,000: how could one think of selling AST 486s that had been bought in at HK$15,000? Lianxiang hoped that AST would lower the price, but AST had been bought by the Korean Samsung and the new bosses did not recognize old favors. The loss continued at Hong Kong Lianxiang in the first three months of fiscal year 1996: HK$9 million in April, HK$8 million in May, HK$7 million in June. In the summer of 1996, Zhang Zuxiang left his position in Hong Kong to return to Beijing. He had spent eight years of his life at Hong Kong Lianxiang. As he left, he came up with a phrase that is accurate to this day: "Crisis upon crisis, but Lianxiang has nine lives."

Liu Chuanzhi was able to get a loan for HK$500 million that gave the company some breathing room. He lowered the salaries of all managerial personnel in Hong Kong by 25%. Wielding a sharp knife, he then dealt with the dispute between Leu Tanping and his subordinates. Leu Tanping received an order to which he submitted: "You are no longer allowed to manage company affairs." Wu Liyi, Ma Xuezheng, and Jia Zhiqiang all admitted to some responsibility. For the second time in eight years the company then began a great retreat. The first time had been in 1991 when they pulled the production center back to the Mainland. They now moved the R&D Center out of Hong Kong and set it up in Shenzhen. The wages of people were lower there, the price of land and housing was cheaper and in one fell swoop they saved RMB 20 million.

Liu Chuanzhi then turned his mind to putting the Huiyang motherboard factory in order. The management of the place that Guo Wei and Chen Guodong had put such efforts into establishing was now a mess. The inside of the factory was a shambles, spare parts disappeared daily. Workers had little motivation and low morale. They had no respect for the managers who had come from Hong Kong. They said these people had no idea of how to manage production. All they could do was delineate conditions for different classes of employees, there was even a different toilet for regular employees and senior managers. One day, a CCTV film crew came to shoot a TV show and a reporter pulled aside a worker and asked him what he thought of Lianxiang. The worker had never heard of Lianxiang. All he knew was that he made RMB 300 per month in wages, plus RMB 80 as a supplement for food.

This kind of thing is not unknown in modern enterprises in the West, but when Liu Chuanzhi heard about it he was very angry. He had always believed in the maxim, "workers are the bosses of the factory." He now criticized the management and fired them all, declaring that Lianxiang would not use colonial methods to manage its factories. Jia Zhiqiang and Ma Xuezheng now came forward to recommend a man named Shi Jianning. They said that he had strong management capability and Liu Chuanzhi soon hired him to manage the motherboard factory. Shi Jianning understood what are known as "Chinese particularities, that is, how to handle Chinese psychology." He especially understood people who lived at the lower levels. When he came to Huiyang he worked and ate together with the workers. He started a night school, a library, and a recreation facility. He organized parties on the weekends, he danced with everyone when there were dances. The workers had only one very simple need, which was that they be treated as human beings. Shi Jianning satisfied this need and workers came to feel that he was "one of us." Things began to change: workers began to smile, items stopped being stolen, the acceptance rate of products rose to 97%.

August still reported a loss of RMB 1 million. Shareholders were leaving the stock in droves. In sixteen days, Lianxiang's share price fell till each share was worth only HK$0.29.

This was the dark before dawn. By autumn, Liu Chuanzhi's methods began to show results. The loss was checked, in October profits were more than RMB 10 million and in the two ensuing months profits were RMB 20 million. The price of the shares rose again and wavered between HK$0.40 and HK$0.60.

Seeing the share price wavering and investors wondering, Liu Chuanzhi decided to make the crisis of the company public. He decided to do it at the annual Christmas Party. His speech this year was radically unlike previous occasions: it was long, inspirational, and quite specific. Before we describe that Christmas Party in Hong Kong, though, we must return to the northern front and understand that arena.

The "Every-man" computer

On September 9, 1996, Beijing Lianxiang and Taiwan Hongji announced that they were joining hands and developing a new generation of personal computers. They gave the new series a compelling name: the "Every-man Computer." China had never had the concept of a computer for everyone. There was "Training for Everyone," "Pig-raising for Everyone," and "Every man a Soldier." All these slogans were thought up by politicians who wanted to mobilize other people's energies to accomplish their own plans. Now, this word "Every-man" was on the lips of the two biggest computer manufacturers on the two sides of the Taiwan Straits. It had a different meaning. From the mid-1990s, supply exceeded demand in China. With money in their pockets, ordinary people became an important force in stimulating Chinese economic development. Commerce lacked the power to drive masses in the direction they wanted, though. No power on earth could force ordinary people to buy what they were unwilling to buy. The only route to commercial success was to offer the best products, to treat customers with gentleness, courtesy and honesty. This was also true of the computer market.

Personal computers had been popular in China for several years, known in China and in the West as "PC." After 1995, the Internet became trendy and China then added to PC something called "NC," net computer. This was a machine specifically meant to allow consumers to get on the Internet. Lianxiang and Hongji now gave their Every-man computer a new acronym, the "BC," or Basic Computer. They lined it up with the PC and the NC in a "Big Three" series.

The computer was designed for the common man, and from this perspective, it was like the "home-use computer." The home-use computer's growth had been slow over the past two years, though, never reaching more than 5% of the market. Yang Yuanqing came up with the "Everyman" concept in order to cultivate a completely new market. In addition, the computer marked an alliance between Taiwan and Mainland computer companies: "Our cooperation with Hongji is a kind of strategic alliance," Liu Chuanzhi agreed, in response to journalists' questions. "One branch in Taiwan, one on the Mainland. Both doing development and sales, therefore we called our new machine the Twin Star. You can see from the name of the computer that our cooperation signifies the joining of hands and moving forward of the two sides of the Straits."

The Computer Design Group: changing the direction of competition
As Yang Yuanqing lowered prices and used the Twin Star as a weapon in his steady advance, Liu Jun started a new era of computer design with the "Scorpio." Early in 1996, the company set up a Computer Development Department and Liu Jun became its Manager. The first thing he did was to bring in a person named Yao Yingjia and allow him to implement an unconventional plan. Yao was a highly talented graduate in the field of Industrial Arts. His head was full of marvellous designs and he scorned the clunky look of computers at that time. "Why can't we make computers more fashionable?" he said. Nobody had a good answer. All computers in the world looked as though they had come from the same mold: a square monitor, a rectangular CPU. Yao was now given permission to change all this, which thrilled him. "You won't regret it," he guaranteed his boss, then flew out of the room to start sketching the computer in his mind. He was to become a pioneer in the industrial design of China's computer industry.

The concept of "industrial design" is often misunderstood. In general, it refers to the outer structure and materials of products, not their internal functioning. It is a hot subject in universities these days, but ten years ago only two institutions taught such courses in China, the Central Fine Arts Academy and the Beijing Science & Engineering University. Nobody in China paid attention to industrial design—the outer aspect of products was not seen as important to customers and particularly so in the field of computers. Computers had not yet become consumer goods in the general consciousness of Chinese. People asked about the CPU, the internal memory, the hard drive and so on; as for the outside, they just wanted a box that was a safe container. The rigid, serious, cold look of computers had not changed much in twenty years. Yao Yingjia firmly believed that this was not right. He felt that computers should be practical in use and beautiful in appearance.

Yao had studied interior design, but he was passionate about computer design. Liu Jun now set up an Industrial Design Center within his Computer Development Department and appointed Yao Yingjia to head it. The Center soon had over eighty employees. This was a pioneering effort in China—there was not another industrial design center in the entire country, let alone in the computer industry. Yao's breakthroughs in this field started from a base of zero.

The first popular-model computer in China was born in 1996. It was called the Scorpio. Yao gave it easy, fluid lines and a soft and pleasant form—it looked friendly. Personal computers with a trendy exterior became one aspect of social trends in the 1990s and Lianxiang was very much at the forefront of this movement.

A second innovation within the Computer Development Center was the new Lianxiang R&D Department. Liu Jun was later to say that only after the personal computer R&D Department was set up did Lianxiang truly have its own R&D. "The establishment of Lianxiang's R&D capacity was the process of a gradual evolution," he said. "It took some time, but 1996 was without doubt the starting point."

Like all computer manufacturing in China, Lianxiang's R&D started out with systems testing. "Testing was the first link in R&D," explained Liu Jun. "You found the bugs, then modified the system. In the early days, we did what I call backwards engineering: first you designed something and then you sold it to the customer. Then we started to do what I call "forward engineering:" we found out what the customer needed and then designed to those specifications."

Liu Jun realized that the "customer interface" had been sorely neglected in the process of building computers. The company had several hundred people working night and day on capabilities, functions, files, quality, and so on. The very first link between customer and computer had nothing to do with these things, however: he saw the "customer interface" as a kind of bridge to the customer. In concrete terms, the interface included the monitor, the keyboard, and mouse, but also the menu and graphs on the screen. Although the Windows operating system was already popular throughout the country, Liu Jun discovered that many people had no idea where to start. They didn't know where to move that tiny arrow when they first sat down. He decided to develop a set of software applications that would allow customers to enter the world of the computer the moment they turned the computer on.

A young man named Han Zhenjiang led this effort. As a designer, he hoped to avoid the use of text as much as possible. He wanted to use symbols to express all functions: the result was to make the computer into a kind of "home." When you turned on the computer, it was as though you were sitting in a place in your home: you wanted to watch television, you put the mouse indicator on the television on the screen, to listen to music, you touched the radio. Multimedia technology was just coming into China at this time and the personal computer market had also entered the multimedia age. The software interface was named "Lucky Home" and it quickly made a sensation.

Lucky Home was an applications software that "hung" on top of Windows. It became a bridge between the Chinese customer and the Microsoft operating system. The little mouse on the screen could speak pure standard Chinese, it could even correct spelling mistakes, which made both children and parents happy. Liu Jun followed up this success with other efforts and soon developed a Lucky Office for commercial users. He had not intended for these software packages to make money— he bundled them into the package, hoping they would encourage consumers to buy Lianxiang computers. In the last few months of 1996, the Scorpio sold at least 20,000 computers, each equipped with a Lucky Home. This became the first home-use computer that actually brought the company profits. Before this, at least ten home-use computer systems lost money but at least put the word out about Lianxiang. After this, home-use computers began to earn serious money for the company.

Enterprise Planning Office

By the year 1997, people began to recognize that Yang Yuanqing had made two great contributions to the company. First, he had rescued the declining prospects of China-brand computers. If it had not been for his efforts in 1994, 1995, and 1996, China's computer market might have been monopolized by foreign brands. Second, he drastically reformed the sales system of the company, setting up a highly effective agency structure and turning products in the direction of home-use customers.

Yang Yuanqing felt that his greatest contribution was in a different arena. Due to his efforts, the older generation of leaders at Lianxiang now had faith and confidence in the next generation.

Not all young people sitting in senior-management positions were content, however. Liu Xiaolin was particularly unhappy. He had been forced to leave the Computer Administration Department by Liu Chuanzhi and was transferred to the position of Deputy Chairman of the Enterprise Planning Department. Sales of computers were up 101% in this one year, market share now exceeded 10%. The company was surging into first place in the Mainland market and Yang Yuanqing's three-year goal had been accomplished in just one year. Liu Xiaolin had long since left the Computer Administration Department, however, so none of this could be credited to him.

What Liu was finding hardest to accept were the new sedans being driven around by people in the Computer Administration Department. Yang Yuanqing was awarding these to top performers as a form of bonus. China had not yet entered an age of private automobiles and most people thought that owning your own car was an impossible dream.

Liu Xiaolin later kept saying that his luck was bad. His subject had been computer technology, but he asked to be put in sales when he came to Lianxiang because he believed that "Sales is King." He was asked to leave sales not because his performance was bad—in fact, it was outstanding. Liu Chuanzhi had his reasons for transferring him to the Enterprise Planning Office. This is a vital department in the company. Liu Chuanzhi set up the structure and staffed it with young people because of the bipolar situation in Beijing and Hong Kong. He was losing one by gaining the other, and he needed capable people who could be a substitute for himself on the Beijing side. Liu Chuanzhi felt that the Enterprise Planning Office was an excellent place "to deploy troops, array soldiers." He wanted Yang Yuanqing and Guo Wei to stay in the front and deflect attacks; he needed Liu Xiaolin to be in the rear helping "devise strategies in the council tent."

Nobody ever says the full name of the Department inside the company. It also does not appear on company documents. Company employees simply say it is "the people next to Liu Chuanzhi." In Liu Xiaolin's words, "The Department was just an extension of the brains and hands of the boss." The General Managers of the many Departments had to submit reports to its Deputy Chairman, Liu Xiaolin. He appeared to have tremendous power, but he felt that his role was a kind of contradiction. He was not a General, since he did no real work. He also was not a Minister, since he did not wield real power. He was extremely busy, but looking back he seemed to have done nothing. This year he had designed a new compensation system, reviewed the manuscript of Chen Huixiang's book, helped the President expand the contents of his "Three Elements of Management," and led the company's cadres in how to create a team. Liu put considerable work into these team-creation study sessions. Some people criticized them as being too tough on people: building a team was turned into a military exercise. Some journalists in particular had the impression that Lianxiang was capable of causing "physical and mental suffering," and that Liu Chuanzhi could "rectify" people at will, criticize them till they were forced to reform. Liu Xiaolin responded to these comments as follows. "Handling a company is handling people." Your troops are more important than your products. And for a company to have staying power, you need people to lead the troops. Liu Chuanzhi believes that when you bring young people on board, you have to pulverize them, kind of grind them up, train them to fit the Lianxiang mold."

In governing a company, as in governing a country, there will always be some people who benefit and others who feel wronged. Liu Xiaolin lost out in terms of the Computer Administration Department, but on balance he benefited in the long run. Handling the Enterprise Planning Department in Beijing satisfied his ambition, while Liu Chuanzhi felt at ease and returned to Hong Kong to rescue that situation.

Christmas party

1996 was on its way out. The Christmas Speech was being held two weeks early, since the company felt it was important for all to know at the earliest possible time that the company had weathered the crisis.

It was customary for the company to hold a Christmas party in Hong Kong, and for Liu Chuanzhi to summarize main events of the year in a brief speech. This year Liu contravened custom: his speech lasted forty-five minutes.

"Results of this past year show a relatively large loss. What should I tell everyone in this annual address?" he began. "I personally bear a responsibility for this situation. Due to my mistakes, I caused the shareholders to suffer tremendous losses, and I am ashamed of that. I caused the employees of Hong Kong Lianxiang material harm and mental distress. I feel very badly about that as well." He then showed slides detailing the accomplishments of Beijing Lianxiang. He told the depressed Hong Kong employees, whose salaries had been cut, that the employees of Beijing had seen a 40% per year salary increase over the past three years. He said that there would be another large increase this year.

Several hundred guests stood in the audience, including the Deputy Director of the Hong Kong Branch of the Xinhua News Agency, and the President of the Chinese Academy of Sciences, Zhou Guangzho. Zhou was aware of how difficult times were for Hong Kong Lianxiang, so he had determined to give Liu Chuanzhi moral support by flying down from Beijing just to hear this speech.

Liu Chuanzhi continued, "The reasons for Hong Kong Lianxiang's losses can be summarized in one sentence: the company did not make necessary changes after becoming a listed company. It used small-company management methods to try to manage a listed company. Senior management did not do adequate research and analysis, they decided important issues in an offhand, almost frivolous manner. They did not clearly delineate the responsibilities of department positions. Without clear-cut responsibilities, generals and commanders were not in harmony. The General Manager's office was lax in the extreme in the way it examined and approved financial matters. All these sound like hollow words, but in fact each sentence has been paid for with a tragic price. Can we use the excuse that the market changed too fast? No: this was brought on entirely due to our own management failures. Hong Kong Lianxiang is like a car on a road: it overturned not because the road is too narrow or the cars are too many. It crashed because we ourselves drove the car off the road."

Liu Chuanzhi then talked about the "rectification" under way in the company. He announced that the company had already gone through its hardest period. He went on to bring all the "family faults" into public view, contrary to tradition. This terrified the senior managers, but proved to be the right thing to do. Investors like honest enterprises. The next day when the stock market opened, Lianxiang shares rose to more than HK$0.30, and on the third day they reached more than HK$0.50.

The brevity of Christmas celebrations was an indication that the company would be going through some major changes. In early 1997, Liu Chuanzhi put into action a plan that had been gestating for several weeks.

Aligning Beijing and Hong Kong
The plan was born in Silicon Valley, in America. In November of 1996, Liu Chuanzhi led a group of senior managers to visit America and they held a one-day conference when they reached Silicon Valley. Everyone discussed the situation of the "southern front"; none felt that the crisis of Hong Kong Lianxiang would be easy to surmount—the accumulated losses of two successive years had reached HK$245 million. The only way out was to depend on loans for support. AST was bankrupt and sales of motherboards had declined by 62%, leading to the collapse of the company's two primary profit streams. The company had no new business lines, it could not miraculously expand in new directions, and just patching things up was not going to restore profitability. Completely new, sweeping measures were required.

Liu Chuanzhi discussed the possibility of uniting or, more accurately, "conforming" Beijing and Hong Kong. Ma Xuezheng proffered two scenarios:

1. Beijing Lianxiang buys Hong Kong Lianxiang.
2. Beijing Lianxiang's resources are consolidated into Hong Kong
    Lianxiang.

Liu Chuanzhi favored the second approach. "The best solution would
be to put the Beijing Lianxiang business into the listed company, and
combine them to create a China Lianxiang."

He told the group that he had evaluated the prospects and determined
that only this would have any chance of saving Hong Kong Lianxiang.
Bank loans would temporarily cover the losses. He had received a "precious
promise" from both the Chinese Academy of Sciences and the State
Capital and Resource Management Bureau: they had agreed to support his
decision to consolidate. The two large Hong Kong shareholders, Leu
Tanping and Wu Liyi, were the greatest remaining obstacles. Liu decided
to remove Wu Liyi from the positions of Executive Board Member and
Vice-President. He decided to annul Leu Tanping's positions of Vice-
Chairman of the Board of Directors and General Manager; he would only
allow him to serve as member of the Executive Board. Leu, Wu and
another Hong Kong person were in control of 208 million of the company's
shares, however. They also had voting rights on the Board. Ma Xuezheng
raised her concerns. She asked Liu Chuanzhi, "If these two unite in
opposition, what then?" This was precisely Liu's problem. "There are five
on the Executive Board," he said. "The Beijing side includes me, old Zeng,
and old Li. Even though we have three votes to two, if they don't agree it's
going to be hard to do it."

He decided to try. Back in Hong Kong, he paid a call first on Leu
Tanping, then on Wu Liyi. He used his finest persuasive talents. The three
had managed company affairs together for eight years. Today the "family"
was big, the enterprise was big, Liu Chuanzhi was famous in China and
Leu and Wu were famous in Hong Kong, yet they were now talking about
parting ways.

Leu and Wu were intelligent men. They knew the situation, they
accepted Liu Chuanzhi's arrangement. They resigned from all positions in
the company, keeping only their shares. In order to expand their holdings,
they had borrowed US$5,525,800 from the company and they knew that
Liu Chuanzhi had suffered on this account. They were willing to listen to
Liu Chuanzhi's arrangements and to support him. Liu said, "our stock is at
its lowest right now, only HK$0.30. I believe in Lianxiang's future, though.
We can wait until the share price goes back up to the issue price of
HK$1.33 as the date of our transaction, and then you can either pay for

the debt with shares or you can keep the shares and repay the debt and interest from other funds." Leu and Wu agreed. They had received western educations and had been raised in Hong Kong society. They had learned the Western style: when the music was right they would stay together, when they could not accept it, then they would leave.

Share prices began to rise. By January 29, they had reached HK$1.15. Four months later, Lianxiang's share price had gone up sufficiently that Leu Tanping and the others smoothly repaid their debt and exited the company.

All Board members of the company held a meeting in Number 505 of the headquarters building of Beijing Lianxiang on February 3, 1997. Decisions made at that meeting were as follows:

1. Beijing Lianxiang and Hong Kong Lianxiang will be consolidated to become China Lianxiang.
2. The main parts of Beijing Lianxiang's business will undergo an asset valuation. With appropriate resources, Beijing Lianxiang will purchase shares of Hong Kong Lianxiang.
3. After the consolidation, Beijing Lianxiang will become the majority shareholder of Hong Kong Lianxiang. Its share holdings will go from the original 42% to more than 60%.

The Board of Directors bestowed control of the consolidated company on Liu Chuanzhi. He became Chairman of the Board of Directors of China Lianxiang, as well as its General Manager and Chief Executive Officer. In addition to Li Qin and Zeng Maochao, the Board of Directors included Yang Yuanqing, Ma Xuezheng, and Guo Wei. The significance of these positions to the young people was great, for this strongly presaged the company's future power structure.

On July 1, 1997, at midnight, Hong Kong was returned to the ancestral country, China. Prince Charles did not linger after the ceremony in which political power was transferred from England to China. Together with the last British Governor of Hong Kong, Peng Dingkang (Chris Patten), he boarded the British Royal Yacht "Britannica" and left the harbor. At the same time, lanterns were being lit and firecrackers were exploding in thirty-five large cities through the Chinese Mainland. Central squares of these cities were bright as a new dawn as several hundred million Chinese people celebrated throughout the night. In Beijing, Li Qin told a reporter at the Lianxiang Headquarters, "Today is tremendously significant for the development of the Lianxiang Group. We have a long relationship with Hong Kong. We will, as we have always done, raise high the flag of the nation's computer industry." On the Hong Kong side, everyone thought that everything had been put in order and all they had to do was wait for the Eastern wind. Once an order came down from above, success was bound to follow. Nobody dreamed that what came down instead was an investigation.

The Investigation Group arrives
The Investigation Group came into Lianxiang three times in July of 1997. They came to investigate Liu Chuanzhi. The ten men in the group included representatives from the Chinese Academy of Sciences, the Central Disciplinary Commission, The State Audit Administration, and the Ministry of Control and Supervision. These men were at quite a senior level. As the newly appointed Head of the Academy of Sciences, Lu Tongxiang, said at the initial meeting of the group: "This investigation is at the request of Comrades Zhu Rongji and Luo Gan and at the request of the Ministry of Control and Supervision's Auditing Administration. They have asked the Academy of Sciences to organize an investigation to get to a thorough understanding and then submit a report to Central."

What *Zhongnanhai* wanted to "get a thorough understanding of," according to Lu Tongxiang's explanation, was "whether or not there has been any behavior that violates discipline in the investment conduct and the shareholdings of Hong Kong Lianxiang. This has been raised in several letters written by people." Everyone knew that the main person involved was Ni Guangnan.

Ni Guangnan had continued to express his views while Liu Chuanzhi was engaged in the problems of the north and south fronts. Ni no longer believed that the Academy of Sciences could avail itself of the "public" to deal with the conflict between himself and Liu Chuanzhi, so he wrote letters "exposing" Liu and submitted them directly to the State Certification Supervisory Committee, the State Investment Bureau, the Ministry of Control and Supervision, the Central Disciplinary Commission, and the Central structures of the Communist Party.

Now that Zhu Rongji and Luo Gan were also paying attention to this case, the atmosphere was tense. Zhu Rongji was known as the "iron-faced Chancellor". He opposed any actions that moved the public resources of state-owned companies into private hands. Luo Gan was the member of the State Council responsible for political and legal affairs. Any statement he made generally led to swift and severe consequences. Liu Chuanzhi thought that the problems with Ni Guangnan had been resolved; he did not imagine they would erupt in even worse fashion.

Ni Guangnan did not deal in intrigues and plots. As per the principles of Communist Party organizations, he did things in an open manner, not transgressing the laws and powers of citizens. Lianxiang's share price had risen, so he calculated that "state-owned assets had lost quite a few hundreds of millions in the shares given to the Hong Kong merchants."

Zeng Maochao tried, in his capacity as Head of the Computer Institute, to get Ni Guangnan to stop writing the letters, but both Ni and his wife were adamant. His wife retorted: "They can pull down Chen Xitong, why can't they pull down Liu Chuanzhi?!" Chen Xitong was Mayor of Beijing who was put in jail for corrupt practices, so this allusion was meaningful.

When the Investigation Committee reappeared, Tang Dandong was first to know the reasons. He was the Responsible Person of the Laws and Regulations Department. He was in charge of supervision and control if the company had any illegal behavior among employees. Zeng Maochao therefore reported to him what had happened. Tang read all the materials marked as "secret," he read the written instructions from *Zhongnanhai.* "Ni Guangnan is an absolute gentleman," Tang once said, "a scholar, a high-level intellectual very much respected by people, without the slightest pretensions, and also very concerned about young people." He knew that Ni Guangnan and Liu Chuanzhi had differences in their approach to work. "He had his approach and Liu-zong had his own, to the point that there was violent debate, but none of us thought such debate was very strange." Yet things had now progressed to this point—Tang was perplexed. "What Ni Guangnan was saying touched on the fundamental fiber of a person. He was attacking Liu's quality as a human being. The charges had become a matter of criminal activity. I never could understand why Ni did this."

From the standpoint of Party discipline and national law, Tang knew that this matter could not be contained. If it got to a point of no return then Liu Chuanzhi would have to go to jail and the company too would be finished. Tang had assumed responsibility for legal matters of the company five years earlier. Most of his time was spent on lawsuits. He had managed at least ten disciplinary actions, he had fired more than a dozen employees, he had sent criminal actions against four employees to the courts, he had been involved in over a dozen contractual disputes. Nothing had ever happened like this before.

Patent infringement case 287
The summer of 1997 was a dramatic period in the history of Lianxiang— war on two fronts, verbal swords crossed in the courts, many people embroiled in sharp conflict.

During the same week the Investigation Committee came into the company, Tang Dandong read the final legal judgment of a particular civil case. The patent infringement case brought by Wangma had finally ended in Wangma's defeat. After a painful three years and one month, Tang Dandong was relieved of a heavy load.

The decision of the appeals court was sent down on July 20, 1997, with a registration number of "1994 Superior Court #30". Its text totalled 7,297 words. The presiding judge, Cheng Yongshun, and two other judges, Cheng Jinchuan and Sun Suli, may have created the longest document in the history of Chinese court cases in the 1990s. Its conclusion and judgment are paraphrased as follows:

"This case does not constitute an infringement of the patent called "superior five-stroke character model." The court supports the reasoning of the Defendant. Although the defendant used 4th-edition technology of the five-stroke method in his Han-card, the two patents are not reliant on one another; one does not "cover" the other. The decision of the lower court contained mistakes with regard to ascertaining the facts and utilizing legal procedures. We hereby correct those. According to the "People's Republic of China Patent Law, Article 59, "PRC Civil Litigation" Regulations Number 153 parts 2 and 3, we rule as follows:

1.   To cancel the civil determination of the Beijing Intermediary People's Court of 1993 Zhongjingchuzi #180;
2.   To reject the appeal of the Wangma Computer Company of Beijing.

First-Court litigation fees of RMB 12,025 and other litigation fees of RMB 5,400 are to be born by Beijing Wangma Computer Company (already paid); Second-court litigation fees of RMB 12,025 and other litigation fees of RMB 9,562.6 to be born by the Beijing Wangma Computer Company."

Wang Yongmin did not accept the decision of the final Court of Appeals. He went instead to the realm of public opinion for sympathy. "To say that the five-stroke method is a commonly owned property—does that mean it somehow dropped from heaven?" he repeatedly asked reporters. He also declared this to be "a scandal" in the Chinese high-tech field. Public opinion too, however, had turned against him.

Liu Chuanzhi again survives a crisis

Liu Chuanzhi did not relax after having won this first case of Chinese intellectual property rights. He even felt some compassion for his opponent in the courts because the resolution of his own pending case could not be predicted. Zeng Maochao accompanied the Investigation Committee to

Hong Kong. After some preliminary issues with regard to jurisdiction, the Investigation Committee went through all documents of Hong Kong Lianxiang. "After all this ruckus, getting into every filing cabinet," one reporter said, "if this guy really had done anything wrong he would have been put in jail eight times by now."

On August 18, 1997, the Investigation Committee issued an eighteen-page report. Its primary points, confirmed by the thirteen attachments, were all unfavorable to Ni Guangnan. The Chinese Academy of Sciences submitted these documents to *Zhongnanhai*. At the same, the Academy made a report to Zhu Rongji and Luo Gan. It said that the Investigation Committee had talked to people in Beijing, Shenzhen and Hong Kong, it had searched through company accounts and it had read all documentation. Its conclusions were:

1. The investigation had not uncovered any individual problems of illegality or breach of discipline, including among Hong Kong personnel. All problems raised in the report of the Joint Investigation were related to work and "not sufficient to be called problems."

2. The reasons for Hong Kong Lianxiang's losses in 1995 had been investigated and clarified. Measures taken to improve the situation were already in place and effective.

3. Loans made to Hong Kong parties to use debt to own shares were based on objective conditions at the time and on the need for Beijing Lianxiang to hold a dominant share position. The two times that share ownership was modified were within the scope of normal operations and within the bounds of legal procedures. State-owned assets had not gone missing.

4. Opinions of the State Audit Bureau and the Ministry of Examination and Control were in accord: there was indeed a need to adopt further measures to strengthen and improve enterprise management in both Beijing Lianxiang and Hong Kong Lianxiang.

Attachments to the report gave more details on the split between Ni Guangnan and Liu Chuanzhi. There did not seem to be much difference between this report and the conclusions of the 1995 investigation group. State Council-member Luo Gan accepted this conclusion. On September 10, he wrote "Approved" on the first page of the report. He agreed with the Party Organization within the Chinese Academy of Sciences: the organization should continue supporting the Lianxiang Group and should further strengthen its management and supervision. At the same time, he submitted his own opinion to Zhu Rongji. Zhu approved Luo Gan's opinion in writing on the spot: "Agree to the opinion of Comrade Luo Gan." So that was that.

Ni Guangnan continued to maintain that the Investigation Committee and the Chinese Academy of Sciences were covering up for each other. On September 22, he wrote Zhu Rongji a letter. He said that some people in the Investigation Committee overtly agreed with the concluding instructions but actually opposed them in private, that the work of the investigation had met with tremendous obstacles. He made it clear that by these "obstacles" he meant Zhou Guangzho.

On October 10, Zhu Rongji therefore handed Ni Guangnan's letter over to Luo Gan for review. Luo Gan then met with the Head of the Chinese Academy of Sciences, Lu Tongxiang, and asked him to handle the matter. He indicated that the Investigation Committee had already made its determination on the issue and that the State Council would not endorse Ni Guangnan's letter.

Four days later, Lu Tongxiang submitted a written request to Ni Guangnang, asking him "to come and seriously discuss this matter, so that we can explain our Investigation's conclusions and listen to Ni Guangnan's opinion. If there are no new circumstances, then there will be no further investigations. The results of our meeting will be reported up to Comrade Luo Gan."

Liu Chuanzhi had again weathered the storm. Lianxiang's Board of Directors did not plan to discuss this matter further. After three revisions, a draft of their opinion was completed, called "Declaration of our opinion on the repeated accusations brought by Ni Guangnan against Liu Chuanzhi." Its main points were as follows:

"1. Ni Guangnan cannot conduct himself properly despite his accomplishments and honors.
2. Liu Chuanzhi's policy was correct with regard to the technology decisions in the company, specifically with regard to integrated chips and switching systems.
3. The true motivation behind Comrade Ni Guangnan's litigation was that he was unhappy he did not have decision-making power in the company.
4. Comrade Ni Guangnan's methods have brought tremendous loss to the company. In 1995, Hong Kong Lianxiang was facing problems while Comrade Liu Chuanzhi had no recourse but to remain in Beijing to comply with the investigation and to deal with contradictions with Ni Guangnan. Just when the stock market

was going through violent changes, the leadership of Hong Kong Lianxiang weakened substantially. Ni Guangnan's actions had a direct relationship to all this. The suit brought by Ni Guangnan delayed the study and approval of the Leader's evaluation of the proposal to unite the two Lianxiangs; this meant that the unification proposal missed the opportunity of a relatively low stock price of Hong Kong Lianxiang: this one item lost the company many hundreds of millions of Hong Kong dollars.

5.   Since the Party Organization of the Chinese Academy of Sciences removed Comrade Ni Guangnan from his leadership position, this resolved the leadership team's hidden issues of disunity. Beijing Lianxiang has achieved breakthrough development as a result. Business income and profits have grown at 100% over the plan for three years in a row."

The Dell revolution

1997 was a year of major events in China. Deng Xiaoping passed away in the spring; Hong Kong was returned to China in the summer. In fall, the Congress of Party Representatives, held once every five years, convened. Chinese people like to point to "major events of the country," and the same is true within computer circles. In 1997, China became the largest personal computer market in the Asia-Pacific region outside Japan. By that time, 176 manufacturers were producing 244 different models with annual sales of more than three million machines. This represented a six-fold increase over the past seven years. Lianxiang had been the solitary China-brand name among the top ten in the market in 1995; now, two years later, Great Wall, Tongchuang, and Founder had been added to the list. The newest brand was the Hong Hubo produced in Shanghai. Its advertisements were ubiquitous in China.

Foreign computer brands reached the peak of their market penetration in China in 1993. At that time, they held 73% of the market. After this came a rapid decline until the share was down to 40% in 1996. AST was already completely out of the running. The other most famous brands only began to react to the Lianxiang Pentium one year later. For a number of years Lianxiang had been inching closer to the foreign manufacturers. Liu Chuanzhi had said, "We must be willing to eat their dust." Now, foreign companies were finding that they were behind Lianxiang, eating dust. Compaq announced a price-lowering strategy. IBM declared in an ad: "Now IBM prices can be compared to the others." It was already too late. Lianxiang's market share had already increased to 17.6% while IBM's stood at 11.8%. Compaq was even worse off: in 1993, its share of the personal computer market in China had been 18.6%, by 1997 it was 5.9%.

Just as people lose their will to win when they are in the midst of a crisis, it is easy to forget about crises when you are winning. None of these computer companies thought that there would be a storm brewing after the lull, nor that the "after the lull" occurred not in China, but in the wilds of northern Texas.

Michael Dell is a genius when it comes to sales. He was still a first-year college student when Lianxiang Company was born in 1984. That summer, he sold around US$180,000 worth of personal computers, and he then refused his parents' request to stay on in school. He dropped his studies to start his own company. He began to buy components and assemble personal computers, then printed up his own name card and went around selling the computers to customers at a 15% discount. His computers were well received, and after making his first fistful of money he went to the bank to get a loan and quickly expanded operations.

By 1994, the capital of Dell Company had reached US$3.5 billion, and its customers included large enterprises and small-scale commercial organizations. Two years later, his business expanded to include government organizations and educational institutions, and the company's assets increased in 1997 to US$12 billion. The flourishing electronics industry allowed Dell an opportunity to expand. Within six months Dell formed the largest personal computer sales company on the web, with a sales turnover that grew 20% every month. "In this industry, speed is everything," said Michael Dell.

Dell's secret was not that it used technology that was better than the technology of others, but that it allowed its salespeople to access the customer directly. It firmly believed in the direct sales method and so became a challenge to the traditional distributed-sales or agency method. Michael Dell said the Internet was the ultimate direct selling method. Every day he would discuss with sales personnel how to sell US$ one million worth of computers that day. The American media began to pay attention to Dell. One news item said, "The direct sales method invented by Dell has brought a rare revolution to the American computer industry." Dataquest even called Dell "the Industrial Revolution's third wave." It predicted that "this revolution is going to change the current competitive structure of business." Dell himself became the "Best Manager" in America's *Business Week*. He was forcing giant computer companies to respect him.

Unfortunately, Chinese became aware of this only after several more years. In 1997, Yang Yuanqing was the only one mentioning Dell. He said that Lianxiang was adopting sales policies that incorporated the smallest inventory and the shortest channels, something like the Dell advanced model. At the same time, Liu Chuanzhi said, "When we started out with eleven people in a Guard's Post, we were proud of our size. Today our feelings are the opposite: we feel that our company is small. In competing with large overseas companies, we are like a little boat bobbing on a vast sea. We can be overturned by a tsunami any time." Liu was describing the insecurity of not being able to feel your way to the edges of a situation, while Yang Yuanqing's description of Dell was just a fleeting mention. Nobody paid much attention. In 1997, the Chinese computer industry had not yet tasted the true flavor of "sailing on that great ocean," and it did not know the significance of the direct sales method. It also did not know the name Michael Dell, just as, three years earlier, nobody in America had heard of a man the same age as Michael Dell named Yang Yuanqing.

Summing up the compensation system of the 1990s

Lianxiang had steadily been moving forward in personalizing the benefits funds of individuals. People were happy that they could enjoy "benefits" two times the amount of their wages, and not have to pay taxes on them. Unfortunately, nobody realized that there were hidden dangers of corruption in this system.

Awkward matters first showed up in a company recruitment meeting. Potential recruits asked how much income they might get. Company officials found they had no way to explain it themselves. Each person's "benefits fund" could only be calculated at the end of the year when accounts were closed and it was known how much money there was. Many factors needed to be concealed, moreover—they could not be put on the table and talked about openly. The Finance Department had begun to receive a lot of strange expense receipts for which employees wanted to be reimbursed. A person who had not purchased a house, for instance, came in with expenses for remodelling his home. Another person had purchased four cellphones in one year. The company had originally hoped that employees would use the Benefits Fund to purchase housing or old age pension insurance, but many months went by and nobody responded. It turned out that buying a house took many years of saving and short-term benefits could not resolve the problem. The pension plan was even less in accord with real needs. Inflation was extreme and in order to avoid a run on the bank, banks set interest rates extremely high. Cash was a better investment, so employees withdrew their funds from the company.

In the summer of 1993, Tang Dandong investigated into the wages and salary conditions of the computer industry in China. He found that the monthly cash salary of a Sitong Company employee was RMB 1,000, at IBM it was RMB 2,500, while at Lianxiang it was a mere RMB 700. With twice that amount in benefits, the Lianxiang employees' total income was not that low, but Tang Dandong still felt that the company compensation system was not competitive. In 1993, the company decided to take a shortcut, after it had progressed only one year down the road, in personalizing the Benefits Fund.

Employee compensation is the main fulcrum for motivating a company. Tang Dandong submitted a report to Liu Chuanzhi, Li Qin, and all members of the President's Office, enumerating the many faults of the current employee compensation system as well as the possibility of improvements. This motivated the company to set up a new system.

In China, enterprise policy is generally a reflection of government policy. Lianxiang's early goal had been to expand "benefits," while now its goal was to contract "benefits" and increase the cash-payment part of the wages. The reason for this was that two major changes had appeared in the government's policy that created an opportunity for compensation reform. First was that the government got rid of the "5-3-2" policy: the new policy said that an enterprise must take a minimum of 20% of profit and put it into a "development fund," the rest could be distributed as the company wished. Secondly, the government changed the "individual income adjustment tax" into the "individual income tax." In the experimental district of ZGC, the starting point of taxable income was RMB 600 per month; the lowest tax rate was 5%, the highest was 40%. Compared to the previous tax on bonuses of 300%, this tax was something that both employees and companies could live with. There was no longer any need to spend so much time and effort evading taxes.

The new system included seven components: Research and development, production, management, finance, sales, engineering, and logistics or "back office." Each component was further divided into 19 grades and each grade had a fixed compensation standard. The new system's primary goals were twofold: to make transparent and resolve the greatest limitations of hidden income; and, within the company, to widen the disparity in incomes. Its practical consequences were that the ratio of benefits and wages turned completely around: from two to one the ratio became one to two. An average monthly cash income for an average employee therefore rose by 128%, to RMB 1,600.

This compensation system that had taken a half-year of hard work to set up was in place for only six moths before it met huge challenges. Since 1993 results were terrible, employee incomes were greatly reduced. The average compensation for a person in 1992 had been 19,823; in 1993 it fell to RMB 15,761. In 1994, the company put its hopes for revitalizing the computer business on Yang Yuanqing. Liu Chuanzhi did as Zeng Maochao had done to him many years earlier: he handed over to him control of administrative policy and human resources. Yang Yuanqing was not satisfied with that, however, for he knew that the compensation system was a key factor in dissension among his ranks. He went a step further in asking to have greater power over distribution of profits. Liu decided to copy the system of the 1980s in China, during its economic reform period: China broadly adopted a *cheng-bao* system, which meant that organizations guaranteed a certain minimum payment to the government and kept any profits made above that minimum. This was a tremendous incentive. Liu now said he would hand twenty percent of gross profits to Yang Yuanqing to keep for distribution to employees, after Yang had met his sales and profit targets. Other administrative departments in the company were allowed to adopt the same plan.

Two years later, in actual implementation of the system, most employees found that their purses were bulging. The average income in 1994 increased to RMB 35,569, six times the average salary in large cities at the time. In 1995 it again increased to RMB 40,936. The reason for such a large jump was that the bonuses received by employees far exceeded their fixed income.

The difference in incomes in the company was substantial. The fixed compensation in the original system constituted the total income for employees in some departments, while in others it was hardly worth mentioning. Reasons lay in the disparity between business results of departments. For example, in 1995, the average compensation for the highest-paid person in the Notebook Department was RMB 228,468. The CAF Department came in second place, with RMB 128,376. The lowest-paid department was the Han-character systems Department, with an average of RMB 29,150. For young people who wanted to buy housing, this disparity gave low-salaried people a tremendous debt burden. The President's Office had to adopt some way to temporarily increase their income, while saying that they had to repay as soon as business results were better.

With "profit distribution rights" now in his hands, Yang Yuanqing kept back 20% of sales profit and awarded those employees with special merit. Liu Xiaolin worked hard on compiling a set of bonus-system rules for the Computer Administration Department, but to a large extent decisions on bonuses were in the hands of Yang Yuanqing. In 1996, when the Lianxiang computer counter-attack was largely successful, the income of Computer Administration Department managers greatly exceeded that of managers at Headquarters. The income of Yang Yuanqing himself was higher than the President of the company, Liu Chuanzhi. Incomes of salespeople became the best proof of the statement that "Sales are King." As for employees working in the so-called "back office" of the company, they received their incomes through thick and thin, but did not get any increase for three years in a row.

In early 1997, the Human Resources Department invited a group of specialists into the company and asked them to develop a unified compensation system. The experts brought with them a kind of evaluation system that they said was in common use internationally. The key thing about this system was that it rated all positions in the company by three factors: Scale of responsibilities, including influence on the company and number of people managed; Scope of responsibilities; and Degree of complexity, including difficulty of problems being resolved, and environmental factors.

Compensation was only one of many Lianxiang systems, but the improvements in this one system helped take the company into a new era. The rating factors for each person were different and they helped determine the relative values of various positions. Changes in the 1990s led to two distinct trends—average incomes increased and the cash component of incomes increased, and compensation differentials among positions increased. Employees with the same academic qualifications and length of service might have radically different figures on their wage slips. Among senior management personnel, the difference might be significant, depending on responsibilities and performance. In the early 1990s, the differential in total compensation was roughly one to two, by 1993 it was one to three, by 1994 it was one to eleven, after 1997 it was one to thirty.

To company employees, this provided short-term motivation, but not long-term motivation in terms of ownership of shares. Liu Chuanzhi now decided to implement his long-held dream. He wanted to transform the shareholders' rights that the company had received five years earlier into actual shares, and at the same time, to put in place a stock option system that would have a middle- and long-term motivational function. He called this plan the Employee Shareholders' Association.

Employee Shareholders' Association

Liu Chuanzhi had reason to be satisfied as he looked over the course of the past five years in the company. Computer sales were ranked Number One in the Chinese market; the agency business had performed with great vitality. Company profits came in a steady stream, the company had RMB 230 million of net assets, it paid the government RMB 178 million in taxes, and gave its administrative supervisor, the Chinese Academy of Sciences, RMB 27.8 million. Employee incomes were speeding upward. The company's share price shook off its gloom and by November 8 had returned to HK$2.38 a share.

After the furor surrounding the accusations of Ni Guangnan, the Securities Committee prepared a plan for Lianxiang that allowed north and south Lianxiangs to consolidate and again be listed on the stock market. The asset consolidation of Beijing and Hong Kong was completed on the very last day of the 1997 fiscal year, namely March 31, 1998. Total Beijing Lianxiang assets were determined to be HK$2,092,500,000.

By combining its shares into Hong Kong Lianxiang, the Lianxiang Group Company's ratio of shares rose to 73.4%, while the public shareholders' ratio went to 26.6%.

Theoretically and from a legal standpoint, from being a solely State-owned entity, Lianxiang had now evolved into being an entity with combined ownership by the Chinese State and by public shareholders. No matter how much wealth was created by company employees, however, none of it belonged to them. The greatest obstacle to realizing an employee shareholder system was the relationship between the company and the "State," or the Chinese government. Way back at the beginning, the Chinese Academy of Sciences had permitted Lianxiang to retain a portion of dividends, but the Academy did not have the power to allow the company to turn this "dividend distribution right" into a "share ownership right." According to China's system, only the Ministry of Finance and the State Assets Management Bureau can represent the State in determining the ownership of State assets.

Zeng Maochao's old position as Head of the Computer Institute now proved useful. Zeng went about calling on his many friends. He was able to secure various connections. The Ministry of Finance agreed to allow the company to have 35% of the State-owned shares, but it said that employees of Lianxiang had to purchase these with cash. This method of putting a portion of shares into employee hands had been broadly adopted in the great wave of China's state-owned enterprise reform. Since employees often did not have large amounts of cash, authorities could either value the state assets at an extremely low price, or they could just transfer the assets for no payment. This had brought on tremendous corruption to the point that there are few examples in China of successful transitions from state to private. Instead, many organizations have been investigated by the government's auditing authorities. Liu Chuanzhi did not plan to do it this way. His principle was, "since we need to reform, we will, but we do not want to become sacrificial victims of reform."

Liu Chuanzhi had sowed the seeds for this day five years earlier. Despite getting 35% profit-distribution-rights at that time, he never distributed a penny. He had the Finance Department record this sum in an account every year, and it accumulated year by year until it was a significant sum. At a price of RMB 1.6 per share the company now purchased the State-owned share portion of 35%. It allowed employees, overnight, to become the owners of their own enterprise.

Liu Chuanzhi's beliefs with regard to the company distribution system were the combined result of socialist and capitalist factors. He believed that company profits should be divided and shared by all employees for he knew that a high-level compensation system would attract high-calibre employees. Liu felt that the profits and losses of a company were determined less by ordinary workers than by the management team. Regular employees' income should be, relatively speaking, quite stable—it should not jump up if company profits rose dramatically, and at the same time regular employees should not bear the responsibility for company losses. The management team's income, on the contrary, should rise and fall with company fortunes. An outstanding management team should not be linked solely by beliefs. It also should have sufficient benefits, sufficient salary, a good work environment, and part ownership of the enterprise's assets.

Due to these beliefs, Liu Chuanzhi espoused a system whereby all company employees were allowed to enter an Employee Shareholders' Association and, moreover, were accorded dividend rights. After going through the two new issues and a reduction in shareholders, publicly-held shares in the Lianxiang Group (Stock 00992) constituted 43%, while the Lianxiang control-shares Group constituted 57%. Within the 57%, the Chinese Academy of Sciences held 65%, the company's Employee

Shareholders' Association held 35%. According to the final decision of the Board of Directors, among the shares held by the Employee Shareholders' Association, fifteen "people who had made special contributions" were to hold 35%; one hundred people who had "historical contributions" were to hold 20%, and later employees of the company were to hold the remaining 45%.

All members of the Employee Shareholders' Association were given a red booklet in which was recorded the number of shares owned by the employee. According to newspaper reports, Liu Chuanzhi's own shares totalled 1,698,600,000, among which were 10,266,000 shares and 6,720,000 options. Liu Chuanzhi's own shares constituted 3% of the shares held by the fifteen special contributors. From this, the percentage of total Lianxiang shares owned by Liu Chuanzhi himself can be calculated: 1.4% of all shares.

Shares held by the Employee Shareholders' Association were in a different category from publicly-held shares, for they could only be granted to people within the company. They could not be sold on the market. The dividends were therefore the more practically significant part of this arrangement to employees. After the financial accounting for each year the company would pass the appropriate dividends to the Chairman of the Board, Zeng Maochao. The Chairman of the Board would distribute the dividends according to the number of shares owned by each employee. By fiscal year 1997 figures, Hong Kong Lianxiang made HK$26,110,000 and Beijing Lianxiang made RMB 33,910,000, so the figures are as follows:

> (HK$26110,000 + RMB 3,3910,000) x 57% x 35% x 35% = the share of the fifteen special contributors' dividends.
> (HK$26110,000 + RMB 3,3910,000) x 57% x 35% x 20% = the share of the one hundred historical contributors' dividends.
> (HK$26110,000 + RMB 3,3910,000) x 57% x 35% x 45% = the share of several thousand later-arrived employees' dividends.

Lianxiang's stock option system was also set up in this period. It derived from rules of the Hong Kong Stock Exchange, which specifies that the company had the right to take 10% of all shares on the market and reserve them for distribution to its own employees. At the time, all employees who had more than three years of seniority were entitled to receive one stock option authorization.

The two systems, stock option rights and Employee Shareholders' Association shares, were different in character. Employees owned the shares at 80% of their value on the date of issue. After June, they had the right to sell 25% of the shares on the market, after six months they could only sell an average of 25%. What an employee made off the shares was the difference between the price on the day he received the shares and the day he sold them. If share prices did not increase and even declined, the employee would earn no benefits, but neither did the employee need to pay out anything. As for stock options, as soon as an employee left the company he lost these, so that another name for "stock options" was "golden handcuffs." This logic was invented by large Western companies that hoped that employees would focus on the long-term development of the company. Every time the company shares went up, the stock option holder had the opportunity to make considerable profits. Microsoft stock options are a good example: in the 1990s, several thousand people made tens of millions of US dollars, and several dozen people made hundreds of millions.

Lianxiang's compensation system gradually stabilized and matured. The income of employees now included four aspects:

1. wages: including wages for one's position and wages for results
2. bonus: as determined by each person's work results
3. share dividends: as determined by the entire company's annual operating profit
4. stock options: as determined by the long-term development circumstances of the company.

In 1997, all this was "talking about soldiers on paper" when it came to stock options and share dividends. The first time stock options were actually issued was the beginning of 1999, while share dividends were only truly realized in the year 2000.

Global recognition

In January of 1997, when Lianxiang announced that its computers held the largest market share in the Chinese market, many people were not convinced. The debate about "Who is Number One" raged for several weeks. According to the statistical data of IDC, the IT market intelligence company, the difference among the top three in the personal computer market was tiny, less than one hundredth of one percent. By the end of 1997, Lianxiang had survived the toughest crisis in its history, winning a war on both north and south fronts. And, according to the newest IDC market report, Lianxiang had sold 435,860 computers, an increase of 111%. It now had a market share of 10.7%, having pulled far ahead of the Number Two in the market, IBM. Lianxiang became globally recognized as "Number One in sales in the Chinese market." In addition, the Shaoyang notebook computers that it produced were now entering the market and ranked among the top five, while its Wanquan Server, put out in 1995, now ranked among the top ten in sales in the Asia Pacific region.

In 1997, 2,210,956 motherboards for personal computers were sold on the international market, only some 47% of the peak period. Lianxiang began to put computers into the international market, but in small quantity: by company records, only 347 computers left the country, given to people as gifts by senior Chinese officials when making state visits. The gifts went to Mongolia, Cameroon, Mozambique, Zambia, Côtes d'Ivoire, Morocco, Romania, Chechnya, and Tunisia: the political import of these computers was greater than their economic significance.

In the fall of 1997, a large forum was held in Beijing called "China and the World march in step together." At this conference, the Hewlett-Packard representative noted that, "Lianxiang truly is the rising star of the Chinese market." Yang Yuanqing regarded Hewlett-Packard as his "teacher" and not out of politeness—it was simply a fact. Yang must have felt that this sentence was the greatest reward a teacher could bestow on his student.

A good manager recognizes that individuals should receive recognition of their achievements. At the end of 1997, Liu Xiaolin received an unexpected award. When Yang Yuanqing was evaluating merit and distributing company benefits, he thought of those who had made real contributions. He allocated RMB 130,000 to Liu Xiaolin, which was exactly the price of a Jedda sedan. Liu did not hesitate a moment—he handed the money over to an auto dealer and drove the car home.

9

GODFATHER OF CHINA'S INFORMATION INDUSTRIES

When you and another chicken are the same size, the other one will always think you are smaller than he is. When you are a rooster, and the other guy a little chicken, you might think you are pretty big but the other guy thinks you are about the same size. Only when you are an ostrich will others admit you are bigger. Be careful not to overestimate yourself.

Liu Chuanzhi

Newly appointed Premier Zhu Rongji took the questions of several hundred reporters as though they were a fresh spring breeze blowing on his face. He talked of reform, development, impediments and risks. He talked of science and technology revitalizing the country. He spoke of new mechanisms, of opening the Chinese telecommunications market, of how "the government is determined to streamline state-owned organizations during this term, and to cut the number of people employed by them in half". He also declared, "no matter how treacherous the territory ahead, how full of landmines, we will not turn back. We will exert ourselves to the utmost until the very end." Under the influence of his dramatic phrases, one could imagine all of China rising to meet the challenge.

In spring of 1998, a reform government had taken the helm again. Li Peng had governed for ten years from the northern compound of *Zhongnanhai*; things were now changing. Zhu Rongji summoned Liu Chuanzhi to discuss concerns of Chinese enterprises. Liu told him frankly that the endlessly changing government policies and overall system had brought tremendous risk to enterprises. He described, as an example, how the central government had levied a super-high tax on bonuses, how he had tried to evade these taxes and been fined, how the government had soon after retracted its policy and eradicated the tax.

Liu was by now a representative in the Ninth National People's Congress. He voted for Zhu Rongji because he felt that "the country should be handed over to intelligent, upright, strong and energetic people to govern." The first thing he did after being made an NPC representative was to persuade organizers of the NPC and the National People's Consultative Committee to move several hundred Lianxiang computers into the Great Hall of the People. Foreign computers had always been used at these two annual events, and nobody had ever objected. As soon as Liu Chuanzhi came in, he said; "If the NPC doesn't even use China-made brands," he said, "how can we talk about revitalizing the country?"

Moving Lianxiang computers into the Hall was symbolic. Sales were moving upward anyway under the leadership of Yang Yuanqing. The recently concluded Winter Vacation Sales of the Lianxiang 1+1 were highly successful. A new model called the Heavenly Lute became the new star of the market, selling around 8,000 machines every day. "Hug a Heavenly Lute and take it home," as the *S&T Daily* wrote in its February 4 report, and this became the thing to do for families during Chinese New Year. On February 26, the company began to promote its First-generation New Concept Computer: the Lianxiang Wentian 301. Wentian means "ask the heavens," linking the concept of a computer with the Internet. This "Ask the heavens" put CPU and monitor together into one entity, with Hitachi helping to develop liquid crystal technology for the monitors. This was the first time Chinese people had seen such monitors used on a desktop computer. Although the screens were small—they came in two sizes, 13.3 inches and 12.1 inches—and the prices were expensive—RMB 25,800 and 19,800—they were inspirational.

The enthusiasm of customers attracted the attention of market research experts. They had decided that the brand of "Lianxiang" was worth RMB 357.4 million in 1996; now they raised that to RMB 418.1 million. In a February 1998 study on the value of Chinese brands, Lianxiang was still far behind such brands as HongtaShan (RMB 35.3 billion), Changhong (RMB 18.2 billion), Haier (RMB 11.8 billion) and Yiqi (RMB 727.6 million), but it had surpassed the famous Qingdao Beer. Thousands of articles announced the entry of Chinese enterprises into the age of brand competition. Lianxiang was the only computer brand to enter the ranks of the top ten brands in China.

The value of the Chinese name *Lianxiang* as a brand was rising, but not the English trademark "Legend," the name by which Lianxiang was known to foreigners. When the company took this English-identity trademark to be registered abroad, it had a rude awakening. Others had long since registered the name. By the beginning of 1998, senior management realized that it was a serious mistake not to have done a timely registration of the trademark overseas. The conclusion of a meeting in the Number 505 Conference Room was that "it is not realistic to continue to use the Legend brand to enter the North American market." After the consolidation of the Hong Kong and Beijing companies, the name of the consolidated company was changed to the Lianxiang Group Company. This supplanted the former Beijing Lianxiang Computer New Technology Development Company. In Hong Kong, the "Hong Kong Lianxiang Control-shares Limited" was changed to Lianxiang Group Share Company Ltd. Despite the conclusion in Number 505, though, nobody was willing to give up the banner of "Legend." Only three years later did the company again address this problem and begin to reconsider the name. By this time, it had to pay an even greater price for the delay.

New fiscal year

Since 1994, when the company was listed on the Hong Kong Stock Exchange, the company's fiscal year ran from April 1 to March 31. In the fiscal year that had just passed, the company's record was not too bad: sales income of RMB 12.5 billion. Approximately 62% of profits for the year came from Lianxiang computers. The company no longer served as agent for foreign computer brands, since its own computers already held a 10.7% market share and, under these conditions, no foreign enterprise was willing to hand over its computers to Lianxiang. Lianxiang still carried out enormous agenting of other products in the Chinese market: 34% of Toshiba Notebook computers, 30% of Hewlett-Packard inkjet printers, and 35% of Hewlett-Packard laser printers were sold by Lianxiang.

"1997 was a year in which the company went sideways, consolidated," Li Qin said. "1998 will be a year in which it takes off." The word "take-off" had been discussed in advance with Liu Chuanzhi, for Liu picked up on it in a speech in which he detailed what the signal was going to be for "take-off" after the "run-up approach."

Despite its impressive growth, the company could not stop to catch a breath, for competitors were following closely behind. Manufacturers within China were mobilizing forces, "Tongchuang" being the closest of the pursuers. In the last twelve months, it had sold 200,000 computers, and was described by the *Weekly Computer Report* as the fastest growing computer enterprise in China. The birth of Founder had preceded Lianxiang's by less than one and one half years, yet this company was now selling at least 10,000 computers every month. Qinghua Tongfang announced that in the next three years it would expand production capacity to 500,000 machines. Shida declared that in the next twelve months it would produce 100,000 machines and enter the ranks of the top eight national manufacturers. Changhong had originally made televisions, now it set up a computer planning group and a person named Ren Dongwei declared that "Changhong will be attacking the information-industries with all its might, first with monitors, then with complete machines, and finally with Internet products." The television industry enjoyed a saying at the time: "change TV production lines a little and you can produce computers." Many headlines declared: "Tiger comes out of the mountain", "Full-scale attack on the information-industries market" and so on. None of the competitors was specifically aimed at Lianxiang, but the ambient threat was enough to make the company sit up and take notice.

The concern was expressed in a proposed revision of that old advertising line, "If humanity loses Lianxiang, what's the world going to do?" People said this line had great vision, but did not make clear what Lianxiang was actually doing. Some felt the line should read, "If humanity loses Lianxiang, what are computers going to do?" Others said that this was changing an ad about the entire entity into an ad about one of its parts, and thereby diminishing it.

If one had asked the President of the Asia-Pacific region of Dell Company, Phillip E. Kelly, to answer this question, he might have responded, "If computers don't exist in the future, what's the world going to do?" In the last week of February, this man visited Beijing, which made Chinese finally pay attention to Dell. A journalist named Li Sun from *Weekly Computer News* interviewed Kelly, and he declared, "The first to enter the market is not necessarily the one who wins. For years, Dell was Number 32 in the Asia-Pacific market, but now has jumped to Number Nine. This is not Dell's ultimate goal: Dell intends to keep going at the same pace and in a few years China will see Dell succeed." This young American company of the same age as Lianxiang clearly was pointing its spear in the direction of Number One. The journalist's article ran with the headline: "Direct Sales King plans to monopolize China."

In the first week of the new fiscal year, Lianxiang's share price rose to RMB 3. By the end of the second week, the company increased its shares in the Hong Kong market by 150,000,000 shares and raised HK$450,000,000 in new capital. This was the first share expansion since the company was listed. The offering was oversubscribed by four times and Lianxiang shares rose dramatically the following day. This also indicated that the "consolidation of Beijing and Hong Kong" of several months earlier had been well received by the market. Senior management was delighted with the success of the offering, but was soon to realize that the taste of "having money with no place to spend it," was no better than "not having any money to spend."

A trip to Taiwan, and strategic changes in the company

Changes that occurred in Lianxiang in the spring of 1998 were intangible yet highly significant. The company had pursued others—now it was being pursued. Secondly, in the past it needed money but lacked funds, now its pockets were bulging but it didn't know where to spend the money. In the past, the company was small but sounded big and felt that it could go anywhere it wanted, now the company was large but strangely hesitant about stepping out. The new generation of young people that had entered the company in the 1980s was now mature. Yang Yuanqing's success in the market had helped generate trust from the older generation. On April 15, the company's new roster of senior management appointments sent a powerful message: other than Liu Chuanzhi, Li Qin, Zeng Maochao, and Cao Zhijiang, the frontline commanders were all young. They included three senior vice-presidents: Ma Xuezheng, Guo Wei, and Yang Yuanqing, five vice-presidents: Zhang Rongzong, Chen Guodong, Jia Zhiqiang, Wang Xiaochun, and Wu Minwei, and ten Assistants to the President.

The biggest change of all, however, was that the company was reconsidering its strategic direction.

By the spring of 1998, the currency crisis that began in Thailand had been going on for eight months, enveloping the entire western rim of the Pacific. The free market systems of Southeast Asian countries were infected. The crisis stormed through Malaysia, Singapore, the Philippines, and Indonesia, Korea and Japan and even China's Taiwan and Hong Kong were unable to escape. The storm wavered on the edges of China's coastline but did not come up on land. Nonetheless, it threw a shadow over Zhu Rongji's hard-won "Chinese Economic Revitalization". The growth rate of the economy declined, retail sales declined, currency deflated, the unemployment rate rose. Officials of the Ministry of Foreign Economic Relations and Trade (MOFERT) guaranteed to the Premier that although

China's exports would not continue to grow as they had the previous year at 20%, they could achieve 10% growth. The first-quarter statistics of the Statistical Bureau, however, proved otherwise: the figure was actually negative.

Like Zhu Rongji, Liu Chuanzhi felt there was much he wanted to do but was unable to accomplish. He was aware that for the past ten years he had learned too little about the world. He felt as though he had been sitting in a well looking up at the sky. This feeling became particularly acute when he led a group of senior management personnel to visit Taiwan in April of 1998. By protocol, this eleven-day trip was a return visit for the trip by Hongji's President, Shi Zhenrong, to the Mainland. The agenda mainly revolved around the information industries in Taiwan, and included visits to production centers, industrial research institutes, software associations, the most famous of Taiwan's manufacturers, the Xinzhu S&T Development Center, and the "Father of Science in Taiwan," Li Guoding.

The group was seeing Taiwan up close for the first time. Lianxiang managers observed the technological level of Taiwan's industrial production, the professionalism and nimbleness of its management. They noted that 70% of the spare parts produced were sold overseas. They saw that all the computers coming off the production lines were IBM, HP, Compaq, and Dell. "Turns out what we call "foreign brands" in China are really all being manufactured by the people of Taiwan!" Chen Guodong exclaimed. "These people are truly phenomenal. We on the Mainland are far behind them. You can only understand if you see it in person." One day the group visited a factory under the banner of the Guangbao Group, and saw that the production line was compiling notebook computers for a foreign manufacturer. The manager of this company explained that when the American company attacked its brand the machine immediately became its product. Liu Chuanzhi asked, "Why should they want it to be made by you?" As soon as he picked up the product to look at it, he didn't need an answer. "This thing is truly made well. American companies will undeniably order it. This is Taiwan's strength."

However, Taiwanese manufacturers envied Lianxiang's huge China market as well as Lianxiang's sales network. "The land is so incredibly big, and has such a fast-growing computer market," said Shi Zhenrong. Liu Chuanzhi wanted to know why the Hongji Company had not marched into the American market since it had such tremendous capacity. Why, instead, was it willing to use its own production lines to do value-added for foreign brands? Shi Zhenrong told him that Hongji had tried to put its own brand into the American market. It had spent millions of US dollars on the effort, and all for nothing. He warned that creating an international brand was not easy.

The last stop on the Taiwan journey was Sun Moon Lake, where the company held a one-day conference. All of the visitors from China now had a visceral understanding of Lianxiang's greatest asset: its good fortune was to have been born on the Chinese Mainland. The group then began to discuss what had been regarded as the company's key strategic focus: "advancing overseas."

Liu Chuanzhi confessed that he had been strongly affected by the visit to Taiwan. He told the others that they should now reconsider the "advance overseas" strategy, a dream the company had held for some ten years. "What do we rely on for success at Lianxiang? We rely on the advantages of our own native turf. Producing and selling in China, we get support from the government as well as the people. We are supported by media. There is a good analogy for the way we should use our resources. How do Israelis irrigate in a part of the world that has so little water? They calculate how much water the plant cells lack, and then they put every drop where it counts. Americans irrigate like mad, but indiscriminately. So what's my point? My point is this: First, we want to ask Yang Yuanqing to reconsider, to think about whether it is worthwhile taking our brand overseas. Second, we want to think about how to make our brand even better in the Chinese market."

The results of this Sun Moon Lake Conference became Lianxiang's Five-part Strategy. People were to talk about it for years to come.

1. A pluralistic approach to information industries, not just one-track.
2. Emphasis on developing the market within China.
3. Investment in Canadian manufacturing.
4. Investment in Canadian R&D.
5. Strengthening investment resources.

Liu Chuanzhi had always felt that formulating strategy was the primary element in managing the company. Company files hold copious amounts of information on the subject. Looking through this material, it becomes apparent that four of these five items were not new. Senior management had repeatedly proposed them. Only the second item constituted a major revision: the "advance overseas" strategy was now out.

Yang Yuanqing shelved the huge "advance overseas" strategy. Plans for two teams to investigate the Hong Kong and European markets were cancelled. The industrial investment company led by Cao Zhijiang stopped most of its projects. Chen Guodong let go of the attempt to woo businesses into the Huiyang Industrial Park. The company began to focus.

Global commercial leaders

In the fall of 1998, "proud corn and waving wheat" were growing from northern China to the great Northeast. South of the Yangtze River, rice fields were rippling by the thousands, yet it seemed that this traditionally agricultural country had entered a strange new world. Everyone was enraptured by the marvelous allure of the Internet. Everyone wanted to partake of a virtual digital life. The leaders in Zhongnanzhai were consumed with the headaches of state-owned enterprises, defunct manufacturing industries that they swore to "revitalize." Party propaganda organs sent journalists out to sing the virtues of model labor heroes to counter this materialistic trend, but the person of greatest news value this year was Liu Chuanzhi. Chinese journalists were now describing him as "the godfather of Chinese information industries." *Time* magazine ranked him as Number 14 in its top twenty-five most influential leaders in the world.

Foreigners wondered what this Chinese entrepreneur was all about. While it may be true that Liu is "the godfather of China's information industries," one could also say that he allowed Chinese to have extreme and unrealistic hopes about the "digital economy." Both "information industries" and "digital economy" were trendy terms in 1998. Liu led the charge and was among those to encounter the bubble. But if he had not, fourteen years earlier, led a group of people in a new direction, it is very possible there would be no Chinese voice in this arena today.

China is moving towards "information industries". Lianxiang's first step in this direction was to expand its software development, for the rest of the business was going well. In 1998, Lianxiang sold 763,365 computers, an increase of 75% over the year before. IDC's reports showed Lianxiang's market share on a par with the three big firms in Asia. In home-use computers, it was Number One in Asia. In 1998, Lianxiang became the "best agent" for Hewlett-Packard in China for the tenth time. The company then teamed up with the world's second largest software enterprise, Guanqun, to establish a new software company, called "Lianxiang Guanqun." It set up headquarters in the four main regions of China; it set up a strategic partnership with the Yongyou Company; it bought 30% of Jinshan Software Company (Kingsoft). This was the first time a hardware company had gone so thoroughly into the software arena. The peak of activity came in the fall of 1998, when Lianxiang and IBM signed an agreement to cooperate in developing software. This astonished the press. Journalists unconsciously began to put Lianxiang and "Big Blue" together in the same breath, although, as Liu Chuanzhi noted at the time, Lianxiang and IBM operated on totally different scales. To some this was not important. *Time* magazine explained why it put Liu Chuanzhi in the same ranking as global commercial leaders by saying that his goal was to surpass Hewlett-Packard and IBM. "Today China, tomorrow the world."

China was on the doorstep of the Information Age in 1998. The common belief was that "we are going from an industrial to an information society." The government began to use the term "Information Capacity" to evaluate the country's prosperity. A group of scholars came out with a report called *Research report on China's Information Capacity*. Among twenty-eight countries in its comparison, America came first with 71.76 points; China's information capacity was 6.17, ranking it next to last. This conclusion issued from the government's Social Sciences Foundation.

The scientific community in China was amazed at Lianxiang's rapid growth and was also curious about the field of information industries. On October 10, fifty Academicians of the Chinese Academy of Sciences and the Engineering Institute came to Lianxiang's operations base on the northern side of ZGC. These men were the best of China's scientists. They noted that "it is a rare opportunity to stand here at the window of Lianxiang, from which we can view the future of China's information industries."

Not everyone believed that this information age was the trend of the future. Doubts came initially from the leaders of the Chinese scientific community. The Chairman of the State Science Commission, Song Jian, publicly expressed his concern about this mad pursuit of the "Information Society." He thought it had the potential to deceive people. On November 25, 1998, in the *Chinese Science News*, he published an article that said, "We must be alert and not be deceived by the casual approach of these authors." This angered many young people. One took up the challenge and wrote an article called; "A Fraud or a Trend". "Some reject the so-called Information Society," he wrote, "saying it is the misleading deceit of some authors. No-one in this field in my generation is anything but appalled by this." He recalled the words of the founding father of modern China, Sun Yatsen: "Mighty are the great trends of the world: those who go with them flourish, those who oppose them die."

This debate was far from having the emotional force of other recent debates in China, however, particularly "is it called socialism or is it called capitalism?" and "are we for a planned economy or a market economy?"

Instead, this debate seemed to be a struggle between the older and younger generations in China. The 1990s were a decade of declining agriculture and flourishing commerce. Moving too far in this direction, however, was known in traditional terms as "taking the branch for the root, or getting things backward." Educated young people increasingly disliked traditional industries, they disliked farming; they liked cities. They disliked "blue-collar" and liked "white-collar," they disliked workers' clothes and liked trendy fashion, they disliked an assembly line and liked an office, they disliked the noise of machinery and liked the sound of popular music. Their parents' generation had believed that the only true security lay in physical production of goods, while these young people had a kind of fanatical belief in the power of information and knowledge. Many things indicated that the world was moving in their direction. America was experiencing an economy of high growth, low inflation, and high employment. Things seemed to be booming and the Internet seemed to be the reason.

In China, no matter what the issue, somebody is always talking about it while somebody else is actually doing it. Lianxiang did not want to be rolled into this debate about "misleading fraud" or "major trend." The company's understanding of the information industry was well explained in comments made by Li Qin at a conference. "Let us take a look at how big the cake is in the information industries market," he said. "In 1998, the growth rate in the global computer market is slowing and should be between 14 and 17%. The Asian currency crisis made demand for information markets smaller than predicted and this unfavorable influence will continue for at least five years. The growth rate of the China market is also not optimistic. In 1997, the growth rate of China's information industries was 41.3%, while this year it is only 27%." This evaluation was closer to the mark than many.

The ERP Project: "Enterprise Resource Plan"
In November 1998, the company officially initiated its "ERP Project." This was an unprecedented reform in the company, involving more than 6,500 people, costing RMB 20 million, and extending over fourteen months. Its purpose was to improve the company's internal management procedures. The process was managed by two women—one young and one old. The older woman's name was Gong Guoxing. Forty years earlier she had been Liu Chuanzhi's classmate and she later became his wife. Twenty years earlier she entered the Computer Institute with him, more than ten years earlier she became one of the Founders of Lianxiang. She

was modest and self-effacing in nature. As the Chinese phrase goes, she was "able to endure both hard work and criticism." The younger woman was Wang Xiaoyan. She was willful, and daring. She could "endure hard work but did not take well to criticism." Everyone said that the computer industry was a man's world, but Lianxiang included quite a few women. Women held one-fourth of its senior management positions. These pages have already mentioned Hu Xilan, Zhou Xiaolan, Ma Xuezheng, Qiao Jian and Wang Lijie, all of whom were outstanding. In 1999, the two women in the company who most attracted attention were Gong Guoxing and Wang Xiaoyan. Gong led the way in recommending that ERP be adopted; Wang took this idea and made it reality.

The term "ERP" needs some explanation. It can be directly translated as "Enterprise Resource Plan". It is a set of enterprise management systems software that was developed by a German company, called SAP, in the mid-1990s, that has been adopted by various large enterprises in developed countries. Lianxiang was the first enterprise in China to express an interest in adopting it. Companies in China had no advanced management systems at the time; software programs developed by companies like Yongyou came only later. Lianxiang researched the world's most advanced management systems and deliberated carefully for twelve months before making a decision to adopt ERP to replace its old management systems. Everyone knew the tremendous risks involved, since the new systems were totally different from a management style that had been in place for years.

The President's Office held an "oath-swearing meeting" to confirm corporate-wide support for the effort. This very Chinese term indicates a meeting in which everyone pledges support for an action, in this case casting off the old and taking in the new with a positive attitude. The reason for "casting off the old" was that while the company's business kept growing, its management systems were stagnating. Barriers between departments meant that information could not be consolidated. Reconciling accounts at the end of every month was a headache. In needing to change, Li Qin drew the analogy of a mature person wearing the clothes of a child. "A child keeps growing bigger, and his original clothes get too small," he said. "If you don't do something, sooner or later there are consequences."

The President's Office was resolute and the oath-swearing was vigorous. Liu Chuanzhi called on all employees to participate in the process, "put your back into it, conquer all difficulties, set up your own confidence in certain victory." Still, months went by and the matter proceeded slowly.

Liu Chuanzhi and Li Qin had selected Senior Vice-President Zhu Linan to lead the Project. This brilliant young man from Suzhou had been poached from a company three years earlier in Shenzhen. He later played an important role in many policy decisions in the company, and was third in line in the succession to Liu Chuanzhi after Yang Yuanqing and Guo Wei. Zhu Linan's horizons were broad, he knew his subordinates well enough to deploy them well, he had a sense of propriety. Clearly, he was qualified. Yet he lacked a full understanding of the details of the business, such as Yang Yuanqing had. He also was unwilling to spend his own time on the implementation process. After he became the Chief Commander of the ERP Project in 1999, his first thought was to transfer Gong Guoxing over to finish the details. Gong was at that time Vice-Chairman of the Enterprise Planning Office. She had successfully established the first information management system for the company in the early 1990s, and she was familiar with ERP. Zhu Linan hoped that she could supplement his own shortcomings with her experience and prestige.

Gong Guoxing smoothly completed negotiations with the German SAP Company. At the time, almost everyone was opposed to ERP. The General Managers of the three main departments in the company looked dubiously at Gong Guoxing and asked the same thing: "Is this thing going to work?" The company had weathered many storms under its old system: business was bigger now, but the old ways seemed to operate well. Although there was a localized Chinese edition of ERP, people doubted if it was really adapted to Chinese conditions. One problem was that the immediate concerns were so great that managers could not deal with less urgent distractions. Every morning, managers wanted to look at sales reports. They did not want to change their well-established procedures.

Everyone in the company had an opinion and the debate raged. To understand why, one must understand China's corporate management systems at the time. Almost all companies were divided into departments, each of which governed itself. Lianxiang had spent ten years trying to break through the ramparts between these, and had formulated a "Department connections system" that ran to more than one hundred articles. The company's management thinking focussed on coordination among departments, but the core concept of ERP was integration. It required all employees to comply with same-behavior rules and it treated the company as one entity. Its basic management concept was known as "process." This was a little like a large river, into which all the tributaries flowed from their mountain sources. Each drop of water had its position as it flowed from the upper to the middle to the lower reaches, joining the main channel of the great river, finally entering the East China Sea. From the moment an employee entered this "process," his responsibilities and rights were dictated by it. The old familiar ways had to be thrown away and he had to use new methods. All of the various resources of the enterprise were now to be integrated: capital, technology, people, rights, sales channels and so on. Where every one of many thousands of employees was at each moment, what they were doing, how they were doing it, had to be clear. There could not be wasted space and there could also not be duplication in activities. Naturally there should also not be any conflict.

Lianxiang's own employees were the first problem. The second problem related to cooperating with the Germans. SAP Company was encouraged that Lianxiang had adopted its system. Its ambition was to enter the China market and the company no doubt felt that Lianxiang's use of its software was an intangible advertisement. SAP was unaware of the many "Chinese Characteristics" in Chinese enterprises, however. It did not know that these were things that could not be contained in any advanced management software from outside China. After being made aware of this, SAP Company asked a famous consulting company in to help, confident that it had a greater understanding of China, but it too was unable to penetrate the mysteries inherent in Chinese enterprises. As one small example, when a person named Wang Lijie in the Finance Department mentioned "internal bank", the foreigners were mystified. "A bank is a bank," they said. "Why do you say internal and external?"

Although Gong Guoxing supported the company's decision to apply ERP, she knew it was risky. As Liu Chuanzhi, her husband, feared, "If we don't implement ERP, we're just waiting to die. If we do implement ERP, we're looking for death!" For many weeks she tried to persuade managers who, like herself, had some confidence in the new system but nevertheless felt that the end results of implementation at Lianxiang would be minimal. Her gentle, uncombative nature, her willingness to take a step backward— so admirable a trait in Tai Chi Chuan and traditional Chinese philosophy— made it impossible for her to break through the company's "psychological barrier" and managers' passive opposition.

Days were going by without any progress. Gong finally lost patience. She marched into Zhu Linan's office. "I'm not doing it any more," she said. "I quit." Zhu Linan tried to calm her down with a cup of tea while he decided what to do. Finally he asked Liu Chuanzhi and Li Qing if he could take someone from the Administration Department to actively promote ERP. The two bosses immediately said, "take whomever you want." He chose Wang Xiaoyan.

Wang Xiaoyan was at the time a Vice-President of the Lianxiang Computer Company, and also Yang Yuanqing's assistant. Her role was a little like Secretary General. She could manage anything, so she was known as "Yang Yuanqing's General." She was forthright, sharp-witted, self-confident and stubborn. She liked difficult tasks. She could slice through those who opposed her like splitting a piece of bamboo. Most importantly, she was a manager of the company's actual business, so she knew the ropes. She had initially regarded this ERP plan as being a waste of the Department's energy, and this very opposition was what made Zhu Linan set his sights on her. "The biggest obstacle to promoting ERP in the company is Wang Xiaoyan," he said. "But if you want to succeed, she has to be the one."

Zhu Linan told Yang that, in exchange for Wang Xiaoyan, Yang could substitute any person in Headquarters for her. Yang Yuanqing nominated Liu Xiaolin to be brought back into the Computer Department.

The two men agreed to this trade on the spot. Many years later, when Zhu Linan discussed this subject he was still happy at how it all worked out. "The thing I am most proud of was getting Wang Xiaoyan to come over," he said. "If it had not been for her, I would have had to put 120% of my energies into this affair and it wouldn't have been accomplished half as well as she did it."

Wang Xiaoyan was delighted with the new mission. In April 1999, her arrival was the turning point for ERP: a situation that had been stalemated for months suddenly changed. She got the President's Office to allocate RMB 3 million to her for special awards for those who contributed to promoting ERP. For the past years several years she had trained directly under Yang Yuanqing, who liked to "whip a cow into action." He put high demands on those he considered especially capable. Wang now used all of this on her team in successfully implementing ERP.

Bill Gates' Venus Plan and criticism from patriots

1999 was the tenth year of Lianxiang's attack on the personal computer market, and it was a year of steady improvement. Adept at utilizing current affairs, Liu Chuanzhi began to use the terms "climate," "topographical advantages," and "favorable geographic position" to realize the company's market plan. But it was impossible for him not to be hurt at times by public opinion. On March 10, he made a brief trip to Shenzhen that unexpectedly drew him into a hornet's nest of national debate.

The situation arose out of a meeting between Liu Chuanzhi and Bill Gates in Southern China. Bill Gates had come to China earlier that week and he arrived in Shenzhen on the same day as Liu Chuanzhi. All but a few businessmen had been excluded from the speeches being held at the Wuzhou Hotel. Liu Chuanzhi was among those invited, he appeared promptly at 9am and with him were the President of Sitong, Duan Yongji, and the President of Haier, Zhang Ruimin. They wanted to hear Bill Gates talk about "Enjoying the Digital Life," and they also wanted to take over this slogan and work it into their own products.

Gates described the benefits of the arrival of the digital age. "The speed of telecommunications on the Internet doubles every one hundred days. In 1994, the number of Internet users in the entire world was only three million, by 1998 it was already 153 million. The increase in the rate of Internet users is as much as 29% in America and Canada, in Europe it is 5%, in east-Asia regions and South America it is only 1%. In Africa, there are only around one million people using the Internet. China has 2.1 million people currently using the Net with a penetration rate of less than 2% and the use of personal computers is also less than 2%. You have a mature consumer electronics market, however, and an unbelievable VCD market of around 40 million."

He then announced a plan that was to stimulate Chinese debate for a full year: "Under these circumstances, the Microsoft China R&D Center is going to invest US$40 million in the next five years, with Windows CE as a platform, to enter the market in China with Chinese-language hand-held home-use-style computers."

Bill Gates called this new plan the "Venus." He declared that these marvelous products would be on the market in the second half of 1999. After he finished speaking, Lianxiang announced that it would be creating set-top boxes that would be compatible with the Venus Plan for accessing the Internet. These boxes were lightweight and ingenious. They had tremendous functions that allowed you to connect to cables, to receive and send electronic messages, to handle Chinese-character files. Moreover, they were compatible with the newest Chinese VCD standards. The presenter of this Lianxiang product declared that the set-top boxes "merge information products and home-use computers into a new generation of products."

Liu Chuanzhi and Bill Gates were not in close contact and the relationship between Lianxiang and Microsoft was fairly formal. It could not be compared to Lianxiang's relationship with Hewlett-Packard or Intel. The Chinese phrase "gratitude and resentment" described the relationship over the years. Lianxiang had been the largest buyer of Microsoft operating systems among computer manufacturers in China, but its purchases of Windows licenses did not increase at the same rate its computer production did. In fact, most computer manufacturers in China only installed Microsoft operating systems in a small percentage of their products. They sold the rest as a "shell" without installing any software. Salespeople would generally offer two prices to the purchaser: if he wanted to install a Windows operating system, then he had to pay RMB 300 more. Salespeople would say that the customer had to decide whose operating system he wanted to use. Most home users would not pay an extra RMB 300 to purchase the license for Windows, but they still hoped to use Windows: this left considerable room for pirated copies. Virtually every computer maker in China was aware of this, but turned a blind eye to it. Intense competition in the market made cost of goods the key to a sale: Lianxiang could do nothing but copy the same approach.

Senior management of Microsoft was at a loss as to what to do about this piracy. The company didn't care about the smaller makers. Instead, it put the full force of its anger on Lianxiang. Liu Chuanzhi had tremendous respect for Bill Gates and the company he led. He told a CCTV reporter, "Personal computers are having a revolutionary effect on how we live and work. My 80-year-old mother uses a personal computer to send emails to her grandson. All of this is because Microsoft put out Windows, an operating system that uses a graphic interface. Without Microsoft's hard work, personal computers would be nothing like as widespread as they are today."

Clearly, if the two could work together, the world's largest software company and a Chinese hardware producer with the most product in the Chinese computer market, it would be advantageous for both. That afternoon, Bill Gates and Liu Chuanzhi met again. They announced that they had established a "partner relationship." They said they would have "even greater cooperation" in such concrete projects as hand-held computers and set-top boxes. When Bill Gates left China, Liu Chuanzhi gave him the first hand-held computer based on Windows CE, developed jointly by the Lianxiang Central Research Institute and the Microsoft China R&D Center.

Liu Chuanzhi felt that helping the common man enter the Internet age was a virtuous thing to do. In describing the proposed set-top box in an interview after the conference, he casually noted that Lianxiang might sell several tens of millions, at a price approaching RMB 5,000. He didn't realize that he was describing a monumental cake, one worth at least RMB 200 billion. A domestic uproar ensued. Computer manufacturers, home-use electronic appliance makers, government officials, media, nationalistic patriots surged forward. "It was like the gold rush in California," said Sohu Company President Zhang Chaoyang. Everybody wanted to get in on the act. The biggest critic of the plan, however, was a man named Fang Xingdong. Within forty-eight hours he had published an article called "Venus Plan: good or bad?" "Where is the banner of "national industries" going to float off to?" he asked. Then he ridiculed China's information technology companies as having strong government backing but lacking their own virility, to the point that they were willing to lay down a carpet for Microsoft to walk in and take over China. Monopoly control by Microsoft was feared. The Venus Plan was seen not as a goddess but as a Trojan Horse.

Much of the criticism seemed aimed at Liu Chuanzhi. Only one person named Xia Hong came to Liu's defense. He noted that "Liu Chuanzhi has said, "our approach is to broaden our "face," to stabilize our technology, then layer by layer to pile up the ramparts. It is not to ram a stake in the ground, a very tall one that will blow over the minute a breath of wind comes by."

Irrespective of how Chinese enterprises regarded the Venus Plan, whether as Trojan horse or as goddess, each proceded according to its own self-interest. On March 26, Microsoft signed twenty cooperative agreements with twelve Chinese enterprises. When the *Science Times* reported, "The Venus Plan has stirred up a lot of anxiety in our country's consumer electronics industry," Liu Chuanzhi explained, "The market does not wait for anyone. You can't say "I'm going to stop the market for awhile and ask everyone to wait for me." Nonetheless, the Ministry of Information Industries soon convened an "emergency meeting" outside Beijing, to discuss The Venus Plan and China's information industries. Many senior enterprise managers attended. It looked as though the government was now fixing its attention on Venus as well. Some "experts" lost no time in pouring oil on the flames by saying that Venus was a scheme cooked up multinational corporations: "They are sizing up the China market and getting ready to have their clothes tailor made." Vigorous opposition to Venus began to come from all quarters of China. More and more people questioned Microsoft's motivation. Some people said that China's consumer electronics market had become the goal of monopolists. Others said that the Venus Plan was the first battle in Microsoft's war against China. Their purpose was to grab all of China's market for pocket-sized computers, handheld computers, set-top boxes and so on, in one fell swoop. They would then control the platform for China's new generation of information industries. Others recommended that China's information industries set up strategic alliances with science and technology units, to defend against Microsoft's "technological invasion" of today and its "market monopolization" of tomorrow. The Kaisi Software Group under the control of the Chinese Academy of Sciences' Software Engineering Center began to think of uniting with the Great Wall Company and other large-scale enterprises in China, to raise the flag of a "War of Resistance." They had already announced, twenty-four hours earlier, that they would be calling their product the "Neuwo Plan." *Neuwo* is the Chinese goddess of an ancient Chinese myth.

To pit "Venus" against the "Neuwo" was to make the whole affair both ludicrous and alarming. The media entered the fray. A Beijing TV host declared, "This is a war of great disparity in strength, but it's also a battle that is worth fighting." The *Science Times* report said, less politely, "Our "local goddess" is going up against a "foreign goddess," which has the makings of a tragedy."

Into this situation came grievous news from Europe. On May 8, a NATO plane, with five guided missiles, bombed the Chinese embassy in Yugoslavia. Three people died. When the news reached Beijing, anger was immediately directed at Americans. Many people shouted slogans such as "down with American imperialism." Beijing streets had not seen this kind of thing since the end of the Cultural Revolution. Students made a surprise attack on the American Embassy in Beijing. IBM's organizations in China did not escape, though posters were put up around university campuses among which one said, "Boycott American goods, except for computers!" Microsoft made computer software but this was, after all, American goods. Microsoft's President for Greater China stayed in his apartment in Beijing for days, not daring to emerge. He sent an email to all company employees, saying, "Your safety comes first. The company's interests come second. If needed, the company can instantly shut down."

Liu Chuanzhi had considerable powers of intuition but could not have imagined that things would come to this. He had always been the "standard-bearer of the flag of national industries;" now he feared being called a traitor. After five days he felt he should let the public know his views. He called in reporters and declared: "Lianxiang was involuntarily rolled up in this Venus issue. I myself have no interest in any dispute." Journalists asked what he thought of the "Neuwo Plan" and he said, "This kind of attempt is very admirable, it takes a certain kind of courage." He then reminded people, "enterprises must keep their eye on the market, they can't tackle things by technology alone. Real "patriotism" is not a mere slogan. You can't measure it by how loudly somebody shouts "patriotic slogans." I personally feel that I am imbued with patriotism but I am first of all an entrepreneur. Entrepreneurs must be realistic, walk on firm ground. I have to be very clear about exactly how I myself, and also the company, manifest our patriotic ideals.

"There's no problem in advocating national products, but you can't allow a change in public opinion to railroad you. You particularly can't demand the formation of "protective" standards. Enterprises cannot simply use the word "patriotism" to get people to pull money out of their pockets and put it down on second-rate, high-priced products. Criticizing consumers who do not buy national goods by saying they are unpatriotic is not rational."

"Yang Yuanqing is up here too"

After five years of running the Computer Administration Department, Yang Yuanqing was confident and successful. Sales were Number 1 in the market, and in the Computer Administration Department profit margins were high. With astonishing energy, Yang Yuanqing had taken the company to a pinnacle, and several dozen managers, more than 600 workers, and more than 6,000 salespeople had contributed to the process. The 34-year-old Yang Yuanqing had become famous throughout China and reporters referred to him as "Lianxiang's Little Commander-in-Chief."

The abrupt rise of Lianxiang's computer business brought about the company's and also his personal success, but he had not yet enjoyed its warmth when people were already saying that personal computers were passé. They said the world had entered a "post-PC era." Three men who had founded Internet portals in 1999 were being considered the new stars: Wang Zhidong who founded Sina, Zhang Chaoyang who founded Sohu, and Ding Lei who founded Wang Yi.

Outstanding people often make the mistake of paying overly close attention to their own sphere of operations while neglecting outside developments. They are slow to react. Yang Yuanqing's interest in the Internet came only slowly, and this was similar to Bill Gates on the other side of the Pacific. While people around Gates had long since become aware that the Internet was an unbelievable thing, Gates did not see it. Sometime in 1995 he suddenly woke up. When he did, he sent an email to all 30,000 employees, admitting that he had made a grave mistake.

In China, many thought that the Internet was a trick being played on them by crafty Westerners. They found it hard to imagine the value in such a digital network. They could not comprehend how using a keyboard to transmit information might serve any purpose. Wasn't it good enough to send parcels through the post office? Wasn't it good enough to talk to one another by phone? Why should one spend so much money to lay in a line and buy equipment? Yang Yuanqing had been putting all his energy into lowering the cost of his computers, expanding his sales, beating IBM in becoming Number 1 in China. He first saw the Internet when he went on a visit to America in November 1996. By chance, this was precisely when Netscape was listed on the stock market and all of America was mesmerized by the New Economy. Wherever he went, Yang heard people discussing how much Netscape's share price had risen. Everyone encouraged him to visit an Internet company. According to Liu Ren's record of the occasion, when he did visit an Internet company, and stood before a bank of computers, his first feeling was confusion; he couldn't understand the use of this whole thing. He couldn't understand the concepts that they were talking about, all the new words such as website, homepage, IP address. The impression that remained from this visit was that one could look up the *People's Daily* on the Internet. This was mildly interesting, but he couldn't see how it had anything to do with Lianxiang. "I had not yet progressed very far at the time," Yang Yuanqing later said, "I kept on thinking it would be fine for me to just keep on selling computers."

A former American classmate had given him some addresses and told him various marvelous things about "electronic mail." So he sat in his own office at Lianxiang and wrote that classmate a letter. Internet access was available only to key people in the Research Department at that time. Yang Yuanqing had a dial-up account. "I still didn't know the depths of this thing, I didn't even know how much it cost to send one email" he said. So the first email in his life was brief, to save money: "Yang Yuanqing is up here too. Don't forget me."

For the next three years, his interest in the Internet was limited to using email. Even in 1997, when Lianxiang computers were used on the Yinghaiwei Company's website, he still did not see how combining these two things might be an opportunity. He saw the tremendous enthusiasm that the Chairman of the Board of Yinghaiwei Company, Zhang Shuxin, was pouring into the Internet, but he didn't take it to heart. At that time, content on the Internet was pitifully small and there was no evidence to show that the Internet would make customers buy computers.

By spring of 1999, the situation was different. The Internet linked up terminals of some 56,210,000 computers and some two hundred million users. In China, it linked at least 1,460,000 computers and four million Internet accessors. By the end of 1999, these two figures had doubled. As Andy Grove had said, this was an "age of ten-speeds." Using fifty million users as a benchmark, radio reached fifty million users in 38 years, television in 13 years, cable television in 10 years, personal computers in 6 years, and the Internet in only four years.

China's central government now convened an "Internet Project Mobilization Conference", which signalled that the Internet was recognized and accepted by the authorities. Schools, companies, news media, all began Internet Projects. In 1998, the United Nations News Commission declared the Internet to be "the fourth medium." Xinhua News Agency said in a news brief that "Chinese and foreign experts point out that in ten to twenty years the influence of the Fourth Medium will surpass print media, radio and television." As a tool for electronic commerce, on average, transactions completed via the Internet doubled every 100 days. China's largest software sales organization, the "Alliance of electronics commerce," put out a website named in honor of Mount Everest: "8848," which was the height of the mountain in meters. The site quickly became the most famous e-commerce website in China. The company listed in Hong Kong as Lianbang Company "Zongyi Shares", the price rose from RMB 10 to RMB 35 and became Number One among Chinese Internet listings.

Yang Yuanqing could see the way things were going, but by nature he was stubborn and it was hard to change his mind. He particularly disliked this term "post-PC." "The Internet is a great tool," he said, "but it isn't everything. To make it real, you still have to go through a physical thing, something in the physical world. And making a physical object that works is not as easy as just setting up a website."

In terms of fundamental values, Yang Yuanqing more closely resembled the generation of people that included Liu Chuanzhi. He was rather removed from the younger enthusiasts. However, Yang Yuanqing was already changing. And as he said to the journalist Liu Ren, "It's not too late to do the Internet in China. In fact, it's just about the right time. If you go in too early, you just have to spend a lot of money on paving the road for others to use."

Yang Yuanqing's call to lead the troops into the Internet World can be traced to a specific date, May 5, 1999. His report to the New Fiscal Year Oath-swearing meeting had a stirring title: "Meet the Challenge of the Internet." Yang said that all of China was to hear the footsteps of Lianxiang now as it marched into the Internet World. He finally believed that the Internet would become "the third revolution in Information Industries." At the same time, to Yang Yuanqing, a concrete sales figure was more important than "guiding-principle slogans." He urged his staff to open up an e-commerce system as fast as possible, to meet the peak sales season of summer vacation. On June 28, the system was ready. Reports started coming in: on the first day: more than 10,000 people came to the website and purchased RMB 8,5000,000 worth of computers. This was what he had hoped for. In Xi'an in June, he described the "Internet New Life" for consumers, in October he came to Nanjing University and described the "Future Internet Age" to students. Using a set of slides, he said as many felicitous things as he could think of to say about the Internet, which everyone wanted to hear.

In some respects, Yang seemed to have adopted the habits of Liu Chuanzhi. If something had not been thought through clearly, wait. Don't act on it, and don't talk about it. Unfortunately, Yang did not follow this resolution through to the end. If he had, he would not, one year later, have dived headfirst into the Internet Bubble, and taken such a huge fall.

Final resolution of the Liu—Ni conflict
By the fall of 1999, the conflict between Liu Chuanzhi and Ni Guangnan had entered its final stages. The efforts of the two Board meetings of 1995 and 1997 had not resolved the conflict. Ni Guangnan had not surrendered, verbally or psychologically. He continued to believe that truth lay on his side. After getting no response from his letter to Premier Zhu Rongji, Ni Guangnan no longer trusted the central government and he proceeded to bring his case before the Academicians of the two Academies and the National People's Political Consultative Committee. He hoped that they would help in promoting an investigation of Liu Chuanzhi. On September 12, 1998, eight Academicians united in presenting a case to the Chinese Academy of Sciences. They "expressed their deep sympathies for the treatment of Comrade Ni Guangnan," and they felt that the "nature of the issues reflected by Ni Guangnan was quite serious." On March 11, 1999, twenty-eight NPPCC members wrote a letter to the Chinese Academy of Sciences asking to be allowed to go together with eight Academicians to the Lianxiang Group, "to make a contribution to resolving the split."

These activities of Ni Guangnan actually caused him to lose all support within the Academy of Sciences, as well as any remaining respect and sympathy among the Board of Directors at Lianxiang. On September 2, 1999, for the first time the Board made this whole event public. The Board announced that it was dismissing Ni Guangnan. In his capacity as Chairman of the Board, Zeng Maochao announced the decision while at the same time handing RMB 5 million to the Chinese Academy of

Sciences for exclusive use by Ni Guangnan as funds for investment as he developed new work within a new unit. The Board said that this money was in consideration of his contributions. Ni Guangnan was not grateful. "Lianxiang has no power to dismiss me," he said. He refused to participate in a meeting at which the dismissal was to take place. Five days later, when he knew that the matter was irretrievable, he drafted a statement:

> "Board of Directors of Lianxiang:
> I have received your notice of my dismissal. Please give me an opportunity to respond, and please do not dismiss my work accomplishments. I did two major things in my ten and one-half years in the company as Chief Engineer: 1. Continued my ten years of scientific results in the Chinese Academy of Sciences through directing the development of the Lianxiang Han-card, 2. Directed the development of the Lianxiang System computers, using my experience in developing eight computers for the Computer Institute of the Chinese Academy of Sciences. While in office I led our comrades in developing several dozen large-scale projects and national-level new products. I hope that these work results will not be implicated by your action".

Ni then drafted a "self-criticism", a term commonly applied during the Cultural Revolution when people were required to "reach into themselves and pull it all out, make full confessions of their psychological state". An excerpt follows:

> "Lianxiang Board of Directors:
> This dismissal has made me deeply reflect, and I feel that I have a tremendous responsibility. The "Fiftieth" is coming up [anniversary of the founding of the PRC, in October, 1949], and I don't want to influence the mood of celebration. I have determined to do this self-criticism, and to conclude this affair as soon as possible. I feel that the basis of unifying the split should be the Investigation Report of the Academy of Sciences as approved by Central [the Communist Party].
> I respect this Report and do not again intend to raise this matter to my superiors.
> I am willing in this regard to:

> 1. Publicly apologize to Comrade Liu, because I mistakenly understood his motivation. I looked on the arrangement of debt for shares as a way of running off with company funds.

2. Stop bringing any more suits. Please have those organizations involved make an accounting of the economic losses resulting from these actions. I am willing to bear all costs.
3. Is there any possibility Academy leaders might make a slight adjustment to the conclusion regarding me of June 1995? Specifically, change "lodging a false accusation" into something like "causes for the matter being investigated proved to be without evidence.""

Liu Chuanzhi and I cooperated closely for some ten years. Although misunderstandings have occurred in the past few years, they are still a short chapter in a long story. Since nobody has acted out of self-interest it should be possible for everyone to return to having a common objective, to "mutually dissolve old enmities with a smile."

Liu Chuanzhi did not attend this meeting of the Board of Directors, for he was in the hospital at the time. He maintained a proper manner but he no longer could bring himself to use the word "Comrade" in addressing Ni Guangnan in the Board's response:

"The Lianxiang Group expresses its appreciation for this positive attitude of Mr. Ni Guangnan. Previous contradictions have both personal and systemic causes. Bygone matters are now past. The Age of a Knowledge Economy that the country is now facing needs good minds. The Lianxiang Group hopes that, on the basis of conscientiously summarizing the lessons of this experience, Mr. Ni Guangnan will actively look ahead, make joint efforts, contribute his forces to the development of the Chinese information industry."

There the matter ended. Only one detail of the storyline was left to be resolved: that RMB 5 million. What was to be done with it? The company's intent had been that all those who put meritorious work into the founding of the enterprise should get shares in the company. Liu Chuanzhi felt, however, that his mind-purification had not reached such a state that he could allow Ni Guangnan to enjoy this privilege. From an organizational point of view, members of the Employee Shareholders' Association had to be company employees: the decision by the Board of Directors to exclude Ni Guangnan from the list of "company Founders" stripped him of the right to hold Lianxiang shares. This decision later become one of the key points in the dispute, for quite a few people cried "unfair" on behalf of Ni Guangnan. In the Board's opinion, this RMB 5 million was sufficient recompense to Ni Guangnan. "That was an extremely large figure at the time, much larger than the financial amount that shares would have been," Liu Chuanzhi said. "What's more, employees had not yet got the shares in their hands, whereas this was cash."

Ni Guangnan did not see it that way. He did not argue on behalf of his own shares, but he refused to accept the RMB 5 million. "This 5 million is not in compliance with any kind of law or regulation, and I don't want it," Ni said. He spoke frankly on another occasion, "They say that this RMB 5 million is for me to carry on work in a new unit. What would I want that for? The government is supportive: if I want funds for research I can apply to the government anytime."

This was a man who lived for his reputation. He would go to any lengths to prove his rightness, he would even hurt old "war comrades" without compunction, but he never sought personal "benefit." Most people who knew him agreed with this. Several people maintained that he took a certain percentage of the income from sales of the Han-card, but Liu Chuanzhi always believed that Ni Guangnan was not a person in pursuit of money.

The "Heavenly Auspicious:" Lianxiang's Internet computer

On November 28, 1999, the "Heavenly Auspicious" was born. This machine enabled one-stroke access to the Internet, so qualified as what Yang Yuanqing thought of as an "Internet computer."

It also had epoch-making significance in terms of design. Its exterior was imaginative and its use of color was courageous. The monitor and keyboard had fluid lines, while the CPU looked as though it was flying upward like an ocean wave. The Heavenly won Intel Corporation's award for creative computer design, and also the COMDEX computer exhibition award in 2000, the "Oscar" of the information technology industries. This was the first time that Chinese had ever won the design award in the world's most prestigious forum. What's more, the award was given in the cultural context of America, outside the aesthetic mindset of the Chinese market.

The value of the Heavenly was not limited to its shape and color. Its functions had undergone a revolutionary change. It controlled the decibel level at below 30, had a keyboard designed into the monitor, and modified the structure of the keyboard by adding seven keys so that it had easy Han-character indicators. Among these the most important key was one called "Fly to the Net." This "one-key Internet access" was much touted in ads. An additional row of keys on the right were somewhat like the dial on a radio, they were "channel keys" that took one straight to such things as Education, Lifestyle, Entertainment, and Stocks.

For a computer to have its own web-accessing function was a great advance at the time. Before this, accessing the Internet was a complex process for a common person. First you went to the Public Security Bureau to register. Then you went to the Telecommunications Bureau to attest to your identity. After you had bought a piece of equipment you asked technical people to come connect it to your computer. Finally you were able to dial a regular telephone number and enter the Internet world. Every time you used the code you would pay a fee, however, and you might have to dial eight times before you got through. Then you would find that you did not know what website to go to, you didn't know how to navigate to what you wanted. The Heavenly was created to resolve this whole set of difficulties. Consumers could take it home, turn on the power source, push the "Fly to the Net" button and be connected.

The company's advertising staff had been preparing for the Heavenly's debut for a full year. They had learned that good marketing people do not sit back and wait for customers, they actively create consumer trends. A Lianxiang team travelled to around 300 cities from 1998 to 1999. As soon as they got to a location, they would gather a group of children together and play the song "Descendants of the Dragon." They did not neglect this crucial step, even in such places as Sichuan and Tibet. After the song, they would extol the virtues of the "Internet Life," and declare that the new century about to start was the "Internet Century." It was fine to have all Chinese become aware of the Internet, but to have them actually enter its domain was difficult. The promotion group therefore told its audience throughout China that it had a way to resolve the problems: it was called the Heavenly. Not yet finished, the Heavenly was not unveiled at these market-building exercises. It was hinted at, as some kind of marvelous secret. When the advertising staff could finally reveal the secret, they invited more than 2,500 people to the Heavenly debut, including over 500 reporters. This enormous Press Conference was held in the Beijing Exhibition Hall.

Liu Xiaolin was an important character in the drama of creating the capabilities of the Heavenly. He had returned to the Computer Department from Enterprise Planning and he took up the task of smoothing relations with Telecommunications branches throughout China. He understood that it was not enough just to resolve technical obstacles to allowing consumers smooth access to the Internet. One first had to pass the hurdle of local Telecommunications companies, so he asked Yang Yuanqing for permission to attack this problem. While Liu Jun, Head of Technology for Lianxiang Computers, worked day and night on technical issues, Liu Xiaolin spent most of the time flying from one city to the next. He took his team to the China Telecommunications Companies of all of China's provincial cities and regions, and he signed a "telecom" agreement with each one. He negotiated agreements that allowed Lianxiang to bundle all of the Internet account numbers and devices for dialing-up into each machine, and that also allowed each user to have unlimited free access for a period of one year. Lianxiang would pay all fees to the local China Telecom in a one-time fee.

"Everyone had been saying how hard it was to do any business with China Telecom," Liu Xiaolin later said, "but nobody had really tried. Yuanqing and Liu Jun thought of this thing first. I was just the one to implement it." By the end of 1999, the Heavenly covered 100% of larger cities, and 70% of small and medium-sized cities in the country.

Proudly marching into the 21st Century

At the end of 1999, the Lianxiang billboard at the Baishiqiao Bridge in Beijing was exchanged for a new message that symbolized the company's vitality. For fifteen years, the company had been through every kind of crisis imaginable. Many privately called it the Lianxiang of Nine Lives. The official "Fifteen Great Events in Fifteen Years" managed to avoid all the failures, however, while it recorded only the glorious moments. Lianxiang now stood at the gateway to the new century. The Asian currency crisis was over, China and the US had signed an agreement on China's entry into the WTO, consumers were again buying things.

The Great Hall of the People was selected to be the venue for the fifteenth anniversary of the company. On December 3, seven thousand Lianxiang employees descended on the huge building on the western side of Tiananmen Square. They hung out horizontal banners, put up ornamental columns, set up computer displays, the company trademark, several hundred fresh-flower wreaths, sixty small water fountains, 450 spotlights. When all was ready, Liu Chuanzhi walked up on stage to speak. Dissatisfied with a draft prepared by assistants, he wrote the speech himself. He began:

> "History is like a book, bound together one page at a time. Young people who were born in 1978 have begun to appear among our ranks. They find it hard to imagine what was written on pages that have long since been turned. They listen with envy to their older

siblings discussing which make of car to buy. They simply cannot imagine the hard times their parents went through twenty years ago. The Founders of Lianxiang also could never have imagined that the company they founded would be the best proof of the Opening and Reform of the People's Republic of China."

Heavy snow covered Beijing in the last two days of 1999. People at the company were busy: Gong Guoxing was doing the final work on the ERP Project. Yang Yuanqing was also happy that week. The Heavenly had amazed people with its success, taking the share price of the company up 10% in the space of thirty days. By December 31, it had reached RMB 19.3. A practical man, Yang had never liked to spend money but he now indulged the advertising staff. The staff went on to spend RMB 6 million promoting the Heavenly in 300 cities. They spent RMB 10 million on press conferences promoting Heavenly in 27 major cities, and they spent another RMB 10 million on ubiquitous ads. A four-page ad was created by the Diantong Advertising Company: the first page played up how hard it was to get on the Internet, then a red thread guided the reader's line of vision to a second page. This page showed the now-famous shape of the Heavenly and the familiar line, "one-key access to the Net." The third page called itself "Purple" and introduced various amazing things about the Internet. Only on the fourth page was the price: the 2000 model for RMB 9,988, the 6000 model for RMB 12,988, and the 8000 model for RMB 17,988.

These prices were not considered cheap at the time, but consumers were hooked. They didn't care about the money. The very first Heavenly was sold at auction on the web. After 55 bids, it finally went to the Beifang Engineering University in Beijing for a price of RMB 14,701. This was higher than the price on the market, but the bonus was personal letters from Liu Chuanzhi and Yang Yuanqing. The Heavenly sold 15,000 machines in the next thirty days, bringing the company RMB 200 million in gross revenue and RMB 40 million in gross profit. In the coming year, the machine sold another 400,000 machines, with a total sales revenue of roughly RMB 3.75 billion. Lianxiang's market share of home-use computers rose from 30% to 40%. The bright red model was bought by many farming families as a dowry to accompany the bride. Although more than 99% of farming towns still lacked any means to access the Internet, people liked the bright red color and the "Heavenly Auspicious" name.

Part Four

(2000-2004): Change or Die

HALF PEACOCK, HALF TIGER

Remember the saying: "Modesty improves a man whereas pride goes before a fall."

Liu Chuanzhi

On the last midnight of the twentieth century, Yang Yuanqing and Guo Wei were in their offices, anxious and harried. The millennium bug, meant to shut down computers globally, was foremost in their minds. Neither of these men was yet forty years old, yet they had been in the company for twelve years already. They were loyal and dedicated, and right now they were worried. One was in charge of the branded-products business, the other in charge of the agency business. As the globe celebrated the arrival of a new millennium, people around the world watched the scene via satellite. The international date line is in the Pacific Ocean, so January 1 broke in China before Europe or America. Irrespective of nationality, ethnicity, or religious belief, everyone celebrated the arrival of the New Century and the New Millenium. Yang Yuanqing and Guo Wei took no note, for they were focussing all their attention on the very last plan of the last century. In the past ten years, they had brought Lianxiang computers to a 20% market share in China, had spread that blue trademark in a circle, surrounded by a square, throughout China. This success now became their biggest problem. They were worried that the "thousand-year bug" was crawling through the systems. In order to try to catch it, they dispatched hundreds of engineers to the terminals of especially vital computers. They spent the entire night awake.

Assessment of the new century

As the first light dawned on the New Century, Lianxiang had a total of more than 10,000 employees. Their average age was 28. All of the pain of the past seemed now a sharp contrast to the glories of today. Western media were describing Liu Chuanzhi as a hero who carried all before him. *Fortune* Magazine, in its January issue, said that Liu Chuanzhi was "the victor in a live-or-die market". *Time* magazine pointed out that making computers was not the first step in Liu Chuanzhi's success but it was what attracted most attention since he had created China's most profitable private computer company.

From financial statements and reports of the company, this seemed accurate. Meanwhile, Liu Chuanzhi's influence was becoming worldwide in scope. He became the "Man of the Year in Asian Business" in *Fortune* magazine, the "Asian Star of the Year" in *Business Week*, the "Business leader with the most global influence" in *Time* Magazine. His name was now ranked alongside the most famous businessmen in the world. In China, journalists gave him a vivid title, "The godfather of IT." The only one who could be compared to him was Zhang Ruimin, who had hung the English trademark of Haier over Fifth Avenue in New York and on the Ginza in Tokyo.

Ten years earlier, when Liu Chuanzhi said he wanted to "recreate a Hongji on the Mainland," many people laughed at him. Now, Liu Chuanzhi and Hongji's President, Shi Zhenrong, were in the same ranks. The biographies of these two Commanders-in-Chief have similarities. They were born in the same year, belong to the Year of the Monkey, are talented in high-tech fields. Both trained in electronics, moved from science to management, took control of their companies at the same time. For both, 1989 was a year of decisive significance, though at the time Lianxiang had no computers, no brand, no assembly line, no agents. The flag of "Lianxiang" had not even been raised. The company's greatest hope was that the government would allow it to produce computers. By now, the company had plenty of accolades. Media reports put an international spin on the company's ranking: "Number Eight among global information technology companies," "First in the Asia-Pacific market." As the new century started, the entire world began to be aware of the abrupt rise of China. Some started to describe a China Century, which to them was a China Threat. Others felt this was a China Phenomenon. China had become the greatest manufacturer in the world, with eighty commodities that were ranked First in the world. Although computers were not among these, when you considered that many foreign-brand computers were manufactured in China, it was not far from first place. When a Vice-

President of IBM saw the value-added computer assembly industries of the Pearl River Delta, he exclaimed, "If the road from Dongwan to Huanggang ever stopped, the world's computer industry would shut down." The President of a Japanese company noted, "The moment China enters the market for a product, we prepare our retreat." He was talking about color TVs, refrigerators, air conditioners and home appliances, but Lianxiang was taking this list further with computers.

A statue of Mao Zedong still stood imposingly in front of the Beijing Chemical Engineering University. It looked out over the cars streaming along the northern Third Ring Road. Just across the Ring Road from Mao was a huge billboard, 40 meters long, gazing at the great man. It held the azure-blue trademark of Lianxiang and the Lianxiang motto that was now known throughout China: "Each year, each day, we are advancing." A young man in a red t-shirt gazed upwards, his eyes full of dreams. After selling the first one million machines, Lianxiang had sold another two million within two years. All this seemed to indicate that the market was firmly in the company's grasp.

Liu Chuanzhi kept a keen eye on the stock market in the spring of 2000. Computers coming off the company's assembly lines were the same as computers around the world, but he saw the NASDAQ (National Association of Securities Dealers Automated Quotation) continue to go up for sixteen months in a row, while his own shares, registration number "00992," were always in that troubling category of "high business results, low share price." Stock analysts reminded him that investors did not like this. Now, as NASDAQ was attacking the 5000 benchmark, investors around the world seemed hungry. This seemed to be a golden opportunity. On the last day of February, Lianxiang began to implement a share distribution that had long been planned: it granted 35 million shares to institutional investors, then it issued 50 million new shares at a price of HK$33.75 per share. The company announced that it would put 85% of the funds gained from floating the shares into realizing its "Internet strategy." This included purchasing Internet content providers, buying copyrights, developing a new generation of Internet access equipment, and promoting e-business. Liu Chuanzhi said to Hong Kong reporters, "the Internet market is developing fast and the Lianxiang Group has to grab this chance." This was what investors wanted to hear. The "00992" received strong confirmation from the market. On June 23, 1999, Lianxiang had returned only HK$936 million from an issue of 130 million shares; now it issued only eighty-five million shares but returned HK$2.807 billion. The *Beijing Youth Journal* marveled at this as it noted, "The market appears to want Lianxiang to be an Internet Company and not a Computer

Company. In this latest stock issue, it has given Lianxiang a vote of confidence."

The momentum was just beginning. On March 3, 2000, Liu Chuanzhi and Li Zekai announced, that Lianxiang and Yingke Digital were going to cooperate on developing a "Broadband Internet Business." Thirty-five-year-old Li Zekai was the son of Hong Kong magnate Li Kashing, considered one of the richest men in Asia, and was also the boss of "Yingke." Li Zekai had just completed the purchase of Hong Kong Telecom and was now linking up with Liu Chuanzhi. The news immediately pleased the market. On this day, "00992" closed at HK$45.2, an increase of 28%, entering the ranks of the top ten values in the Hong Kong stock market. The company's total capitalization now exceeded HK$80 billion, of which HK$17.7 billion had been gained in the last eight hours.

On March 4, "00992" continued its ferocious rise and for a moment reached HK$59.5. By the end of the day, the share price of Lianxiang had appreciated 41% in two days, and 2000% over one year earlier.

Yet "00992" was still rising. On March 6, 2000, it reached HK$69. This was good tidings to those who had bought in to the Lianxiang share issue: if in January, 1997, you bought HK$10,000 worth of shares, over the past 38 months, due to both the investing and the rise in price, your investment would now be worth HK$2.33 million.

The rise in the markets flamed ever higher, until March 9, when the NASDAQ broke 5,000. Wall Street acclaimed this historic new record. It had taken only 46 trading days to go from 4,000 to 5,000. Stock commentators predicted in the newspapers that before the end of 2000 the NASDAQ would reach 6,000. Some warned that the market was overheated. Others said that bubbles were already coming off the high-tech stocks, and that sooner or later they would burst. Few paid serious attention to these warnings.

In the spring of the year 2000 Liu Chuanzhi began to discuss with his most trusted advisors the possibility of dividing the company in two. In the last week of the 12th month of the lunar calendar, before the New Spring meeting, Senior Vice-President Zhu Linan said to the Head of the PR Department, "You have to create a PR masterpiece out of this occasion." Except for Yang Yuanqing, Guo Wei, and a few of the senior managers of the company, few grasped the import of Zhu Linan's words.

Successors
Conscious that the company's fortunes were ascending by the day, Liu Chuanzhi decided that this was an opportune time to leave the field. He

began to discuss retiring with those immediately around him. "I can't continue to charge ahead on the front line," he said. "When the business was slipping in the past few years, I certainly couldn't think of leaving. But now that the company is headed for high places, it is time for me to go." Everyone said he was still young. He replied, "I am too busy and too tired. I just don't have enough physical and mental energy—my body doesn't keep pace with what I want to do." Liu liked to sit peacefully, reading books, chatting with people. He liked to discuss things without any calculated benefit from the conversation. But he was exhausted when he got home from work every night—any kind of conversation was out of the question. "If someone could just replace me, be responsible for the more than 10,000 employees, be responsible for the company's profits, I could relax."

The issue of succession is always sensitive, whether with regard to a company or a country. In the past year, names of various successors were discussed within a small group of five people; this was an absolute secret within the company. Within the Lianxuang Culture, keeping secrets was easy to do, but this did not help Liu Chuanzhi resolve the most difficult question. In recent history, Mao Zedong had become enemies with his colleagues because of this issue. He chose four different people, one after another, that did not work out. Deng Xiaoping saw many carts overturn in front of him, and learned from the lessons, but he too could not avoid a struggle over this issue. In the late 1980s, Liu Chuanzhi had already begun to cultivate a new generation of younger people. Many setbacks later, they were his salvation. Young people gave outstanding performances in the late 1990s, and a succession structure gradually formed.

Among the "three important elements of management" that Liu Chuanzhi was fond of discussing, the most important was to establish a team. He liked to say "a small company manages affairs, a large company manages people." Implied in this was his fundamental belief that a company is not formed of such material things as money or technology, but rather of people. This kind of thinking, that put people above all else, was unique among Chinese entrepreneurs. When Liu Chuanzhi described four types of management personnel, though, this was not his own invention but borrowed from Jack Welch, at the time Chairman and CEO of General Electric.

The company needed senior managers who were both able to achieve a predetermined goal, and able to accept the company's values. The reason the situation became more complex was that Liu Chuanzhi had two of this kind of person—Yang Yuanqing and Guo Wei.

Having more than one candidate for a position is common in outstanding companies. The Chinese method of dealing with it is to force the two of them to work together. Westerners always choose one or the other, and make the loser leave. Among the countless stories about Jack Welch that Liu Chuanzhi could recall, one is about how Welch chose a successor from among three people. "That was the toughest and most painful decision I had to make," Welch said once. "The process almost drove me crazy." Yet he chose one, forcing the other two to leave.

Liu Chuanzhi did not plan to do it this way. He was not willing to let either one go. Guo Wei had achieved success early, as a young man, while Yang Yuanqing's ascendancy came later. Guo Wei was nimble and sharp, Yang Yuanqing was weighty and trustworthy. Guo Wei floated in indecision, Yang Yuanqing's feet trod on firm ground. Guo Wei had an endless stream of ideas but was not confident he could always succeed: he was particularly bad at turning a good idea into a detailed plan and then implementing it. Yang Yuanqing did not have so many ideas, but he had an indomitable will. He carefully evaluated the road ahead and then he reached his goal. Guo Wei had worked for a long time beside Liu Chuanzhi, he was a good talker and good at understanding what Liu meant, and Liu Chuanzhi felt closer to the man. Outsiders felt that Liu Chuanzhi was inclined towards Guo Wei and even Yang Yuanqing could not help but think this himself. In terms of character and a sense of ethics, though, Yang Yuanqing and Liu Chuanzhi shared certain qualities. They were both "round on the outside, square on the inside." Despite their humility they were autocratic. Having decided upon a course of action they were undaunted by setbacks. From a company standpoint, Liu Chuanzhi was inclined towards Yang Yuanqing, from a personal and emotional standpoint, he was inclined towards Guo Wei.

Liu Chuanzhi once used the analogy of a peacock and a tiger to describe different kinds of leaders: the peacock excels at displaying its own beauties, and uses this to seduce people into following him; the tiger depends on his own internal strength, and subdues all with his imperious authority. Liu felt that Guo Wei was a "peacock-type," while Yang Yuanqing was the epitome of a "tiger-type." He was asked, "And you? Which type are you?" His response was, "Half peacock, half tiger."

Yang Yuanqing and Guo Wei

The matter was resolved in a quintessentially Chinese fashion. Liu Chuanzhi hoped to keep both these two young people. The part of the company led by Guo Wei had 3,000 people, produced 30% of the annual revenue and 20% of its profits; "Lianxiang Computer" led by Yang Yuanqing had 7,000 people, brought in 70% of the revenue and 80% of the profit. Lianxiang's computers were undeniably the company's primary business, a business, moreover, that Yang Yuanqing had brought about himself. His familiarity with the computer-manufacturing process far exceeded that of Guo Wei. Another little-noticed but important factor influenced Liu's decision to make Yang Yuanqing senior to Guo Wei: Yang Yuanqing excelled in doing one thing over the long course of months and years, he excelled at beginning something and he excelled at finishing it. Guo Wei excelled at doing many things in the course of a year. He always appeared at the key moment in the key place. He was either good at starting things or at finishing them, not both. There was virtually no one thing that he had taken from beginning to end.

"We'll do an experiment," said Liu Chuanzhi to Yang Yuanqing and Guo Wei. "I'd like to ask the two of you to work together, with a positive attitude."

Although Yang Yuanqing and Guo Wei were both Vice-Presidents in the company, they had never worked together before. Indeed, they felt more like competitors. Neither had prepared in any way for the prospect of cooperating. Now that the President wanted to "try an experiment," the two agreed verbally but found it difficult psychologically. Business conflicts in the company became more pronounced and they soon recognized that they could not work together. Yang Yuanqing was focussing on selling more Lianxiang computers, while Guo Wei wanted to do "agenting" and shouldered a whole raft of "best agency" brands. These two goals conflicted. As Yang Yuanqing said, "Our own Lianxiang brand was just getting stronger and agenting the brands of other companies might affect that." Guo Wei noted, "Why should people use us as their agent when Lianxiang has its own brand? We once worked closely with Hewlett-Packard, for instance, but HP cancelled all of our agency contracts for their computers."

Each was in charge of his own affairs. Neither was happy. Both came to Liu Chuanzhi to express their grievances. Liu Chuanzhi realized that these two would not get along, and the situation now came to a head. All he could do was accept the fact that "one mountain cannot accommodate two tigers." He had seen too many personal disputes, and he knew that under these circumstances urging "accommodation" would be useless. After considerable deliberation, Liu and the Board of Directors concluded that, "the friction between the two men is unavoidable. It's not that they fight because their basic nature is bad, but they have different goals. It would be best to separate them."

The inability of the two Little Commanders to cooperate, and the conflict between those parts of the company that each represented, became the primary reason Lianxiang split into two parts. Yang Yuanqing felt that the business factor was of greater importance in the split, while Guo Wei felt that the human factor was paramount. Liu Chuanzhi voiced the opinion that dividing the company was "caused by the need to develop the company." Later he admitted that this had been said for the benefit of the stock markets. "I decided in the end to have Yang Yuanqing succeed me. Still, I couldn't bear to make Guo Wei leave, so I had to build another stage for him."

Splitting up a company because of personnel issues was rare in Chinese commercial history. The boss of any Western company would find it hard to understand. Before Liu Chuanzhi made up his mind, he asked for advice from consultants and met strong opposition. "If Americans knew your reasons for splitting the company, they would think you had gone mad," said one senior consultant. Investors in the Hong Kong capital markets also found it hard to accept, so Liu Chuanzhi led Zhu Linan to Hong Kong to try to explain. "Other companies much bigger than you haven't split up," was the response. "You are only US$2 billion, and you want to split?" In unanimous agreement, the consultants recommended reorganizing the business, and choosing one person to head it. "As for the other, let nature take its course." These consultants seemed to think of Lianxiang as an American company. Americans would never make an enterprise revamp itself just because of one person. In China, however, this was not a matter of one person but of the entire phalanx of people under that person.

Liu Chuanzhi did not change his thinking for this reason. "Better to have a sharp knife cut the Gordion knot than a dull knife try to cut meat," he said. "Neither side wants to submit to the other, right? Then give each one plenty of room to maneuver, see what the market says." He said these things to his Senior Vice-President, Zhu Linan, who could understand his concerns. "Both were his beloved generals," Zhu later told the author. "Both were capable of managing a large company. Naturally there were other considerations. For example, if Liu let one go, then he would instantly have created a competitor to himself, which wouldn't be good for the company either." Zhu emphasized that it was corporate interests rather than individual emotions that led to the action.

Liu Chuanzhi's decision was final. Facing a significant possibility of failure, he used all of his intelligence and authority to divide the two Commanders. He split in two the company that he had worked so hard to create.

The company divides itself in two

Zhu Linan became a critical person in the process. This Senior Vice-President of the company was in charge of more than 1,000 people in the corporate headquarters. In terms of corporate power, he was on a par with Yang Yuanqing and Guo Wei. He could not compare to the other two in terms of revenues, though, since he was not in charge of a profit center. As a result, the grade level of his position was slightly lower, and he was not an official member of the President's Office. Because he was not in the core power circle, he faced no conflict of interest and could be objective. He played an important role in the process of analyzing the company. In Liu Chuanzhi's eyes, Zhu Linan was a "commanding talent."

Legally, the company had to wait until 2001 to accomplish the split, though the de facto division started in the spring of 2000. The basic idea was that Yang Yuanqing would command all business related to Lianxiang brands, while agency business and systems integration would come under Guo Wei's banner. Dividing a company that had over a dozen subsidiaries, several dozen business lines, more than 10,000 employees, RMB 2 billion in assets, and RMB 20 billion in sales is, as one can imagine, not easy. Liu Chuanzhi talked daily to Li Qin, Zeng Maochao, and Ma Xuezheng, hoping to keep side effects to a minimum. He held countless meetings though he knew that the most important things could not be discussed at meetings. Yang Yuanqing and Guo Wei had always been important in the decision-making process, but this time was different: the two were in direct conflict. Liu Chuanzhi was aware that Zhu Linan maintained his friendship with both of the Commanders and was skilled at handling human affairs. He felt that Zhu could help him resolve the thornier issues.

At the beginning of 2000, the Administration Commission asked Zhu Linan to attend important meetings and he then became a kind of bridge. He went back and forth between Yang Yuanqing and Guo Wei, transmitting their thinking to Liu Chuanzhi and Liu's back to them. Senior management in the company knew that he represented the President: only he himself did not feel this way. "I wasn't really "representing" him," he said, "I was just helping him out."

Telephone conversations between Zhu and Liu became the oil that lubricated the process of dividing the company. Yang Yuanqing and Guo

Wei haggled over every ounce as they negotiated the corporate division. One would write up lists of demands, the other would not give an inch of territory. They were like canny traders at a country fair, one side demanding an exorbitant price and the other offering a pittance. It looked as though they were going to take each other down in the process. The final result was that Yang Yuanqing inherited the greater part of the business. Only 10% of the assets, 20% of the employees, 20% of the business lines and 20% of the sales revenue were split off to be under Guo Wei's name. When this result was publicly announced, it elicited tremendous debate. Some said that Liu Chuanzhi placed excessive trust in Yang Yuanqing while cold-shouldering Guo Wei. In Liu Chuanzhi's mind, however, this was not the division of wealth of a family, but a one-hundred-year plan for a company's business development.

Guo Wei did not care so much about having fewer assets and employees as he cared about the loss of the name Lianxiang. Ownership of the brand "Lianxiang" became the thorniest issue in the process of separation. When the company divided into two parts, Yang Yuanqing controlled the business lines carrying the brand name. He inherited the title of the company, its trademarks and associated intangibles valued at RMB 4 billion. The stock market's "00992" also became a part of his holdings. Guo Wei tried hard to find a name for the company he was to lead that incorporated the name of the parent, such as "Lianxiang S&T." He cited the example of Founder which had a "Founder Computer" and a "Founder S&T." But Yang Yuanqing adamantly refused to let Guo's company use the word "Lianxiang." From the standpoint of the stock market's rules, using the name was impossible. Zhu Linan tried to persuade Guo Wei to let go of the "Lianxiang" name, but he failed. Liu Chuanzhi finally had to order him to "find another name, run on another platform". Guo Wei and the senior management under him understood the reasoning, but found it emotionally hard to accept. For the past twelve years, they had put their lifeblood into this brand. Now they were not Lianxiang people any more.

The road to success for an enterprise does not allow for tears. Guo knew this and, in fact, had come up with a tentative new name for the company months earlier: "Shenzhou Shuma." In English, this is translated as Digital China; in Chinese the term *shenzhou* carries overtones of "sacred land," a common classical-Chinese term for China. Some said this name was no good because the two characters *shenzhou* were too traditional and too Chinese. Others said the word "digital" was too trendy, it seemed a little opportunistic. Guo Wei stood firm. He successfully persuaded the officials of the Bureau of Industry and Commerce to let him use Digital

China to register the company, and he announced his new dream to the world: to start another famous brand name.

"We are actually *zhong-guo shuma*," he told the author. "But the government wouldn't let us use the words *zhong-guo*, the name of the country, as the start of the registered name, so we changed it to *Shenzhou*." In Chinese corporate nomenclature, the first word of an official name must be the place of registration, such as Beijing Shenzhou Shuma. Only state-owned companies can use "zhong-guo" or "China" as their initial word.

Digital China

On April 3, 2000, Guo Wei received a license to operate as "Beijing Shenzhou Shuma, Limited" from the National Bureau of Industry and Commerce. The swearing-in ceremony of the new company was held the day before. Guo Wei now had RMB 600 million in capital and around 3,000 employees. He had the agency relationships of the original Lianxiang company, plus the e-commerce and systems integration businesses.

Liu Chuanzhi gave him a calligraphy scroll inscribed with the four characters "Create Glory Yet Again". Vice-President Lin Yang told him, "The first hurdle the new company has to get over is that of hurt feelings." Another Vice-President, Hua Zhijian, expressed the pervasive mood at the time: "the anxiety level was high, one slice of the knife and they were separated, without knowing what the future would bring."

The immediate present was hard enough. Several hundred contracts had to be revised, the words "Lianxiang" had to be deleted and all stamped with Shenzhou Shuma. At the time, Guo Wei wanted to believe that Shenzhou Shuma and Lianxiang were still brothers. Business partners had no idea who Shenzhou Shuma was—only when he said "Lianxiang" did people comprehend.

Guo Wei understood the magic of image promotion, and he had experience in fraternizing with the media. So he asked several PR companies to come up with a trademark for Digital China. The results were uniformly unsatisfying. Not until a Hong Kong branch of the Land Company, an American graphic design firm, entered the picture did things look better. The Land designers were extremely professional. They announced that they needed to talk to the highest level of management, to get a clear idea of the company's future and to understand the dynamics of the company's founders. After much discussion, they proposed that the company use the concept of "infinity" in expressing the values of the new company. Guo Wei and his several assistants agreed. Land designed three trademarks around the concept of "infinity," and asked them to choose one. The third was ingenious: it was a bright red line swirling in a kind of dance, a bit like the Milky Way in outer space, also like two clasped hands. It had a dynamic tension to it, and gave the impression of something boundless. Guo Wei and his senior managers were absolutely taken with this last design and spent HK$700,000 to buy it. "That was more than ten times the price of a design inside China," Hua Zhinian said, "but it was worth it."

A journalist named Li Tong from the *Nanfang Weekender* was the first to announce Lianxiang's split to the public. Most people were still focussed on the issue of Lianxiang's succession and were still debating the merits of the two contenders. Only this sharp journalist caught the significance of Lianxiang's split and recognized that it was related to the succession issue. He added a subtitle to his story, saying that one of the resulting companies was an Internet company, while the other one also seemed to be an Internet company. In implying that Lianxiang was keen to enter the Internet world, he was sadly prophetic.

Internet year
The Internet bubble had been gestating in the rest of the world. In China, the final act was yet to come but it was being rehearsed at Lianxiang. The older generation at Lianxiang had built the company with slow and careful deliberation; they had taken an investment of RMB 200,000 and turned it into RMB 13.5 billion. The younger generation was smart, stubborn, and determined: investors in the stock market confidently gave them another HK$30 billion. The company stood at the peak of the computer business; now it sighted another peak just ahead. Moving in that direction was irresistible.

Nobody noticed that the Internet wave was retreating. The historic declines of the NASDAQ and Dow Jones averages came in the first two weeks of April. On April 3, two weeks before Lianxiang released its own internet site, which it named FM365, the NASDAQ fell 349.15 points, its highest fall in one day in history. It closed at 4333.68 on that day, after a decline of 7.64%. On April 13, the NASDAQ plunged to 3764, but worse was to come. On April 14, the Dow Jones average fell by 617.78 points, or by 5.6%, while the NASDAQ fell another 355.49 points, by which time it had fallen 34% from its peak. That was a Friday, so all over the world people were calling it "Black Friday".

In China, however, the Internet pitch was still titillating people and they were still investing. The portal Sina had been listed on the NASDAQ in America: the company issued four million common shares at an issue price of US$17, and was considered a tremendous success. Media on the Pacific side of the ocean acclaimed the issue as "the first internet-portal stock issued from the Chinese Mainland." Spurred by this, Lianxiang kept spending money on the FM365 launch.

Chinese economists like to say, "when a butterfly ripples the air over New York, several days later you get buckets of rain in Beijing." Thinking back on it, the "butterfly wings" of spring, 2000, were not too effective. On this side of the Pacific, it looked as though nobody doubted that we were already in the golden age of the Internet. Shangdi, north of ZGC, a place formerly famous for its "Sino-Japanese Friendship People's Commune" of the 1970s, had now become the heart of the Internet age. Founder, Yongyou, Orient Electronics, Huawei S&T and others were all concentrated here. Lianxiang built itself a huge new building in Shangdi and leased another six buildings. Every day, eight busses sped among them carrying employees and inter-office documents. The Frontline Building, where FM365 was headquartered, was the most active. It attracted cabs from Beijing in a steady stream, lining up to catch passengers at the front door, all of whom, said the drivers, were rich.

Succession and passing the banner
Despite declines in US markets, Lianxiang continued its plan to launch an Internet presence in late spring, 2000. It declared that the division of the one company into two was a success.

The oath-swearing meeting on May 12 became a historic occasion of passing the banner from one generation to the next. Over the past sixteen years, the number of Lianxiang employees had increased from eleven to over ten thousand. Their average age had dropped from 45 to 28. The two new young Commanders stood together for the ceremonial transition. In order to accentuate the importance of this event, the PR Department prepared two azure-blue banners, which they planned to have Liu Chuanzhi personally bestow on the two men.

That Yang Yuanqing and Guo Wei were successors was long since known to all. The only remaining question was who would be their deputies. The mystery was soon revealed: the deputies were not to be one person but a group. The Board of Directors appointed a large number of Vice-Presidents, almost all of whom were young.

Over 3,000 people attended the May 12 meeting. A red carpet went up the stairs from the first floor to the second, on which was written, "One heart one mind: create another miracle." Applause unified the audience, focussing people's attention. Flashbulbs popped, orchestral music resounded through the hall. Li Qin announced, "The Internet age has begun!" This Number Two man in the company went on to enumerate the contributions that the older generation had made over the years. "Chinese enterprises are the product of a movement from a planned economy to a market economy," he said. "One word can sum up this macro-environment and that word is transition."

Liu Chuanzhi also spoke at the event. "We old warriors have been through hundreds of battles," he said to the young people, "and we want to accompany this passing of the banner with some words of advice. In brief: "Be humble." There are no problems that you won't be able to resolve, but at the same time don't let self-congratulation blind you." After this warning, he expressed his hopes for the future.

"After ten or twenty years, when the Chinese economy has doubled another two times, some extremely large enterprises will appear in China. You will be among them. I hope that Yang Yuanqing and Guo Wei will be walking into the White House, meeting with the American President and discussing global economic development, just as Jiang Zemin has been seeing Welch and Dell these days. We are not just saying these things. We must resolve to be that ambitious."

The new and the old lined up together on stage. The "receiving the banner" ceremony took the event to its climax. Young stalwarts dressed in white brought out the banners. Spotlights sprang to the center of the stage, blue light flashed as Liu Chuanzhi gave the banners in turn to Yang Yuanqing and Guo Wei. One had the words "Lianxiang Group" written on it, the other "Digital China."

"The future depends on you." Liu Chuanzhi told his two successors. The inheritance that these two were receiving from the older generation was impressive: 10,678 employees, 21 overseas branches, 20 subsidiaries within China, 2000 service and sales network organizations, RMB 13.5 billion in assets, RMB 2 billion in annual revenues, and a market capitalization of HK$66.6 billion. The Lianxiang brand of computers also now held 30% market share.

The older generation at Lianxiang had been highly successful and they wanted to enjoy the results of their work. Liu Chuanzhi had been preparing for this day for the past seven years. Now, for the first time, the Founders received those red "share certificates." For the first time, they received dividends: RMB 12 for every share. Due to the explosive increase in the stock price of Lianxiang, they became millionaires overnight. As per the options timetable allowed in their contracts, over one hundred employees now sold the first group of shares and mostly used the funds to buy themselves new homes.

"I have seen quite a few successful entrepreneurs," said a journalist with broad experience, "and I've seen quite a few Founders who became wealthy in their own right. But to make not only yourself wealthy but everyone who founded the company together with you, and what's more, in a legal and open way... well, Liu Chuanzhi is the only one I have ever seen like that."

Shares are not cash, however. They change value daily and shortly after spring 2000 was over they began to decline. Within two months the NASDAQ had declined by more than 1000 points. Lianxiang's share price dropped by more than half from its price of HK$70. Even if it had dropped by "more than half," though, the share price was still over 30. Less than one year earlier everyone had bought those options for a price of HK$1.8.

Company policy: Turning a corner at high speed

Lianxiang was now trying to turn a corner at high speed, from being a manufacturing company with a tangible product to being a virtual floating Internet economy. This was counter to Liu Chuanzhi's established way of thinking. He had always said that fast-moving cars need to turn in a broad arc: if you turn too fast you'll overturn.

People who have been successful in China over the last twenty years generally have the following aspects in common: they have faced few legal restraints, they have had no supervisory control in the form of government interference, and they have been bold to the point of recklessness. Cautious people who succeeded were rare. Liu was one of those exceptions. One of his habits was revealing: half a day of every week he would devote to sitting quietly and thinking. This is not strange to others who have been successful including the President of Sitong Company, Duan Yongji. "Whatever he did, he had to think it through first," noted Duan. "He would only start to do it once the concept was mature." In Duan's estimation, "This was his strength, but it could also be a shortcoming. You lose the opportune moment when changes happen so fast and you insist on clarifying every detail before getting started."

Liu Chuanzhi disagreed. "It may look slow at the start," he said, "but when you are ready to move, you can work fast. It is far more effective than rushing at something with your arms flailing. As they say, "what good is it to be in a hurry if you are trying to go to the bathroom at the same time you're digging the hole?""

Right now, though, even Liu Chuanzhi could not sit still. He had seen too many startling new things in recent months. The success of the Heavenly was one, cooperating with Li Zekai was another. To a man who had always relied on material facts, it was an education to watch share prices rise so strongly on the basis of no business results. The madness of investors was unanticipated, but perhaps this was just a sign that the Information Age had arrived. Both old and young generations in Lianxiang were clear about one thing: a phenomenal market would be formed as the computer industry tied up with the Internet. Although the business model had not yet been thought through clearly, the stock market seemed to hope that Lianxiang would participate. "We became aware," Liu Chuanzhi told a reporter for the *Southern Weekender*, "that our customers included not only those who bought products but also those who bought our shares and the rules of the game had changed," he added. "There was a change in the way the market evaluated enterprises."

Liu Chuanzhi began to feel that if he thought things over too rigorously, he might well be too late. He told Senior Vice-President Ma Xuezheng to go to America on behalf of Lianxiang, to prepare to "List on the market a second time." At the same time, he decided to support Yang Yuanqing in moving resources toward the Internet. He felt that he stood on unassailable ground, especially since he had HK$3 billion of investors' cash in his hands. If he did not invest in FM365, where was he going to put it?

Lianxiang had worked hard for many years as a hardware supplier. When it had just occupied the hardware market and still had not won long-term security, it was viewing future prospects and thinking they were boundless. "On the other side of the Pacific, the Internet is thundering and the rains will shower down profits on China sooner or later," Liu Chuanzhi said. The strategic plan that Lianxiang spread out before the media at the time looked as though everything could be accomplished. It said: We will become the best Internet equipment provider - like IBM; We will become the best Internet service provider - like America Online; We will become the best Internet content provider - like Yahoo in America and Sina and Sohu in China.

Those who had strong hopes for the company had always said it could become the "Chinese IBM." IBM now seemed to be spurned by Chinese public opinion, however. The better model was AOL. AOL was the world's largest Internet company. It was only a decade old yet had just accomplished the largest merger in world corporate history, spending

US$184 billion to purchase Time Warner, a company that owned *Time*, *Fortune*, CNN, and Warner Brothers. All signs seemed to indicate that not only could virtual become real, it could win over what was real.

Sound the battle cry and attack!

A kind of psychosis began to invade the company. Former successes became the best medium for propagating the disease. The new team tried to apply the model for success in computers to all other endeavors, and they were radical, inflexible, and self-confident as they pressed forward. They overlooked an essential rule for succeeding in the Chinese environment: reap once you have seen the results. Over-shooting is as bad as not going far enough.

Competition between the two Commanders was partly to blame for what happened. Yang Yuanqing and Guo Wei had been racing each other for years, and their competitive psychology was now being taken even further. Both were young, and full of ambition. Neither had ever faced failure.

Liu Chuanzhi failed to recognize that the competition between the two men would pour oil on the already flaming Internet plans of the company. Thirty-seven-year-old Yang Yuanqing soon put forth what was to become his infamous "3-year plan": sales would rise by 50% every year, profits would go up by 40% every year, by 2003 total revenues would reach RMB 60 billion. "We can't get to the core technology arena for the time being, but we will definitely be there in three years."

Funding kept on rolling in and the money kept being invested. The headquarters building had not yet been completed when it seemed too small. The company bought more land in Shangdi and doubled its square footage by further construction, the result of inflamed emotions and pockets bulging with money. In spring 2000, the "capstone" ceremony was held for the building. It had cost RMB 2.8 billion, and taken only five months to construct. In the center of Shangdi, it became the gem of the Beijing base of Lianxiang. The building was sheathed in dark-green glass set in silver-grey frames. It had shiny marble floors, crystal chandeliers. The southeast side of the third floor was the President's area where Yang Yuanqing and his assistants each had a large office in the power center of the company.

The sales force seemed to be in a daze because of ongoing good news in the market. The sales record on computers was so good it was hard to believe. On July 1, the first day of the summer sales push, 16,000 computers were sold. Salespeople brazenly thought this summer's sales might double. They asked the supply department to plan accordingly and they asked the factories to crank up their assembly lines.

The entire company was working overtime. Though tired, they were jubilant. Factories were at full throttle, production lines in Beijing and Huiyang were producing 18,000 machines a day. Finance people were busy drafting reports and their eyes gleamed when they saw the figures. In the past four years, inventory levels dropped from 72 to 22 days' supply worth of computers, overstock losses went from 2% to 0.19%, the accounts receivable waiting period went from 28 days to 14 days, the bad accounts ratio went from 0.3% to 0.05%, travel and entertainment expenses dropped 10%, cost of sales dropped 50%.

For the first quarter of 2000, home-use computers sales increased by 201% and now enjoyed a market share of 42% in China. Income from computer sales reached HK$3.232 billion, not Yang Yuanqing's planned increase of 50% over the previous year but rather 97%. Return on investment also rose 1%. The reputation of "00992" kept rising. By the time summer vacation was over, investors were euphoric. First-quarter profits went up 136%; in the second quarter they went up 135%. Lianxiang's computer sales figures were three times what they had been the previous year, and the company entered the ranks of the world's ten biggest computer manufacturers.

Now it was the turn of the investors to be in a daze. Most of the entire world's information technology enterprises were in a precarious state. High-tech stocks were dropping in a straight line, whereas at its height, Lianxiang's "00992" did a share split of one for four, turning a price of 62 into a price of 15. Although the company's half-year results were superlative, most people did not believe that Lianxiang was an "unearthly paradise," and Lianxiang's share price now dropped 5.7%. This should have been a signal: the world's retail market for computers was in a depression. It was indeed true that a butterfly fluttering its wings in New York could stir up a storm in Asia.

The management of Lianxiang was still immersed in a happy trance, and with some reason. Several months earlier, when Yang Yuanqing received the banner from Liu Chuanzhi, he swore that in 2000 Lianxiang would sell 1,880,000 desk-top computers, 300,000 hand-held computers, 120,000 notebook computers, 40,000 servers, 80,000 printers, and 3,000,000 motherboards, and raise the overall market share to over 30%. Actual sales figures seemed to be even more phenomenal. In 2000, Lianxiang sold 2,428,105 desktop computers, an increase of 93%. The bonus system of the company did not have semi-annual bonuses—the usual way for managers to award their staff's outstanding performance was by putting fruit out on the front counter in the office. There were many fruit feasts in the company in those months, and the hallways were full of laughter. After the half-year results were released, Yang Yuanqing was so happy that he thought these "fruit feasts" were inadequate reward. He issued each of his "soldiers" a personal computer with a value of more than RMB 6,000.

In this golden season, *Business Week* in America ranked Lianxiang Number 8 among its "global S&T top 100." Inside China, Lianxiang was seen as the only enterprise on the Chinese Mainland to be included in the world's top ten S&T enterprises. As many Chinese reporters saw it, Lianxiang was not far from being one of the biggest companies in the world. Yang Yuanqing must have had the same thought. He led a group of ten Vice-Presidents on a trip through America. After visiting twenty of the most famous information technology companies, the Commander returned to his office in ZGC and announced that sometime between 2005 to 2010 he would be taking the company into the ranks of the World 500, as the Fortune 500 is known in China.

Staff working on FM365 in the Frontline Building were concerned. "Their sights are set on information-industry giants like IBM, HP, Microsoft, Cisco, and Oracle," an employee of the website complained. "They seem to have overlooked Internet companies."

FM365 personnel had become accustomed to flattery and attention. Profits garnered from computer sales were spent primarily on their efforts. In the first six months after April 18, the company spent RMB 40 million on FM365.

A saying at the time was "run towards the Internet Age," which echoed that statement by Mao Zedong forty years earlier, "run towards Communist ideology." Global Internet competition seemed more of a hundred-yard-dash than a marathon. People talked about becoming a publicly recognized leading portal within eight months. Yang Yuanqing set the timeline for Lianxiang's portal at the annual business planning meeting: "within one year, to enter the front ranks within China." Doing it themselves was not going to be fast enough. The logic at the time in the Internet world was, "Those that have money buy those that don't." Lianxiang had money: wouldn't it be best just to go out and buy a leading website? Yang Yuanqing agreed. The company spent US$35.37 million to buy Yingshitong, in order to create the country's largest financial website. Yang put RMB 5 million into New Orient, to cooperate with that famous

Toefl specialist to create an Education Online. He spent RMB 10 million to organize "the future "biggest" Chinese software company" together with Computer Associates. A discussion began in the company as to which of the three large Chinese portals would be best to buy out.

Liu Chuanzhi began to feel uneasy. From the winter of 2000, he began to express his concerns. Investors and the press were getting overly inflated expectations about Lianxiang's forecast earnings. "I don't want people to demand a superheated standard of us," Liu said. "We don't weave dreams."

This statement was really directed at Yang Yuanqing. On the other side of the Pacific, high-tech stocks in America were plummeting: Dell dropped 32%, Intel dropped 31%, Microsoft dropped 23%, the NASDAQ index dropped 39%. Two hundred and ten Internet companies closed their doors, putting at least twelve thousand people out of work. By the start of winter, the bad weather had come to China.

11

WINTER

*This industry changes constantly. Risks can spring up, huge risks
that destroy everything you've done. Be careful, we are living in
a "10-speed" age.*

Liu Chuanzhi

The weather was cold the week that several thousand employees
moved into the new Shangdi building at the end of 2000. On
that day, Ying Qi said goodbye to Beijing and headed south.
This young Beijing native had for the past several months
been in charge of setting up the production line in the Lianxiang Building.
Now the company planned to build a new production base in Shanghai
and Ying Qi had been appointed its General Manager. 2000 sales results
had been good; Ying Qi was confident as he moved into 2001.

Situation trumps people
One key to market success is to enter when the industry is approaching
takeoff. Between 2000 and 2001, however, Lianxiang's computers were
past their peak. The first thing Ying Qi learned on arriving in Shanghai
was that the most recent figures didn't meet target. He thought this was
a fluke, but bad news followed. The first month of the new fiscal year saw
completion of only 80% of the plan, the second month only 40%. Ying
Qi's work experience at Lianxiang had been superlative: in agenting AST
computers he was a "model salesman," in managing production he took
Lianxiang's daily output from 30 machines to 3,000. The East China
market now saw twelve months of not reaching targets. Ying Qi mandated

lowest limits, and he pushed people so hard that they resigned. He brought two experienced salesmen down from Beijing to help. All was in vain.

The East China market's results were simply a shadow of the gloom overlying the entire market—the other six sales regions in China were equally bad. Lianxiang's salespeople frantically tried to find ways to differentiate their products: all of the "electronics and information technology" companies were marching in step, though none admitted it. Only Ren Zhengfei, that outstanding and outspoken entrepreneur from Shenzhen, was willing to declare that the emperor had no clothes.

Ren Zhengfei was the head of the Huawei Group, a company that produced broadband equipment and program control switchboards. Like Lianxiang, Huawei had enjoyed success in the soaring '90s: Huawei had taken its sales revenue from RMB 100 million to RMB 22 billion. In China, this kind of success story was generally hotly pursued by the media, but to everyone's astonishment Ren Zhengfei refused to be interviewed. Some said it was because his company had secrets that it could not divulge. Others said that his personality and his discretion allowed him to hide away in China's southeast, working hard with his head down. By February of 2001, this man who had never been willing to speak publicly could stand it no longer. He wrote an article that was published on the Internet, entitled, "Huawei's Winter." Superficially it was written to Huawei's employees. It was also a warning to anyone in the IT industry who considered himself successful, rich, and self-important: "For ten years, the thing I have thought about every day is failure. I don't look at success. I have no sense of glory or misplaced pride, what I have is a sense of crisis. It may be because of this that we still survive today. We all have to consider together how we are going to survive, for then we may at least live a little longer. A time of failure will definitely come, and everybody should prepare to meet it." He wrote a postscript: "Remember: all things at their extreme must turn back on themselves. This is the way of *taiji*. The market for Internet equipment can be so hot that people don't believe it, but so too can it be unimaginably cold. With no foresight, no preparation, some will die of cold. The one with a cotton-padded coat will be the one who survives."

The "winter" described by Ren Zhengfei drew a loud response. At the time, most people felt that "the Chinese economy is excellent and is unto itself." Asian and Western situations were not seen as comparable—after all, the view was excellent on the China side. Zhu Rongji had been managing the Chinese economy for ten years, and the country's rapid development had been proceeding for twenty years. Superficially, all was well. In fact, the dirge of information-technology industries had been playing for some time. Sohu and Wangyi, both listed on the NASDAQ, had sunk to the level of "junk shares." Ericsson, Nokia and Motorola were stopped dead in their tracks, losing money unless they started firing people. The most tragic of all was Langxun. This huge enterprise with a Nobel research lab, 30,000 researchers and 100,000 employees, saw its stock fall 99% over the course of twelve months. It had to fire 50,000 people. Wu Xiaopo wrote a book at the beginning of 2001 that narrated the path of failure for China's ten largest enterprises. This book, "The Great Failure", instantly became a bestseller. The TCL Group's Chairman of the Board, Li Dongsheng, hero of the home electronics market, noted, "not only will competition become more violent, it will become more complex." The Xiwang Group's Chairman of the Board, Liu Yongxing, was at the time ranked first among the wealthiest people in China in *Fortune* Magazine, but he too had become a pessimist.

For a time, Yang Yuanqing tried to keep Lianxiang at peak performance. He used all possible means to encourage consumers to buy computers: lower prices, rebates, "gifts", free travel, but none of these worked. Vice-President Yu Bing went out on the road to see what was really happening. He travelled throughout the provinces and came back with the conclusion that "2000 was the tail-end of the legend of Lianxiang's computers." The glorious results of that year had overdrawn sales from the three years to come. All Yang Yuanqing could do was admit that his plan for this new fiscal year had been over-ambitious. He held a meeting in April of 2001, and told all employees, "Lianxiang's winter is not coming. It is here."

Lianxiang control shares

Meanwhile, Liu Chuanzhi was travelling around the world with his wife. After passing on the company banner, for the next fifteen months he spent the most carefree time of his life. He had no pressures, and no longer any insomnia. He went to the zoo in Guangdong. He paid a call on Aomori Shrine in Kyoto. He went to Italy to listen to opera, he went to France to see Versailles and Chartres. He lectured at the International Academy of Management in America, speaking in front of 6,400 scholars and entrepreneurs. Finally he came back to Beijing to discuss Chinese painting with friends, why the Emperor's images had identical faces, why in Chinese culture there was a need to feign compliance in public but oppose in private, how there could have been traitors during the War of Resistance against the Japanese. He also discussed the political system in China today, the culture, the religion. This kind of unrestrained talk was something he had not enjoyed for years.

The world was changing: after 9/11 and, for the first time since the end of the Cold War, its direction seemed to shift. Powerful America was drawn into war with a group of terrorists willing to sacrifice themselves for their perceived greater cause. The recovery of the global economy stopped, further chilling the already frozen Internet economy. Chinese, always planning for the future, became aware of the fact that the collapse of the Twin Towers gave China more opportunity to extend its own influence in the world. Two events in summer and autumn of 2001 brought Chinese closer to humanity around the globe: in July, Beijing gained the right to host the 2008 Olympics; in September, China completed discussions on entering the World Trade Organization and became its 143rd member.

On the day that the application for the Olympics was approved, Liu Chuanzhi was in France on holiday. He seemed able to put himself outside the distractions of events only at a great distance. He had been prominent during his tenure as President of the company. Now that he had retired to behind the scenes, he was, unfortunately, still famous. Despite passing on responsibility for Lianxiang to others, he still was in charge of a very considerable asset: Lianxiang Control Shares.

In the summer of 2001, the Lianxiang Group Control Shares Company that Liu still headed had around RMB 2 billion in cash. At a ratio of ten to one, the shares of Digital China had been disengaged from those of Lianxiang's "00992." On June 1, 2001, Digital China was listed on the market independently with a registration number of "00861" which signaled the completion of its separation from Lianxiang. "Lianxiang Computer" and "Digital China" were then set up independently. As the parent, the Lianxiang Group Control Shares Company still existed. It evolved from the company that had been created back in 1984, that laboriously named "Chinese Academy of Sciences Computer Technology and Research Institute New Technology Development Company". It sat at the top of the organizational structure.

Lianxiang Control Shares had its own office in the Rongke Consulting Center at the northern edge of Beijing's 4th ring road. At the beginning, the term "control shares" indicated its 57% of shares of Lianxiang Computer and its 51% of shares of Digital China. Liu Chuanzhi and Li Qin served as President and Standing Vice-President of Lianxiang Control Shares, and they also respectively became the Chairman of the Board of Lianxiang Computer and Digital China. Two new stock issues of "00992" in 1999 and 2000, as well as the decision by the Chinese Academy of Sciences to decrease their shareholdings, allowed the company to receive around RMB 400 million in cash. Lianxiang Computer and Lianxiang Control Shares each got one half. Every year, Lianxiang Control Shares received around RMB 200 million in dividends derived from the profits of Lianxiang Computer.

One of the qualities of capital is that "small money" and "big money" are different. A change in quantity brings with it a change in quality. When you are managing a small business of RMB 200,000, it is not so hard to make 10% in profit. If you try to make RMB 2 billion return 10%, it gets harder. The tremendous increase in share prices in 2000 brought the company both benefits and hardships. Financial resources rolled in, but Liu Chuanzhi could not let the money just stay idle: not investing the RMB 2 billion was no good; not making a good return was no good. This money came mostly from the capital markets, which were not a charity, and Lianxiang's earlier quick returns on its computer business had inflated expectations. Computer assembly is a fast-in fast-out trade, however. The circulation of money from production to sales is one cycle every seven days: the process does not require large infusions of cash. As a result, idle money became a problem and a source of pressure to Liu Chuanzhi.

Venture capital

Liu Chuanzhi's sole experience in getting investment resources in the past had been to open channels to good relations with banks. At that time, he wanted to get money. Now he had to think of ways to spend money.

He began to find models, throughout the world, of those "who knew how to spend money" and he hit upon Jack Welch, Chairman of the Board and Chief Executive Officer of General Electric. Welch had written an autobiography in 2001 in which he detailed the purchasing activities that increased the company's market capitalization by thirty times in the course of twenty years. Liu read of the rapid expansion of General Electric, and when he visited America he went to pay his respects on Jack Welch. Welch was not there but this did not affect Liu Chuanzhi's willingness to be influenced by him and to learn from him.

"Liu Chuanzhi's strongest point is that he excels at learning," Zhou Guangzho, Head of the Chinese Academy of Sciences, once said. "Today, he is like night and day from when he first started managing the company."

From the day in 1984 when he set foot on this new path, Liu Chuanzhi was absorbing things daily. By 2001, now 57 years old, he discovered that his previous knowledge was insufficient. He had noticed the term "venture capital" and knew that America had a "venture capital association." In 1991, that country's venture capital totalled only US$3.4 billion; this increased to US$10 billion by 1996. 60% of the 1,502 enterprises that had received venture capital belonged to information technologies industries. This impressed Liu. From his own experience, he knew how hard it was for a company to accumulate capital in its early stages. This method of financing was used extensively in America—perhaps it could be adjusted in appropriate ways and implemented in China. At this point, Liu again thought of Zhu Linan.

After helping the company complete its division, Zhu had remained in the Lianxiang Control Shares Company and become indispensable to Liu Chuanzhi. He was capable of greater responsibilities: Guo Wei had tried to persuade him to come over to Digital China; Yang Yuanqing hoped he would join Lianxiang Computer. Neither of these Commanders succeeded, for they failed to understand that Zhu was a kind of commanding genius himself who could not be an assistant to anyone else. Only Liu Chuanzhi saw this at the time. In no hurry, he waited till Zhu Linan had first refused Guo Wei, then Yang Yuanqing, before saying to him, "I want to give you a new stage."

Together they established the Lianxiang Investment Company, and Liu Chuanzhi appointed Zhu to be its President. He gave him US$30 million in initial investment funds, which soon was increased to US$200 million. In the remaining few months of 2001, Zhu Linan invested in one company after another within China. By the end of 2001, he had purchased the shares of at least eight enterprises.

The company's investments adhered to a strict evaluation of three considerations: topic selection, cultivating and managing the project, and exit. Zhu Linan was determined to paint a new and beautiful picture on this white sheet of paper called venture capital. Liu Chuanzhi too was tremendously excited about it and had to work hard to keep himself from "pulling the painting over so that he could paint it himself". This financial manager known for his "caution" had not abandoned his traditional approach. He paid particular attention to the personal character of the Founders of each potential investment. He invented a set of investment principles, new concepts steeped in a strong brew of tradition. 30% of the investment decision depended on the industry in which the company was situated; 20% on the technology and internal qualifications of the company; 50% on the Chief Executive Officer. Those in whom he invested were all supposed to be some kind of Liu Chuanzhi. Unfortunately, this world does not have that many Liu Chuanzhi's and it is impossible for a venture capitalist to be successful every time.

Even so, Liu Chuanzhi's dream was to create several more Lianxiangs. He hoped to use this new kind of venture-capital entity to do so. He evaluated the overall environment and then, like the Jack Welch he so admired, marched with full confidence into virgin territories.

He set up the Beijing Rongkezhidi Real Estate Development Company, Ltd. with Chen Guodong in charge of "calling in soldiers and buying horses to lead the charge." He set up the Zhiqinmeiji Company engaged in the business of logistics and delivery. He set up "Jinbailingcanyin Ltd.," a food service company that won the contract to supply lunch every day to the many tens of thousands of employees in ZGC district.

When the company divided, Yang Yuanqing wanted to carry forward Lianxiang's traditions, while Guo Wei wanted to establish a "second Lianxiang." Liu Chuanzhi could now say that his "third Lianxiang" was the Lianxiang Investment Company, while his fourth Lianxiang was Chen Guodong's Rongkezhidi, and perhaps there were also a fifth and a sixth. He knew that to realize these dreams he had to walk on firm ground, and he had to rely on the foundation and support of the Chinese culture. He created another mantra for both himself and employees: "Repay the country with your efforts: make this your responsibility. Exert yourself to become a person that others trust and respect. Be the leading enterprise in your industry. Be an internationalized control-share company that is influential on a global scale."

Diversification

As Liangxiang Control Shares was implementing a diversification strategy in its venture capital field, the Lianxiang Group led by Yang Yuanqing began to diversify in information technology. Several years later, Yang Yuanqing spoke of his thinking at that time: "Our main problem was how to take Lianxiang to a new level, from being a one billion US dollar company to being a four billion US dollar company. There were only two possible routes: one was internationalization, the other was diversification. We felt that diversification was easier than internationalization." Everyone knew that countless dangers lurked in the Internet, but there was much to tantalize as well. For a company that was keen to enter the ranks of the

World 500 and that had US$3 billion, recently increased to US$10 billion, this was particularly true. Yang Yuanqing agreed that winter was on its way, but he was still in attack mode. "You have to think about what is going to happen when spring comes," he echoed Liu Chuanzhi. He told his 7,000 soldiers, "We have to use the purifying nature of this winter. At the same time we have to prepare good seeds for planting in the future."

His first seed, FM365, was born at an inopportune time. Instead of becoming one of the four big portals, as he had hoped, it ranked Number 15. The second seed, Yingshitong, bought with US$35.37 million, languished. Internet companies had become the "Bermuda triangle" of investors.

The shift in the company's strategy towards diversification was manifested in a reorganization. The Lianxiang Group now had six basic business lines: consumer information-technology products, commercial information-technology products, hand-held products, information carriage, information technology services, and contract production of components.

Lianxiang began developing a vast array of commercial goods, including digital appliances. Yang Yuanqing's senior managers said that when people mentioned Lianxiang in three years, they didn't want them to think only of personal computers. In addition, Lianxiang jointly invested in a website with America Online. It cooperated with Siemens on joint development of hand-held equipment. It worked on faster broadband internet access service—the target for this business being the 3000 cable operators in the country. All of these were headline news in information technology in 2001. When a Vice-President of Microsoft came to Beijing to discuss a plan for "digital homes" with Lianxiang, the assumption that Lianxiang would be doing something big in the home-electronics field swept the country.

Going into services became a new goal. Liu Chuanzhi hoped it would become a source of profits, and within at least five years contribute 15% of company income. He also noted that the company had no choice but to pursue this direction, so that it was investing 20% of funds into projects outside the scope of physical products. Lianxiang was transitioning from being a computer hardware supplier to becoming an information technologies service company.

Age of mutual enjoyment

Debate over Lianxiang's diversification strategy raged. One newspaper article wrote that "Lianxiang wants to do all three things at once: selling televisions, setting up TV stations, doing television channels. It won't let go of any of them." Most people felt at the time that having multiple product lines was a necessary trend of the new century. Many saw the West as far ahead of China in this regard.

Others felt differently—they emphasized that multinational companies no longer tried to package everything themselves. They aimed for elasticity, nimbleness, a flexible operational capacity, with alliances, joint investment, and outsourcing methods to establish their competitive advantage. If the secret of the industrial age lay in monopolization, then the secret to the information age seemed to lie in cooperation. Qin Shuo, Editor-in-Chief of the *Southern Window* and author of the book called the "Bureau of Great Changes", continued to say that "an enterprise cannot get involved in too many industries, and the market cannot have a titan who can do everything." Companies in the "World 500" were no exception. Nike had already become a "brand operator," handing all of its production over to others. Ericsson stopped its mobile phone production lines everywhere except for China. Kodak outsourced its digital processors to IBM. IBM outsourced its global network systems business to the more professional AT&T. Microsoft monopolized operating systems but did not attempt to assemble computers. Intel did not say, "since we monopolize microprocessors, we should be able to take the entire computer business into our own hands."

The underlying logic of Lianxiang's new strategy was the opposite. The company's attitude was, "since we have the huge advantage of personal computers, why can't we occupy the entire market for Internet access? Since we can occupy the Internet access equipment business, why can't we operate portals? Since we can operate portals, why can't we provide Internet content?!"

A valuable lesson
The FM365 fiasco provided a valuable lesson. The company spent US$25 million on it, and several hundred employees worked flat-out for twenty months. They poured their knowledge, enthusiasm and creativity into the effort. The company was oblivious to one simple fact, however: success in one arena does not guarantee success in another.

The efforts of Liu Chuanzhi and others in the older generation deeply influenced company morale. Computers were not merely machines to Lianxiang, they were a symbol of the company's spirit. They had proved that traditional Chinese ethics and modern market systems could work together. At the cusp of the new millenia, Chinese yearned for absolutely new high technology, and computers seemed to satisfy this desire. Computer assembly and sales constituted Lianxiang's main profit center, however, so the company's culture was still that of a traditional manufacturing industry. When Lianxiang decided to launch itself into information-technology service industries, it came up against problems.

FM365 began to look like a failure in the fall of 2001. By October 2001, the joint venture with America Online was not only not helping the website but hastening its demise. Eventually, FM365 could not be propped up any longer. On November 1, the company announced it was dismissing employees. This was the first large-scale reduction in employees on the Mainland in Lianxiang's history. Three out of every ten of those people who had worked so hard for a year and a half in the Frontline Building were let go. The rest left within the next few months and the large building became empty. A number of highly credentialled commentators had applauded Lianxiang's Internet launch. Now that they saw things going south, they began to ridicule Lianxiang's strategy as being a "Great Leap Forward." The analogy was to a fatal move on the chessboard: the term Great Leap Forward had been used in the 1950s for that mad and disastrous policy of "constructing" the country, so it was particularly painful to see it used in this context. Many felt that to put a charge of fanaticism on Liu Chuanzhi was inappropriate. This man was the embodiment of caution. He had always said, "Don't do it if you haven't thought through it first." Unfortunately, at the time he too believed that Yang Yuanqing's website would succeed.

Yang Yuanqing was later to say, "I felt incredibly strong and capable. If the general direction was right, in a business sense, I would take on a business and try to do it. It didn't matter how large the disparity between that business and our capabilities. The difference between computer assembly, information technology services, and Internet is very large. Take our website: it required a new talent and new a new kind of system. But we were immature in our thinking. We all grew up studying a different kind of management. To us, "management" meant things like making sure workers did not urinate inside the factory. Or knowing how to tie your tie and be presentable. We had not yet studied the chapter on management strategy."

"Lianxiang" and a new advertising tactic

In 2002, Yang Yuanqing became increasingly aware that he had another problem. He had to relinquish a Lianxiang trademark that had epitomized the company. The English name of Lianxiang had always been "Legend." It was perfect, but for that very reason it was already in use by many people in many countries. It could not be registered in most places overseas. Years earlier this had been discussed after the President's Office received a report from the Legal Department—at that time an unwillingness to let go of the brand held the upper hand. Yang Yuanqing had been in secret communication with officials of the Olympic Commission and he planned to make Lianxiang a sponsor of the 2008 Beijing Olympics. He decided he could no longer allow this situation to continue.

In the end, the company took the two first letters of the old English name and added "novo" to it to form a new word, "Lenovo." Yang Yuanqing felt that the new word implied "creating a new Lianxiang". He decided to combine this Latin-derived word together with the Chinese name for the company: in China, Lianxiang is written in Chinese characters, Lenovo in English. Yang kept the original color of the trademark, azure blue. He liked blue, for it reminded him of Big Blue, or "Blue Giant" as it is known in Chinese, IBM.

On April 28, 2003, the "Legend" banners that had waved over China for fourteen years were changed simultaneously to "LianxiangLenovo." The square surrounding a circle was gone. Huge outdoor billboards announced the change, as well as golden time ads on TV. At least 200 million Chinese saw the nightly news broadcast, after which they saw the word "Legend" dissolve and melt into silvery watery. "LianxiangLenovo" rose, surrounded by the brilliant rays of a sunrise. For eight weeks, the ad was broadcast for thirty seconds every day.

Over the course of ten years the company's ad policies had matured as Lianxiang successfully combined China's traditional qualities and a more contemporary emotional makeup of the people.

The Shenzhou-5 manned spacecraft was being sent on its voyage just at this time. Lianxiang spent RMB 18 million for insertion of an ad in CCTV time slots. The new name, Lenovo, floated in a blue sky, together with the ad copy: "transcending depends on how you think." This reinforced the idea that you can create whatever you can imagine and, if you are imaginative, anything can be done.

The promotion of the company's new name was a success. By the time 2003 was drawing to a close, the name had penetrated people's consciousness. Promotion costs were high, over RMB 200 million, but this was a small percentage of the company's entire expenditure on ads.

The Threat of Dell

Dell graced itself with the halo of "international quality, local price," in an advertisement broadcast in China on August 28, 2001. One of its computers, equipped with a liquid crystal display monitor, was cheaper than Lianxiang's by RMB 401. The media generally felt that a frontal assault on Lianxiang had begun; later events were to prove that this was correct.

Yang Yuanqing did not take this sniper's shot from behind seriously at first. He was mostly in America these days, learning about multinational companies, clarifying in his own mind the blue-sky thinking of how to enter the "World 500". Nobody among Lianxiang's senior management seemed to think that Dell constituted a threat. This complacent attitude, in addition to a series of policy mistakes, began to impede the company's progress. Liu Chuanzhi was a master at handling sudden crises but he had never dealt with this kind of creeping danger. He underestimated his opponent. In the oath-swearing meeting of 2004, he said, "Let's allow Mr. Dell to get to know us. He'll find out who Yang Yuanqing is!" This drew loud applause from the audience.

Within two years, it became obvious that Dell was a dangerous opponent. As the "dragon-headed elder" in the Chinese computer market, Lianxiang discovered it had to deal on its own turf with a powerful invader. Dell's starting point can be traced back to 1984, coincidentally the same year that Lianxiang was founded. In May of that year, Michael Dell left college in Texas and founded his own company. He initiated a direct sales model in the computer industry that was stamped with his individual character: he believed in the power of "direct contact." After succeeding in the North American market, he quietly transplanted his direct sales to China. All of this happened in the mid-1990s, just as Yang Yuanqing was rolling up the China market with his agency model. Nobody believed in the efficacy of direct selling systems in China. The saying among computer manufacturers at the time was, "Dell? That company owns nothing but a screwdriver!"

Michael Dell silently watched Lianxiang's strategies but continued to keep faith in his own ideas. By February 2002, he was able to announce that the "direct sales method" had the highest efficiency rate in the global computer industry. In 2001, Dell Company sales were Number One in the world for the first time, and enjoyed a 14% share of the total global market. In the United States, Dell's market share exceeded 25%, but its greatest victory was achieved in China. Assembly workshops that the company had set up in Xiamen produced 1500 computers a day, and over the past two years Dell's sales in the China market had been growing at an average of 50% a year. From 2002 on, the rate would rise to 60%. Dell was seen to have the most advanced sales and service system in the world, so that even a crisis like 9/11 represented a minor disturbance.

In 2000, the Chinese computer market belonged to Lianxiang; after that, everyone began to notice the looming shadow of Dell. The expansionist policy of Lianxiang fragmented that company's resources, while Dell now deployed a troop of 600 people to fill any cracks with their direct sales. As 2004 began, the situation was clearly changing. Although Lianxiang computers still took 27% of the China market and were ranked Number One in sales, senior management of the company was disturbed to discover that this figure had dropped 3 points from the 2000 level. In the third-quarter of 2003, Dell surpassed Lianxiang to be Number One in the commercial-use computer sector. The Research Director of IDC, Bryan Ma, felt that this latter figure was significant. He announced, "Dell has won the support of government and educational organizations in China—in the past this market segment usually chose Lianxiang."

Lianxiang now recognized that it had a problem. "Computers are our lifeline, we rely on them for survival, they are the basis of our search for breakthroughs. This foundation must be firm," Liu Chuanzhi announced. "Due to the threat of international competitors and our overly dispersed strength over the past three years, the foundation at our feet is cracking." In the mid-1990s, under the banner of National Products, the Chinese government had purchased Lianxiang computers. Now they were replacing those with Dell.

Liu Chuanzhi had always felt that Lianxiang had the benefit of home turf on its side in its competition with foreign brands. It now looked as though the positions of host and guest were being reversed. Dell's assembly lines in Xiamen were able to lower costs of production to a point low enough to compete with Lianxiang, and this was key to winning orders from government and educational organizations. "We hope to make the growth rate in the Chinese market three times that in the entire industry," said Bill Amelio, Dell's Senior Vice-President. "And we intend to keep it at that rate."

Direct selling versus Agency selling: Which is better?
Although direct selling is not the entire Dell story, it is the most extraordinary part. All aspects of Dell's core culture, standards, process, organization, discipline, results, are imprinted with the direct-sales method.

Direct sales moves the product directly into the hands of the customer from the manufacturing line. Agenting means that the product has to move through a series of connections, so-called agencies, including wholesale and retail. It is hard to imagine that a manufacturer can place tens of thousands of products in a one-to-one relationship directly with consumers, so in the modern market, agency selling has become the most common model. Only when Dell appeared did someone, for the first time, put direct selling and mass production together. Dell's results are impressive. Proponents of this method declare that it is sounding the funeral bell on a system of indirect selling that lasted for over one hundred years.

Lianxiang's senior management does not agree with this conclusion. "Different sales methods have different qualities," Yang Yuanqing has noted, "and should be used on different market segments. Our competition with Dell is not in fact about direct or indirect selling. The sales method distinction is superficial. The true competition is in whose total process is superior, more efficient, can hold more market segments. Dell's advantage lies with large enterprises, particularly in mature industries. The company can offer these customers a "long-term customer plan." For dispersed customers, such as households, the advantage is on our side."

"Dell is an extremely admirable company," Liu Jun, Senior Vice-President of the Lianxiang Group, has noted. "We are constantly studying it. We are well aware that we are going to have a tough battle ahead." In charge of home-use computers, Liu Jun has remained secure in his own realm. Though Dell had been victorious in the commercial-use market, Lianxiang seemed impregnable in the home-use arena. From 2000 to 2003, Dell made three concerted attempts to apply its success in the one market to the other. These were termed the "three encounters" by Liu Jun, and in every battle Lianxiang countered the thrust. Dell bought inexpensive computers from Taiwan and stuck on its own label, then sold them cheaply hoping to gain price advantage. "We took measures," Liu Jun said. "They have not been able to find any way to beat us."

Dell appears now to be in the process of trying to set up some channels for agency selling. Moreover, it is placing Dell computers in more and more retail shops. Just as it is applauding its Direct Sales method globally, in the China market it is quietly changing. Dell has never publicly admitted to its agency business, but indications show that there are indeed certain "national circumstances" in China that make for problems with any other selling mode. Consumers like to compare prices and goods, and the practice is to hand over the money with one hand while taking the goods with the other. Chinese do not believe that a stranger on the end of a phone line is worthy of confidence. They do not like to pay any money for a service visit. To them, time is not important—the most important is not to be "tricked."

Winter of 2003

Winter of 2003 was the "twenty-year winter" in Lianxiang's history. It was long and it was cold. To computer industries around the world, this winter had gone on for much too long. In three years, global personal computer sales had dropped 24%. The situation in China was better but the increase in sales was only 12%. Lianxiang's diversification strategy produced mixed results: over three years, operating revenue had increased 25% while profits had risen 50%. In the world's computer assembly industry, it was one of only two companies that was making money. The other was Dell.

The *Economic Observer* commented that, after a period of rapid growth, Lianxiang appeared to be "stuck". "It has hit the ceiling." But Lianxiang's problem was not that today's numbers weren't good but that its ambitions for tomorrow were too great. Yang Yuanqing pressed on with plans for joining the "World 500".

12

SITTING ON THE MOUNTAIN TO
WATCH THE TIGERS FIGHT

Two years ago I said, "We'll let Mr. Dell get to know us a little better. He'll find out who Yang Yuanqing is!" Today we have a rather clearer understanding of "who Dell is." We are taking this blow well. It has cleared our heads, turned us away from blind self-confidence. To sum up my lessons: Study Dell. Learn from Dell. Then send the troops out to beat Dell. We will see what the outcome is.

Liu Chuanzhi

On a day in January 2004, Liu Chuanzhi went to the Naval Hospital in Beijing to visit a patient and was shocked by news that he heard there. This hospital had signed a contract with Lianxiang to treat its employees. Years earlier, Liu had been treated here for Meniere's Disease by Dr. Li, who was now seeing more and more Lianxiang employees come in with problems. "Those young people under you are killing themselves," Dr. Li said to Liu. "They are nothing but walking medical problems."

He showed Liu Chuanzhi a list of employee names and ailments: high blood pressure, heart disease, liver problems. Liu was aware of the difficulties in managing a large company, but he had not imagined that, in the space of three years, every one of his managers would come down with serious physical illness. They all shared one symptom: insomnia, and when anyone fell asleep he had nightmares about company affairs.

Liu had once promised to "soothe their wounds." He could not say such a thing and not do something about it now. At the spring meeting of the company he gave his most emotional speech to date. He talked of the dangers of the storm in the market, he talked about how neither of the companies led by Yang Yuanqing or Guo Wei had met their targets, and then he changed his tone. "The reason I asked you all here is that I want to let you know that we are a large family, the Lianxiang family. If I am truly going to represent the older generation in saying something to you young people, I just want to say... take care of yourselves. Because Dr. Li.... Dr Li told me..."

He could not go on. His voice choked up. The young people in the audience had prepared to hear a stern reprimand, not this scene. "This is the second time I ever saw him as emotional as that, " said Liu Xiaolin later. "The first time was when he and Ni Guangnan parted ways."

Health problems were not the only issue facing the company, however.

Lianxiang crisis, and staff reduction

Nine-lives Lianxiang had weathered many crises over the years. Liu Chuanzhi never seemed to lack the resolve and courage to overcome them. As his father once said about him: "He is stubborn. He has the kind of spirit that just forges ahead." Liu's father had died several months earlier. Before dying, he reminded his son, "When you encounter hardship, everything depends on your will to carry on." His father's encouragement and advice served as a lifelong support for Liu Chuanzhi, and he remembered it now.

"In order to reform, we have to pay the price," Liu told the company in a meeting in early 2004. For many years he had described the company as a ship on the ocean: he now saw that the ship had sprung leaks and that the situation was grave. "The choices we face are: one, everyone sits on the ship and we all go down together; two, one group first gets up on shore and quickly gathers material to plug the holes and in the end everyone gets up on shore. It may be, however, that only some of the people get on shore. The rest might get their feet wet, or even get hurt more seriously." All kept thinking of this warning until March 11, 2004. On that day, in the space of three hours, Lianxiang laid off 600 employees, around 5% of the company.

Staff reductions are a common practice in Western countries when a company faces problems, but they are extremely rare in China. In Lianxiang, a rapid turnover was common. The company had an "elimination through selection" system and an employee whose performance was not up to standard would either be let go or would voluntarily leave to find another position. Every year around 5% of employees left the company. This staff reduction was different. The company called it a "strategic reduction", which meant that people were being asked to leave not because their performance was bad but because the company's strategic direction had changed.

The media believed that this was the first-ever reduction in the company's history. This mistake gave the impression that Lianxiang was in tremendous trouble and about to close up. Public opinion has a kind of "domino" effect, a phenomenon that exaggerates some parts of a story, which in turn exaggerate others. Journalists began to wonder what secrets Lianxiang was hiding; others estimated that the reductions were reaching 10% of the total. Wang Xiaoyan, the Vice-President of Finance, firmly answered all questions: "The total is 5%, and Lianxiang has no need to hide it." She complained that people with an axe to grind were attacking the company now that it had grown so big. "No matter what happens with Lianxiang, these guys take a magnifying glass to it," she said.

The process of deciding to streamline forces was not as complex as described in the media. The matter could be traced back to the company's taking the diversification route: employees hired en masse when the company was at its peak had not brought with them commensurate business results. As a percentage of sales income, people's salaries were 2% of the total in 2000 and 3% in 2003. The increase was eating up the company's profits. Lianxiang began to experience the most common symptom of "big-company blues": bloated personnel, weighing down the company.

At a senior management meeting in early 2004, the subject of "pioneering reform" was put on the agenda but Wang Xiaoyan was more concerned about next year's budget. The company had already captured any potential sales in the market, administrative expenses and rent for the buildings had been pushed as low as possible, whatever could be cut had been cut. No other actions could be taken to get to the profit targets expected by investors. "I have pretty much wrung the towel dry," Wang Xiaoyan said. "I can't get out another drop of water."

This situation led most observers to believe that the staff reduction was a result of financial considerations. Ma Xuezheng, Senior Vice-President, disagreed. "Staff reductions and our finances are two separate things. This action related to business operations." She went on to say, "It seems to me journalists inside China don't understand this too well—they just don't get it. Go ask financial experts on Wall Street, or go ask any of the ten

largest investment firms in the world. Tell them to look at the financials
of Lianxiang. You will then realize that Lianxiang's staff reduction and our
profitability are not related. The reduction relates directly to our adjustment
of business lines."

Whatever one says, Lianxiang fired many people. This was meant to
put business back on the road to glory but, to employees, it was disaster.
The Human Resources Department decided that not a single department
could avoid firing people. The company decided on its new structure and
new positions in February, and employees soon discovered that positions
outside the core business were drastically reduced. The General Manager
of the Human Resources Department, Qiao Jian, became the busiest and
most traumatized person in the company. She had spent years promoting
the company's image to the public, now her sole task was to close the
doors and secretly peruse lists of "who should be let go." The lists were first
drawn up by the managers of each department. They then went through
a confirmation process by the Human Resources Department. If all of the
people on the list were let go, salary costs to the company would be
lowered by 0.8%. Department managers were on the lists as well, not just
common employees.

The reduction was accomplished briskly. It was mobilized on March 6,
lists of names were handed over on March 8, they were confirmed on the
9th and all measures were prepared on the 10th. The reduction took place
on Thursday, March 11. There were no arguments, there was no debate.
There was no need for any explanation or comforting. All those who
received the order to "leave" had nothing to say. All they could do was go
silently. People who had sat next to colleagues were gone in a second,
leaving behind empty offices. A kind of eery silence remained in the
building, as if everything had died.

The emotional impact on employees was unprecedented. "I could see
it," said Qiao Jian. "Everyone was traumatized, those who left and those
who stayed." She felt it would help if employees talked about their
feelings, so in the first week, when people were most upset, she instructed
the Human Resources Department to "evaluate people's attitudes."
Unexpectedly, results showed that over 80% of employees "felt the
reduction was essential." Only 4% felt that the reduction should not have
occurred. These statistics comforted her somewhat. "I think this will blow
over fairly quickly," she reported to her boss.

"The company is not our family"
All morning on March 11, Mao Shijie watched his colleagues leave the
Lianxiang Research Institute. Thirty people left from the Research Institute

and twenty more were transferred to other positions. Of nine employees in his department, three remained. Mao had many things to say about this but they stayed bottled inside until he sat down to write the following in his diary late that night:

"Today was face-to-face meetings. They used the two little conference rooms on the first floor of B-building. People went in one by one. The leaders first confirmed their past accomplishments. Then they explained the meaning of "strategic staff reduction," told them how much compensation they would be getting, handed over a sheaf of materials prepared in advance, and asked them to sign a contract dissolving the employment relationship. It took twenty minutes on average.

"Those who were getting fired knew nothing about it before hand. Before each meeting, the company had prepared everything in advance. When they were called in, people's mailbox, HR card, IC-cards, were cancelled. Once they got the news, they had two hours to leave the company."

Mao went on to describe specific circumstances. Then he asked, "Whose mistake is it, that all of a sudden the company decides "we don't want to move in that direction?" I don't know. All I know is that the ones hurt most were lower-level employees.

"The reduction came down hardest on new employees and also on old Lianxiang people who had been with the company a long time. There were some who had been with the company ten years, were pushing fifty. Like everyone else, they had to go, and they went.

"In these three years I've been at Lianxiang, I've seen it expand and seen it contract. We used to talk about "High-tech Lianxiang", "Service Lianxiang", "International Lianxiang". All of that is pretty much gone. High-tech is now applied science, and who knows if it will succeed. The IT service team has been absorbed into another group and it will be hard for them to keep their jobs. The software design center will soon have no ties to Lianxiang. The company is being attacked on all sides and the damage is heavy.

"Whose fault is it? It is the leaders' fault! They evaluated the prospects, decided the direction. These things were supposed to make big money, for after all, how could Lianxiang fail? I don't mean to do anything about it, but I feel that it's us common employees who are getting shafted, bearing the brunt of their mistakes.

"I feel I have a deeper understanding of things than a lot of people. The relationship between employees and company is all about benefits. You should never in a million years think the company is your family. At the same time, I also feel that Lianxiang doesn't owe me anything.

Lianxiang gave me a good working environment, the opportunity to learn things, and pretty good pay. But, the company is the company. Everything it did for me was done so that I would make a contribution to it."

These diary pages were copied by someone and found their way to the Web. There, the account became notorious and soon someone added a headline:

"Lianxiang employee personally experiences the Great Lianxiang Firing: Company is not Family." Any remaining faith in the "Big family of Lianxiang," so extolled by the company, was soon gone. Within five hours, at least 104 people had appended their own comments. All seemed to consider the staff reduction a cruel scandal. Some asked why the mistakes of leaders should be paid for by regular employees. Some said that the same sort of thing was happening daily in China, just not on such a big scale.

Liu Chuanzhi was shaken by the event. Evidence indicates that he knew about the staff reduction only a few days before Mao Shijie. After the company split in 2000, Yang Yuanqing and Guo Wei were given policy control over the two separate companies. Liu Chuanzhi and Li Qin had periodic communications with them. In order not to distance himself too far from the frontline commanders, Liu Chuanzhi assigned a PhD named Qiu Jin to be his assistant. She had long been in the Lianxiang Group and had a good idea of what he needed to know. He asked her to keep him informed, but other than matters of financial budgeting and adjustments in shares, he had never interfered with Yang Yuanqing's decisions.

"Decision-making power rests with him," he said in response to a journalist's question. "Yang Yuanqing looks on me as a consultant, he is willing to discuss things with me but I only talk principles. I never say "cut forces" or "don't cut."" Liu Chuanzhi supported Yang Yuanqing in this action, but he believed that Yang Yuanqing's firing methods "were a little too precipitous. Done badly, this thing could damage the family culture that we worked so hard to build. We "take human beings as the essential, the core."" He was still considered the spiritual leader of the company, and everyone wanted to know what he thought.

April 16, 2004 marked the oath-swearing meeting of the new fiscal year of the Lianxiang Group. Liu Chuanzhi came on stage and presented frank views on the company staff cuts. He did not beat around the bush. Without adornment, his speech responded to the concept of "The Company is not Family."

"A piece called "The Company is not Family" was written by a Lianxiang employee and put up on the Net. It is tactful and sincere. I felt badly after reading it. Among people who were let go were old-timers with whom I had worked many years ago. Not one of them made a phone call to me to object. They accepted it in silence, which made me feel even worse. More of these employees were directly under Yang Yuanqing, and I know that his heartache was greater than mine.

"I believe that the most basic principle that an enterprise has to respect and follow is that of growth. Only by growing can an enterprise be responsible to its investors, its employees, and society. With growth as its main principle, if an enterprise is to advance, it must adopt an internally competitive system. While employees at Lianxiang should feel a certain sense of security, they should also feel the pressure to compete and struggle to excel. Therefore, in a very real way, it is indeed necessary not to take the company as your family. At home, children can have all kinds of defects, make all kinds of mistakes, but parents forgive them in the end. An enterprise cannot behave in the same way.

"The author of this piece "The Company is not Family," mentions that strategic adjustments were the fault of leaders who then forced regular employees to take the brunt of the consequences. I stopped to think for a long time when I read this point. I think that what he said is right. This time, some of those employees who were let go were related to policy mistakes of the leaders, to faults of strategy formulation. This is a bitter matter. We should say to those employees who were let go, with extreme honesty, "I am sorry." As the Chairman of the Board of this enterprise, knowing that growth is a fundamental requirement, how should I ask Yang Yuanqing and the others to do their work? One way is to proceed with extreme caution, avoiding any losses. Another way is to seek breakthroughs, creativity, and, following that path, we certainly will make mistakes. We are fighting this war under extremely difficult circumstances, under great handicaps relative to the situation of foreign enterprises. Nevertheless, we must struggle, we must fight, we must go all out. With near-zero experience, we are entering a new realm. We are throwing manpower and material at it in order to try to succeed. Since we don't see the direction clearly, and have not mastered the methods, we hit our heads, lose blood, pay a sad and a heavy price.

"I don't know how many mistakes I made in the fifteen or so years that I was directly responsible for the company. I paid a price for them, but the leaders were lenient and didn't call me to account. My mistakes changed the course of many people's lives.

"When I think of these things, I ask myself, what should I have done? Today I have come up against a similar situation. The question I need to answer now is, "what demands should I place on Yang Yuanqing?" And in the end I feel that all I can say to Yuanqing is: 1. Keep your goal firmly in mind. Remember your responsibility; forge ahead. Create! Break through! There is no other way. 2. Covet your resources, especially your employees. Keep firmly in mind that people are fundamental, they are the core: manage them knowing that they are the primary value. 3. Go to war. If you win seven out of ten battles, you will be an outstanding commander.

"With apologies, I must say to the author of "The Company is not Family" that the standpoint from which we evaluate problems is different. If Yang Yuanqing can look at issues from the perspective of the larger picture, the growth of the company, then this is the best way to "take people as the core value." It is the most fundamental way to be responsible to employees. If Yang Yuanqing evaluates issues from a regard for only a portion of employees, then the enterprise will sink under the weight of familial emotions. It will be unable to grow and China will lose Lianxiang. The rhythm of forward movement must come from battle drums.

"As representative of Lianxiang's senior management, Yang Yuanqing is taking on a tremendous burden. Employees are saying to him, "we are giving you the best years of our life. Lead us well, do not make mistakes!" Shareholders are clamoring, "Grow! Profits! Development!" Others in our industry are waiting to grab any opportunity to deal us a fatal blow. On this shameless battlefield, the slightest loss of attention will lead to a split skull. As one with experience in this regard, I know how it feels. Because of this, all of us—shareholders, employees—must be strict in our demands on those responsible for managing the enterprise. We must criticize, must raise opinions; at the same time, we must applaud, say well done. We must, top to bottom, unify and be of one heart. When we win a victory, we must not be proud; when we lose, we must encourage each other. Then we raise the battle song once again."

Top sponsor of the International Olympics
Two weeks after completing the reduction in forces, the company held a large press conference at which it announced that Lianxiang had become an international partner of the Sixth International Olympics Commission. At the same time it became a "Top Sponsor" of the 2006 Turin Winter Olympics and the 2008 Beijing Summer Olympics. This helped considerably in pulling employees out of their depression.

As with the force reduction, Liu Chuanzhi did not participate in planning for this affair but he undoubtedly was in favor of it. He had always been a sports enthusiast, once putting RMB 10 million into sponsoring the Chinese Women's Soccer Team, and he had hopes for organizing a Soccer League though he later gave this up as being unrealistic.

In 2000, the world's most outstanding athletes and sports journalists converged on Sydney where the 27th Olympics were held. Chinese had felt that their capital city should obtain hosting privileges for this Olympics; Lianxiang even put up RMB 12 million to support the Beijing government's application. Unfortunately, the international image of Beijing was not good at the time. Americans obstructed the Chinese application and the 2000 Olympics were given to Sydney. Liu Chuanzhi and Beijing government officials were disappointed but the defeat was probably a good thing: Lianxiang in the 1990s had insufficient resources to contend for being a top Olympics sponsor. When Beijing finally did get hosting rights for the 2008 Olympics, Lianxiang was rich and its fortunes were soaring. The previous RMB 12 million had not been spent in vain— Lianxiang and the Beijing Olympics Commission had become close partners. The investment was the first step in the direction of the company's eventual stride through the doorway of the Olympics.

Officials of the International Olympic Committee came to Beijing at the end of 2002, and the municipal government found an opportunity to present representatives from Lianxiang. This was the first time Lianxiang had contact with officials of the Committee, and the company came prepared. Management had set up a small team and formulated a plan for "taking the Olympics." It was ranked "Absolutely Secret". In the past, if a project being researched by the company was secret, then it was given an English letter, such as "A-plan," or "B-plan." This time, since there were seven years between 2002 and 2008, the team decided to call the plan "007."

The three members of the team worked for one year under conditions of utmost secrecy. They studied everything there was to known about the Olympics, its traditions, its procedures. They then selected the best athletics services company in the world, and invited it to Beijing to become Lianxiang's consultant. In due course the team came to know that "global partner" meant the highest level of partnering with the International Olympics Committee. They learned what steps an enterprise must take in order to do this, what the price would be, and what benefits would result. In February 2003, Ma Xuezheng led a team to Lausanne where they met with the President of the International Olympics Committee, Jacques Rogge. They did not know that they were the first Chinese enterprise ever to come to this quiet town. They did not know who their competitors might be, and they could hardly imagine that they would be successful.

The first action after the Lausanne meeting was to extend an invitation to Rogge to come visit Lianxiang. From years of experience, the company knew that a visit by senior officials would enhance solidarity within the

The Lenovo Affair

company and improve the company's image abroad. Unfortunately, Rogge was busy handling the 2004 Olympics and hadn't time to work on 2008. He expressed strong interest in Lianxiang, however, and he sent over a video in which he was standing under the five flags at the International Olympic Committee headquarters as he said with great warmth and enthusiasm, "We would be delighted to see a Chinese brand become our Computer Technology Sponsor."

The implication of this was that Lianxiang would have exclusive rights, and that other computer manufacturers would be excluded. In the two previous Olympics, this position had been held by IBM. IBM was now withdrawing from the "partner plan," which allowed Lianxiang to be considered. The Olympics had been resumed for some one hundred years but this "partner plan" had begun only in 1984. That year, an enterprise had to pay US$4 million to be a partner. The price kept rising till by 2003 the average sponsorship fee had reached US$65 million. There were only eleven technology-sponsor corporations at this level for the 2008 Olympics. They formed the list of "Top Sponsors," and included such companies as Coca-Cola, General Electric, Kodak, MacDonalds, Matsushita and Samsung. For the first time, Lianxiang's name was ranked together with these multinational corporations.

The signing ceremony was held on March 26 at the Peking Hotel. The Executive Board member of the International Olympic Committee and the Vice-Chairman of the Turin Olympic Organizing Committee sat on one side of the table. On the other was the Chairman of the Board of the Lianxiang Group, Liu Chuanzhi, and its President, Yang Yuanqing. A number of gold medallists attended, as well as the Secretary General of the Beijing Municipality, Liu Qi, and the National Planning Commission Chairman, Yuan Weimin.

For several weeks after this, the name of Lianxiang and the five circles of the Olympics were jointly flown over streets of all major cities throughout China. All of the billboards were blue and white, accentuating the words "Lianxiang becomes the global partner of the International Olympic Committee."

The term "patriotic" perhaps goes too far, but a certain non-commercial sentiment was involved in this process. As Liu Chuanzhi said, "It would be unacceptable if the Olympics were held in China and not a single sponsor was a Chinese company." Lianxiang's azure blue banners therefore flew in concert with the crimson red of the national flag, and to great acclaim. Our country has a distorted approach to sports. Westerners are inclined to look on sports as a game, something that stimulates and amuses. Chinese take sports as a symbol of patriotic devotion and national strength. Officials, experts, scholars all were happy to give their views on the subject. The Beijing Vice-Chairman of the Olympics Preparatory Committee, Liu Jingmin, said, "The Lianxiang Group has come up with a new model for taking Chinese enterprises out into the world." The Corporate Vice-President and CEO of the Greater China Region of Microsoft, Chen Yongzhen [Tim Chen], said that he "felt very proud on behalf of Lianxiang." After journalists had loudly extolled Lianxiang, they began to look for the flaw in the plan. The most important issue, of course, was how much this was going to cost: how much Lianxiang would pay for this opportunity to "raise its eyebrows in public." Although the public was keen to know what the figure was, Yang Yuanqing was determined to keep it confidential.

Senior managers of the company respected the privacy agreement and did not give out a figure, but in China, this kind of thing is impossible to keep quiet. Guesses of the media covered a wide range, but gradually approached a realistic figure of US$65 million. Although this was much lower than an earlier estimate of US$80 million, it still made people gasp. They looked at Lianxiang lined up with the other mighty companies, and felt that this was an ugly duckling trying to be a white swan.

The media started asking if the company in fact had sufficient resources. Someone researched precedents of other Olympic sponsors: for every dollar of sponsorship, it seemed they spent three more dollars "to form a complete set". Lianxiang in the end would have to invest US$260 million. Lianxiang's total profit for one year was only roughly US$150 million. Newspapers sounded the alarm. People said, "Top" is a trap."

Middle and small investors in the stock market got nervous. Liu Chuanzhi had to meet with journalists and confirm that, "as the largest shareholder, we wholeheartedly support this affair." He also noted, "There are risks, but they are not as big as some think. Some have said that this is a gamble on our part: I say emphatically that it is not. Lianxiang does not take up things it doesn't win."

Journalists were not satisfied with this response, however. They went looking for Yang Yuanqing. Yang explained that the investment was not all in cash. More important was the supply of goods and services. He then took on a sharper tone: "If you understand Lianxiang at all, you should know that this is an extremely conservative company. It is not a very aggressive player. We never put all of our eggs in one basket, and we never play with dice."

Three years earlier, the concern that Lianxiang had insufficient means might have been valid. Now, in the spring of 2004, Lianxiang's problems were not financial. The advertising budget already surpassed

RMB 600 million every year, and in addition, Yang Yuanqing held around US$300 million of cash in his hands. His greatest worry was not that he had insufficient funds but that "our products may not be qualified for such a huge event. When the Olympics start, if the athlete falls down the hill, namely us, we will be the laughing stock of the entire world."

The things that most concerned Yang Yuanqing and his senior management were technology, workmanship, management, service, cooperation—all of which formed the quality of a company's total operations. After all, Lianxiang was replacing IBM at the Olympics. For whatever reason, this was a point that very few thought about at the time.

Focussing on computers

Yang Yuanqing's so-called "2004 passionate transformation" was a two-edged sword. On the one hand, it was a "strategic retrenchment," on the other it was "commanding a global initiative." It combined a reduction in forces and a courageous Olympics initiative.

Ma Xuezheng had said, "the staff reduction has nothing to do with the finances of the company, it has to do with its business operations." Looking at reports of senior managers at the time, we can see that this statement is valid. Researchers in the company were by now trained to be sharp-eyed and effective. They could analyze the pros and cons of any project. Investors would have been delighted and alarmed to see these reports. They analyzed twenty-three projects in the company and came to the conclusion that none of them had come up to target over the past three years. At the end of 2003, the reports consolidated the results into clusters of data that showed just how much of the company's resources these projects were swallowing every day. The company's prosperity relied almost solely on Lianxiang computers, which brought in 80% of the sales volume and 90% of the profit.

Lianxiang computers were synonymous with the "nation's computer industry." On computer sales, the company continued to maintain a net profit of over 5%. In the China market, Lianxiang was facing the encirclement of many other manufacturers, however, and its market share had been going down one percentage point per year for the past three years. When it was selected as the prescribed computer of the Winter Olympics in 2006 and the Summer Olympics in 2008, market faith in the brand was briefly restored, but all indicators showed that the company must now concentrate its resources on Lianxiang Computers.

Yang Yuanqing candidly admitted that the "diversification strategy led us into the woods. It was ill advised." He swore to "rally back to the mountains and rivers." In March 2004, staff reduction and contraction of business lines proceeded at the same time, but senior management did not like the term retrenchment. After considerable discussion, someone finally found the word "focus". All decided to use that as a word that allowed for ongoing retrenchment without harming company morale. "We have recognized that computers are the foundation of Lianxiang's development," declared Yang Yuanqing. "Only by expanding this business can we move to the next step, setting the stage for becoming both international and diversified. Because of this, our first step is to focus all of our management resources on guaranteeing the success of computers."

Liu Chuanzhi later reiterated this to employees, "The adjustment of Lianxiang's strategic line is mainly "to focus". The business focus is on the field of personal computers. This will, however, be a multi-staged process." In private conversation, he did not deny the fact that the company was retrenching but he clarified, "Retrenching means focussing. It's the same thing."

The company's retrenchment plan looked severe. In 2000 the company had six major business lines. By spring of 2004, these six were slimmed down to three, called A, B, and C:

A: Information products business line. This included home-use electronics, commercial-use computers, notebook computers, and servers.
B: Lianxiang mobile. This included hand-held computers and mobile telephones.
C: IT services. This included consulting, development and integration of applied software, operations security, outsourcing, and training.

The A-type businesses held 80% of the company's sales revenue and 100% of its profit. Resources were concentrated here as much as possible in order to guarantee a 15% annual growth rate to investors. B-type businesses still belonged to the realm of loss-making endeavors but represented the company's future hope. In the summer of 2004, the company sold the C-type businesses to Yaxin Company, more thoroughly expressing its determination to focus. Lianxiang pulled out of the Huizhou motherboard production factory completely and stopped its involvement in mobile phone manufacturing at Xiamen.

"Business lines" had always been described in the company in the form of a graph. The graph of 2000 was "two large pillars and four small pillars." Now, in 2004, business lines were described by the Vice-President, Lu Yan, as a football field. "Our "front line" is A-type businesses," he said.

"Our centerfield is B-type. There is also a rear defense, which includes the company's purchasing platform, its logistics, its information support, financial support, and central R&D systems."

Internationalization

The term "retrenchment" did not in fact totally explain the nature of Lianxiang's strategy in 2004. "We are not yet an international company," Yang Yuanqing said on March 26 of that year, "but we are in the process of expanding overseas." Many people were perplexed by this and took it to mean that the Olympics Partnership implied a strong desire to expand abroad.

A popular commentator on Sina.com noted that, "Investors and experts are raising doubts about Lianxiang's overseas strategy. China has the world's largest potential market. Managing this market well would guarantee Lianxiang a stable growth. Unduly wanting to expand overseas would require tremendous expenditure and is not wise." This author also pointed out that 90% of Lianxiang's sales revenue was coming from China itself. This figure somewhat overestimated Lianxiang's capabilities overseas. Speaking more precisely, Lianxiang's annual export revenue was around US$100 million, only 2% of total income.

"Take the internal market as the core focus," senior management had concluded after travelling around the world in 1997 and 2000. Their reasoning back then was still valid in 2004. They were modifying their tune now with the Olympics strategy not so much out of expansionist leanings as out of a realization that the best defense is an attack.

In the same week that Lianxiang became an Olympics global partner, Yang Yuanqing began to say that the company was entering a "second round of competition." This was going to be a more bitter fight than the struggles that Lianxiang had been through in the 1990s. "Chinese industries truly are dancing with wolves. As a result, you are either eaten by wolves or you become a wolf." Yang went on to explain that becoming a wolf meant becoming an enterprise that is internationally competitive. "In our view, a high growth rate is hard to sustain if you only try to maintain your position in the China market." Several weeks later, in a discussion with the author, for the first time he explained the logic of a strategy that both "focussed" and "expanded."

"A 50% growth rate in the future cannot be expected but we do hope to maintain a 20% growth rate. There are only two ways to do this: one is diversification, the other is internationalization. What we are emphasizing this time is that we are more focussed, that is we are strengthening our competitiveness in personal computers as our core business. Before 2000, in the first round of competition with foreign manufacturers, we were highly successful and home-use computers were tremendously successful. Within this success lay some illusions, however. We overestimated the protective qualities of our home turf, of "the China marshes." It's not the same now. The marshes have turned into superhighways. Foreign manufacturers can transfer their business models and competitiveness directly to China, they don't have to take anything out of the envelope. As a result, the market inside China has become an international market. No matter where you are in the world, you must now be an enterprise that is internationally competitive. Internationalization has therefore become a key goal for us."

Liu Chuanzhi excelled in recognizing the way the wind was blowing and using the latest changes in national circumstances to his own advantage. He used the trend towards globalization of the 1980s to formulate his "advance overseas" strategy. He used the nationalistic wave of the 1990s to mobilize Chinese officials to "vitalize national brands." By the 21st century, the difficulties his successors faced in controlling the balance between "diversification" and "internationalization" was meaningful: it indicated that China's economy had gradually disengaged from political control. It had disassociated itself from official government channels. Enterprises now had to rely substantially on the laws of a market economy to survive.

Pressure on both ends of the market: the struggle between "powerful dragons" and "local snakes"

Several months into 2004, Lianxiang was facing an increasing squeeze from two different directions. Strong competitors were proliferating in the high-end market as IBM, Toshiba, Dell, Fujitsu, and Hewlett-Packard crowded into notebook computers. Dell and Hewlett-Packard fought for the desktop computer market. HP had been pushed into a corner in the late 1990s by Lianxiang but was now staging a comeback. Dell was a latter-day hero.

All name-brand products leave an anthropomorphic impression in consumers' minds. Computers are no different. IBM is a middle-aged man, quite stable, rather dignified. Lianxiang is a young man, full of passion and vitality, rather seductive. Hewlett-Packard and Dell are somewhere in between these two, both fairly stable but also energetic. Lianxiang's hold on home-use computers seemed firm, but on other important battlefields it was meeting powerful challenges.

Three years ago, Lianxiang would not have faced this tough a situation. "Things are different now," IDC's Deputy General Manager for China, Wang Ning, explained. "Lianxiang is facing a huge strategic shift. The year 2004 will be critical for the company's future."

Most analysts felt that Lianxiang was facing pressure from Dell. Lianxiang's own employees recognized that Dell was the worst enemy but there were many others. Lianxiang was being attacked from both sides, by low-priced name-brands and by what were called "local snakes" in its regional markets.

Guangdong had always been the largest regional market outside of Beijing and Shanghai, but in the past three years Lianxiang's market share there had dropped by eight percentage points. "Local snakes" were particularly strong and were gradually eating away Lianxiang's share.

One of the most aggressive was a company called Seven Delights. Lianxiang transferred a man named Tang Xionghua from Wuhan to Guangzhou in the spring of 2004 to become the General Manager of the Guangdong region. Tang watched the business closely for an initial two weeks and it didn't take him long to discover that Seven Delights was everywhere. In Chinese, this name was particularly evocative in the southern-Chinese context. One hundred kilometers away from him, in Shenzhen, a colleague named Wang had already had his bitter fill of Seven Delights. He now warned that "even strong dragons can't get local snakes."

In order to try, TCL joined Lianxiang in an alliance. TCL was a well known Chinese television manufacturer; at this time, it was just getting started in the computer business. Without any specific agreement, TCL and Lianxiang came together to force the tiny Seven Delights to the wall. The two companies used the most basic of competitive techniques: price-cutting. Seven Delights' sales results began to falter, its Exclusive Red outlets were getting fewer, yet somehow Lianxiang's market share did not begin to rise. It kept going down. At its peak in 2000 it was 32%, by May of 2004 it had dropped to 21.3%. Lianxiang's territory was now getting nibbled away by many other "local snakes". Some of these merely assembled machines and did not even brand their products.

The computer market in China has seen many strange things in its 20-year history, but one of the strangest was this instance when the smaller computer-assembly companies "sat on the mountain to watch the tigers fight". They were happy to exploit the competition between bigger forces. These companies found marvelous opportunities in the cracks between famous brands and they now expanded their market share by at least 10%.

These "computer-assembly companies" were originally retailers of computer parts. Many had made their initial capital in the wave of a particular kind of corruption in the 1990s, which involved importing without paying for licenses and taxes. Smugglers piloted fishing boats into the open seas outside customs borders, where they took on product. They then "found ways", i.e., paid bribes, to avoid customs and brought the products into the Chinese Mainland. Inside China, slightly more cautious computer manufacturers were not willing to do direct smuggling themselves, but they were willing to buy things from these people. The business was called "hauling goods". Computer-assembly companies relied on "hauled goods" to build up an initial sum of investment. By 2004, many "assembly companies" began to go legitimate. After learning the tricks of the trade from branded computer makers, they established standards for their own machines and set up servicing and repair systems.

To attack, or to defend

Lianxiang influenced the times in which it existed, and the company was also influenced by the times. Under most circumstances, senior management reacted to events and did not initiate them. Yang Yuanqing, just now mobilizing the "passionate transformation", prepared to meet strong market pressure. His capabilities and his persistence were extraordinary, but the process took time. At the company's Annual Results press conference in Hong Kong on June 2, he admitted that: "Transformation can't be accomplished in one leap. It requires a certain process." He asked customers and investors to be patient. He promised that: "within a few Quarters, everyone will see the results of this transformation."

Investor psychology was unstable. The next day, "00992" dropped HK$0.225 to HK$2.15, lowering Lianxiang's capitalization by HK$1.665 billion. The company's sales agencies were fighting a loyal battle but the painful price wars had taken profits down to 1% margins.

"We need to attack," decided Yang Yuanqing. "Our attack means a transformation of our business model. We need to be closer to customers, cultivate the customers, manage the customers." Salespeople were all waiting for high-sounding words. This time he was low-key. He just told everyone, "get prepared for a very tough fight."

The tough fight soon began. Lianxiang's ability to make the market submit was still very strong, and it relied on the ability of Lianxiang computers to lower price daily but still maintain a sufficient profit margin. On June 18, viewers of CCTV watched a 15-second Lianxiang ad on Golden Time. "I believe in Lianxiang," was the message. "My needs are exactly the same as its needs. Seeking excellence is what has made Lianxiang the Global Partner of the Olympics." This phrase was a kind of advance notice: the company's "summer sales battle" had begun.

This was to be the largest promotion activity in Lianxiang's history. Within the space of one month, RMB 100 million was spent. The country's eighteen sales regions and 108 sales networks were plastered with ads promoting over one hundred kinds of products. The company's electronic order-form system opened on the first day of the summer sales activity, which meant that all orders could now be transacted on the web. Fax machines were no longer necessary, people no longer had to hand record orders into their own computers and work overtime. Salespeople were still attentive. Nobody was willing to drop his guard. "We have sworn that in the summer-season market of 2004 we will make a beautiful massacre," one of the company's internal publications declared.

June 19 was the first day of concerted sales activities. In eight and one-half hours, the company received 10,000 orders. It looked as though the sales tide had turned—the trend persevered and good news was passed back to the market. The Lianxiang brand rose steeply in value. Now ranked Number 4 among the 500 most valuable brands in China, it was said to be worth RMB 60.165 billion. This evaluation came from the "World Brand Summit" jointly organized by the World Brand Laboratory and the World Economic Forum. The Summit published a list of the top ten brands on June 28, 2004.

People had criticized Lianxiang as lacking core competency. If the World Brand Laboratory and World Economic Forum were correct, the company was doing something right.

By the end of the first quarter, on June 30, the company's operating revenue had gone up 10% to RMB 5.878 billion. Profits had increased 21.1%. Yang Yuanqing announced that this result was in accord with the company's own forecasts and had exceeded the market's expectation.

The company's Board of Directors continued to maintain a cautious attitude. In July, it lowered the compensation for members of the Board by an average of 40%, and it lowered Yang Yuanqing's compensation by 50%. This stimulated a positive response from the stock market and it also aroused vigorous efforts among the employees. Yang Yuanqing kept the heat on them. "Don't think that when you've handed over the product to the distributor, that's the end of your responsibility," he told them. "Keep the relationship with the real customers, the end-users." He asked his staff to revisit at least 100,000 Lianxiang customers whose warranties had

Brand	Organization holding the brand	Brand value (billions of RMB)
Haier	Haier Group Company	61.237
CCTV	CCTV	60.851
Baogang	Shanghai Baogang Group Company	60.574
Lianxiang	Lianxiang Group Limited Company	60.165
Zhonghua	China Sinochem Group Company	57.689
Hongtashan	Yuxi Hong Ta Tobacco Group, Limited Company	52.968
China Industrial and Commercial Bank	China Industrial and Commercial Bank	47.235
Zhongtie Gongcheng	China Railroad Engineering Company	45.148
Zhongguo Renshou	China Life Insurance Group Company	42.767
Zhongguo Yidong	China Mobile Telecommunications Group (Mobicom)	39.129

expired, and he too personally went to see an old customer to resolve a computer problem.

Orders began to increase as the days became warmer. Business seemed to revive. Production lines were busy: the three assembly lines at the Shanghai Production base were at full speed, where daily quantities went from 1,800 to 5,000 machines a day. On August 11, Yang Yuanqing announced that the company results had exceeded market forecasts, setting a new record. By now, Lianxiang had the capacity to produce 15,000 computers a day. This tremendous capacity kept the three production centers of Beijing's Shangdi, Shanghai's Jinqiao, and Guangdong's Huizhou busy. Supply now generally could not keep up with demand and the lines had to move to two shifts—a situation the company had not enjoyed in over two years.

Yang Yuanqing now put his energies into assuring high employee morale. "Can our team stand firm as they move forward?" he asked himself. "This was my greatest concern at the beginning of the year. It was gratifying to have come through the most difficult period." He led the President's Office in a face-to-face discussion with forty employees. This was intended as "a forum for frank discussion, no holds barred, no limits."

One employee asked him what he thought about having his compensation cut in half. He said, "That cut was right. Lianxiang's compensation system is well designed, for what I take home depends on the results of the company. I hope that this year I'll be making more because that means everybody else will as well."

Another employee asked him, "If the transformation is successful, what will we get? What about Lianxiang in 2008?"

"Lianxiang will be much better in 2008 than it is today," Yang Yuanqing responded. "Depending on its growth, all of us here will benefit. In addition to receiving a stage on which to operate and enjoy personal growth, we'll see an increase in wealth. I hope that in 2008 all of you here will be enjoying a comfortable home and a car. If you already have these, I hope you'll be able to trade in for a bigger home, a better car. This is not merely a dream. It is a goal that, through our common efforts, we should be able to reach."

13

TAKEOVER OF IBM-PC

L et us now return to the beginning of this book. The negotiations between Lianxiang and IBM continued throughout the summer and fall of 2004. They were held in a building in Zhongguancun, the area in northwest Beijing known as China's Silicon Valley. China hoped that one day this fledgling Silicon Valley, with its 6,000 IT companies, would surpass the real one in California. It perhaps also hoped that this negotiation might represent an important step in this process.

Measured in terms of the recent wave of mergers in global companies, however, this deal between Lenovo and IBM was a small affair. The PC division of IBM was far from being important in IBM's overall business. It was near the bottom of the company's technology chain and its annual revenues came to only around 15% of IBM's total revenue. At the same time, though, the deal had tremendous symbolic significance. To China, this acquisition was not only unprecedented in Chinese history, it was a portent of China's gaining superiority in a fierce competition.

In American eyes, the deal was clear evidence of a Chinese threat. China was the challenger, or at the very least the competitor. Only a few years earlier, this threat had been a nebulous potential. Now it had become crystal clear and tangible. Officials of America's Committee on Foreign Investment in the United States (CFIUS) must have been thinking in these terms when they raised the possibility that China would use the acquired company to steal American classified technology. America's Justice Department and its Office of Homeland Security shared similar concerns. Some said that they feared Lianxiang would establish the headquarters of the new company in North Carolina's Research Triangle, so that the Chinese could easily enter IBM's research labs there. The

Chinese might even take the opportunity to use Research Park facilities to obtain and interfere with American information on US government computers. American media seemed to have the same opinion. In the several weeks of late 2004 and early 2005, news broadcasts focussed endlessly on Chinese people's apparently evil intentions. *TIME* magazine gathered evidence from officials at the Federal Bureau of Investigation, the FBI, which, according to statistics put forward, said that over 3,000 Chinese companies in America were suspected of gathering information on behalf of the Chinese government. In California's Silicon Valley, Chinese spy cases dealt with by the FBI were reportedly increasing at a rate of 20% to 30% every year. Cross-cultural issues were clearly a key element in the negotiating process, and public opinion played a role.

The initial motivation for the deal came not from the Chinese, however, but from the Americans themselves. Three years earlier, when IBM's Senior Vice-President John R. Joyce went to China and raised the idea of acquiring IBM-PC for the first time, Lianxiang's senior managers were stunned. They thought they were hearing a fairytale. Had IBM not initiated this business itself, never in a million years could Lianxiang have dreamed it up. Lianxiang's senior management at first did not believe that John Joyce's proposal was in earnest.

Joyce resolutely promoted the idea until Lianxiang realized that IBM was sincere. In the fall of 2003, the two companies finally commenced serious discussions. The critical element that brought the two sides together was the fact that each one faced problems and needed to find a resolution. The resolution being proposed seemed to be of strategic benefit to both sides. For many years, IBM-PC had been a debt-laden division. Its accumulated losses now exceeded US$500 million. The division was enveloped in low morale. As one of its managers said, "We're just working for our own rice bowls every day, not much more." IBM's strategic turnaround plan included a decision to divest itself of the lowest parts of the technology chain and, as a result, IBM had been looking for precisely this opportunity. At the same time, Lianxiang had its own problems. As described earlier, it already held a 30% share of China's PC market, so that its ability to continue to grow at a fast rate was capped, while efforts to diversify had not been successful. The dream of Lianxiang's management was to stride into the world, to reach global markets, but this had not proven to be easy. Lianxiang now wondered whether swallowing IBM's PC Division might not be a good first step onto the global stage.

Negotiations seemed at first to be an exercise in futility. This was simply, however, the blackest darkness before dawn. John Joyce was the key negotiator in putting forward IBM's position. Yang Yuanqing was the man on the Lianxiang side. As Chairman of the Board of the Lianxiang Group, he played a decisive role in the acquisition. Considerable evidence indicates that the deal initially faced serious opposition from some members of Lenovo's Board of Directors. At the time, Lianxiang's annual sales revenue from PCs was a mere US$3 billion, roughly one quarter of the income of IBM-PC. Many said that this was a farce, it was the pitiful sight of a small fish trying to eat a big one. Done badly, it would undoubtedly result in strangulation. Liu Chuanzhi had always been proud of his cautious, steadfast approach. He felt that this quality was what had enabled him, over the course of twenty years, to turn nothing into something substantial. When it came to strategic choices, he took few major risks.

Up until early spring of 2004, therefore, Liu Chuanzhi felt that the risks of this acquisition were too great. He felt that Lianxiang would be unable to support the burden. It was at this point that the frontline negotiators played a key role in the process. They discovered that the cost-management of IBM's PC Division had serious problems. As a result, what was in fact a fine production line was unable to turn a profit. "We looked at the accounting, line by line," Liu Chuanzhi later said. "And we finally came to believe that in IBM's hands the PC division would continue to suffer annual losses, while in Lianxiang's hands it could be profitable." He then added, "We also found that this was not a question of wringing a few more drops out of the towel, it was a question of getting bucket-loads more water."

Rays of dawn light now broke over the negotiations. From the summer of 2004, Lenovo began to seriously consider "eating" IBM's PC division. From then on, critical negotiating points concentrated on technical details rather than the overall principle of whether or not both sides wanted a deal. Both sides were now intent on finding a solution. Coming from completely different cultural backgrounds, they were now being drawn by a common thread: their own self-interest. They now knew that the self-interest of each would intersect at a certain price.

The patents and the brands held by IBM's PC Division were subjects of negotiation, but the most vexing issue was simply that of price. IBM held to its asking price of US$1.5 billion. Lianxiang was only willing to put up US$1.1 billion. For the entire summer and fall of 2004, negotiators on both sides went back and forth between these two figures. At the beginning of December, 2004, both sides finally reached an agreement: for US$1.25 billion, Lenovo would purchase IBM's global PC business. This figure included US$650 million in cash and US$600 million worth of

Lianxiang's shares. In addition, Lianxiang would assume the PC Division's US$500 million worth of debt: this debt would now be the obligation of Lianxiang.

Although the matter went forward under conditions of extreme secrecy, on the Friday of the first week of December 2004, the American side was the first one to divulge some news. This was immediately picked up by the *Wall Street Journal* and the *New York Times*, whose articles stirred waves of interest on both sides of the Pacific. "These are marvelous times," said a senior person at IDC. "This is a marriage between the very symbol of western capitalism and a Chinese company owned in part by the Chinese government. It's too bizarre."

It truly was bizarre. Everyone knows that IBM invented personal computers. It put out the very first personal computer in 1981; in 1986, it put out the first batch of notebook computers. Today, more than one hundred million people have computers carrying the IBM trademark. More importantly, IBM is a symbol of America's vitality. Lianxiang, in distinct contrast, was a latecomer to the PC business. It was born in a country administered by the Community Party. More than one-half of its assets belong to the Chinese government. Lianxiang has just begun the process of trying to graft western-style business management onto stubborn Asian traditions. Until a few hours before the deal was done, very few Americans had ever heard of it.

That weekend in December 2004, Lenovo became the focal point of mass media in both the East and the West. The name began to appear in western newspapers. Accurate news was sandwiched in with surmise and guesswork. Journalists on both sides of the Pacific were trying to get the inside story, hoping to verify the rumors, but the companies on both sides stayed locked up tight as a drum.

Nobody could deny this was a "snake eats elephant" story: a company with annual revenues of US$3 billion was reportedly purchasing a company of US$13 billion, and, in so doing, entering the ranks of the World 500. Some people said it was a joke, others said Lianxiang would be strangled to death. The most famous people in the personal computer market disapproved of it, at least on the surface. The President of Toshiba Company said, "I can't see any benefit to a merger with IBM." The Executive Vice-President of Hewlett-Packard, Duane Zitzner, said, "for a company born and bred in China suddenly to be making products for American or French markets... well, they will face substantial logistical complexities and supply chain problems." The most important competitor to Lianxiang,

Michael Dell, noted that the transaction might not be able to escape the fate of many other mergers, namely an inability to consolidate the two parties.

The reason for the delay in announcing the news was that the final link of the chain was not yet complete. The two companies still needed permission from their two governments. Lianxiang had asked the Chinese government to approve this transaction, but the formal request was still in Zhongnanhai, waiting for instructions from Central. Those familiar with all the inside considerations were sweating it out. According to China's enterprise system, if the Chinese government does not approve a deal of this magnitude, then it has absolutely no hope of going through.

Neither side had imagined, however, that the final obstacle would not be the Chinese government at all, but officials of the Committee on Foreign Investment in the United States.

At the beginning, the new company was to be called New Lianxiang (in Chinese). Lianxiang bought the IBM-PC division, while IBM became Lianxiang's second largest shareholder. Lianxiang's acquisition includes all research, manufacture, sales channels, customers, brand and patents of all IBM notebook computers and desktop computers. It also includes two R&D centers located in America and Japan, as well as 9,600 employees distributed over 160 countries in the world. Overnight, Lianxiang has become the world's third-largest personal computer manufacturer, with US$13 billion in annual sales revenue and 7.6% of the global market for personal computers. Dell and Hewlett-Packard are currently ahead of it, but are firmly in its sights.

In legal terms, this without doubt was an asset exchange, but in terms of actual operations it was more a form of strategic cooperation between the two companies. Very notable was that it was premeditated and implemented step by step. We now know that for the past two years every action taken by Lianxiang, including changing the trademark, changing the English name, adjustments in corporate strategy, the retrenchment, the reduction in forces, focussing on personal computers, becoming an Olympic Partner, selling off its information services business, stubbornly persevering in the middle and lower ends of the market, all of these were to lay a foundation for its strategic objective. All of this was quietly proceeding just as the company was being denigrated by the Chinese media. "Lianxiang lacks vision, lacks a dream," said the critics. "It has no virility, it is simply a mediocre operation." Now, with the situation suddenly changed, nobody used the word mediocre any more. Journalists, scholars, officials, all began to use that new phrase: Snake eats Elephant. This was pregnant with patriotic fervor, and it also contained a measure of sneering ridicule at the West.

Irrespective of how anyone described the deal, Lianxiang and IBM did sit down together and eventually achieved an accord. The one-meter thick stack of papers signed by the two parties represented the last page in the twenty-year drama of Lianxiang. The much-planned "twentieth celebration" was deferred time and again as everyone waited for confirmation of this deal. Without this merger, no glorious exclamation mark could be put at the end of this twenty-year period. The final signing ceremony was meant to be imminent; journalists were jostling to get invitations to the event. Senior management of Lianxiang kept their eyes cast in the direction of Zhongnanhai. Straining their vision as the hours went on, they wondered how Central would decide in the end.

Word arrived: four Premiers and Vice-Premiers had finally signed. In the course of one day, an emissary from the Lianxiang Group had succeeded in getting them all to approve the acquisition.

On Wednesday, December 8, at 4:50 in the morning, I met Liu Chuanzhi at the main entrance to the Lianxiang Group. The man I had been researching and trying to understand for the past year seemed much the same. The lines on his face were more pronounced and he looked tired, but he was also radiating a kind of energy. After another four hours, he would be announcing the news to the world.

"You must be pretty happy?"

He smiled, and said simply, "Yes. This is a most astonishing thing."

Suddenly I became aware that there was indeed a tremendous change in this key figure in our story. As described in this book, twenty years earlier this man was not deemed to have the qualifications to shake hands with the IBM Sales Manager for the region. When Liu Chuanzhi determined that Lianxiang would become "the IBM of China," his company had exactly eleven people in it and his monthly salary was less than US$60.

This early morning in the winter of 2004, Liu Chuanzhi assembled eighty of his senior managers in the third-floor round conference room of the Lianxiang Building, and outlined the future of New Lianxiang. From this time on, he would be resigning from the position of Chairman of the Board of Lianxiang Group. Some people said that this was an indication of his leaving the company completely. In fact, the blood of Lianxiang still flows in his veins, and there are still new dreams in his heart. Moreover, Liu Chuanzhi is generally able to turn his dreams into reality.

Night was coming down on the American continent on the other side of the Pacific when all employees of Big Blue received an email from the Chairman of the Board and CEO, Sam Palmisano:

"Dear employees of IBM: I have some important news to share with you…"

This news split open the stillness of the night. "I worked for years for IBM," one employee cried. "And now I work for a company that I've never heard of!" Another employee wailed on the company's internal website: "our pension funds are going to be turned into RMB."

On this side of the Pacific, the dawn rays were beginning to shine. Liu Chuanzhi and Yang Yuanqing walked together out of the Lianxiang Building, and went to the Five Continents Hotel on the northern Fourth Ring Road. From this venue they confirmed news that was already circling the world. At the beginning of 1985, as a sales agent for IBM, Liu Chuanzhi had for the first time attended an IBM conference; unsure of himself, nervous and excited, he sat in the very last row of seats. Now, before more than 500 Chinese and western journalists, he announced that, representing Lianxiang, he had signed documents purchasing IBM's personal computer business worldwide. He felt the gaze of the world upon him, and like twenty years before, felt both nervous and excited. "This realizes the dreams of two generations of people at Lianxiang," he said. "At the same time, it marks the start of a new beginning."

The company's twentieth-anniversary celebration was held on December 15 at the Beijing Workers' Stadium. It was a tremendous event that went on for over two hours. The words of Zhou Guangzhao, Chairman of the Chinese Science Association, best express the sentiment of the occasion: "Lianxiang's accomplishments today do not amount merely to forty billion RMB in assets; they are not measured merely by the six billion RMB that the company annually provides the nation in taxes. These are not the main contribution of the people of Lianxiang. Their main contribution has been to create a new path for China: in science and technology, to lead our conceptual framework through a total change. This is of historic significance."

Journalists caught the messages of Liu Chuanzhi and Zhou Guangzho and turned them into a new beginning for all of China's IT industry: a new stage of made in China. Articles on this theme proliferated. Americans, already sensitized by their experience with Japanese purchases of US companies some twenty years earlier, began to be worried. They began to wonder if this acquisition by a Chinese company would not compromise American national security.

On January 27, 2005, the Committee on Foreign Investment in the United States formally began its investigation into Lianxiang. It hoped to reach a prompt conclusion. Negotiations now began among Americans themselves. IBM clearly needed this transaction more than the Chinese did. The company therefore made a promise to the Committee: it would forbid any employee of Lianxiang from entering IBM's research facilities at the North Carolina Research Triangle, and it would prevent the Lianxiang Group from obtaining IBM's list of customers among American government institutions.

At a safe distance across the river, the Chinese watched the developments with complex emotions. Some were worried that this child of an American and a Chinese company would die stillborn death before it had even emerged. Others were more sarcastic. They said that the components of IBM-PCs were mostly made in China anyway, and that the only way Chinese could use IBM notebooks in a military application was to throw them out of airplanes onto the heads of enemy soldiers.

Another six weeks went by. On March 9, the American Committee on Foreign Investment in the United States finally completed its investigation of the purchase of IBM-PC by Lianxiang. People in both companies drew a long breath and announced the results. "There is absolutely no change in the terms of the agreement on the acquisition; there is absolutely no change in the price." The Chairman of the Board of Lianxiang, Yang Yuanqing, added that Lianxiang "has the right, under its existing form of business, to sell any products of the new company to all levels of the American government. Lianxiang employees in America have not been restricted or hindered in any way." He denied that the company had made any concessions in the course of being investigated. However, before a large group of journalists he publicly promised that the new Lianxiang would "satisfy American national security needs." He added that, "Wherever Lianxiang goes in the world, it will respect the local laws and obligations."

In the past century, misunderstandings and distrust between the Chinese and the American people have been common and even, at times, led to open conflict. In the future, misunderstandings will undoubtedly continue. Nonetheless, one detail proves that the ice has been broken and that nothing can restrain this Asian country from striding into the western world. In the few weeks before Christmas in 2004, while company employees were immersed in a sense of victory, Yang Yuanqing made this announcement to his senior staff: "I want you all to know that we will be adopting English as the official language of New Lianxiang."

Over twenty years, Liu Chuanzhi, Lianxiang and China have traversed a remarkable period of history. In retrospect, the process seems organic: a plant pushing upward toward the light. However, the transformation of China was not pre-ordained; individuals and specific events propelled the action. Lianxiang's purchase of IBM-PC has been one such event, for it has drawn a clear benchmark on the course of history. Interpenetration of China and the West will define the coming century. Liu Chuanzhi and Lianxiang are a part of the mechanism that has changed China's thinking about its relationship with the world. Their role as agents of change will now pass to others, including those who find themselves playing a part in the unfolding drama of globalization.

INDEX